Mastering
Foreign Exchange &

i

FT Prentice Hall

FINANCIAL TIMES

In an increasingly competitive world, we believe it's quality of thinking that will give you the edge – an idea that opens new doors, a technique that solves a problem, or an insight that simply makes sense of it all. The more you know, the smarter and faster you can go.

That's why we work with the best minds in business and finance to bring cutting-edge thinking and best learning practice to a global market.

Under a range of leading imprints, including Financial Times Prentice Hall, we create world-class print publications and electronic products bringing our readers knowledge, skills and understanding which can be applied whether studying or at work.

To find out more about our business publications, or tell us about the books you'd like to find, you can visit us at **www.business-minds.com**

For other Pearson Education publications, visit **www.pearsoned-ema.com**

PEARSON

Prentice Hall

market editions

Mastering Foreign Exchange & Currency Options

A practical guide to the new marketplace

Second Edition

FRANCESCA TAYLOR

FT Prentice Hall
FINANCIAL TIMES

An imprint of **Pearson Education**

London • New York • Toronto • Sydney • Tokyo • Singapore
Hong Kong • Cape Town • Madrid • Paris • Amsterdam • Munich • Milan

PEARSON EDUCATION LIMITED

Head Office:
Edinburgh Gate
Harlow CM20 2JE
Tel: +44 (0)1279 623623
Fax: +44 (0)1279 431059
Website: www.financialminds.com

First published in Great Britain in 1997
Second edition 2003

© Pearson Education Limited 2003

The right of Francesca Taylor to be identified as Author of this Work has been
asserted by her in accordance with the Copyright, Designs and
Patents Act 1988.

ISBN 0 273 66295 3

British Library Cataloguing in Publication Data
A CIP catalogue record for this book can be obtained from the British Library.

Library of Congress Cataloging in Publication Data
Applied for.

10 9 8 7 6 5 4 3

Typeset by Mathematical Composition Setters Ltd, Salisbury, Wiltshire.
Printed by Bell & Bain Ltd. Glasgow.

The Publishers' policy is to use paper manufactured from sustainable forests.

Contents

15 e-Foreign exchange   249

Francesca Taylor, Taylor Associates

16 Multi-bank electronic trading: a brief history and current use   257

Ted Sanborn, Currenex

17 Innovations in e-fx   271

Anneliese Widdows, Citigroup

18 Electronic procurement of foreign exchange: the corporate perspective   279

Neil Cotter, LogicaCMG

Appendices

The author

Francesca Taylor, is the Principal of Taylor Associates, one of the City's leading financial training companies, established in 1993 and specializing in FX, derivatives, capital markets, risk and treasury skills training. She has personally trained in major UK and international corporations, government agencies, American, European and UK banks and building societies.

Francesca's career commenced with one of the UK's largest companies – BICC plc, where she learned her treasury, FX and money market skills. In a typical day she would liaise with banks, transact money market and foreign exchange deals and advise on risk management. The City beckoned and Francesca joined Midland Bank, becoming Team Leader in the Financial Engineering Group, concentrating on marketing, selling and troubleshooting the whole range of currency and risk management products to a client list including, central banks, major and minor commercial banks, corporates and supranationals. In addition, it was Francesca's responsibility to educate and train the bank's own client base in the uses and applications of a growing number of currency risk management instruments. Francesca then became a Treasury Consultant advising her own clients on all aspects of risk management. Notable clients included major utilities and engineering companies. Following this, she spent some time as an interbank swap broker with Sterling Brokers.

During her career Francesca has followed each of the four major groupings within banking and finance. She has been a corporate, a banker, a broker and a consultant. This leads her to be ideally placed to offer product education and independent training.

Her company, Taylor Associates, has been highly successful since inception and now offers a wide range of FX, treasury, risk, general finance and complementary soft-skills courses to banks and non-banks alike. Delivery is by traditional face-to-face training, e-learning or a blend of both. Francesca is a popular speaker at major conferences in the UK, Hong Kong, Singapore, Malaysia and Australia.

She is an Associate Member of the Association of Corporate Treasurers (AMCT), holds a Masters Degree in Management Science from Imperial College, London, and has a BSc in Geology.

The contributors

John Austin is Deputy Head of Financial Trading at IG Group, the UK's leading private client margin trading company. For the past two years he has also been head of IG Group's margin FX desk.

Tom Buschman is development manager for central treasury operations of the Shell Group. Previously he was responsible for Shell's central foreign exchange and money market activities. Before coming to London, he worked for Shell's Dutch Pension Fund and held various managerial finance positions for the Shell Group in Brazil. In his current role he is responsible for a number of projects around the implementation of effective straight-through processing and centralized risk management of Shell's treasury operations. He is the founder and coordinator of the TWIST integration standards initiative. TWIST involves well over 50 trading platforms, market infrastructure providers, professional service providers, banks and corporates that together drive towards straight-through processing of financial transactions, commercial payments and working capital management.

Neil Cotter has been Group Treasurer of LogicaCMG (formerly Logica) since 1999. LogicaCMG is one of the largest IT services businesses in Europe with over 21,000 employees. Prior to this he was responsible for bank relationship and funding management for ICI. Neil was originally employed as an IT consultant before moving into corporate finance and, latterly, treasury. He retains a special interest in technology and its interaction with the corporate treasurer. Neil is a qualified accountant and treasurer.

Joseph De Feo joined CLS as President and Chief Executive Officer of CLS Bank International and Chief Executive Officer of CLS Group in June 2000. For over seven years, Joseph was a member of the Barclays Bank Executive Committee and managed the IT and Operations strategy of the group. This spanned personal, commercial and investment banking, as well as a substantial asset management business. Prior to working for Barclays, Joseph was with Morgan Grenfell & Co. as Director, Systems and Operations, where he was involved in, among other things, establishing a strategy to restructure the securities aspect of the business. He has also held various positions at Goldman Sachs & Co. and Chase Manhattan Bank.

Tina Kane, Head of Corporate Communications, EBS, has worked with the company for over 12 years, initially as an external financial PR consultant and for the last seven years as the inhouse PR and Communications manager. She has extensive experience of global financial markets having worked with a number of major banks and financial institutions prior to joining EBS and covering a range of subjects, in addition to foreign exchange, including global custody, fund management, managed futures funds and reinsurance. Previously a director of a leading City PR company, she has also been involved in the flotation of a number of UK companies on the London Stock Exchange.

Simon Lee spent 11 years in the FX market both as a trader and a technical analyst and has experience in trading index and fixed income futures, with banks such as Midland Bank, SEB, Sakura and Allied Irish. For the last seven years he has been working in sales & marketing within the data vending business, initially with Knight Ridder then Bridge and is now the EMEA Marketing Director for Moneyline Telerate. He plays rugby and is kind to small animals.

Dr Yuval Levy has been the Chief Technical Officer of SuperDerivatives since 1999. He is in charge of all the development, as well as the whole complex network structure of the application service that SuperDerivatives provides all over the world. In his previous career, Dr Levy was a prominent scientist in solid-state physics, specializing in heavy computation consumption applications. He has developed many inventions with day-to-day applications, as well as heading large computer centres for the laboratories he worked in. Dr Levy decided to switch to the world of finance, where he has specialized in the area of pricing derivatives and computation models.

Andrew Medhurst has worked for the HSBC Group since 1987 in London, Hong Kong and Tokyo. In 1993, after roles in fixed income sales and asset swaps, he subsequently became an interest rate and currency derivatives trader. Since 1998 Andrew has worked for the Emerging Markets Structuring Group which offers multi-product structuring capability, using financial instruments and derivatives to help HSBC's UK and European customers manage risk more effectively, reduce volatility of their earnings, and attain their objectives in the difficult environment of emerging markets.

Ted Sanborn, VP Product Management at Currenex, joined the company in January 2000 with 16 years of experience in the financial markets and financial information products. Prior to his role at Currenex, Ted was a Director of Product Management in the Information Products Division at Reuters PLC. In this position, he had responsibilities for product strategy and design for an international product line of financial information services for professionals. Other experiences include six years with Freddie Mac, a leading issuer in the US mortgage-backed securities market. He has an MBA and Bachelor of Science in Finance from Virginia Tech.

Derek Taylor is the Managing Director of Taylor Associates Financial Training. He has personally trained in banks, brokers and corporations worldwide. Recently he has been working with a number of online brokers both in the US and Europe. Derek joined Midland Bank and became one of their youngest managers at the age of 22. He then joined the dealing room and swiftly rose to supervise interbank trading in major currencies, specializing in GBP/USD and USD/JPY. Derek is an Associate of the Institute of Bankers, a member of the Forex Association and a member of the Society of Technical Analysts.

Anneliese Widdows has worked for the foreign exchange division of Citigroup since 2000. Her principal role is to assist in the marketing of Citigroup's foreign exchange products and services to its corporate and institutional customers. She specializes in producing product specific literature for Europe, Japan and North America. Anneliese has a BSc in Environmental Science from Kings College, London.

Acknowledgements

Special thanks go to my contributors who are all current market practitioners with 'real' jobs and who have gone out of their way to find the time to sit down and write a chapter based on their experiences. They are:

John Austin, Head of Foreign Exchange Trading, IG Markets
Tom Buschman, Treasury Centre Development Manager, Shell Group, and Founder and Coordinator, TWIST
Neil Cotter, Group Treasurer, LogicaCMG
Joseph de Feo, Dr, President and Chief Executive Officer, CLS Bank International
Tina Kane, Head of Corporate Communications, EBS
Simon Lee, Marketing Director, Moneyline Telerate, EMEA
Yuval Levy, Chief Technical Officer, SuperDerivatives
Andrew Medhurst, Assistant Director, Emerging Markets, Structuring Group, HSBC
Ted Sanborn, Vice President, Product Management, Currenex
Derek Taylor, Managing Director, Taylor Associates
Anneliese Widdows, Marketing Executive, Citigroup

I would like to offer my grateful thanks to Lee Oliver and David Simmons for providing additional market information. Thanks also to Lawrence Galitz who has let me reprint his derivation of the Black and Scholes option pricing formula. The Bank of England's new code of conduct (NIPs code) is included with their kind permission and we have also reproduced market statistics from the Bank for International Settlements in Basle and FX-week.

With the brave new world of FX upon us, the time is right to revisit the market. I have tried to make this book as informative as possible by giving all sides of the story: the theory and the practice, the buy-side and the sell-side, the vanilla and the exotic. By including examples, diagrams and a multitude of screen dumps I hope I have de-mystified the subject.

Finally, I want to thank my husband Derek and my son Alex, for their total support throughout this project. None of this could have been achieved without the help of Barbara who ensured that things ran smoothly at home while I wrote this book and the various pets who sat and watched while I typed the manuscript.

Preface

The last ten years have seen a revolution in the global foreign exchange markets. The changes, whilst radical have been well and truly adopted into the market psyche.

This is a completely new book on *Mastering Foreign Exchange and Currency Options* in the twenty-first century, rather than simply just a second edition. In addition to all the chapters explaining the fundamentals and changes to foreign exchange and currency options, we have lots of new up-to-the minute contributions from:

- Citigroup
- CLS Bank International
- Currenex
- EBS
- HSBC
- IG Markets
- LogicaCMG
- Moneyline Telerate
- Shell Group and TWIST
- SuperDerivatives

If you had been in and around the FX markets 7–10 years ago, but had not done much in the area since, you would be astonished. The style of trading has changed – dealing rooms are not quite so frantic, or so noisy. The inexorable push of technology has led to single and multi-bank portals, the introduction of new market initiatives such as STP, CLS, EBS, ECNs and e-fx, continues. New acronyms are also entering our vocabulary, such as 'TWIST' and CFDs. I make no apology for not defining any of the terms here – read this book to learn about them!

Without information and the information providers, none of this would be possible – we have all come to rely on instant real-time information, relayed across the capital markets and displayed straight onto our desks. Dealers often having a choice of four to eight screens to watch – which begs the question, just how much information can the human brain absorb? Chapter 6 from Simon Lee of Moneyline Telerate charts the progress of the information industry from carrier pigeons to the present day and looks at the value of information to both the professional trader and the occasional day-trader. Likely future developments are also explored.

The easy access to historical data through the databases of the information providers leads to the increasing use of technical analysis to support or initiate trading decisions. This is now very marked with traders and fund managers happily discussing Fibonacci retracements and Japanese candlesticks. A revised chapter on Technical Analysis (Chapter 20) from Derek Taylor, here at Taylor Associates, is included to de-mystify some of the strategies and techniques. Can you honestly say you know what an Elliott wave is or the significance of 'three black crows'?

Every three years the Bank for International Settlements (BIS) based in Basel, undertakes a survey of the FX and derivatives markets. The latest data is drawn from the 2001 survey and covers the period either side of the introduction of the euro. Appendix 1 lists the 49 contributors to the survey and if you would like further information, either contact your local central bank direct or look at the website, www.bis.org.

The importance of world capital flows, linked to large bond and equity issues has consolidated although the global downturn has meant a temporary downturn in the amounts traded. The rise in the importance of the emerging markets cannot be overstated and Andrew Medhurst of HSBC has written a chapter (Chapter 9) giving many practical tips and background details for dealing in these markets.

London as a financial centre continues to dominate the turnover figures, see Figure P.1, although the volumes have declined since the previous survey of 1998.

The expansion in FX over the last 10 years has not been uniform across the user groups, Figure P.2 shows the growth of FX across two key sectors:

Figure P.1	**FX markets around the world**

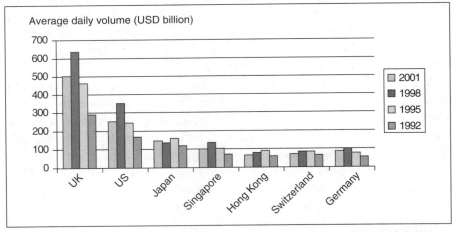

Source: BIS, *Triennial Central Bank Survey*, published March 2002, based on FX and Derivatives Market Activity in 2001

- Corporate FX – USD 137 bn *per day* in 1992 increased to USD 156 bn in 2001.

- Institutional FX – USD 96 bn *per day* in 1992 increased to USD 329 bn in 2001.

I am often asked why so much business is transacted in London when other centres such as New York, Frankfurt and Sydney are just as available.

The easy answer is, 'it's traditional', but seriously, the pool of experienced staff in both front, back and middle office functions is second to none in London. English is now the universal language of finance and here in the UK we have the benefit of the time zones in our favour making it possible to speak to the Far East and the west coast of the US in the same day. When you combine those factors with London also being the centre of the Eurobond market the pre-eminence is natural.

We have included, as Appendix 3, the new code of conduct from the Bank of England (known as the NIPs code – Non-Investment Products code), this succeeds the old London Code of Conduct and was drafted following the introduction of the Financial Services and Markets Act 2000.

The BIS survey is discussed in more detail in Chapter 5 by Tina Kane from EBS as she reviews the changes of the last 10 years from a broker's perspective. Currently in the forefront of the e-fx revolution, as well as being one of the early initiators with the Reuters/EBS platform, EBS have a unique insight.

However, for me the startling point is how much FX business is still concentrated within so few major banks. In the UK, 17 banks transact more than 75% of the business, and in the US it is just 13 banks accounting for three-quarters of the business.

FX sector growth

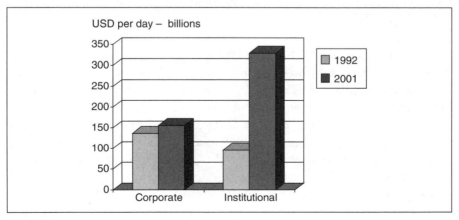

Source: BIS

Figure P.3

Derivatives volumes

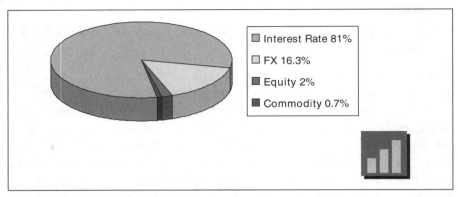

- Interest Rate 81%
- FX 16.3%
- Equity 2%
- Commodity 0.7%

Source: BIS, Basel, June 2002

Although volumes in FX have fallen from their high point in the 1990s, the latest BIS survey shows an increase of 39% in OTC currency option transactions. Both vanilla and exotic transactions need state-of-the-art pricing models, and at the last count there were in the region of 70 different currency option structures with new varieties being regularly developed. Yuval Levy of SuperDerivatives, one of the leading players in this market, has contributed a chapter (Chapter 14) on exotic options and the increasing transparency which is now available in the pricing. The simpler exotic structures are also explained with practical examples to aid further understanding.

Figure P.3 shows the over the counter (OTC) derivatives market transactions broken down by asset class.

Whilst the interest rate derivatives continue to dominate the market, currency derivatives now account for approximately 16.3%, equivalent to USD 18 trillion out of approximately USD 110 trillion.

In the first edition of this book, our attention was focused on the onset of EMU and its likely repercussions, together with radical new systems and technology. Well, the euro is with us now, and the technological advances continue.

The whole concept of e-foreign exchange is with us. The 'sell-side' of the market – the FX portals and e-fx banks are live and trading and Ted Sanborn of Currenex has allowed us a look at the world through their eyes, illustrating Chapter 16 with screen shots of their system. Anneliese Widdows of Citigroup, another of the market leaders shows us the range of additionality that is possible, such as 'benchmarking' and 'white labelling'. Indeed some say it will be the add-on features that will ensure the ultimate success of these e-fx ventures.

We are fortunate to also have contributions from two of the 'buy-side' participants – Tom Buschman of Shell Group and TWIST and Neil Cotter of LogicaCMG, who both give us the benefit of their own knowledge in the field of corporate e-fx. It is possible to learn much from their observations and experiences. In my humble opinion we are caught in a 'catch-22' situation. The portals need the liquidity, the liquidity providers want the portals, but the customers are still reticent about committing expenditure to more than one portal, so are all waiting to see which one is likely to dominate. Those of a certain age will remember a similar scenario with video recorders some years ago: VHS versus Betamax.

Many smaller companies look with horror at the increasing technology in this market and I have included a new chapter (Chapter 15), detailing the background to the technological changes we have seen. My intention is to demonstrate that this progress is justified and also understandable as I explain the new terminology, thus making things, I hope, less daunting.

The innovation in FX continues and IG Markets (formerly known as IG Index) have made a very profitable business out of new ways of trading FX. For example, you can now try:

- margin trading;
- spread-betting; or
- FX CFDs.

The retail client has been overlooked for many years by the FX market and the barriers to entry previously meant that you needed to be able to transact in large amounts for traditional bank-based business. With FX CFDs, margin trading and spread-betting a whole new generation of players are now able to put into effect their own currency risk management utilizing these tools. The economic downturn means that many individuals are now at home, keen to manage their own portfolios and take control of their own destiny.

A final note on one of the largest projects ever undertaken in the FX markets – the design and successful implementation of Continuous Linked Settlement (CLS). This payment vs payment settlement system went live in the fourth quarter of 2002, and we are all interested in the impact it will have on the liquidity of the market.

Who said FX had become boring! Fascinating times ahead.

Francesca Taylor

The historical perspective

Francesca Taylor, Taylor Associates

... for the pro-euro campaigners, the introduction of the euro is simply the first step in a progressive process towards EMU (Economic and Monetary Union) – it is not the only step!

■ ■ ■

INTRODUCTION

Foreign exchange (known in the banking and financial markets by its abbreviation, FX) has been with us for a long time; from your schooldays you may recall a mention in *The Bible* of moneychangers and moneylenders outside the temple in Jerusalem over 2000 years ago. The two currencies were the Israeli shekel and the Roman dinari. The Romans were collecting taxes from the Jews in Bethlehem whose domestic currency was the shekel, yet payment was required in dinari. The Romans were setting the tax rates whilst others – the moneychangers – were setting the foreign exchange conversion rate.

Moving forward a little; in the twelfth century a group of wealthy Italian merchants came to London to set up a banking house. They came from Lombardy and left some years later – the result of a dubious credit decision. Although that family is no longer in business they left behind their legacy – Lombard Street in the City of London. Moving on again, in Italy in the Middle Ages, money changing and money lending activities were carried out by prosperous families around the town square where the moneylenders would sit on benches. The Italian word for bench is 'banco', from which the modern word for bank is derived.

More recently the euro has been introduced as the common currency in twelve of the European nations as the prelude to full EMU: Economic and Monetary Union (not European Monetary Union). This is a key point; for the pro-euro campaigners, the introduction of the euro is simply the first step in a progressive process, it is not the only step. Before we travel further along the FX highway we shall briefly consider some of the more notable foreign exchange signposts which are described below.

1880–1914: THE TWO GOLD STANDARDS

A system of fixed exchange rates where currency parities were set in relation to gold. Under the *Gold Specie Standard*, gold was the internationally recognized sole medium of exchange and payment, and any currency value was directly linked to gold. Consequently, certain preconditions had to be met:

- the central bank must agree to sell and buy gold at a fixed price in unrestricted amounts;
- anyone could melt down the gold to put it to different uses;
- a holder of gold was entitled to have coins struck from bullion at the state mint, whatever the amount;
- there had to be unrestricted import and export of gold.

It followed that under this standard the liquidity of a particular currency was linked to gold production, as the face value of the coin and the metallic value of the gold were the same.

Under the *Gold Bullion Standard*, money in circulation was either all paper or partly paper, with gold being used solely as the reserve asset. Paper money could be exchanged for gold, but not everyone wanted the gold equivalent. This meant that the issuing bank no longer needed to have full bullion coverage for every note or coin in issue.

Accordingly, the volume of paper money in circulation was always greater than the holdings of the metal.

1918–1939: BETWEEN THE WAR YEARS

Wars are expensive. Additional finance for wartime economies could be met only by the creation of money. This in turn led to differential inflation in the affected countries and created an obvious disparity in international price relationships. Corrective action required some countries to devalue and others to revalue. Inflation and devaluation were only two of the problems faced: the other main problem was the imposition of exchange controls in the first half of the 1930s. Governments were required to exercise control over currency flows in and out of their country, which in turn led to foreign exchange rationing. The outbreak of the Second World War forced all countries to introduce exchange controls, even those that had not imposed them earlier.

1944–1970: THE GOLD EXCHANGE STANDARD

To escape the danger of the devaluation/revaluation/inflation cycle experienced in the interwar years, the US and the UK tried to create a 'free, stable, and multilateral monetary system'. This became known as the Bretton Woods agreement, named after the location where the agreement was signed in Bretton Woods, New Hampshire. Proposed by the Americans and accepted in July 1944, it created a monetary system resembling the original Gold Standard concept. At the same time the International Monetary Fund (IMF) was established to monitor the operation of this new monetary system. The IMF's main objectives were:

- to establish stable exchange rates;
- to eliminate existing exchange controls;
- to bring about convertibility of all currencies.

Each member of the IMF set a parity for its currency relative to gold or the dollar, and guaranteed to maintain the rate within plus or minus 1% by central bank operations. By 1944 Europe had been devastated by war and was slow to emerge from foreign exchange rationing; consequently liberalization took place very slowly. Currency convertibility eventually came fully into force on 27 December 1958.

The Bretton Woods agreement was effective for many years, although there was a wave of devaluations as early as 1949. The first real strains showed shortly after 1958 when full convertibility had been achieved. The US's massive balance of payments deficit (USD 11.2 billion) in the years 1958–60, caused a run on gold, pushing the price above USD 35 per ounce for the first time since 1951. The central banks formed a gold 'pool' to stabilize this volatile market. Throughout this period economies were growing at very divergent rates, leading to a series of revaluations. In 1961 both the Dutch guilder and the German mark were revalued due to large balance of payments surpluses, and in 1967 the British pound was devalued from GBP 1 = USD 2.80 to GBP 1 = USD 2.40. This caused another run on gold, ultimately forcing the central banks to abandon their 'gold pool'.

In the years that followed, social unrest in France in 1968 cost the Banque de France most of its currency reserves, leading to a devaluation of 11.1%, whilst in Germany massive inflows of capital caused a revaluation 9.3%.

1971–1973: THE COLLAPSE OF BRETTON WOODS

The collapse of the Bretton Woods agreement was swift, brought about mainly by a lack of confidence in the dollar. The American economy ran into trouble following President Johnson's attempt to finance the Vietnam War by increasing the US current account deficit. This caused a dollar crisis in 1971, and on 15 August 1971, the newly elected President Nixon finally abandoned dollar–gold convertibility. In mid-December 1971 the US declared its readiness to devalue the dollar. But only if the major Western European countries and Japan would revalue their own currencies. This cleared the way for a general return to fixed parities.

On 17 and 18 December 1971, and within the framework of the Smithsonian Agreement, the US raised the gold price to USD 38 per ounce, equivalent to a devaluation of 7.9%. Japan and Europe revalued their currencies by up to 7.66%. At the same time intervention points were widened to ±2.25%. Speculation soon started up again and in March 1973 Japan and the hard currency countries of Europe suspended their obligations to intervene in the market. Fixed exchange rates were effectively dead.

THE PERIOD FROM 1973 TO 1999

As a result of the collapse of the fixed rate system many industrialized countries went over to exchange rates that 'float'. At the time this was considered to be a short-term measure but after a few years it became unthinkable to return to the old ways. Most countries have adopted a type of 'managed' floating exchange rate with central bank intervention to try to control the currency if movements become too erratic.

In the years since the breakdown of Bretton Woods it has become increasingly difficult to manage currency risk as exchange rates have moved in a haphazard way, although in the eight years leading up to 1988 there had been two important trends for the dollar. First, way up and then way down, each lasting a number of years. It was hard to get it wrong as the trends lasted a long time. Furthermore, until the Plaza Accord in September 1985, central bank intervention was largely regarded in the market as an opportunity to profit from the central bank's futile attempts to control market forces.

To appreciate more fully the dynamics of the market since 1985, let us examine an earlier period. Between 1979 and 1984 the Deutschmark depreciated almost in a straight line against the dollar from DEM 1.73 to DEM 3.15 or by about 82% (see Figure 1.1) there has probably not been a similar period where it was so easy to 'get it right'.

Towards the end of 1984 there was a general consensus that the dollar was

| Figure 1.1 | **Chart showing the depreciation of the Deutschmark against the US dollar 1979–1984** |

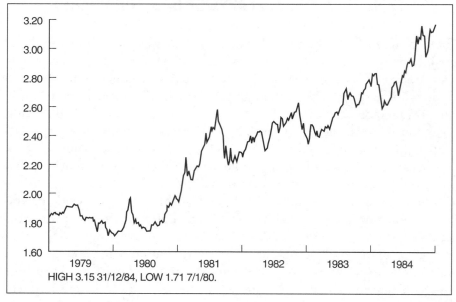

HIGH 3.15 31/12/84, LOW 1.71 7/1/80.

Source: Thomson Financial Datastream

seriously overvalued against most major currencies, and in September 1985 the finance ministers of the world's leading industrialized nations met to launch a coordinated effort to drive the dollar down. There was a deliberate correction (about 50%) to the dollar value but it was over by late 1987.

EUROPEAN MONETARY UNION, 1999 ONWARDS

The euro was introduced as a virtual currency in 1999 with notes and coins arriving in circulation during the early part of 2002. A chart of the value of the euro against the USD (from 1 January 1999 to November 2002) is shown in Figure 1.2.

I wish to avoid the debate on whether the UK will or won't join or whether it is a good thing or bad thing, etc. I believe enough column inches (if not miles) have been written about this and I do not particularly wish to enter the fray. However, Figure 1.2 describes the value of the euro so that the reader can see its initial decline then partial recovery. But are we measuring the decline of the euro or the rise of the USD? Those of you who know me personally, know my views on this matter. Suffice it to say that the euro is here, is trading and affects 300 million people from Paris to Athens, Dublin to Frankfurt. As far as the financial markets are concerned it is just another currency that can be bought/sold on the foreign exchanges.

Graph showing EUR/USD from 1 January 1999 to November 2002

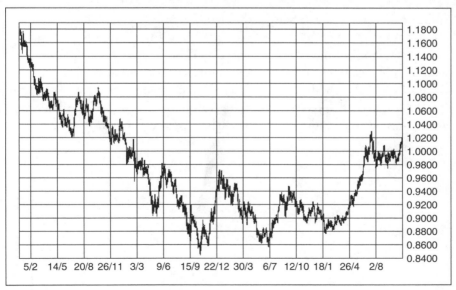

Source: Moneyline Telerate

In conclusion, it has now been clearly established that forecasting exchange rates on the basis of a view about relative fundamentals such as inflation, external accounts, and interest rate differentials is of limited or no value to the hedger, trader, or arbitrageur, and should be reserved largely for end-of-year competitions.

CONTINUOUS LINKED SETTLEMENT (CLS) 2002

In terms of historic milestones we need to mention Continuous Linked Settlement. CLS was introduced in September 2002. This is a system designed to avoid the settlement risk which for many years was an integral part of foreign exchange dealing. It eliminates the risk that occurs if one party to a foreign exchange trade fails to settle with the other. It is only available through CLS bank and links the Real Time Gross Settlement (RTGS) systems in the following seven currencies:

- US dollar
- UK pound
- Euro
- Japanese yen
- Swiss franc
- Canadian dollar
- Australian dollar

Additional currencies will be added in later stages.

For a transaction to be eligible for settlement through CLS it must be a trade where both of the currencies are listed above and the bank(s) in question is (are) members of CLS. For more information see Chapter 21, Continuous Linked Settlement. It is a radical change to the cross-border settlement system which has been used for hundreds of years and at the time of writing has been operational for only a short period.

Background and development of the foreign exchange market

Francesca Taylor, Taylor Associates

The recent survey conducted by the BIS shows a general decline in the volume of foreign exchange traded globally, but estimates that the average daily figure still remains in excess of ...
USD 1,200,000,000,000.
■ ■ ■

INTRODUCTION

What exactly is foreign exchange and what is being bought and sold? When people discuss foreign exchange they invariably refer to the value of one currency in terms of another. A typical comment might relate to the strengthening of the US dollar: this will have little impact on the Americans domestically, but it will allow them to buy foreign goods more cheaply. However, on the international market it will make their exports more expensive and possibly uncompetitive. In essence, our statement concerns the value of the dollar in the global marketplace, in terms of how much of another currency can be bought with one single dollar, or how many dollars will need to be given up in return for a specific amount of a foreign currency.

Individuals and companies do not normally buy and sell currencies for their own sake; rather, they do so in order to pay for something else, such as goods and services. In that sense foreign exchange transactions are essentially a part of the payment mechanism, and it is to the commercial banks that individuals and companies have turned to convert foreign currency into domestic currency and vice versa. Incidentally, the market standard abbreviation for foreign exchange is FX or Forex.

The FX markets in a particular country tend to be located in the national financial centres, near their related financial markets. In the UK the market is in London, with very little activity taking place elsewhere in the country. A client in Birmingham may sell dollars to his local bank in return for sterling under a 'retail' transaction, but ultimately the deal will be priced and processed through the treasury operation of the bank in London, which will have access to the 'wholesale' or interbank markets.

In the US most of the activity centres around New York, although due to the immense size of the country there is a role to play for both Chicago and some of the West Coast banks in the late afternoon. Communication is effected by internet, telephone, fax, and direct dealing information systems such as Reuters, Bloomberg and Moneyline Telerate.

There is no requirement for either of the parties to a foreign exchange transaction to be physically present in a specific location. This is because the foreign exchange markets are found in the dealing rooms of the commercial banks around the world. This is in contrast to some 'exchange-traded' products where both parties have to be physically present in a building known as an exchange. FX is an over-the-counter (OTC) market, where the prices are negotiable, as are the amounts, the currencies, and the maturity dates. Each party must take on the other's credit risk, although with spot foreign exchange transactions this will ultimately become a risk on final settlement of the currencies.

11

Many dealing rooms in the major commercial banks employ over 150 front office traders, sales and marketing staff, and economists – some as many as 350, although the numbers are beginning to decline as banks merge and the technology dominates. The front office is where the deals are struck and where the bank and the client enter into obligations to buy/sell their currencies. This is distinct from the operations departments where the deals are processed and payments made/received. The middle office will include the information technology, legal, audit, financial control, risk and compliance areas. Not all of these traders or support staff will be active in foreign exchange: some will be working within the money markets or deposit markets, or perhaps bonds and equity, derivatives or bullion. One thing is certain, to an outsider looking in, a dealing room can be a chaotic place: traders may be wearing head-sets or speaking into more than one phone. They may be talking into brokers' boxes, and shouting at one another, and anyone else who happens to be passing – all at the same time! Foreign exchange traders, especially in a busy market, are known to be loud, noisy and 'in your face' which can sometimes offend the more gentle souls in a bank.

So just why is there so much going on? If we logically follow through the argument that foreign exchange is part of the payment mechanism, it would seem that the volumes of foreign trade must have increased beyond all recognition. Not so. Thirty years ago dealing rooms were more dignified and much less frantic. The real reason for change is linked to the speed at which international capital flows are moving, not just the volumes of international trade; rather, it is also due to the decline of fixed exchange rates and the introduction of (managed) floating exchange rates and the euro.

The recent survey conducted by the Bank for International Settlements (BIS) shows a general decrease in the volume of foreign exchange traded globally on a daily basis, but estimates that the daily average figure still remains in excess of USD 1.2 trillion (USD 1,200,000,000,000), down from USD 1.5 trillion in 1998. Be careful – when we discuss trillions, the US trillion and the European trillion are not the same. In this context we use the US trillion with 12 zeros. Of this USD 1.2 trillion only about 10–12% is 'real', or non-speculative, although it could be argued that when banks operate in the interbank market they are mostly hedging existing positions, or those recently inherited from clients.

The survey also highlights that in 38% of all transactions the euro was one of the currencies. With trading in FX against the USD accounting for over 90% of the total and the most popular currency pair is still USD/JPY with a share of 30%.

The FX market exhibits continuous trading, conducted 24 hours a day around the world, and far outstrips the volume of actual trade flows.

MARKET PARTICIPANTS

The players within this market fall into a number of specific categories. The **first** group, which dominates the marketplace, consists of domestic and international banks, and which may be acting on their own behalf or for their customers. Central banks comprise the **second** group, and may be active in the market either intervening to support a currency or perhaps to suppress its value, or possibly for reserves management. Customers of banks who need physical foreign exchange to pay currency invoices, or sell forward the proceeds of a trade transaction, comprise the **third** group. They will generally have a real need for the currency. Unfortunately, they may suffer in the speculative flows when the FX traders start to operate. A **fourth** group of players exists: the high net worth (HNW) individuals, who may well be speculating with their own money for capital gain, as do a fifth group, the Fund Managers.

Lastly, there are the foreign exchange brokers acting as intermediaries between buyers and sellers. In the last few years there has been a massive shift towards technology and it is now necessary to divide the brokers into:

- Voice brokers – human beings; and
- Electronic brokers – computers.

For more information on broking generally and electronic brokers please see Chapter 5, The Last Ten Years: Developments in the Foreign Exchange Market by Tim Kane of EBS.

It is also valuable to step beyond these boundaries and approach the market from the perspective of the participant's motivations, are they:

- hedgers;
- traders;
- arbitrageurs?

In short, a hedger will seek to cover (or manage/mitigate) the FX risks, a trader seeks FX risk for profit and an arbitrageur is hoping to make money out of market inconsistencies or price discrepancies.

Generally the professional players can be subdivided into the following groups: the market makers, the central banks, the brokers, and then the clients – both commercial banks and corporate customers.

Market makers

These are the major banks, which will buy or sell a currency on a continuous basis 24 hours a day – not in the same centre! They quote their own prices, i.e. to buy and to sell a specific currency, and they will quote a two-way price. The gap between their bid and offer prices should cover their costs and make them a profit. Most big banks are market makers but not always in every currency. The recent 2001 BIS survey (published 2002) which was mentioned earlier, shows a daily average turnover of USD 504 billion in London, over 31% of the total global turnover. Business in the US and UK is quite widely spread but much of it is concentrated within relatively few major banks:

- In the US, 75% of all FX transactions are conducted with only 13 (was 20 in the 1998 survey) banks.
- In the UK 75% of all FX transactions are conducted with only 17 (was 24 in the 1998 survey) banks.

See www.bis.org for details of the 2001 and previous surveys.

These figures show a marked reduction in the amount of available counterparties, largely due to the onset of EMU and the introduction of the euro, together with the many banking consolidations, worldwide.

When you bear in mind there are still many hundreds of banks in the main financial centres, this is a massive concentration of business with a few major banks. The big market players, as at November 2002, are:

1. Citigroup
2. UBS Warburg
3. Deutsche
4. HSBC
5. ABN Amro
6. Royal Bank of Scotland
7. Standard Chartered
8. JP Morgan Chase
9. Goldman Sachs
10. ANZ

(Source: Risk Waters, *FX Week*)

Central banks

In the UK the central bank is The Bank of England. The Bank's supervision responsibilities passed to the Financial Services Authority in December 2001, it will, however, still intervene on the foreign exchanges to stabilize the exchange rate if required. In the US it is the Federal Reserve Bank of New York which fulfils this role and in Germany, the Bundesbank. The legacy European Central Banks such as Bank of France and the Bundesbank remain responsible for supervision in their respective countries. For a financial centre to operate effectively the market must have confidence in the abilities of the central bank.

The brokers

These are institutions which act as intermediaries, as agents rather than principals, and do not trade on their own account. There is evidence of a declining share of FX market trades going through traditional voice brokers all around the world.

Brokers remain an integral part of the FX market, providing price discovery and anonymity for their clients, together with fat and effective pricing. Over the last few years, there has been a degree of consolidation among the brokers as the smaller firms have been taken over and amalgamated with the bigger firms.

Looking at both voice brokers and electronic brokers, the biggest brokers in Spot FX are:

- EBS
- Reuters
- Prebon Marshall Yamane
- Tullett and Tokyo Liberty
- Intercapital (ICAP)

(Source: Risk Waters, *FX Week*)

The clients – domestic, commercial, and foreign banks

Not all banks will wish to make markets in every single pair of currencies. Often one can find niche banks that may aggressively trade, say, Czech Crown and EUR/USD, but for everything else they rely on the market to provide them with prices. They will need to ask another bank for the price, so in effect they are client banks most of the time. The distinction between foreign and domestic banks is subjective and is relative to where the client is based and regulated.

The clients – the customers

These may be financial institutions, hedge funds, multinational companies based in the UK or foreign subsidiaries based in Europe, or indeed anyone from anywhere, whether it be a major company or a private individual. The distinction between a customer and a market maker revolves solely around who is making the price and who is dealing on the price. Customers can buy or sell the foreign currency against their own domestic currency, or any other, with minimal regulation and with the certain understanding that the deal is being quoted and serviced in a highly professional manner.

Financial institutions

This group of companies can be regarded as institutions in the City of London or on Wall Street, or elsewhere in the world. Their major commodity is money and they buy and sell money or money equivalents, but they are generally not banks. Included in this group are the building societies, the insurance companies, the pension funds, the unit trusts and more recently the firms offering spread betting and contracts for differences (CFDs) in foreign exchange.

Hedge funds

This is an American term that crossed the Atlantic about seven years ago. The name is a misnomer. A hedge fund does not hedge. It is a high-risk investment vehicle that speculates in the currency, equity, and commodity markets. The fund name that is familiar to most market practitioners is the Quantum Fund through which George Soros used to operate in the markets, and through which he made good profits during the ERM crisis of September 1992 (Black Wednesday). There are many other hedge funds that speculate on the foreign exchanges. Hedge funds are now beginning to cause some concern among some of the regulators, as they are often based offshore and are consequently outside the jurisdiction of the central banks.

Multinational or domestic companies

There is a collective name given by banks to companies who are active – and sometimes not so active – in the financial markets: the 'corporates'. A corporate may range in size from BP Finance right down to a small engineering company based in Wigan, Lancashire. It is amazing but some large trading banks treat US investment houses as corporates rather than counterparty banks. Corporates usually have an underlying trade transaction for which they need to buy or sell currency. They will often be trying to 'hedge' or risk manage their positions so as to minimize potential losses or to obviate them completely.

High net worth individuals (HNWs)

A whole industry has grown up with the sole purpose of managing the risks and assets of the private individual. To qualify as an HNW you need to have a fair amount of money that can be placed 'under management': quite how much depends on the individual banks but it is usually assumed to be in the region of a minimum of USD 1,000,000 to USD 5,000,000. The banking service that these clients need will be vastly different from that required by, say, a major European corporate, and is known as private banking. A private bank may well concentrate on large mortgages, income enhancement, asset management, and investments, as well as offering speculative FX trading such as margin trading. This is where the client puts up collateral of, say, USD 1 million, and the bank allows him to 'gear up' and trade anything from five to 20 times his principal amount on the foreign exchanges.

SOME BASIC DEFINITIONS AND QUESTIONS

What is a currency?

Definition

It is a medium of exchange, coins or notes, used to buy goods or services. Most countries have their own currency, issued by an official agency called a central bank or a monetary authority.

What is a foreign exchange rate?

Definition

It is the ratio used to convert one currency into another. A rate of 2.2900 for GBP/CHF signifies that one pound is worth 2.290 Swiss Francs, or that one pound will buy 2.29 Swiss Francs.

What is a convertible currency?

Definition

A currency that can be freely bought or sold with no restrictions, or very few restrictions. Most currencies in the industrialized world are convertible or semi-convertible.

How are foreign exchange rates quoted?

Definition

Generally the SWIFT convention applies, where if a currency pair is written USD/JPY it signifies how many yen per dollar; if a currency pair is written GBP/JPY, it signifies how many Yen per pound sterling. In effect, it shows how many units of the second currency equal a specific amount, usually one unit of the first currency.

What is a foreign exchange transaction?

Definition

A deal where at a given moment two currencies are exchanged at an agreed rate. The exchange can be immediate or within a day or two: this is known as a **spot** transaction. Alternatively, it may be for a future date – which is a **forward** transaction.

Definition **What is the foreign exchange market?**

It is a communication network linking all participants. This is now a global market but centres like London and New York tend to dominate.

Question: *Why are banks involved with foreign exchange?*

Answer: To make money! In theory any individual or corporation can run a foreign exchange operation, unless restricted by law. Banks, however, are well equipped to handle all aspects of foreign exchange activities.

Question: *Is there a formal marketplace?*

Answer: No. The market consists of the trading rooms of public and private institutions, their clients and the brokers. Participants in various institutions may see one another only occasionally.

Question: *Is there a physical exchange of money?*

Answer: Rarely. The vast majority of transactions involve electronic transfers where accounts are simultaneously credited and debited. The recent money-laundering regulations have also encouraged the banks to ask many more questions when they are asked to transact in 'real' money or cash.

Question: *How permanent is a given exchange rate?*

Answer: The rate is valid until there is another rate. This can be a fraction of a second or it can be indefinitely if the exchange rate is controlled by the government. In the market, rates fluctuate constantly as they are affected by supply and demand

HOW FOREIGN EXCHANGE AFFECTS THE ECONOMY

Consumer prices

The prices of all imported products are directly affected by foreign exchange movements. In many countries a significant proportion of consumer goods are imports.

Wholesale prices

Staples and raw materials, from food to oil and metals, are major imports and therefore also subject to fluctuating prices due to foreign exchange developments.

Inflation

The pricing of imports will have a marked effect on inflation levels.

Export industries

The behaviour of the home currency in international markets is an important factor in determining the competitiveness of exports.

For instance, if a currency is overvalued, the price of that country's goods overseas will be relatively expensive, exports will suffer and jobs in export industries could be lost.

Domestic economy

All of the factors mentioned above can affect domestic developments.

Investor confidence

Patterns of savings and investments in the domestic economy can be greatly influenced by the degree of domestic and international confidence in the home currency.

Monetary policies

The pattern of international money flows (in or out), and to a lesser extent central bank interventions, may have a strong influence on the money supply, and therefore on monetary policies.

Interest rates

A change in monetary policies for the reasons shown above may result in changes in prevailing interest rates. For example, the desire to control inflation may lead to an increase in interest rates.

Leisure and tourism

Patterns of tourism are directly affected by currency fluctuations. When a country's home currency becomes strong, it becomes expensive for visitors.

THE ROLE OF THE CENTRAL BANKS

The Bank of England

The Bank of England, often called The Old Lady of Threadneedle Street, or simply The Bank, was founded in 1694 when the newly formed government under William of Orange raised a loan from a group of individuals who in return became the first Court of The Bank of England. It is reputed that this loan was needed to fund the war with France and was for £1.2 million with interest at 8%. Three years later, in 1697, the national debt had increased to £15 million. Two companies were soon contributing to the finances of the UK, making loans to the government in exchange for trading privileges these were, the East India Company and the South Sea Company. By the early eighteenth century these three groups practically controlled all of the nation's debt. The financial crisis of 1720 put an end to this arrangement and discredited the practice of financing the state with company funds. It also led to the increased importance of The Bank of England.

In 1844 The Bank was split into two separate departments: the Issue Department and the Banking Department. The Issue Department was given the authority to issue notes covered by government securities, and eventually became the sole bank with this privilege. The Banking Department is the banker for the government and the repository of the British monetary reserves (which may soon leave Britain's shores for Europe if/when the UK experiences EMU and joins the new European currency).

In 1946 The Bank of England was nationalized by the Labour government and placed under government ownership, the Treasury holding all the capital stock. In its banking role, The Bank will raise and lend funds like any other bank, and its main customers can be grouped into:

- private customers involved with commercial banking;
- banking institutions such as clearing banks;
- overseas central banks and monetary authorities.

The US Federal Reserve System

The US Federal Reserve ('The Fed') was created by an Act of Congress in 1913. Until then there was only a decentralized system of banking providing the cash and credit requirements of the US economy. The Federal Reserve Act provided for 12 regional Federal Reserve banks to be located around the country. Each had its own Board of Directors which selected one person to be on the Federal Advisory Board which would meet in Washington four times a year. A Federal Open Market Committee (FOMC) was established later, controlled by the district banks.

The Federal Reserve has three components:

(1) **The Board of Governors** consists of seven members appointed by the US President, six of them for a term of 14 years; the seventh, the Chairman, serves a four-year term which can be renewed. No two Board members can come from the same Federal District. The Board is responsible for formulation of US monetary policy, the supervision and regulatory compliance of all the regional banks, and the supervision of foreign activities of US banks, and the US activities of foreign owned banks.

The Federal Reserve Districts

1st	Reserve District: Boston	7th	Reserve District: Chicago
2nd	Reserve District: New York	8th	Reserve District: St Louis
3rd	Reserve District: Philadelphia	9th	Reserve District: Minneapolis
4th	Reserve District: Cleveland	10th	Reserve District: Kansas City
5th	Reserve District: Richmond	11th	Reserve District: Dallas
6th	Reserve District: Atlanta	12th	Reserve District: San Francisco

US Federal Reserve Districts

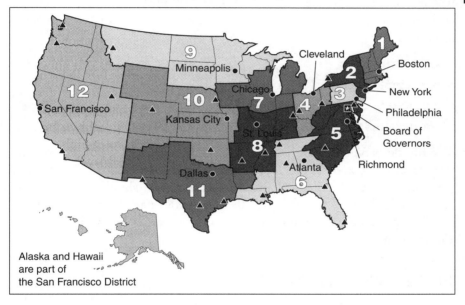

Source: US Federal Reserve Board

(2) **The Federal Reserve Banks** – these are the 12 district banks, through which member banks can borrow funds. The districts are shown in Table 2.1 and on the map – Figure 2.1. The Federal Reserve Banks operate a clearing house arrangement. They also operate as fiscal agents for the US government, and hold deposits for member banks.

(3) **Member Banks** – of which there are about 5,750. Only half of the nation's banks are members and part of the Federal Reserve system. There used to be considerable advantages in being a member bank, but these have diminished as some of the privileges are now open to non-member banks. Privileges used to include access to the wire transfer facilities, receiving dividends on Fed Reserve Bank Stock, provision of aid and information and assistance.

The original 1913 Act paid scant attention to the institution of a national monetary policy to preserve economic stability, so the 1935 Banking Act transferred control of the FOMC to the Board from the district banks. The Committee comprises the seven governors of the Federal Reserve Board, and five of the 12 Chairmen of the Federal Reserve Banks, chosen by rotation. The FOMC operates through the New York Federal Reserve Bank, which carries out the day-to-day dealing operations.

The German Bundesbank

The Bundesbank was established just after the Second World War. A 1957 law ensured that it was independent and required to support general economic policy unless this conflicted with its own functions, which are to ensure:

- stable prices;
- high employment;
- balanced foreign trade;
- constant and reasonable economic growth.

The Bundesbank does not have to be consulted over fiscal policy. The unification of East and West Germany has led to an enlarged Bundesbank council, and the President of the Bundesbank can, should he wish, even attend cabinet meetings. Many of these activities have been largely superseded with the introduction of the euro and the formation of the European Central Bank

The European Central Bank (ECB)

For many people, there is still an element of confusion over the exact role of the European Central Bank, which came into being with the euro and EMU in the late 1990s. The legacy central banks such as the Bank of France and the Bundesbank are still in existence. The European System of Central Banks (ESCB) has been established to coordinate the activities of all these central banks – but an important distinction needs to be made; the non-joiners are not allowed to be decision makers but all the countries are members.

At the time of writing there are 12 countries in the Eurozone with four European countries that have not joined, the non-joiners are:

- Denmark
- Sweden
- United Kingdom
- Norway

The Eurosystem is the name given for the ECB and the central banks of the in-countries, and comprises:

- Belgium
- Germany
- Spain
- Italy
- Luxembourg
- Austria
- France
- Greece
- Ireland
- The Netherlands
- Finland
- Portugal

Basic tasks of the Eurosystem

- To define and implement the monetary policy of the Euro area.
- To conduct FX operations and to hold and manage the official reserves of the euro area countries.
- To issue banknotes in the euro area.
- To promote smooth operations of the payment systems.

(Source: ECB)

Note: all banking supervision remains with the legacy central banks.

Currency classifications

Francesca Taylor, Taylor Associates

The foreign exchange market has its own jargon ... major and minor currencies, 'basket currencies', 'emerging markets', 'cross currencies'.

■ ■ ■

INTRODUCTION

The foreign exchange market has its own jargon as does the currency option market. It is quite likely that you will have heard references to the 'five majors', 'minor currencies', 'basket currencies', 'emerging markets' or maybe even 'crosses'. In this section we will explain the various different classifications. One method of classifying currencies relates to the ease of conversion between them and what restrictions, if any, government or otherwise, might apply to their spot and forward markets. Generally there are three important subdivisions.

BROAD CLASSIFICATION OF CURRENCIES

Major currencies

Freely available in the spot and forward markets.

Minor currencies

Freely available, although the spot market may from time to time lack liquidity. Restrictions can be imposed on the forward market in terms of maturity, i.e. not more than six months.

Emerging market currencies

Spot rates are available, but may be restricted with regard to transaction amount or government intervention. The forward market could be lacking, intermittent, or very expensive. Often currencies transact on a non-deliverable basis, known in the markets as NDFs. For more information on NDFs see Chapter 9, Emerging Market Foreign Exchange by Andrew Medhurst from HSBC.

INDICATIONS OF CURRENCY CLASSIFICATIONS

Major currencies

US dollar, Euro, Swiss franc, Japanese yen, UK sterling.

Minor currencies

Norwegian krone, Singapore dollar, Danish krone, Swedish krona, Hong Kong dollar.

Emerging market currencies

Indonesian rupiah, Thai baht, Malaysian ringgit, Vietnam dong, Chinese renminbi, Philippines peso, South African rand.

MAJOR CURRENCIES

The top five major currencies in foreign exchange trading are the US dollar, Euro, Japanese yen, Swiss franc, and British sterling. They should not be confused with similar abbreviations such as that for the G5 or even the G7 – the Group of seven nations, which comprise USA, France, Great Britain, Germany, Japan, Canada, and Italy. Each of the top five major currencies exhibits complete currency convertibility in large amounts, with an active long-dated forward market, sometimes over five years forward.

MINOR CURRENCIES

These are the currencies where there is complete convertibility but where there may be difficulties executing the full amount in a large transaction, for example in excess of USD 50 million equivalent. Alternatively, the forward market may only go out for perhaps 12 months or a year, or it may be relatively expensive.

EMERGING MARKET CURRENCIES

Over the last few years the term 'Exotic currency' has been dropped and those currencies are now included within the term 'emerging market', which can cover many things. Generally these are the currencies of the newly deregulated Eastern bloc countries, such as Poland, the Czech Republic, Slovakia and Hungary, Russia, Romania, the Baltic states of Lithuania, Latvia and Estonia, together with all of the South American currencies and all of the African currencies. If you then include the old exotic currencies which were typically Far Eastern (Thai baht, Singapore dollar, etc.) you have a currency block which covers a major part of the globe.

CROSS CURRENCIES

The definition of a cross currency is where a foreign exchange market price is made in two currencies, not involving the US dollar. Historically, the US dollar has been used as the medium of exchange, between currencies, but about twenty years ago the FX market started to expand the use of direct 'cross' dealing.

Consider a company based in the UK, selling goods to Switzerland and receiving payment in Swiss francs. Before 'crosses' evolved to their current level, it would have been necessary for the company to sell the Swiss francs for dollars and then sell the dollars for sterling. This would have involved them not only paying away the 'bid–offer spread' but also the possibility of running a potential dollar exposure if the two deals were not transacted simultaneously, not to mention further complications with forwards and options, etc. The major traded crosses are:

- EUR/JPY
- EUR/GBP
- EUR/CHF

Notice that the EUR is an integral part of cross-trading, although other crosses exist such as:

- GBP/CHF
- GBP/JPY

As the growth of cross markets continued, more and more banks were faced with customers requiring both cross currency rates and cross derivatives. By the early 1990s the market had grown enormously, leading to a common trading practice where some cross rates are used to quote other less well traded crosses. For further details on how to calculate cross currency rates see the section in Chapter 7, The Mechanics of Spot Foreign Exchange.

Cross currency arbitrage

This is one of the advantages of cross currency trading. It applies mainly to banks and brokers who are set up for the purpose. In simple terms, if the currency that is being traded is EUR/JPY, and a counterparty sells the bank EUR against yen, the bank has the option of either:

1. selling the EUR on to another counterparty;
2. trading out through the dollar, by selling EUR, buying dollars, then, selling dollars and buying yen.

If you can transact at a better rate through using the direct market (through the US dollar), then cross currency arbitrage is possible, sometimes known as triangular arbitrage.

4

The economics of foreign exchange

Francesca Taylor, Taylor Associates

An exchange rate is determined by the interplay of supply and demand.

■ ■ ■

INTRODUCTION

A foreign exchange rate is the price of one currency in terms of another. A rate will tell us, for example, how many euro are needed to purchase one US dollar. It is always important to remember that an exchange rate involves two currencies and can therefore be influenced by economic, financial, or political developments in either of the two countries in the relationship. As with any price, an exchange rate is determined by the interplay of supply and demand. This takes place in the global foreign exchange market, which in economic terms can be described as a 'perfect' market.

There are four criteria that have to be fulfilled for a market to be 'perfect':

1. There must be freedom of entry and exit from the market.
2. The product must be homogenous.
3. Each participant must be seeking to maximize profit.
4. There must be freedom of information within the industry.

Let us look at each of these in turn.

Entry into the foreign exchange market is generally relatively easy, especially following the abolition of exchange controls in the major economies. Both companies and individuals can trade foreign exchange with very few restrictions, although in their dealings with banks they will be subject to credit considerations, with banks themselves being supervised by central banks or other agencies.

The products being traded are undoubtedly homogenous or identical in that a purchaser of Swiss francs for dollars from one bank would be able to purchase them from any other bank.

There are problems with the third requirement in that the various participants in the market are not necessarily seeking profits in the same way and, in the case of governments, may not be seeking a profit at all. The attitude to profit differs because of the different time horizons of participants. A spot interbank dealer has a profit horizon of only a few minutes, an institutional investor will be judged by performance over months, while a corporate treasurer may simply have a mandate from the company to cover its currency requirements as and when they arise. In this case the corporate treasurer's activities may not even be regarded as being those of a profit centre. Over recent years a new development in the market has been the growth of so-called 'hedge funds'. Such funds use computer-generated technical models to seek profits in any financial market and as such have become important 'movers and shakers' in the foreign exchange market. Unlike banks they are not market makers and are not committed to being active in any one market at any time. Finally, when central banks/governments (collectively called the authorities) intervene in the FX market they are not usually seeking to make a profit but, rather, to influence the value of their currency for the 'benefit' of the economy and society as a whole.

The fourth issue – that of the freedom of information flows – brings in the concept of the 'efficient market' hypothesis. A market is said to be 'fully efficient' if the current price results from a consideration of all available news about the past and influences on the future. There is little doubt that spot rates are based on all the available information and therefore are traded in a 'fully efficient' market but this is not the case for forward exchange rates. These are not based on all available information, but instead are calculated from interest rate differentials plus a risk premium. This will be discussed in more detail later.

WHY BUY AND SELL CURRENCIES?

There are a number of reasons why governments, industrial and commercial companies, financial institutions, and individuals should want to supply and demand non-domestic currencies. The main reasons are:

- trade in goods and services;
- flows of short-term deposits;
- investment in financial assets (bonds and equities);
- investment in physical assets (e.g. factories);
- the use by central banks of reserves.

The relative importance of these has altered over the years and even now varies from time to time and from currency to currency. In the 1950s the bulk of activity on the foreign exchange market was the result of trade in goods and services. With the development of Eurocurrency deposit markets from the mid-1960s onwards, flows of short-term money became an important influence. More recently, the abolition of capital controls, improved communications and technology, together with an increase in the volume of investable funds, such as those of pension funds, has meant that flows of long-term capital into bonds and equities have become increasingly important. Various theories have been developed to try to explain what determines the levels of exchange rates.

IN THE BEGINNING WAS PURCHASING POWER PARITY ...

The oldest attempt to explain exchange rates is the purchasing power parity (PPP) theory. The pen that was used to produce the first draft of this text would be just as useful in New York City or Geneva as it is in London. However, the currency used to pay for it would be different – dollars in New York, Swiss francs in Geneva, and pounds sterling in London. Suppose that the price of the pen was £1.25 in the UK and $1.88 in the US. This would indicate an equilibrium exchange rate of $1.50 per £1. By comparing this with the actual market price of the currency, it is possible to say if the currency is over- or undervalued. In this example just one product was used but, if a basket of many goods is taken, an indication of an equilibrium exchange rate can be obtained. This type of calculation is carried out from time to time by international organizations such as the OECD. The result is, of course, only as representative as the basket of goods that has been used.

Purchasing power parity also gives an indication of the effect that inflation has upon exchange rates. Going back to the earlier example, if over the subsequent year the price of the pen increased by 15% in the UK to £1.44, but rose by just 5% in the US to $1.97, this would give a new equilibrium exchange rate of $1.37 per £1. The value of the high-inflation currency, sterling, would have fallen in terms of the low inflation dollars. This illustrates the importance of looking at economic developments in both countries.

Note that the example of the pen was chosen deliberately as it is the type of product that is universal. One of the drawbacks of PPP is that many goods cannot be transferred from one country to another in order to take advantage of exchange rate differentials. It thus applies only to tradeable and not non-tradeable goods. A car, for example, although cheaper, after allowing for the exchange rate in another country, may have the steering wheel on the wrong side, while differences in television transmission systems mean that a US television will not work in Europe. In addition, there are problems in deciding which is the correct measure of inflation to use when assessing relative exchange rate movements, given that there is a choice of consumer prices, wholesale prices, producer prices, traded goods prices and unit labour costs. Even if a particular index is chosen there may be problems as a result of differing tastes, and therefore index weightings, when comparing one country to another. A further difficulty is that when applying relative price changes in different countries to the exchange rate, it is necessary to start from a year in which the exchange rate is in 'equilibrium'. It is, however, extremely difficult to judge when this occurs at the time, and can only really be confirmed retrospectively. Finally, and most importantly, PPP tells us nothing about the determination of the flows of capital that dominate today's foreign exchange rate market. Many believe, however, that although PPP is of little use in forecasting short-term exchange rates, it is very important over the long term of five, ten, or more years.

Figure 4.1 shows the actual dollar/Deutschmark exchange rate from 1975 to 1996 together with the ratio of US consumer prices to those in Germany. It can be seen that over the period as a whole the exchange rate in 1996 was

Figure 4.1

Exchange rate and purchasing power parity

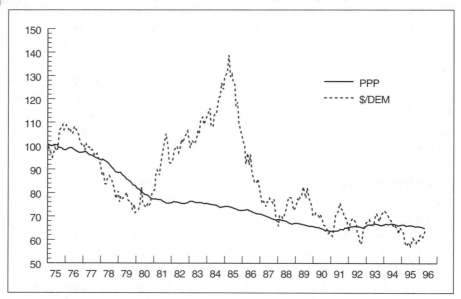

Source: Thomson Financial DATASTREAM

close to where PPP would have predicted, but that there have been times, e.g. 1985, when the dollar was substantially overvalued.

An extension of PPP is the use of 'real' exchange rates which show inflation differentials between countries. There is not, however, agreement as to which measure of inflation should be used, but there is a strong argument that relative wage costs give a good indication of a country's competitiveness. For this reason real exchange rates are taken as a measure of competitiveness.

... AND THEN THERE WERE DEPOSITS

A Eurocurrency deposit is a currency held at a bank outside its country of issue. It is, for example, a sterling deposit at a bank in Paris. This market started in the late 1950s as a result of the unwillingness of state banks in the Soviet Union to hold dollar deposits in the US for fear that they would be 'blocked' for political reasons. Instead the funds were placed with banks in Europe, which then lent them to their customers. The market quickly developed with dollars accumulating as a result of US trade deficits. The attraction of holding the deposits in banks outside the US was that this enabled US monetary controls, in particular bank reserve requirements and restrictions on the rate of interest paid, to be circumvented. Over time the market became broader and is now made up of deposits in all major currencies in banks throughout the world and not just in Europe.

During the 1970s and 1980s a number of alternative approaches to foreign exchange rate determination was developed. These attempted to take into account the increasing flows of short-term deposits that were taking place after the creation of the Eurocurrency market. In addition the increased study of the links between the money supply and prices (known as monetarism) made a move inevitable from purely domestic to international considerations of the impact of money.

This approach is therefore known as 'international monetarism' and looks at the willingness of both domestic and international residents to hold money. With fixed exchange rates, an increase in the money supply is seen as leading to a balance of trade deficit, which is offset by a drop in the country's reserves, which are defined as being part of the country's money supply. This results in a fall in the money supply and the old equilibrium is restored. Under floating exchange rates the analysis is somewhat different. An increase in the money supply is seen as being followed by a rise in domestic prices. With PPP assumed to hold continuously, this leads to an equivalent drop in the floating exchange rate. Observation of real world exchange rates, however, shows that rates frequently diverge from what were assumed to be their PPP levels.

An important development of the monetary model by Professor Rudiger Dornbusch of the Massachusetts Institute of Technology (MIT) attempted to resolve this dilemma. Dornbusch made a distinction between asset markets, where prices can react instantaneously to events, and goods markets, where prices are 'sticky'. In these goods markets prices are slow to react in the short term, although eventually the prices and the exchange rate will move in proportion to the change in the money supply as happened above. There are several possible reasons for prices being 'sticky'. Wages, for example, are often subject to review only on an annual basis, while supplies of raw materials may be bought on long-term fixed price contracts that cannot be readily altered. The analysis is based on the assumption that over the 'long term' PPP will apply, but not continuously as with fixed rates. In these circumstances, in the short term, a rise in the money supply will result in a fall in domestic interest rates (an increase in the supply of any product will generally result in a fall in prices). This fall will make the domestic currency less attractive. It will therefore depreciate, but those holding it will require to be compensated for the lower domestic rates by a future appreciation. The currency will therefore have 'overshot' its long-term equilibrium level, but will, over time, move to this level.

Although this 'sticky price' model is more sophisticated and provides an insight into why exchange rates may over- or undershoot, it has a number of drawbacks. First, it had problems associated with the definition of the money supply and the erratic velocity of circulation as a result of the instability in the demand for holding money. Second, the assumption in many models that PPP held continuously was clearly unjustified. Third, and most importantly, it assumed that wealth was held just in the form of domestic or foreign money. Holdings of bonds and equities were ignored.

FX RATES WITH A FULL RANGE OF ASSETS

The international monetary approach has thus given way to the wider approach of portfolio balance. This has the advantage that it can be adapted to embrace a greater range of assets and it thus includes money, bonds, and equities. Under portfolio balance, it is assumed that investors have a desired mix of money, domestic bonds, foreign bonds, domestic equities, and foreign equities. Furthermore, it is assumed that, although the foreign assets (by definition) are denominated in a foreign currency, the investor is interested only in their value in the domestic currency. Thus a depreciation of the currency raises the domestic value of the foreign bonds.

Let us work through an example of how the portfolio model operates. Suppose that the monetary authority increases the supply of domestic money. This will lead to domestic interest rates falling, which will make domestic bonds more attractive with their price tending to rise. At the same time, however, the lower interest rate will make the domestic bonds less attractive to foreign investors, and this will lead to an outflow of funds and a depreciation of the exchange rate. This in turn will boost the value of domestic holdings of foreign assets. The balance of the portfolio will be restored. A similar simulation can be carried out in the case of changes in fiscal policy. The impact on the exchange rate, however, will be less clear cut. Changes in the issuance of either public sector debt, as a result of budget deficits, or private sector debt, as a result of balance of payments deficits, can also be considered. As with other models, the portfolio approach is best at suggesting how a currency will react to a change of policy or behaviour, rather than predicting exactly where a spot rate will be in the future.

ARE FORWARD RATES FORECASTS?

Another approach is to look at forward exchange rates. By definition, a forward exchange rate gives the price of a currency at a future date. If markets were completely efficient, forward exchange rates would be forecasts based on information such as statistics and political developments that are expected to affect the currency over the period. Studies, however, show that

Figure 4.2

GBP/USD spot and forward rates

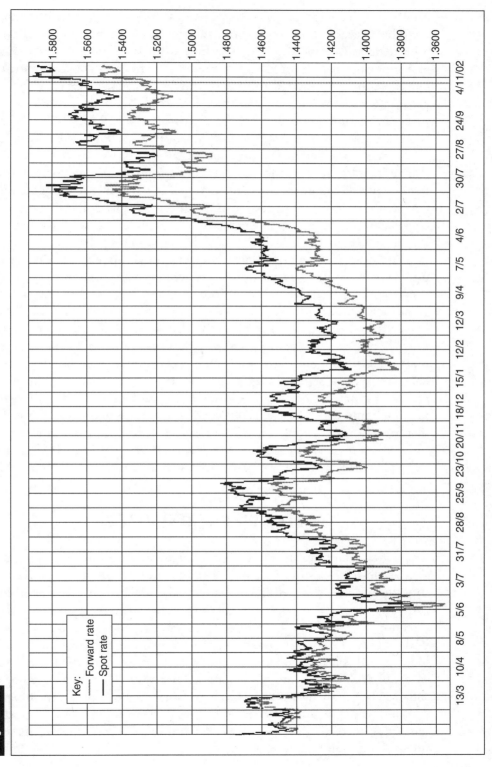

Source: Moneyline Telerate

economic forecasters can, on average, beat the forward rate. Why should this be? The answer is that forward rates are not forecasts but are based on an arithmetic calculation using the spot rate when the transaction is arranged and a forward margin based on the interest rate differential between the two currencies over the period until the contract matures, together with a risk premium. Forward rates at any other price would allow the counterparty to make an automatic profit. (This is discussed in detail in Chapter 8, The Mechanics of Forward Foreign Exchange.) The relationship between spot and forward rates can be seen in Figure 4.2.

The interest rates used to calculate forward rates are not allowed to find their own level but are set to a greater or lesser extent by the domestic monetary authorities, either the government or the central bank, using domestic considerations. They are not therefore set purely by market forces particularly at the very short end of the maturity curve. This is because the monetary authorities have a monopoly on the creation of money and can use this power to determine the level of interest rates in their economy.

On the face of it, then, there is little reason to suppose that forward rates are a forecast, but this raises the question of why interest rates differ from one country to another. As noted above, this is partly the result of differing official policies, and also as a result of differing inflation rates and the credibility of official policy. In brief, and very simply, interest rates can be characterized as being made up of two components: a real return and compensation for inflation. Thus a country with high inflation will tend to have high interest rates, when compared with a low inflation economy. This in turn will result in the high inflation economy having a relatively high forward discount on its currency which will make it worth less in the future. This, of course, is the same prediction as would have been made under PPP.

RELATIVE INTEREST RATES

There are some cases in which an exchange rate is dominated by flows of short-term deposits. One example of this is the euro/Swiss franc relationship. In this case, changes in interest rate differentials may give a good indication of how the exchange rate will move. This, of course, assumes that the direction of causation is from interest rates to exchange rates, but there may well also be a feedback in the other direction. A more sophisticated way of looking at this is to take inflation into account and adjust the interest rates accordingly. However, although domestic residents will be concerned by the inflation rate in their own country, they will not be bothered by the inflation rate in the other country except to the extent that it influences the exchange rate either through PPP or because the authorities try to counter the high inflation through high interest rates.

While considering interest rates, it is important never to forget that exchange rate changes are calculated in simple percentages but interest rates are quoted as a percentage per annum. Thus the return from an exchange rate movement of 1% during a day is considerably greater than that from a three-month Eurodeposit with a rate of say 10% per annum. This explains why the raising of short-term interest rates to extremely high levels does not necessarily protect a currency from expectations that it will be devalued. As can be seen from Figure 4.3 when in late 1992 Irish punt (now part of the euro) call money rose to a relatively high level as a result of speculation that the punt was to be devalued. In some cases overnight rates of as high as 1,000% have been seen in money markets.

As already noted, high inflation countries tend to have high interest rates and depreciating currencies. There are periods, however, when their currency is, for one reason or another, expected to remain relatively stable. This combination of high interest rates and a stable currency encourages inflows of short-term capital. On occasions investors borrow a low interest currency and then convert it into the high yielding currency in order to take advantage of the high interest rates. (Note that because forward rates are based on the interest rate differentials, the protection of a position through a forward contract would mean giving up the interest rate advantage.) By contrast, in volatile market conditions, historically stable 'hard' currencies, such as the

Irish overnight deposit rate

Figure 4.3

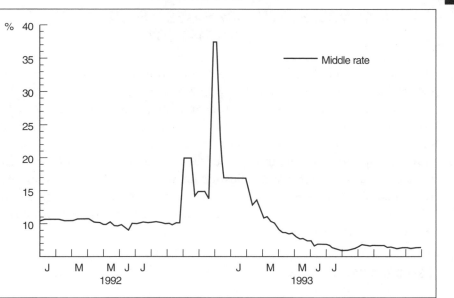

Source: Thomson Financial DATASTREAM

yen or Swiss franc, will appear more attractive despite their relatively low interest rates.

A FEW WORDS ON TECHNICAL ANALYSIS

Another approach to exchange rates is the use of technical analysis, which is discussed in detail in Chapter 20, Technical Analysis. In the very short term, technical analysis methods, such as moving averages, give a good indication of supply and demand pressures in a market. Charts and associated techniques can thus provide useful information. To some extent charts can become self-fulfilling prophecies. If market participants are using similar techniques they will react in the same way at the same time and this will produce the expected movement. The use of chart patterns to make predictions into the future is perhaps more problematic. Essentially chartists are saying that history repeats itself. A similar belief underlies econometric models. Those who look at currencies from a fundamental perspective would argue that, while charts are useful in the short term, they cannot deal with longer-term developments such as changes in fiscal policy. The counter-argument is that time is made up of a succession of discrete short terms and that it is therefore fruitless to make forecasts based on the long term.

WHAT MOVES EXCHANGE RATES – ECONOMIC NEWS AND STATISTICS?

Whichever model of exchange rate determination is thought to be most relevant, it is clear that economic developments are important. Economic news gives an indication of what is happening in an economy and how the economy might develop in the future. Economies are rather like supertankers at sea. They both have considerable forward momentum and are slow to respond to commands, which in the case of the economy include fiscal changes and interest rate adjustments. Because of this forward momentum, markets have a good idea of where an economy is going, but will nonetheless react, possibly dramatically, to shocks from statistics which lead to changes in those expectations.

Economic news

There are various types of economic news.

The stance of a government's economic policy has an important influence on exchange rates. Declarations by governments and central banks give an indication of official policy and may include remarks on the exchange rate. These are studied closely to see if the policies put forward are consistent and credible. Markets are not gullible and are not taken in by promises to carry out policies that are impractical or will be impossible to carry out because they lack public support.

Other business news may also be important. For example, a cross-border takeover may involve a large currency transaction that will not only have a one-off impact on the market, but may also be a precursor of similar deals, especially if a particular country is seen as offering good investment opportunities. Note that investment in physical assets, such as factories and machinery, once made is difficult to withdraw when compared with investment in financial assets.

Statistics

Statistics give an indication of what has happened in the past, and this forms the basis for forecasting what might happen in the future. Statistical releases can be broken down into several different groups.

First come those that deal with the size and growth of the overall economy. Gross domestic product (GDP) measures this, but because it is generally calculated only quarterly needs to be supplemented by other, monthly figures, such as industrial production and retail sales. Growth is an important influence on unemployment.

Second, there are several measures of inflation or changes in prices. Overall inflation is measured by the GDP deflator, while other measures such as the consumer (or retail) price index, producer prices, and import prices give information about what is happening in key parts of the economy. Wage and earning statistics give an indication of the effect of labour costs, with unit labour costs also taking account of productivity changes.

Third, balance of payments statistics give an indication of international flows to and from a country. The current account is made up of trade in goods and services, and also includes payments of interest and dividends. Flows of capital are included in the capital account. Note that not all the transactions included in the balance of payments involve an FX transaction. Exports, for example, may be paid for in the currency of the exporting country or that of a third country, with oil, for example, being paid for in US dollars.

Fourth, financial statistics show financial developments. These statistics include a country's budget deficit/surplus or the public sector net cash requirement (PSNCR) and money supply statistics. It is believed by monetarists that there is a link between money supply and future price inflation.

The strength of this link varies from country to country and is thought by the German Bundesbank to be particularly close in Germany.

Foreign exchange statistics

Information and statistics are available about exchange rates themselves. FX prices are readily available from screens and newspapers, but note that these prices are indicative and do not necessarily represent actual deals. In addition, because the FX market does not have fixed hours of activity there cannot be definitive opening and closing prices as in a stock market or futures exchange. Some central banks hold daily fixings for their currencies against other units, and publish the price at which market supply and demand balances.

Effective exchange rates attempt to show the overall impact of changes in spot rates, by linking exchange rate movements to trade flows. An effective exchange rate index for a country weights the importance of other currencies in terms of volumes of trade. Thus a change in sterling against, say, the US dollar will have a greater impact than a movement of sterling against the Australian dollar. Such indexes are compiled by several organizations and as a result of different weightings produce slightly different results. The overall picture, however, should be broadly similar. In the UK, for example, the sterling index is published at hourly intervals during the working day by The Bank of England, with those for other currencies published on a daily basis.

Surveys of overall activity in the global FX market are carried out at three-yearly intervals by central banks under the auspices of the Bank for International Settlements (BIS). The 2001 survey is discussed in the Preface.

FX market reaction to data releases

In many countries, notably the US and the UK, a calendar of future releases is published, sometimes covering several months ahead. This allows positions to be taken before US and UK figures in the knowledge that they can be closed ahead of the actual release. Markets normally have a forecast of each release and will react only if the actual figure is significantly different from this forecast.

With many statistical releases, the reaction of the foreign exchange market will take place in two stages. The first reaction will be based on economic theory, while the second will depend on how the authorities are expected to react. Thus higher than anticipated inflation could be expected to lead to a currency depreciating as higher prices will make a country's exports less competitive, but the realization that rising inflation should lead to the government raising interest rates will encourage inflows of short-term deposits. Note, however, that higher interest rates will tend to slow the economy and could thus have an adverse impact on equities. Short-term bonds will react unfavourably to higher interest rates, but long-dated stocks are likely to be helped by the government's move to dampen inflationary forces. As the range of transactions in the FX market has broadened, it has become more difficult to judge the reaction to news and statistics. This has made the use of economists and analysis services more important.

Observation of statistics shows that economies move in cycles of boom and bust or peaks and troughs. Various theories have been put forward for these patterns, ranging from the influence of sunspots to the effect of investment. Market reaction to statistics will depend partly on where an economy is within the business cycle. Thus a sharp increase in industrial output may be welcomed when an economy is in recession, as it suggests that a recovery is taking place that will boost company profits, but a similar rise when the economy is booming may lead to concerns over shortages of capacity within the economy and thereby give rise to fears of higher inflation.

WHAT MOVES EXCHANGE RATES – POLITICS?

Politics is another factor that has an important influence on foreign exchange rates. While the business cycle is unpredictable in timing and amplitude, it is played out against the background of the political cycle. In some countries, e.g. the US, this cycle is very rigid, with set dates for elections, but in others, such as the UK, it is more flexible with the government having discretion on the timing of the election, subject to a latest date by which voting must take place. Economic factors are a major consideration for voters and governments therefore tend to try to maximize the 'feel-good' factor of rising incomes and falling unemployment as elections approach.

It would be naive to pretend that markets do not prefer centre-right governments, because these tend to allow the corporate sector more freedom. Generally the market is looking for consistency and continuity of policies. Changes of government or leaders call this continuity into question and this can cause exchange rate volatility. A good knowledge of a country's political system is needed to be able to assess the importance of opinion polls and elections. Thus, in many European countries, voting in the elections for the European Parliament is seen as being an opportunity to register a protest vote, rather than as an opportunity to change the government of the country. A poor result for the ruling party may, therefore, have a minimal influence on domestic politics and policies, unless the poll is very close to the general election.

WHAT MOVES EXCHANGE RATES – INTERVENTION?

Given the importance of foreign exchange rates to an economy, a government has to have a policy on its currency. This will vary from country to country ranging from allowing the unit to float freely, on the grounds that the market knows best, to having a currency that is fixed against another unit. Few currencies are truly floating or completely fixed and most countries undertake 'dirty floating' with reserves of gold and foreign currency used from time to time to influence the value of the currency.

The old Exchange Rate Mechanism (ERM) formed part of the European Monetary System (EMS). Each of the participating currencies had a central rate against the European Currency Unit (ECU), which was made up of a basket of the currencies of the members of the European Union in 1989. These ECU rates were used to calculate central rates, and bands of ±15%, against each of the other currencies. A combination of intervention, interest rate adjustments and general economic policy was used to keep a currency within its band. Should these fail then evaluations/revaluations could take place. (Note that strictly a devaluation refers to an administered change in a fixed central rate, whereas a downward movement of a floating rate is a depreciation.) Thus the ERM was a hybrid system that contained elements of both fixed and floating exchange rate systems.

With the formal introduction of the euro the historic terms of, ECU, EMS and ERM were superseded. The euro is a now a true new currency not just a basket of all the Eurozone currencies, even though at its inception in 1999, weightings etc. were taken into account.

Intervention can be both verbal and actual. Verbal intervention takes place when the authorities make statements intended to influence the value of a currency. Actual, physical, intervention takes place when reserves of gold and other currencies are used to purchase the domestic currency and, by increasing the demand for it, boost its value. However, reserves are finite and unlimited intervention to support a currency cannot therefore be carried out, because eventually the reserves will run out and all borrowing facilities will be exhausted.

Intervention can also be carried out to reduce the value of a currency. The domestic authority can literally produce extra money and, by increasing the supply of the currency, reduce its value. Note, however, that this printing of money has implications for the country's money supply and, if the country is following a money supply target, the extent of this intervention will have to be limited.

Given the size of the global foreign exchange market, the influence of central bank intervention will always be limited. Central banks know that their finite reserves will have only a modest impact and that they will rarely be able to turn around a currency. They can, however, seek to influence their

Figure 4.4

£/DEM and UK underlying reserves

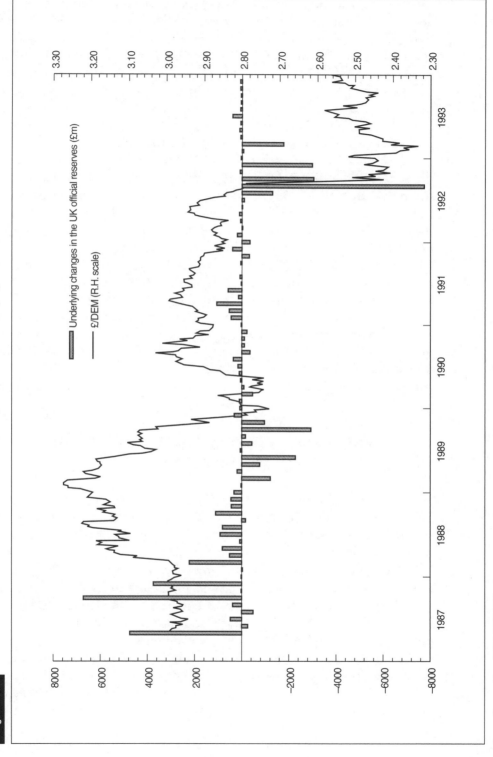

Underlying changes in the UK official reserves (£m)

£/DEM (R.H. scale)

Source: Thomson Financial DATASTREAM

currency and encourage markets to assess whether a movement is justified or not. Coordinated intervention, carried out by two or more central banks acting together, tends to be more effective than when a single bank is acting alone to support its currency. This is because it shows that there is international agreement on the need for the value of a currency or currencies to be altered. Often such action is carried out by the Group of Seven (G7) industrialized countries acting together. Intervention, backed up by appropriate changes in national economic policy, may be effective, but intervention by itself rarely has more than a relatively short-term impact.

Figure 4.4 shows movements in GBP/DEM and the UK's reserves over the period 1987 to 1993. During 1987 the government followed a policy of shadowing the DEM with sterling being sold in an attempt to prevent it from appreciating over DEM 3.00. As a result the UK's reserves rose substantially. There then followed a period of more modest intervention, apart from in 1989 while the currency was weakening. During the period of the UK's membership of the ERM intervention was again relatively modest, but there were very large falls in late 1992 as a result of the government's ultimately unsuccessful attempt to keep sterling within its bands.

A country will try to hold its reserves in the currencies that will prove most effective when it is intervening. Historically the foreign exchange market has been dominated by dollar trading and the US unit has therefore formed the bulk of reserves. Over recent years, however, this has been changing as a result of the growing importance of the euro and the yen.

WHAT MOVES EXCHANGE RATES – SENTIMENT AND RUMOURS?

Sentiment is a word that is frequently used in the FX market, but is almost impossible to define. To some extent it is based on a long-term view of a country and represents confidence that it will maintain policies that have worked for the good of its currency in the past.

In the short term, markets can be moved by rumours. The subject of these can be wide-ranging. There is a suspicion that rumours are sometimes started deliberately in order to take advantage of the subsequent movement in rates, but obviously it is very difficult, if not impossible, to prove or disprove this. It is also possible that some rumours or leaks may be started deliberately by governments or central banks in order to prepare the market for surprising statistics. Once a rumour is denied or disproved, the market will tend to move back to its original position, but often the market will remain suspicious, especially if the rumours are about politics, on the ground that there is no smoke without fire.

WHY DO EXCHANGE RATES MATTER?

Exchange rates have an important influence on economies because of the effect that they have on inflation, trade competitiveness, and employment. The degree of their impact will depend on the extent to which the economy is self-sufficient, with little trade, rather than open to trade. Thus exchange rates have a much smaller impact on the US, where exports account for around 8% of GDP than in the UK where exports are equivalent to about 20% of GDP. The impact on inflation comes because a strong exchange rate will mean cheaper imports and force exporters to contain costs if they are to stay competitive.

A high, overvalued exchange rate will make exports more expensive in terms of another currency but imports cheaper in terms of the domestic currency. Exports will therefore be curtailed, while imports will be encouraged. This in turn will lead to production being increased in other countries relative to domestic output. As a result, unemployment will rise domestically, particularly in the traded goods sector, but fall internationally. A weak exchange rate will have an analogous effect, but in reverse. Note that the exchange rate does not just affect trade in goods, but has an impact on services such as tourism.

Workers have votes, and politicians know that employment is a key issue in general elections. Thus over time there will be a tendency for politicians to try to keep the currency close to, or even perhaps a little weaker than, its equilibrium level in terms of employment in goods and services. This process, however, will be slow and erratic.

Another reason exchange rates matter is that many business leaders believe high exchange rate volatility reduces international trade. It is argued that the uncertainty created by this volatility discourages businesses from selling to other countries. This is, of course, despite the existence of a wide range of hedging products.

The last ten years: developments in the foreign exchange market – a broker's perspective

Tina Kane, EBS

INTRODUCTION

'Once a dealer, always a dealer' used to be the motto of the UK Foreign Exchange Association before its re-branding as the Association Cambiste International (ACI). For foreign exchange traders and brokers, this might mean a wistful look at tourist rates when they are on holiday. But for many an old foreign exchange hand, the lure of the markets is extremely powerful.

Among its many attractions, the foreign exchange market is a dynamic and vibrant place and one that changes rapidly. This has been particularly noticeable in the last decade. Indeed, the market's evolution since 1993 has been so fast that a trader who had decided to take a ten-year sabbatical ten years ago would now find the foreign exchange business almost unrecognizable compared with the environment he once worked in.

Even if the principles and mechanics of the business are the same, the pace and scale of the changes make it extremely likely that anybody returning to the foreign exchange market after such a long break would struggle to survive. Perhaps the old Foreign Exchange Association was prescient when it dropped its motto.

WHAT IS FOREIGN EXCHANGE?

There is nothing particularly complicated about the concept of trading foreign exchange (FX or Forex) as long as it is remembered that money and currencies are little more than commodities. And like all commodities, money has a value that can change.

Indeed, the FX business is built entirely on the premise that the value of currencies *will* change, relative to the value of others (in either direction). Sometimes this happens very dramatically, such as the plunge in the value of sterling on 'Black Wednesday' in September 1992. (Almost exactly a decade later, several South American currencies fell to record lows against the US dollar because of severe economic problems across that continent).

Most of the currencies of the major industrialized countries are free floating, or 'fully convertible'. They can be bought and sold freely with very few or no restrictions. The value of these currencies is determined to a large extent by market forces, although monetary authorities have in the past – and occasionally still do – try to manipulate their relative worth in the marketplace.

Some countries 'peg' their currency's value to another, like the Hong Kong dollar and the US dollar. Others have stringent restrictions on currency transactions, with all deals requiring extensive paperwork showing that they are a necessity for a genuine import or export business.

Typically, money appreciates or depreciates in value against other 'goods' (including other currencies) over a period of time. A good example of this is inflation, for example, the increase in the amount of money needed to purchase goods such as food or houses. Similarly, in the case of two countries with different currencies, the respective units of money have a relative worth against each other.

How that value – the currency's 'external' value – is determined is difficult to define. It is far more complicated than simply comparing the costs of identical products in two different locations. Factors such as two countries' relative growth and inflation rates, interest rates and trade and investment flows all have an influence on the relative value of one currency to another.

Ironically, the perceived value of a currency can itself have an impact on the economy. The reporting of currency movements and their potential impact on national and global economies is often grossly exaggerated (and often completely contradictory).

National newspapers report with great pride on the strength of sterling (the pound) against the euro as if it were a contest. Perversely, these same papers, often in the same edition, will also rail about the damage a strong pound has on British exports and the UK's manufacturing base. This is because a strong pound makes goods more expensive to sell abroad. At the same time, currency weakness is often portrayed as a national and political disgrace.

The fact is that a relatively weak currency can provide a *boost* to exporters because their goods can be priced more competitively overseas. Importers, however, may take the opposite view. A weak domestic currency means imported goods are more expensive and, of course, vice versa.

The 'spot' market

When commentators talk about the FX market, they are generally referring to the spot market. Spot transactions involve buying one currency against another, with a settlement time of two working days ahead. The FX rate is the ratio used to convert one currency against the other. GBP/USD is the symbology representing the 'currency pair' Great British Pounds (GBP) against the United States Dollar (USD), i.e. GBP/USD 1.5 indicates the value (or ratio) of one (1) GBP in US dollars (approximately 1.5 US dollars).

While numerous currency pairs are traded, by far the largest proportion of activity is concentrated in just five 'majors'. These are the US dollar (USD), euro (EUR), pound sterling (GBP), Japanese yen (JPY) and Swiss franc (CHF). According to the Triennial Central Bank Survey of 2001, published by the Bank for International Settlements (BIS) in Basel, the US dollar is on

Currency distribution (%) of reported FX turnover

Table 5.1

	1998	2001
USD	87.3	90.4
EUR		37.6
DEM	30.1	...
FRF	5.1	
ECU and other EMS	17.3	
JPY	20.2	22.7
GBP	11	13.2
CHF	7.1	6.1
CAD	3.6	4.5
AUD	3.1	4.2
SEK	0.4	2.6
HKD	1.3	2.3
SGD	1.2	1.1
Emerging markets[1]	3	5.2
Other	9.3	10.1
Total	200	200

The total for each column comes to 200% as two currencies are involved in each transaction.
[1] Emerging market currencies in this case are: Brazilian real, Chilean peso, Czech koruna, Indian rupee, Korean won, Malaysian ringgit, Mexican peso, Polish zloty, Russian rouble, Saudi riyal, South African rand, Taiwan dollar and Thai baht.

Source: BIS Triennial Central Bank Survey 2001.

one side of over 90% of all FX transactions. The most heavily traded currency pair is EUR/USD, which accounts for nearly a third (30%) of daily FX turnover, followed by USD/JPY (20%), GBP/USD (11%) and USD/CHF (5%). (See Table 5.1.)

Taken together, daily turnover in spot, forward and outright FX is said to be in the region of around $1,200 billion every day, making the FX market one of the biggest in the world.

FORWARDS, OPTIONS, FRAs AND STIRs

There are other FX products besides spot. Forwards, also known as swaps, account for the majority of daily FX transactions. In a forward transaction, a currency is exchanged *now* for another and then 'swapped' back at an agreed *later* date. In effect, one currency is borrowed from a counterparty in return for the loan of another one. The 'forward' price reflects the interest rate differential between the two currencies for the period. In theory, the forward price could be exactly the same as the spot rate, but for this to occur, the two interest rates of the two different currencies would have to be identical for the determined time period. They seldom are.

Outrights

An outright forward is a combination of a spot transaction with a forward adjustment. Importers and exporters often use outrights to manage their future currency exposure by fixing a future exchange rate. They are taking the risk, obviously, that the rate they fixed at is not favourable at the future date. Equally, the rate they fixed at might be extremely favourable at the future date. A good analogy for outrights might be mortgages offering fixed interest rates for certain periods of time as this passes the risk onto the lender of possible interest rate moves.

Currency options, which can be likened to insurance policies, are derivative instruments (i.e. they are derived from an underlying currency price). Purchasers/sellers of options are buying/selling the right to trade at an agreed rate at some point in the future. At the time that the option is struck there is no exchange of principal. At the agreed future date, however, and depending on where the agreed rate (strike price) is relative to the actual rate the 'loser' will pay the difference between the two rates to the 'winner' (the counterpart that had a favourable interest rate move after the deal was struck).

Numerous inputs are required to calculate (or derive) the value of a currency option, including spot and forward rates. A crucial input is, however, a measure of the probability of a currency moving to certain levels. Options often get a bad press but they can be considered as useful instruments designed to minimize rather than increase risk.

FRAs and STIRs

Forward rate agreements (FRAs) and short-term interest rate futures (STIRs) are also derivatives. FRAs and STIRS are similar to the extent that they are both based on the future cost of three-month money (the IMM dates which are the third Wednesday in March, June, September and December) when futures' contracts mature and the settlement is agreed. The key difference between them is that FRAs, like spot FX, trade 'over-the-counter' (OTC) and STIRs trade on regulated exchanges. Strictly speaking, neither of these are FX products, but money market (deposit) instruments. However, FRAs are included in the authoritative Triennial Central Bank Survey on FX, and both products are widely used by FX forward traders as interest rate tools in their own right and also for hedging forward trade exposure.

As well as using STIRs and FRAs to hedge their own trading books, many forward FX dealers also use these products for their own speculative positions because derivative instruments are much less capital intensive. Rather than doing a *forward* trade buying dollars and selling euros, for example, a trader could create the same exposure by selling Eurodollars and buying Euribor (three-month) euro futures.

How a STIR or FRA price is derived
Definition

The price of a STIR or FRA is derived by subtracting the implied interest rate from 100. So if September Euribor is trading at 95.00, the implied future cost of three-month euro deposits is 5% (100 − 95).

FRAs are normally quoted as 1 month versus 4 months (1v4), 2v5, 3v6, etc. Neither STIRs or FRAs are predictors of where three-month deposit rates will be in the future, but are, effectively, forward-forward deposit rates. Due to what is known as the 'net present value' of money, the implied rate tends to be higher, therefore, further out along the yield curve.

Another way of looking at this is 'What is more valuable, £1 million today or £1 million in three years' time?' The answer is that money available *today* can be reinvested, so is worth more.

Geographical spread

Globally, BIS figures show that the UK remains the biggest location for FX business, accounting for over 31% of daily business, followed by the US (15.7%), Japan (9.1%) and then Singapore (6.2%). Most FX activity in the UK passes through the City of London. However, there are strong regional centres in other countries, such as Germany. There, Frankfurt is considered to be the biggest centre, but trading banks exist in Berlin, Munich, Dusseldorf and other cities.

According to BIS, spot turnover increased by 24% between 1989 and 1992 and it then grew by 25% between 1992 and 1995. Ten years on and it's an entirely different story. According to the most recent BIS statistics spot turnover in 2001 was nearly 22% lower (at $387 billion) than in 1998 and even below the volume recorded in 1992. (See Table 5.2.)

Risk

The amounts, prices and maturity dates of FX products are all negotiable and any deal results in both counterparties assuming some degree of *credit risk*. That is, the risk that the counterparty will be unable to fulfil its side of the trade.

Table 5.2 **Global FX market turnover, adjusted for local and cross-border double counting**

	Daily averages in April (billions of dollars)				
	1989	1992	1995	1998[1]	2001
Spot transactions	317	394	494	568	387
Outright forwards	27	58	97	128	131
FX swaps	190	324	546	734	656
Estimated gaps in reporting	56	44	53	60	26
Total 'traditional turnover'	590	820	1,190	1,490	1,200
Memo: turnover at April 2001 exchange rate[2]	*570*	*750*	*990*	*1,400*	*1,200*

[1] Revised since previous survey.
[2] Non-US legs of FX transactions were converted from current US dollar amounts into original currency amounts at average exchange rates for April of each survey year and then reconverted into US dollar amounts at average April 2001 exchange rate.

Source BIS, Basel

There is also *settlement risk* to consider. That is the risk that one side will pay out and its counterparty will fail to reciprocate for various reasons, including liquidation. This was highlighted spectacularly in 1974 when Bankhaus Herstatt had its banking licence withdrawn by the German regulators. At that time, Herstatt had already received Deutschmarks from its market counterparties. Its US dollar correspondent, however, knowing that its 'customer' had had its banking licence withdrawn, refused to make its dollar payments on behalf of Herstatt.

As a result, settlement risk is commonly referred to as Herstatt Risk.

Settlement risk is of particular importance when two sides to a transaction are settling in different time zones. For instance, a counterparty on one side of a USD/JPY deal might pay out yen from his account in Tokyo some 24 hours before it receives the corresponding dollars to its account in New York. This issue has long vexed regulators although a number of schemes for reducing settlement risk, like FXNET, have been successful. The recent launch of the CLS Bank, which utilizes a payment versus payment (PVP) process to ensure that funds are not released until the corresponding payments have been received, effectively eliminates settlement risk for CLS currencies.

Regulated futures and options exchanges generally use a central counterparty such as the London Clearing House (LCH), for all transactions. This largely eradicates credit and settlement risk since transactions are between participants and the CCP.

OTC VERSUS EXCHANGES

Dealing on a regulated exchange is different. These markets, typically, have had clearly defined, restricted trading hours and until recently, counterparties had to be present physically in the same location. This has changed more recently with the increasing acceptance of electronic trading and the creation of 'virtual' borderless exchanges.

If the OTC markets can be defined as 'professional' to the extent that the players are, in the main, banks and financial institutions, exchanges are attractive to – and accessible by – smaller investors, including 'day traders' trading 'PA' (on their own account) possibly because of a lower perceived risk.

Futures and exchange-traded option contracts are for set amounts and fixed maturities. As with OTC options, there is no exchange of principal for futures and exchange-traded option transactions. Exchange users 'post' a margin at the exchange (they 'pay to play'). This is adjusted typically on a daily basis by 'marking' each open position 'to market' (comparing the actual 'price' with the futures price. This is intended as a means of managing exposure and ensuring that no unexpected losses materialize.

However, this advantage of exchange-traded futures and options can also be its primary disadvantage, especially if risk management is lax.

Margins utilize only a small percentage of principal capital, consequently, traders can and may take positions that far exceed those where principal payment is required. There is an old Turkish proverb 'You get twice as drunk on credit' – an apposite analogy.

The much-publicized ING (Barings) trading scandal of a few years ago and the more recent Global Crossing debacle both apparently demonstrate the potential folly of being over-leveraged if the market goes the wrong way and/or positions are not managed properly.

MARKET PARTICIPANTS AND WHAT THEY LOOK FOR

According to the Bank of England's *The Foreign Exchange Market, April 2000* there are three types of participant in the FX market – brokers, banks and customers. There is a degree of overlap between these categories (banks can be customers of other banks, for example) and all three classifications can be further subdivided.

Irrespective of the type of participant, the pattern of business is generally the same between the three groups. Customers deal with banks and banks deal with brokers (or trade directly with each other).

Brokers are the 'middlemen' of the marketplace, matching up buyers and sellers in return for a commission. Brokers do not trade on their own accounts and are not supposed to hold positions or to have any open exposure to market movements. Brokers are interested only in turnover and it is (or should be) irrelevant to them in which direction a market moves.

The **banking sector** is diverse and includes (national) central banks, large international trading houses, regional savings banks (building societies), smaller 'boutique' finance houses and everything in between. Banks can (and do) deal on their own accounts, either to manage their own FX exposure or to take speculative positions in the market.

Larger banks often act as market makers – they will quote, simultaneously, a price at which they are prepared to buy **and** to sell particular currencies (the 'bid/offer spread'). In addition to the actual quote price, the spread will alter depending on factors such as who is requesting the quote ('do we do business with them?') the reciprocal risk (credit) profile of the counterparty ('are they financially sound?') and the counterparty's perceived 'value' to the bank (i.e. 'how much other business do we do with them?'). The higher the perceived risk and smaller the value of the business, the wider the spread will be. Requests for quotes in non-market amounts, whether small or large, also tend to result in wider spreads.

Banks make their money, in theory, from the spread between the buy and sell price, i.e. by selling a currency for more than they bought it for. They may also make money by charging customers a commission, which is typically calculated as a 'basis point' percentage of the total value of the FX transactions.

Customers range from huge multinational corporations to individuals purchasing currency for their holiday and encompass high net worth (in other words, rich) individuals who are prepared to speculate with their own money, importers and exporters, domestic, international and multinational companies and financial institutions such as insurers, pension funds and other asset managers, futures houses and hedge funds.

Different customers want different things from the market. Some access it to convert foreign currencies received for goods back into their domestic currency. Others purchase foreign currency to pay for imported goods. More sophisticated customers might want to transact FX to take advantage of lower or higher interest rates overseas. Yet others may be active speculators.

The FX trading operations of a typical corporate are a good illustration of why currency markets exist. A German exporter to the US, for example, needs to convert the US dollars it receives from the overseas sale of its goods back into euros. If the exporter is paid in one go, it can simply instruct its bank to execute a spot transaction to sell the dollars it has received for euros. However, and as an additional complication, an exporter will not necessarily export goods and/or receive the corresponding dollars at one time, but in several tranches over a period of time.

Alternatively, an exporter could agree a dollar price today for payment for goods that it will export in six months time – a **forward**). This would expose the exporter immediately to FX risk since the dollar equivalent for the goods today may not be favourable in the future.

In the (unlikely) event that absolutely no FX movement occurred over the forward time period (and allowing for any interest rate differential) the exporter could leave its position 'naked' for six months and sell the dollars when it receives them at 'today's' price.

If in that period, however, the dollar were to weaken dramatically, the exporter would receive far fewer euros than it had anticipated for its dollars and would incur an FX loss.

Alternatively, the exporter could do an **outright forward** and lock in an exchange rate. This would reduce its risk, as it would then know exactly what rate it could use in six months time when it sold the dollars. However, should the dollar have strengthened in that period, it would lose the potential to have gained money from the movement in FX prices.

Another alternative would be to use the **options** market. The customer could buy the right to purchase dollars at an agreed rate, thus capping how many euros they would receive in the worst-case scenario. However, by taking out an option, the customer could, potentially, still gain from beneficial FX moves.

In reality, an exporter can never be sure how many goods it will sell overseas and/or when the transaction(s) will take place than it can predict, accurately, the future FX rate. Managing this risk can be complicated and many larger companies have now established their own in-house treasury function to do this, for example:

Example

A dealer buys EUR 10 million, sells $9 million at 0.90.

The euro appreciates to 0.9020 (a gain of just 0.22%).

Trader sells EUR 10 million at 0.9020, buys $9.02 million.

The euro book balances, but the dollar account is now increased by a $20,000 profit.

If the trader does this everyday for the whole year, they will make over $5 million for the bank. It seems simple enough. In practice, however, it is a bit harder to get it exactly right, all of the time.

It is often said that FX trading is a 'zero sum game'. That is, one in which all profits (and losses) cancel each other out. While this may ultimately be true, because different participants work to very different time frames, on some days it can appear that the majority of market participants have booked a profit and vice versa.

THE FX MARKET – 'ERE AND NOW

A foreign exchange dealer who had fallen into a very deep sleep at his desk in 1993 and awoken today would find the dealing floor and the market as a whole changed considerably, if not unrecognizably. The main change on the floor would be the significant reduction in the amount of noise generated (a possible explanation of why he slept for so long!). Today's trading room is undoubtedly a far calmer, less frenetic place to work.

As with so many other markets, the key driver of change in foreign exchange over the past ten years has been new technology. At the start of 1993 the majority of foreign exchange spot activity took place 'interbank' (between pairs of banks). Business was mainly conducted through voice brokers, who acted as intermediaries to match buyers and sellers anonymously (you did not know who you had dealt with until the deal was done) or directly between banks over the telephone or Reuters direct dealing products.

Voice brokers operate by quoting or responding to prices transmitted through a telephone line, with, typically, a loudspeaker at each end. At any time up to 1993 a dealer might have had three, four or more 'lines' to different brokers on his desk, all calling out prices, often at the same time. With prices spewing out from loudspeakers and spot dealers barking orders at the brokers and their colleagues, noise was clearly a key feature of the typical trading floor in 1993 and especially the larger ones that might have upwards of 50 traders.

So what happened? Technology, as previously mentioned, played a major part. So too did the impact of bank consolidation (banks merging with each other or rationalizing their own activities). Another more recent factor for change has been the introduction of the euro in 2000.

In respect of technology, there is no doubt that the introduction of electronic matching systems, known by most dealers as the 'machine' or 'the box', has had the most influence on today's spot markets. Now, instead of hordes of dealers screaming at each other and a cacophony of noise emanating from brokers' speaker boxes, one is more likely to see traders staring intently at an array of computer screens. Instead of having numerous dealers trading many different currencies, electronic matching has allowed banks to use fewer dealers to trade more currencies.

Electronic matching has also enabled many smaller banks, which were formerly treated as customers by the larger banks, to access liquidity directly (subject to credit availability).

This utilization of technology should not have come as a surprise. The FX market has always been quick to utilize technology to make trading more efficient. For instance, the advent of the Reuters' Monitor Dealing Service (RMDS) in 1981 effectively made dealing over a telex machine redundant and in many cases was more efficient than using the telephone, not least because it generated a hard copy audit trail – the forerunner of straight-through processing (STP).

To paraphrase another ACI motto, a dealer's 'word was his bond'.

RMDS introduced for the first time the ability to produce an *independent* record of a trader's activities, obviously a significant improvement on relying on their word and more importantly, their memory, to identify the trades they had done. It also led to the production of deal tickets, the automated entry of trades into risk management systems and to the back office and as such, straight-through processing (STP) of deals.

The popularity of automated direct dealing cannot be overstated. In addition to Reuters' RMDS, Telerate, then the second largest information vendor, launched The Trading System (TTS). In concert with Minex (a consortium of Japanese banks, brokers and corporates) this system had some success in Japan. Quotron, a Citigroup subsidiary, also launched a competing direct dealing product, called FX/Trader. Despite the competitive challenge, however, it was estimated in 1991 that Reuters' direct FX dealing systems had captured around 50% of all FX transactions, worldwide.

Not surprisingly, many banks were uncomfortable that Reuters – a supplier to the market and not a contributor or participant – seemed close to achieving a dominant FX share and, with their announcement of the launch of a new automated matching system (Dealing 2-2), potential hegemony in the provision of automated trading tools to that market. Many banks felt, with some justification, that since **they** were the providers of liquidity to the market they should have a greater influence on how the market operated.

Their response was to establish a consortium – The EBS Partnership, comprising, initially, representatives of eleven of the world's largest market-making banks – to develop the EBS Spot™ dealing system, an anonymous electronic matching system (Figure 5.1). (Coincidentally, EBS selected Quotron as its technology provider and built EBS Spot on the foundations of its existing FX/Trader dealing system.)

Since its launch in May 1993, EBS Spot has captured a significant share of the interbank spot market globally and added three new partners – The Minex Corporation of Japan, Commerzbank in Germany and the Scandinavian SE Banken. EBS accounts today for the majority of brokered business in EUR/USD and USD/JPY, the world's two most actively traded currency pairs. Everyday, an average of around USD 80 billion of business is transacted over the EBS dealing system.

Electronic matching systems like EBS Spot have promoted an unprecedented degree of price transparency in the market – making the market rate visible to a much broader audience than might previously have had access to it. In 1993, banks had access only to prices from brokers and from one another. Customers knew only what banks told them. Often the rates quoted to customers were very different from 'the market' and especially for amounts larger than what was considered regular.

Figure 5.1

Electronic FX matching – EBS Spot™ dealing screen

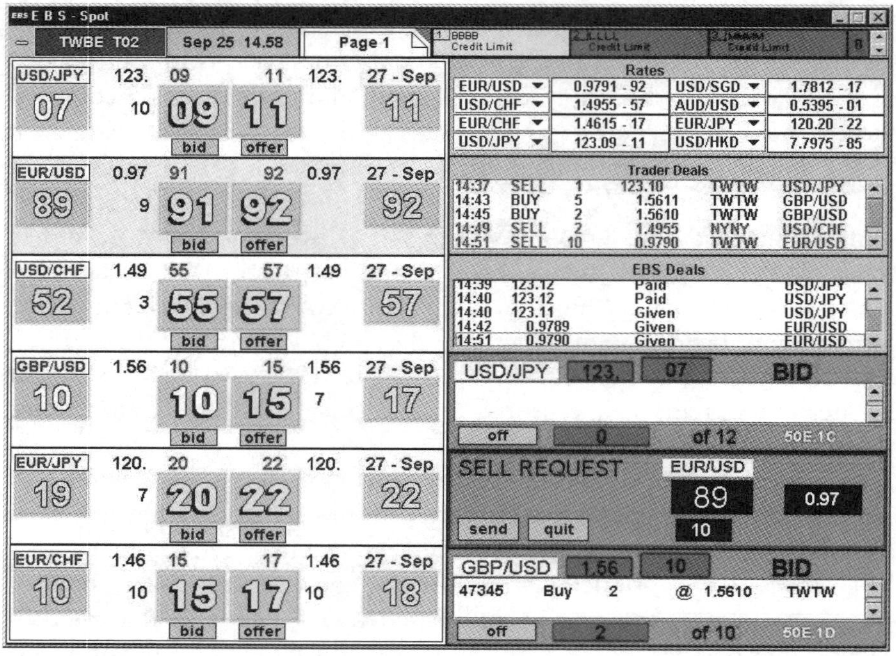

Source: EBS™

As the Bank of England said in 2001:

Electronic trading systems increase the transparency of market prices ... Deals traditionally executed by phone to facilitate price discovery are no longer necessary, leading to a more efficient market, less opportunities for arbitrage, and an overall fall in turnover.

Sarah Wharmby (2001) *Foreign Exchange and Over-the-Counter Derivatives Markets in the United Kingdom*

For many market participants increased price transparency is considered a healthy, positive development. For others, most noticeably the voice brokers, the move to a more 'efficient' market has proved less welcome.

According to another central bank report:

... most voice brokers have been forced into retirement since the mid-1990s, reportedly in great part due to the cost advantage of the electronic systems.

Alain Chaboud and Steven Weinberg *Foreign Exchange Markets in the 1990s: Intraday Market Volatility and the Growth of Electronic Trading*

While this may be a slight exaggeration, one trader stated in October 2002 that spot voice brokers were 'getting a few crumbs off a rich man's table'.

This greater transparency *has* filtered down to corporates and smaller banks, often to the chagrin of the banks providing FX services to them. Other banks, recognizing the logical extension of automated trading services to customers, have embraced the 'new way' and have established their own bank-to-customer electronic pricing and trading systems. Some banks – adopting the maxim of 'if you can't beat them, join them' – are also participants in multi-bank dealing portals like FXAll and FX Connect. The net effect of all of this activity is that customers know, with a much greater degree of accuracy, where the market *really* is and, as a result, are less readily inclined to accept quotes that are significantly away from 'the market'.

The narrowing of spreads and a more efficient, more transparent trading environment is something of a double-edged sword for FX banks. On the one hand, electronic trading has engendered far greater trading efficiency, resulting in lower operating costs (fewer dealers and less back office resources are required) and potentially greater profit margins. On the other, spreads have narrowed considerably, not least as a result of a huge increase in 'matched' prices. As noted earlier, bank customers are much more aware of where the market price is and what the spreads really are. The opportunity to make significant revenues from charging very wide spreads (subject to credit availability) is therefore reduced greatly.

In today's trading environment, the secret of competitive success for foreign exchange banks is **order flow**, and, more precisely *ownership* of order flow. Order flows are 'owned' by customers. In an increasingly level playing field, banks are looking at different ways of enhancing customer value and maintaining customer loyalty. Adding value can range from providing free research to 'bundling' foreign exchange in with other services, e.g. custody for a basis point/percentage commission. Consequently, not all banks compete equally for foreign exchange business.

Another significant change that has occurred in the last ten years is bank consolidation and the associated concentration of business into the hands of a smaller number of banks.

According to BIS, just 17 banks in the UK account for 75% of the total FX business (compared with 20 in 1995). This concentration is even more pronounced in the US. There, just 13 banks account for 75% of the total daily business, compared with 20 in 1995. This aggressive consolidation has led to the disappearance of many well-known US 'names' including Manufacturers Hanover Trust and Chemical Bank, subsumed into US giant, Chase, which in turn has merged with J P Morgan.

The third profound change to the FX markets has been the advent of the euro. Much of the activity in the 12 legacy currencies that now make up the euro consisted of cross trading. Often, a deal would be 'unwound' by trading the two respective currencies against the US dollar. So, someone buying 20 million Deutschmarks (DEM) against the lira at 990 might have traded out of the position by *selling* DEM 20 million against US dollars and then *buying* Italian lira against the dollar. By doing it this way, volumes would have been increased by at least a third, probably by more.

Not surprisingly, the integration of so many trading houses and the elimination of so many active currencies has led to a fall in the total daily turnover in the market. The impact on volume levels as a result of unwinding cross trades can be illustrated as follows:

Example

Bank buys DEM 20 million at 990, sells ITL 19.8 billion.

Bank sells DEM 20 million, buys (approx.) USD 10.25 million.

Bank sells USD 10.25 million, buys ITL 19.8 billion.

Positions all square, profit (or loss) booked: total turnover DEM 60 million.

CENTRAL BANKS

Another impact caused by the euro's introduction (and one that few traders would have imagined in 1993) is a massive diminution of the role in the market of 'eurozone' central banks and particularly, the German Bundesbank (Buba).

Buba built a fearsome reputation as a shrewd market operator and one more than capable of protecting its own currency, the Deutschmark. Buba's forays into the market through the 1980s and early 1990s were legendary and led to a belief that central banks were, in the end, always right. Buba was certainly not the only European central bank to achieve this apparent omnipotency.

Responsibility for intervening in the FX markets for eurozone members now rests with the European Central Bank (ECB) and the role of the once-mighty national central banks might best be described as being little more than that of order fillers.

The Bank of England has also experienced changes over the last decade, not least through being granted independence in 1997. From that point, the Bank – not the UK government – assumed responsibility for setting the level of UK interest rates. Today, The Bank manages the 'Exchange Equalisation Account', which holds the UK's gold and FX reserves on behalf of the government.

Little more than a decade ago, The Bank was active consistently in the FX market. In 1992 it battled in vain to keep the value of the GBP within a relatively tight band against the currencies that made up the European Exchange Rate Mechanism.

The Bank can intervene for the UK government, for another central bank or at the behest of its nine-member Monetary Policy Committee (MPC). The MPC is responsible for setting UK interest rates and has a separate set of reserves that it can use for intervention in the FX market. The MPC does not have to publicize that it has done this at the time of intervention, but it may do so if it thinks that will influence the outcome of its action. At the time of writing, the MPC has never, apparently, felt the need to intervene in the market.

In conclusion, major central banks (with the possible exception of the Bank of Japan) rarely intervene in the FX market. In any event, market watchers believe that the daily trading volume is now so enormous that intervention would, at best, have just a short-term impact. Many traders warn, however, against dismissing central banks as a spent force in the market and they have been described as 'slumbering giants'.

The situation is different for the central banks of minor and emerging market currencies. The way that these institutions react to problems such as speculative pressure has, however, changed. Central banks are no longer prepared to drain their FX reserves in their attempts to see off currency speculators. Instead, they tend to use a combination of 'corrective' methods.

During the Asian crisis of 1998, for example, the Hong Kong authorities saw off speculators by intervening directly in FX, hiking up interest rates temporarily and curtailing stock lending. The result was that speculators had to exit positions to cover margin calls in several markets and a potential crisis was averted.

Changes in forward and derivative trading

Ostensibly, there has been less change in the way forwards and derivatives are traded than common or garden FX. The market is, nonetheless, very different from a decade ago. Attempts have been made to launch electronic trading in forwards, FRAs and currency options. So far, few of these attempts have proved successful. In contrast, STIR activity at LIFFE (The London International Financial Futures Exchange, now called Euronext Liffe) is now transacted electronically and exchanges elsewhere are almost certain to follow London's lead.

While there are some electronic (screen-based) forwards matching and electronic options trading products, they are very different animals to spot. Forwards tend to move at a slower pace, giving participants time to counter-bid and offer in the hope of dealing at a slightly better rate.

In the options markets, brokers still play a major role in price discovery.

One possible reason why all FX products have not migrated in their entirety to screen-based trading like Spot is the fact that market participants have seen what happened in the spot market (narrower spreads, lower volumes) and are, understandably, reluctant to see the same happen to other markets.

There has already been a reduction in overall forward volumes, although not to the same extent as spot. From USD 862 billion to USD 786 billion (a 9% drop) between 1998 and 2001, according to BIS. Another change in this market has been that liquidity now extends far further out into the future than it did a decade ago. Ten years ago, it was very difficult to get good prices for maturities of anything much over one year.

Now, for example, Eurodollar futures (based on three-month US dollar deposits) are liquid for as far out as ten years.

Regulatory imposition

The 1988 Basel Accord on capital adequacy required that banks set aside sufficient capital to cover the risks they took in the marketplace. For various reasons, exchange-traded derivatives require less capital to be set aside. These include the fact that the counterparty to these transactions is a central clearer (with a AAA credit rating) and the fact that positions are traded on margin and then daily marked-to-market. Taken together, there is less settlement risk (since less capital is at risk) and less chance of a sudden large loss appearing.

This is possibly a key reason why the use of interest rate derivatives continues to grow. According to BIS, the daily turnover of OTC FRAs expanded by a phenomenal 74% from USD 74 billion to USD 129 billion between 1998 and 2001 and the volume of exchange-traded derivatives increased by 59% from USD 1,361 billion to USD 2,169 billion.

The FX options market, like spot and forwards, appears, conversely, to have stopped growing. Between 1995 and 1998, daily volume more than doubled from USD 41 billion to USD 87 billion. In the following three years, however, it declined by 31% to USD 60 billion. There is anecdotal evidence that new accounting regulations, such as FAS 133 (for companies that report under US GAAP – Generally Accepted Accounting Procedures), have caused many companies to revert to using outright forwards to manage their currency exposure.

Regulation FAS 133 requires that all derivative positions are marked-to-market on a daily basis and that they are fully visible on the balance sheet. The days when options could be described as 'off-balance sheet' are now long gone. But because options trade OTC, the market is, technically, opaque. This often makes it difficult to mark a position accurately to market, especially for what are known as exotic options.

The way the options market operates has changed little. There is still a thriving voice broker and interbank market. As with forwards, liquidity has moved further out. And even though electronic broking systems for forwards have failed to take off in the interbank market, many banks have had considerable success in providing trading portals for these instruments to their customers.

TRADING PORTALS

Bank-to-customer portals (single and multibank) have met with some degree of success, and particularly State Street's FX Connect, the first and by far the most successful at the time of writing (January 2003).

There is a belief (and some evidence) that such platforms encourage 'stickiness' meaning that customers are less likely to look elsewhere to do their business.

Single bank portals offer bank customers the opportunity to deal electronically with their banks, typically on a 'request for quotes' (RFQ) basis. They can, often, also see bank analysis and other pre-trade information in the same 'container' on their own PC screens. The pricing 'engines' of trading portals are driven increasingly by a live feed of spot rates from EBS and Reuters Spot systems although the actual rates are required to be 'spread' before they can be redistributed in this way.

More recently, a number of multi-bank portals have been launched. As their name suggests, these facilitate multiple price quotes from a number of different banks, as well as providing a greater range of content including analysis, news and charting products derived from many different sources.

For some market observers, there may appear to be a conflict of interest between a bank wishing to assure stickiness from its customers through a dedicated portal and, at the same time, making its prices available in a multiple bid environment from which a customer picks what it perceives to be the best price on offer. The fact is that customers determine what products and services and delivery mechanisms they want to use. It may, therefore, make the most sense for a bank to make its prices available to its customers in this variety of ways.

In a very short space of time the number of multi-bank portals has reduced – with the closure in early 2002 of Atriax – from three to two and this may be an indication that the market does not want to support a myriad of directly competing services in the same arena.

The next logical step for market participants will be to create interfaces between electronic matching (automated direct dealing) systems and bank portals to facilitate the creation of an efficient, automated flow from customer order to bank, through bank trade execution, to bank-to-customer reporting of completed orders. This is *one* aspect of STP or straight-through processing. Settlement is another link in the deal chain.

Settlement – ugly duckling or swan?

Every trade executed has to be settled. For every trade, the right amount of currency has to be transferred by each party to the right counterparty, on the right value date. In the past, this required banks (and their customers) to transfer vast amounts of hard currency in and out of their respective bank accounts. However, in the course of a trading day, major interbank players might buy and sell the same currencies to the same counterparties and this in turn could lead to a situation where Bank A is required to pay the same amount of US dollars to Bank B as Bank B is required to pay to Bank A.

Apart from the inefficiency of making that particular exchange since the end position would be zero or 'net', there are a number of risks inherent in a foreign exchange transaction. Settlement risk, as described earlier, is the risk that one side to a transaction pays out its obligation in one time zone but the counterparty to the transaction fails to make the corresponding payment in a different time zone.

The likelihood of a repeat of Herstatt has spooked the regulators since the 1970s, particularly when volumes in FX appeared to be spiralling out of control. Considerable pressure has been placed on the market by its regulators, and particularly the Bank for International Settlements in its series of Accords (Noel, Lamfalussy, Angell and Allsopp) with the implication that greater capital charges will be imposed on banks if they do not take steps to eliminate settlement risk.

Over the past decade (and longer) a number of initiatives have been deployed to address this issue, with varying degrees of limited success. FXNET, the oldest and the most successful, provides an automated bilateral netting solution, which is a legally binding agreement between pairs of counterparties in which transaction obligations (who owes what to who per currency) are netted continually throughout the trading day.

At close of play, instead of both parties being required to make gross payments to each other, per currency, they have a significantly reduced net obligation to each other, per currency. (In simple terms, all of a bank's dollar or euro or sterling payments *out* to a counterparty are added together and all payments *in* from that counterparty for the same currencies for the same value date are deducted from the total obligation to pay. The concept can most simply be explained as 'I owe you £10 and you owe me £3. I will give you £7 and we are quits'.

Bilateral netting has many advantages for banks with a significant daily FX settlement exposure and today around 20% of all FX transaction obligations are netted via FXNET. In truth, however, no settlement risk solution has yet set the FX world on fire and many never even got off the ground.

In September 2002, however, the CLS Bank was launched (after many delays and considerable budget overruns) to provide a different solution to settlement risk. This is called Continuous Linked Settlement and again, the name is self-explanatory.

CLS operates by linking all of the world's settlement periods and indeed, truncating them, into a period of just five hours. As such, and acting, in effect as a clearing house, CLS receives payments in but does not pay them out until the corresponding payments are also received. In other words, if a bank fails to pay away its euros, it will not receive its dollars. On paper, at least, CLS could eliminate nearly all settlement risk from the market.

The fact that so many banks have spent so much money on getting CLS established suggests that it will be given a large degree of support to succeed. And, in just a few months of operation, CLS cited daily volumes of USD 300 billion plus going through the CLS Bank in the seven currencies in the scheme at the time of launch.

THE FUTURE

Everybody has 20 : 20 hindsight. It takes a brave man or a fool, however, to predict with confidence the shape of the FX market of the future. The only sure things are that there will always be a need for FX and that technology will continue to be used to introduce more efficiency and reduce operational costs.

The Basel II Capital Accord, due to be implemented in 2007, could result in trading institutions having to set aside more cash than they do presently to maintain the 8% capital adequacy ratio demanded by the first Accord. The new Accord may also introduce a measurement to make operational risk part of the equation for the purposes of calculating capital adequacy. This is likely to have a real impact on the FX market, and particularly, currency options.

Electronic trading and broking offers market participants numerous advantages. It can be quicker, cheaper and safer than using a telephone. Deals are booked directly into risk management and back office systems and processed right the way through to settlement, creating automatic records (audit trails) and making it a far harder environment in which a 'rogue trader' can exist, undetected.

In terms of technology, the fact that, up until now, electronic systems have failed to gain a significant foothold in forwards, FRAs and options does not mean that they will not do so in the future. Looking at events in other markets and on the basis that in real life history very often repeats itself, it is clear that even when participants themselves reject automation they cannot always stop its implementation. The incredibly swift transition of many futures exchanges from traditional open outcry systems to electronic trading environments is a clear example of this.

LIFFE, for example, forced through electronic trading at the end of the 1990s despite the *fierce* resistance of its members who claimed, much as they did in FX when spot 'went electronic' in the early 1990s, that it would never work because a 'computer can't buy you a beer' (i.e. it wouldn't work without a human 'touch'). Since then LIFFE has migrated its STIR business to 'screens' and demonstrated that (even allegedly complex) short-end products can be traded successfully in this way.

The same might be said for FX options. Options may be less 'commoditized' than swaps but a fresh approach, such as the hybrid model adopted by ICAP's Volbroker, may well succeed. The possibility of it being able to be used for STP and to provide a clear reference for end-of-day settlement rates suggests that there is a lot of potential in this area.

Another possible trend to consider is whether FX can, and should, move to an exchange model. Arguably, this would, at the very least, enable market participants to make more effective use of their capital.

Historically, it was perceived that daily FX volumes were too big for the market to make effective use of a centralized clearing counterparty. This may no longer be true. For instance, the German–Swiss EUREX exchange clears around 3.1 million contracts (worth around USD 220 billion) each day. This is more volume than is traded currently over EBS and Reuters in the FX spot market.

In an era of 'virtual exchanges' there is, actually, very little that differentiates EBS from a futures exchange like EUREX. Both have vast pools of liquidity in the products that they 'list', both have numerous counterparties accessing the markets from various locations around the world and both are powered by proven and scalable technology. In effect, EBS has already created an 'exchange' for spot trading. The main difference, however, between EUREX and EBS is that the latter does not have a central counterparty for its trades. (The CLS Bank might, however, offer a feasible clearing-house solution for an FX exchange model.)

It is hard to imagine the advent in the *near* future of a *truly* centralized FX exchange, given the continuing development of numerous trading portals aimed at different groups of participants, all of whom demand different things from the market.

Another trend that looks likely to grow is out-sourcing peripheral services, such as settlement and clearing. CLS may well add to this development, as there are relatively few banks that can handle the liquidity demands the system imposes.

There is also talk that the success of CLS could spawn a new intra-day liquidity market. The US Federal Reserve Bank already charges interest on money on a minute-by-minute basis and some believe that commercial banks will start to do the same. Because of the massive amounts involved, lending money for just an hour might prove to be a very profitable business opportunity.

Further consolidation in the banking sector looks to be inevitable and the impact of this on liquidity remains to be seen. The concentration of the market into fewer and fewer hands will still leave rich pickings for some. Anecdotal evidence suggests that many day traders are flocking to FX from equities because of the abundant liquidity the market possesses and the relative ease with which positions can be entered and exited. Already a raft of quasi-exchanges has been developed to cater for this particular market segment.

Last but not least, internet and other technology advances will continue to influence and shape market developments. Banks will seek to garner even greater order flows through distributing their prices online (via single and multi-bank portals) and by bundling their prices with other value-added products and services to encourage customer stickiness.

It seems likely, too, that service providers like EBS, traditional brokers, bank portals *and* the plethora of other contributors to the FX market will seek to develop interfaces between their respective products and services to engender more market efficiency and more customer flexibility.

While the last ten years have seen unprecedented change in the FX and associated markets, there is every chance (without appearing to be too prescient) that the next ten years will see an even more radical shake-up. What is certain, and to quote the poet William Henry Davies, 'We have no time to stand and stare'.

Technology and the markets

Simon Lee, Moneyline Telerate

THE NEED FOR INFORMATION

It may not exactly be the world's oldest profession, but foreign exchange trading is a business that can clearly trace its roots far back in antiquity. And as the money changers of the past carried out their transactions down at the local temple or forum, it is not too hard to imagine that some of the sharper operators would have wondered how they could take advantage of the price discrepancies that they had heard existed in the value of their commodity in the next town.

In essence, this is what data vending is about. The distribution of market rates introduces transparency and facilitates price discovery mechanism.

When business is transacted in just a single location, such as a specific equity on a regulated exchange, it is clearly far easier to discover the value of that particular instrument than if it is traded by numerous participants, in countless offices at a vast array of locations around the world.

When there is no single marketplace, such as in foreign exchange, discrepancies in the value of a particular currency will inevitably arise, if only because of regional differences in supply and demand. The person that has the ability to discover these differences is potentially in a very lucrative position. With this in mind, it is relatively easy to see that the availability of real-time accurate and reliable data has value.

EMBRACING TECHNOLOGY

This was apparent back in 1851 when Paul Julius Reuter opened an office in London to transmit stock market prices between London and Paris. To do this, he used a new cable that had been laid between Calais and Dover. This was an obvious technological advance on the carrier pigeons Reuter had previously used on the Continent.

The embrace of technology has been a recurring feature of the data vending industry right from what can be regarded as its start with the creation of the company that bore Reuter's name. The company soon expanded its network to include the Far East in 1872 and then South America in 1874. In the first half of the twentieth century, Reuters was a pioneer in the use of radio to transmit news and information.

However, in comparison with the rapid changes that have occurred over the last couple of decades, the developments in financial markets throughout most of the twentieth century proceeded at a relatively sedate pace. With specific regards to the foreign exchange market, the fact that most currencies were fixed against each other meant that there was scarcely any need for the dissemination of price data. If a company had a large foreign exchange transaction to make, the price it discovered by reading the *Financial Times* at the start of the month was unlikely to have moved too far by the end of it.

The end of the Bretton Woods agreement in 1973 changed the situation completely. The introduction of floating rates in most of the major industrialized countries introduced a level of constant volatility that had not been seen before on a consistent basis. That, together with the ample liquidity, which further expanded at a rapid rate into the late 1990s, attracted speculators of all sorts. Suddenly, nobody with foreign exchange risk or exposure could really rely on newspapers for their data provision. The market was now too fast moving and, furthermore, it operated for 24 hours a day across the globe.

Whether by chance or design, the fundamental changes that were taking place in the foreign exchange marketplace were being matched by developments in the data vending industry. In 1969, Neil Hirsch pioneered the use of electronic terminals to collect and then distribute commercial paper rates to brokers and traders. Hirsch called his system Telerate and it soon spread out from New York, to Chicago, San Francisco and then overseas to London and Tokyo.

This was the start of real time data transmission, and Telerate expanded further when it was acquired in 1972 by the interdealer broker Cantor Fitzgerald. A year later, Reuters launched its Monitor product for the foreign exchange market. Some data industry watchers have claimed that the Reuter Monitor rescued the company from looming bankruptcy. This may be an exaggeration, but it is clear that the success of Reuter Monitor suddenly gave the company a lucrative revenue stream. Furthermore, that stream started to flow a lot faster as the foreign exchange market expanded rapidly over the next 25 years.

Reuter Monitor later started to carry news, as well as prices from other markets such as equities and fixed income. A significant development was the introduction of the Reuter Monitor Dealing Service in 1981. By tapping into the foreign exchange market, Reuters hit a very rich seam. By 1984 it was able to float on the London Stock Exchange and Nasdaq.

THE NEED FOR COMPETITION

The dealing service gave Reuters a clear advantage over Telerate, which had been sold to money broker Exco for around USD 100 million in 1981. However, Telerate continued to have its fans and it may well have been helped by the support of many institutions that did not want to see Reuters coming to dominate the data vending industry.

Also, Telerate retained several key pages such as the British Bankers' Association's Libor rates, as well as a strong foothold in the fixed income market. Many of these pages were accepted as providing various markets with benchmark rates.

The fact that easily accessible benchmarks were available was also important for many foreign exchange traders. For instance, it was often essential to know what was going on in US government bond market through the 1980s. The US funded its Reaganomic monetary policies by sucking in money from overseas. In simplistic terms, foreigners had to buy US dollars to buy US debt. So if you were trading foreign exchange, you had to keep an eye on what was going on in US Treasuries (see Figure 6.1).

Other systems appeared in the 1980s, such as Bloomberg. This company was founded in 1981 and it soon gained a strong foothold in the bond markets. Of more interest at the time to foreign exchange players was the appearance of screens from Knight-Ridder. This system gained a reputation for breaking market-moving news and it soon had many fans among foreign exchange dealers.

Benchmark treasury rates

Figure 6.1

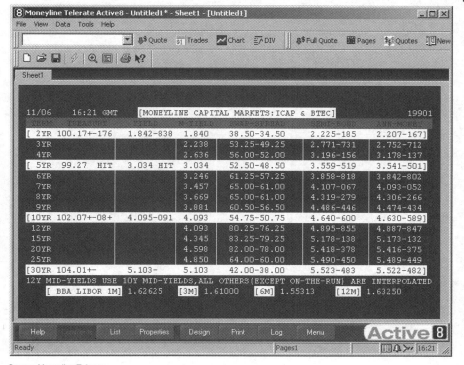

Source: Moneyline Telerate

Desktop real estate

In a perfect world, foreign exchange traders would have been able to pick and choose the best features from all the different platforms on offer. However, to have each system required a separate screen and the issue of desktop real estate cropped up. There was seldom enough space available on a trader's desk to have all that was on offer from the data vendors.

This changed to some extent when Reuters introduced 'Triarch' (Trading Information Architecture) at the start of 1986. At the time the company described it as 'an important distributed processing network designed to inter-connect video and digital trading systems of today with the processors and devices needed to drive the fully automated trading floor of the future'.

What this meant was that multiple data sources could be viewed through a single display. Most of the data vending platforms now have similar prod-

| Figure 6.2 | The user configurable Active 8 platform, pulling in news and prices from customizable sources |

NAME	LAST	T	OPEN	HIGH	CLOSE	LOW
FTSE 100 Index	4035.08	↑	4021.60	4071.60	4028.60	3990.3
FTSE 100 Index LIFFE	4036.0	↑	4000.0	4078.0	0.0	3982.5
DJ Industrial Average	8308.05	↑	0.00	0.00	8308.05	0.0
Dow Jones Industrial Avg Pit CB	8298		8510	8540	8380	8286
S&P 500 Index	878.82 800 to 89	↑	0.00	0.00	878.82	0.0
S&P 500 Stock Index CME	882.50	↑	878.00	884.80	0.00	876.9
NASDAQ 100 Index Adjusted	899.64	↑	0.00	0.00	899.64	0.0
NASDAQ 100 Index CME	906.00	↓	905.00	909.50	0.00	904.0
NASDAQ Composite Index	1263.84	↑	0.00	0.00	1263.84	0.0
E-MINI NASDAQ 100 Stock Index	906.50	↑	905.00	909.50	0.00	903.5
Bond US Treasury Pit CBOT	111 ¹¹⁄₃₂		110 ¹⁶⁄₃₂	111 ²⁰⁄₃₂	111 ¹⁶⁄₃₂	110 ²⁄₃₂
Euro Bobl EUREX	109.27	↑	109.36	109.45	0.00	109.1
Japanese Government Bond 10	141.03	↓	141.15	141.20	0.00	141.0
Long Gilt LIFFE	119.84	↑	119.95	120.12	0.00	119.7
CAC 40 Index	3135.86	↑	3102.76	3175.50	3126.60	3068.1
CAC 40 Index EURONEXT-PARIS	3143.0	↑	3100.0	3182.5	0.0	3077.5
DAX Index	3424.17	↑	3396.80	3462.70	3398.99	3348.6
DAX Index EUREX	3431.0	↓	3402.0	3469.0	0.0	3352.5
MIB 30 Index	24392	↑	24164	24576	24287	24078
FIB 30 Index IDEM	24425	↑	24215	24600	0	24070
SMI Index EUREX	4946.0	↑	4880.0	4994.0	0.0	4828.0
DJ Euro Stoxx 50 Index EUREX	2516.0	↑	2497.0	2540.0	0.0	2461.0
FTSE techMARK 100 Index	739.98	↓	746.24	748.52	747.87	739.4

NAME	URITY DESCRIPT	LAST	CLOSE	NET.C
Australian Dollar Pit CME	Sep02 Future	0.5476	0.5475	-0.0024
British Pound Pit CME	Sep02 Future	1.5816	1.5814	0.0148
Canadian Dollar Pit CME	Sep02 Future	0.6442	0.6442	0.0028
Japanese Yen Pit CME	Sep02 Future	0.8646	0.8545	0.0113
Swiss Franc Pit CME	Sep02 Future	0.6795	0.6794	0.0125
Euro FX Pit CME	Sep02 Future	0.99590	0.99590	0.01570
Short Sterling LIFFE	Sep02 Future	96.040	0.000	0.000
Short Sterling LIFFE	Dec02 Future	96.140	0.000	-0.030
EuroSwiss LIFFE	Dec02 Future	99.240	0.000	0.010
EuroSwiss LIFFE	Sep02 Future	99.250	0.000	0.000
Three Month Euribor LIFFE	Sep02 Future	96.780	0.000	0.005
Eurodollar 3 Month Pit Only CME	Sep02 Future	98.2300	98.2325	0.0425
Eurodollar 3 Month Pit Only CME	Dec02 Future	98.3350	98.3400	0.1150

96.130 Short Sterling LIFFE

98.3350 Eurodollar 3 Month Pit Only CME

96.855 Three Month Euribor LIFFE

99.240 EuroSwiss LIFFE

04/09/2002 11:50 Aberforth Partners - SAR - Brandon Hire PLC
04/09/2002 11:50 JPMorganFlemJapSmlr - Net Asset Value(s)
04/09/2002 11:50 DJ MARKET TALK/EU: Wanadoo Sate From Web Ad Spending Slump
04/09/2002 11:50 DJ Interbank Foreign Exchange Rates At 06:5C EDT / 1050 GMT
04/09/2002 11:50 DJ Interbank Foreign Exchange Rates At 06:5C EDT / 1050 GMT
04/09/2002 11:50 Market Talk/Merrill Lynch senkt Umsatzprognose für Hugo Boss
04/09/2002 11:50 KLSE Cl 7014 MY; Changes in Sub. S-hldr's Int. (29B)
04/09/2002 11:49 KLSE Cl 7014 MY; Changes in Sub. S-hldr's Int. (29B)
04/09/2002 11:49 KLSE Cl 4103 MY; Changes in Sub. S-hldr's Int. (29B)

moneyline telerate   CREDIT SUISSE FIRST BOSTON

	GB;FTSE	FR;CAC	NL;AEX	DE;DAXX
4	4034.10	3134.40	348.06	3420

Active 8

Source: Moneyline Telerate

ucts that do this. Moneyline Telerate, a company that can trace its origins back to Telerate and Knight-Ridder, uses what is known as the 'Moneyline Trading Room Systems (MTRS)'.

Moneyline Telerate is probably the most open of the big data vendors. Other companies' front and middle office products can sit easily on MTRS. The system also allows companies to input their own data or news into Active 8, its proprietary front-end display and analysis product (see Figure 6.2).

Active 8 gives users total flexibility, which can be an important consideration for those clients that have their own extensive databases. This is particularly important on hard to obtain information, such as that on certain emerging market currencies. In contrast to Moneyline Telerate's open approach, certain other systems rigidly control the data that is input and then displayed on their product.

USE OF DATA

Different users have different demands from the data available. It still remains true that the provision of data helps the price discovery mechanism, especially when a market is not centralized. However, it is important to note that few professional bank traders would completely rely on a third party screen rate to tell them where the market is. As professional traders, it is their job to know that. But to a day trader, accurate indicative rates can be extremely important, simply because they are unlikely to have access to the same resources as a bank dealer.

The fact that professional traders should know where the market is was true back in the days before the electronic matching systems, which have introduced yet further transparency to the major spot markets, and it remains true today. A spot dollar/mark trader in 1985 would not have relied on Reuter Monitor to tell him where the market was. However, someone trading a currency that was highly correlated to the Deutschmark may well have done, especially if they did not have access to the money brokers. The brokers played a very important role at that time in the price discovery mechanism. Similarly, a forward cable trader might have used and still use third party data to work out things such as sterling cross rates.

Another consideration that has already been alluded to is that certain markets are often strongly correlated to others. For instance, through much of the 1980s, the dollar's performance was highly correlated to that of US treasuries. As treasuries rose, and therefore interest rates fell, there was greater demand for dollars, confounding the textbook economists (see Figure 6.3).

Presently, equity markets and sometimes even high-profile individual stocks can have a significant effect on foreign exchange. If the US stock

Figure 6.3 **Chart showing the sometimes strong correlation between $/¥ and the Dow, and a statistical measurement of correlation (r²)**

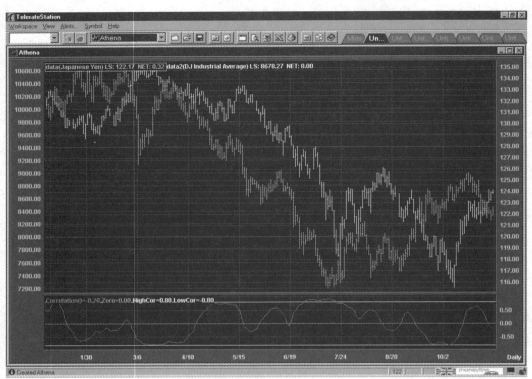

Source: Moneyline Telerate

markets plummet, the reasoning goes that foreign investors will liquidate their holdings, sell their dollars and repatriate their funds. Therefore, most foreign exchange traders will want to have access to live rather than delayed equity prices. At other times oil or another commodity might be significantly influencing the market. What is important is that the customers can access the data they want almost at the moment they want it. So an institution may seek to cut overheads by having delayed feeds for its non-core market data. However, if one of those markets then starts to bear heavy influence, the customer should be able to reverse the decision swiftly and upgrade to live data.

What this shows is that financial markets seldom move in isolation. So, although a foreign exchange dealer may be completely aware of which currency is moving at a particular time, he will need to source data from another market either to explain or even anticipate the move.

THE VALUE OF DATA

It is easy to see that live data has greater potential value than delayed prices or news. In the early days of live data, most of the banks and some of the brokers gave their prices away for free. Nowadays few do. For instance, looking at a different market, prices from the London Stock Exchange that are delayed by 15 minutes are available free. Live prices cost each user £4 a month. This is a relatively modest figure, but access to what is known as Level II data costs £150 a month for each user. Level II data shows the bid and offer, as well as the depth of the order book. Such information is probably very important to an equities market maker, but it is of limited value to a foreign exchange trader.

Value of the business

It is difficult to put an actual value on exactly how much data is worth. Given the respective volumes of trade transacted, it is clear that live rates from one of the big electronic matching brokers is potentially of more value than indicative rates from a voice broker. But how much more is open to debate. Another way to get a feel for the value of the market is to analyze how much revenue is generated by the data vendors, or to look at the valuation of the data vendors themselves.

According to Risk Waters, the market data industry pulled in USD 6.8 billion in revenues in 2001, down from the USD 7.2 billion generated in the previous year. Of that, around 40% was derived from selling equity market services, 40% from fixed income and 16% from foreign exchange. Not surprisingly, the professional trading community accounted for the vast (52%) portion of revenues, followed by what Risk Waters terms the investment sector, comprising both buy- and sell-side analysts, portfolio managers and corporate customers, and then the retail sector (14%).

Globally, there are around a million screens in place. Reuters has approximately 320,000, Bloomberg is said to have 172,000 and Moneyline Telerate now has about 50,000. Other non-global players make up the balance.

The full-year results to the end of 2001 for Reuters, the market leader, illustrate that data vending can be extremely profitable. The company's pre-tax profit came in at £304 million, with the information division accounting for 47% of the total revenues.

Although these figures look impressive, 2001 was a very challenging year for all the data vendors. Most posted slower annual growth rates as consolidation impacted on the industry's core customers. The slowdown was severe enough to trigger the collapse of Bridge Information Systems, which at the time was the global number two behind Reuters in terms of screens.

Bridge's bankruptcy illustrated how competitive the business is and also, because of its history, how difficult it is to value a data vending business. Although not especially well known in Europe, Bridge could trace its history back to the start of real time data provision. Bridge was founded in 1974 and its early focus was to provide equity market data to the institutional trading markets. However, after it was bought by the private venture capitalist firm Welsh, Carson, Anderson & Stowe in 1995, Bridge went on a rapid expansion programme. The company 'merged' with several well-known vendors, including Knight-Ridder Financial and the legendary Telerate. But although it gained a large global presence, the growth by acquisition of the company came at too high a cost and it collapsed under a mountain of debt. (See Figure 6.4.)

This was not the first time the value of a data vending business had been seriously miscalculated. Dow Jones apparently had the opportunity to buy Telerate a few years after it was founded for just USD 1 million but declined. It eventually acquired the company in 1990 for USD 1.6 billion,

| Figure 6.4 | **TelerateStation developed by Bridge and still one of the most technically advanced platforms available; only Active 8 is currently more advanced** |

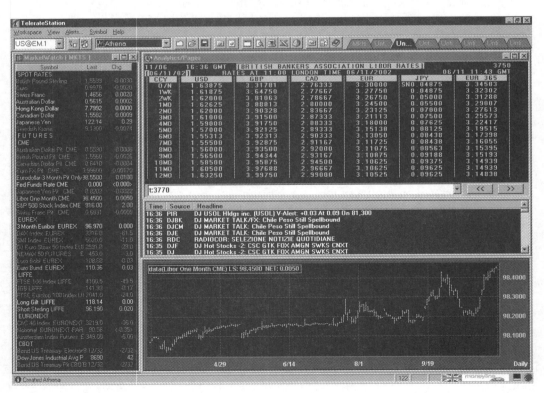

Source: Moneyline Telerate

only to sell it for a rumoured fraction of that (USD 600 million) to Bridge in 1998. What Dow Jones found was that it had bought a company with a fantastic brand name. But after years of under investment, this alone was not sufficient to generate meaningful revenue. It proved a very expensive mistake for Dow Jones.

THE FUTURE

The collapse of Bridge and the continuing slowdown has led some industry watchers to question whether the data vending industry is now a fully mature one with little room for any fresh expansion. Obviously, consolidation among the world's banks and financial institutions has had and may continue to have, a negative impact on the industry's revenue stream.

Some have also asked whether the distribution of free data by many internet sites will lead to further pressure on the vendors. The internet cannot be ignored. Free data will certainly suit some market participants who previously may have paid for it. But it is unlikely to prove acceptable to the high-end and middle-tier customers who provide the bulk of the data vendors' revenues. Those transacting multi-million dollar trading strategies want to know the data they have based their decision on is reliable, timely and authenticated. In addition to just data, high-end and middle-tier customers normally require additional functionality, such as analytics. The provision of all this in a single package is where market data vendors come into their own.

This is what a product such as Moneyline Telerate's Active 8 does. It combines numerous sources of information and analytical applications. Customers have the choice to access around 65,000 different pages of financial information, comprising contributed data from more than 60 countries and 1,200 market-making institutions. Furthermore, the overall package presented can also include news and research from over 100 different sources, bond and option analytics, as well as powerful and flexible charting services.

Far from being the threat originally feared, the internet actually offers great potential to the data vendors. As a medium of delivery, the internet is now almost unrecognizable from what it was just five years ago. It is more robust and connection speeds are much faster. This allows the vendors to use the internet as a delivery mechanism for traditional and new generation browser-based products, such as Moneyline Telerate's Webstation product (see Figure 6.5). At present, these products may not carry the full range of functionality that a workstation such as Active 8 does but this is likely to change. Increasingly, customers no longer associate the internet with free services.

Figure 6.5 **The high power, internet delivered Webstation. Impressive functionality available to anyone with access to the internet**

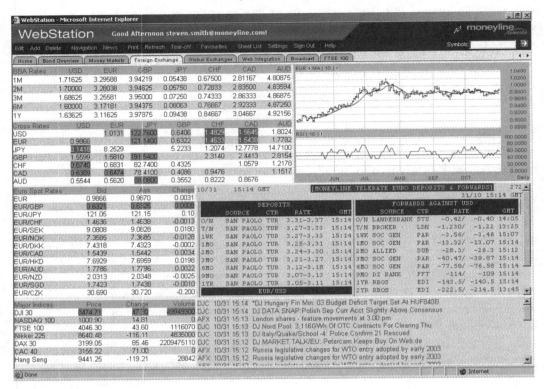

Source: Moneyline Telerate

Even during times of consolidation and a slowdown in the financial industry, the vendors will seek to use technology to maintain and even expand revenue streams.

Biggest not necessarily the best

For the data vendor, there are advantages in size and widespread market coverage. But there are also disadvantages. Scale can certainly hinder the rolling out of new products, which in turn ultimately leads to higher costs for the vendor and potentially the customer, through having to maintain widely dispersed legacy products. There are still numerous niche players exploiting smaller markets that the big vendors see as unprofitable. For participants in these markets, the data also remains key. A platform can have all the bells and whistles and leading edge technology available, but if the data is poor quality, users will inevitably look elsewhere.

The industry will certainly remain competitive, and if the past is any indication, it will continue to embrace new technology. Another lesson to remember is that the client base is reluctant to see the establishment of effective monopolies or duopolies. Therefore, companies such as Moneyline Telerate, which has a philosophy of partnership with its clients and which does not compete with its customers' transactional services, will continue to find customers amongst the financial community of the future. They will do this by providing a neutral, technologically advanced platform, rich with reliable data and state-of-the-art functionality.

The mechanics of spot foreign exchange

Francesca Taylor, Taylor Associates

It is a zero sum game – almost!

■ ■ ■

INTRODUCTION

The spot foreign exchange markets are driven purely by supply and demand. Nevertheless, it is important to remember that demand can be artificially stimulated by rumours, expectation, intervention, and even charts (technical analysis). It is also quite likely that a number of influences will operate simultaneously, thus masking any individual effect. Market confidence is also a key factor, as without it the traders in the banks may start to have second thoughts about the ability of the market or a particular bank to fill their respective orders. It is a zero sum game – almost! The overhead that used to be paid by the central banks is now being funded by the corporation and the private individual.

Throughout this book I shall use the SWIFT (Society for Worldwide Interbank Financial Telecommunication) codes for the currencies. When discussing exchange rates I shall also adopt the market convention, where references are made in relation to how many units of the second currency are equivalent to one (or a specified) unit of the first. For example, USD/CHF will be quoted as the number of Swiss francs per dollar, and EUR/JPY the number of Japanese yen per euro.

TIMING

Spot FX is generally dealt or transacted today (the dealing date), for value two business days later (the value date); that day must be a business day in each of the two countries to apply. The term value date is used to denote the day on which funds must be received or paid with 'good value' into a nominated bank account. Over the Christmas and New Year periods, where some countries often have different scheduled bank holidays, it is quite possible for the value date on a spot deal to be four or five actual days away to cover the two business days in each territory, and longer if a weekend intervenes. Two business days are required to transfer the currencies – this allows for the different time zones and for the completion of all necessary settlement procedures. It is now universally agreed that with the increasing use of technology two days is overly long for the settlement of a spot transaction, but it has become a tradition.

There are some notable exceptions. A trader dealing USD/CAD without qualification would expect delivery on the next working day. This is known as 'Funds'. A spot price can, however, be requested as an alternative. In order to keep the value dates the same, some FX transactions involving the Australian market, if dealt early enough in their morning, are for one working day ahead only. This provides continuity with the US market, where the actual day of the week has not yet changed. After midnight London time, all Australian market prices will have the usual spot value.

Other complications arise when dealing in some of the Middle East currencies; this is where the banks are closed on the Friday but open on the Saturday, by when the rest of the market is closed. Consider a USD/SAR spot transaction dealt on Wednesday for value Friday, but the local Saudi market is closed. This deal could have a split settlement date, with the dollars settled on the Friday and the Saudi riyal settled on the Saturday; alternatively, it may be dealt Wednesday for value Monday, and have the same value date as a spot deal that was dealt on the Thursday for value Monday.

Cross currencies, which are currencies that are not traded through the dollar, for example euro against yen, also require two business days for the settlement. So in the case of euro and yen, we would need two clear business days in Japan, and Europe. There is, however, a strong argument that we will also require two business days in the US, as many cross currency traders may trade out of or into their positions through the dollar, and if the US markets were closed, there would be a mismatch on settlement.

CONTINUOUS LINKED SETTLEMENT

The new market initiative to reduce the settlement risk on foreign exchange transactions is now operating in the market. Continuous Linked Settlement (CLS) will simplify the operational procedures involved in finalizing payments on FX transactions. It is designed to eliminate the settlement risk known in the market as Herstatt risk, named after the German bank which was closed in 1974 by the German authorities. At the end of the European day they were closed down and therefore unable to make outstanding dollar payments to their US counterparties.

However, following the events at Allfirst in the US and a decline in FX turnover of approximately 20% over the last few years, some in the market feel that other risks are perhaps the ones that should be addressed, i.e. market risk, operational risk and ultimately replacement risk.

CLS is a payment versus payment matching system, and will therefore eliminate the exposures suffered when there is a time gap between when currency is bought and sold. Two major factors will influence the viability of CLS; will the system work as it is intended and who are the companies and technology behind the initiative. One of the likely knock-on effects will be the market moving a to a one day settlement on traditional FX deals away from the current two day spot value period and possibly eventually to same day settlement. For further detail on CLS, see Chapter 21, Continuous Linked Settlement.

QUOTATIONS

Direct vs indirect

Foreign exchange has very specific ways of quotation and it is necessary to become familiar with these. Domestically, most countries use a method known as direct quotation: this is when the foreign currency is quoted in dollar terms in the US but in yen terms in Japan, etc. There are exceptions to the rule: in the UK, for many years everything was quoted against sterling, with sterling as the base currency. This was because for many years the UK did not have the decimal system and it was easier to quote that way. Eventually, in 1971, the UK adopted decimalization, but this method of quotation still exists. When the euro joined its international counterparts in 1999, the central banks decided that the euro would always become the base currency. Thus not £1 = 1.5485 euro but, EUR 1 = 0.6457 pence.

In the US all domestic prices are quoted on a direct basis in their equivalent dollar terms, so, for example, a Swiss franc may be worth USD 0.6727, but on the international foreign exchange markets the same rate would be quoted the other way around as USD/CHF at 1.4865. Internationally, it is convention in the global FX market to quote most currencies against the dollar, with the dollar being the base currency.

Generally, most currencies are quoted against a US dollar base, except currencies like UK sterling, the Australian dollar, and the euro, where they themselves are the base against the various 'foreign' or 'quoted' currencies. Using the dollar base simplifies currency trading a great deal: it will allow a trader to compare rates more easily. They could ask a German bank in Madrid their rates for Swiss francs, and they could also inquire the same of a Japanese bank. Both rates will be quoted back to them as indications against a dollar base currency, rather than, firstly, a quote against the euro and, secondly, a quote against Japanese yen.

Should anyone need to, the way to convert an indirect quotation into a direct quotation is to calculate the reciprocal: this is rarely required for major currencies but is occasionally used for minors. An example is shown below.

Example

Consider a USD/CHF quotation of 1.4856–61.

This can be converted to CHF/USD by taking 1 and dividing by 1.4861 equalling 0.6729, and by taking 1 and dividing by 1.4856 to make 0.6731. These rates will still be quoted in line with market practice, with the smaller number on the left, see the section below: Procedures and practices – banks.

In the case of CHF/USD the two sides of the quotation need to be reversed, resulting in 0.6729–0.6731. The important factor here is that as the quotation is reversed the bank also operates in the reverse manner. So, the bank, instead of buying the dollars and selling the CHF on the left-hand side of the quotation, as is normal, with the direct quotation the bank buys the CHF against the dollar on the left, and sells the CHF against the dollar on the right.

Changing the price

Tip *When a market maker quotes a client, whether it is another bank or a corporate client, the price will only be good until it changes. It is not uncommon for a trader to want to change their price before they have managed to voice their rate. Among market makers and major clients it is market practice when quoting two-way rates to quote only the last two figures. For example, if the GBP/USD rate is 1.5305–08, the trader will quote 5–8. In a fast-moving market the trader may get as far as saying 'five–eig ... change'; They do not complete their quotation as they wish to change their price. Their next price may be, say, 06–09.*

There are some markets and some times where the foreign exchange rates are fairly stable and where the trader may be happy with their price for hours, but as soon as you hear the all important words of 'change' or 'off' you know the price is changing.

Significant figures

Another area where mistakes can be made concerns how many significant figures should be quoted after the decimal point. Generally most currencies run to four figures after the point, with some rates being bigger than 1 and some smaller than 1, some examples are shown below:

GBP/USD	1.5898–02
USD/JPY	121.92–97
EUR/USD	0.9881–85
USD/CAD	1.5183–89

FOREIGN EXCHANGE MARKET INFORMATION

Because foreign exchange prices move very quickly it is important for all market participants to have access to up-to-date prices, preferably 'real-time' prices and feeds. These can be provided by the various commercial operators, such as Moneyline Telerate, Reuters and Bloomberg. Publications such as the *Financial Times* also carry a very good market page within the Companies and Markets section, covering FX and money rates. But, remember, this information is historical as it is a day old before it appears in print. A selection of various data forms is shown in Figures 7.1 and 7.2.

> When dealing on the telephone with banks, it is vital that the client does not put the bank's dealer on 'hold'. If the bank is placed on hold while a second call is made or received (usually because the client is seeking a competitive quote), and the dealer shouts 'change', no one will hear the new rate. This can lead to confusion.   **Tip**

UK pound spot and forward

Figure 7.1

POUND SPOT FORWARD AGAINST THE POUND

Nov 18		Closing mid-point	Change on day	Bid/offer spread	Day's Mid high	Day's Mid low	One month Rate	One month %PA	Three months Rate	Three months %PA	One year Rate	One year %PA	Bank of Eng. Index
Europe													
Czech Rep.	(Koruna)	47.8514	-0.1431	325 - 702	48.0040	47.7710	47.8061	1.1	47.7069	1.2	47.2167	1.3	-
Denmark	(DKr)	11.6435	-0.0063	404 - 466	11.6586	11.6095	11.6384	0.5	11.6228	0.7	11.5448	0.8	103.3
Hungary	(Forint)	370.629	-1.2650	317 - 941	371.870	370.317	372.338	-5.5	375.736	-5.5	390.266	-5.3	-
Norway	(NKr)	11.4604	-0.0037	566 - 642	11.4793	11.4321	11.4901	-3.1	11.5499	-3.1	11.7506	-2.5	106.6
Poland	(Zloty)	6.1642	-0.0378	590 - 693	6.2209	6.1541	6.1791	-2.9	6.2054	-2.7	6.2693	-1.7	-
Romania	(Leu)	52967.9	-35.80	307 - 052	53115.0	52855.0	-		-		-		-
Russia	(Rouble)	50.3407	+0.0748	328 - 486	50.3805	50.2531	-		-		-		-
Slovakia	(Koruna)	65.1970	-0.1529	506 - 433	65.9180	64.9450	65.3288	-2.4	65.4108	-1.3	65.7686	-0.9	-
Slovenia	(Tolar)	359.766	-1.1550	533 - 999	361.505	358.877	-		-		-		-
Sweden	(SKr)	14.2108	-0.0460	056 - 160	14.2381	14.1705	14.2132	-0.2	14.2156	-0.1	14.2062	0.0	78.5
Switzerland	(SFr)	2.3010	+0.0015	998 - 021	2.3036	2.2933	2.2949	3.2	2.2822	3.3	2.2282	3.2	114.7
Turkey	(Lira)	2493948	-34661	018 - 877	2527572	2488018	-		-		-		-
UK	(£)	-	-	-	-	-	-		-		-		105.9
Euro	(€)	1.5677	-0.0010	673 - 680	1.5699	1.5631	1.5669	0.7	1.5644	0.9	1.5511	1.1	82.81
SDR	-	1.183900	-	-	-	-	-		-		-		-
Americas													
Argentina	(Peso)	5.6214	-0.0232	133 - 294	5.6294	5.5588	-		-		-		-
Brazil	(R$)	5.6435	-0.1827	386 - 484	5.8243	5.5927	-		-		-		-
Canada	(C$)	2.5095	+0.0140	092 - 097	2.5163	2.4945	2.5072	1.1	2.5027	1.1	2.484	1.0	74.7
Mexico	(New Peso)	16.0861	-0.0850	840 - 881	16.1910	16.0545	16.1443	-4.3	16.2725	-4.6	16.9938	-5.6	-
Peru	(New Sol)	5.6815	-0.0050	805 - 824	5.6824	5.6758	-		-		-		-
USA	($)	1.5813	+0.0024	812 - 813	1.5827	1.5777	1.578	2.5	1.5713	2.5	1.5441	2.4	113.0
Pacific/Middle East/Africa													
Australia	(A$)	2.8079	-0.0011	075 - 082	2.8123	2.7996	2.8099	-0.9	2.8139	-0.9	2.8286	-0.7	74.5
Hong Kong	(HK$)	12.3331	+0.0185	323 - 338	12.3441	12.3061	12.3097	2.3	12.2633	2.3	12.0946	1.9	-
India	(Rs)	76.1847	+0.1133	032 - 661	76.2661	76.0610	76.2565	-1.1	76.4173	-1.2	77.2181	-1.4	-
Indonesia	(Rupiah)	14223.3	-29.40	150 - 317	14279.1	14203.8	14193.53	2.5	14133.17	2.5	13888.69	2.4	-
Iran	(Rial)	12626.3	+18.8000	267 - 259	-	-	-		-		-		-
Israel	(Shk)	7.3924	+0.0290	842 - 005	7.4005	7.3718	-		-		-		-
Japan	(Y)	191.513	+1.2790	452 - 575	191.680	190.230	190.888	3.9	189.598	4.0	184.048	3.9	132.2
Kuwait	(Kuwaiti D)	0.4761	+0.0005	758 - 764	0.4764	0.4749	0.4753	2.0	0.4737	2.1	0.4674	1.8	-
Malaysia	(M$)	6.0088	+0.0090	086 - 089	6.0135	5.9960	-		-		-		-
New Zealand	(NZ$)	3.1771	+0.0161	757 - 785	3.1805	3.1650	3.1822	-1.9	3.1923	-1.9	3.2319	-1.7	90.0
Philippines	(Peso)	84.4467	+0.1729	203 - 730	84.4730	84.3579	84.5445	-1.4	84.8999	-2.1	86.9417	-3.0	-
Saudi Arabia	(SR)	5.9302	+0.0086	297 - 307	5.9351	5.9178	5.9208	1.9	5.9036	1.8	5.8544	1.3	-
Singapore	(S$)	2.7897	+0.0053	891 - 902	2.7906	2.7834	2.7822	3.2	2.7677	3.2	2.7057	3.0	-
South Africa	(R)	15.1227	-0.0900	163 - 291	15.2085	15.0675	15.2414	-9.4	15.483	-9.5	16.4886	-9.0	-
South Korea	(Won)	1912.36	+4.2600	215 - 258	1918.23	1900.99	1913.33	-0.6	1915.4	-0.6	1920.87	-0.4	-
Taiwan	(T$)	54.9564	+0.1606	467 - 660	54.9777	54.8314	54.8493	2.3	54.6003	2.6	53.5361	2.6	-
Thailand	(Bt)	68.6025	-0.1034	766 - 284	68.7990	68.4120	68.5141	1.5	68.3328	1.6	67.6526	1.4	-
U A E	(Dirham)	5.8080	+0.0087	062 - 097	5.8125	5.7957	5.796	2.5	5.772	2.5	5.6761	2.3	-

Bid/offer spreads in the Pound Spot table show only the last three decimal places. Sterling index calculated by the Bank of England. Base average 1990 = 100. Index rebased 1/2/95. The exchange rates printed in this table are also available on the internet at **http://www.FT.com**

Source: Extract from the *Financial Times*, 19 November 2002

Figure 7.2	US dollar spot and forward

DOLLAR SPOT FORWARD AGAINST THE DOLLAR

Nov 18		Closing mid-point	Change on day	Bid/offer spread	Day's Mid high	Day's Mid low	One month Rate	One month %PA	Three months Rate	Three months %PA	One year Rate	One year %PA	J.P. Morgan Index
Europe													
Czech Rep.	(Koruna)	30.2618	-0.1357	508 - 727	30.3930	30.2350	30.2966	-1.4	30.3628	-1.3	30.5798	-1.1	-
Denmark	(DKr)	7.3635	-0.0150	618 - 652	7.3817	7.3406	7.3757	-2.0	7.3973	-1.8	7.477	-1.5	102.4
Hungary	(Forint)	234.390	-1.1500	200 - 580	235.470	234.200	235.965	-8.1	239.135	-8.1	252.755	-7.8	-
Norway	(NKr)	7.2477	-0.0131	455 - 499	7.2695	7.2285	7.2817	-5.6	7.3509	-5.7	7.6102	-5.0	105.5
Poland	(Zloty)	3.8983	-0.0298	951 - 014	3.9405	3.8935	3.916	-5.4	3.9494	-5.2	4.0603	-4.2	-
Romania	(Leu)	33497.5	-72.50	750 - 200	33555.0	33425.0	-	-	-	-	-	-	-
Russia	(Rouble)	31.8360	-	320 - 400	31.8475	31.8320	-	-	-	-	-	-	-
Slovakia	(Koruna)	41.2313	-0.1582	033 - 593	41.7150	41.0850	41.4013	-4.9	41.6303	-3.9	42.5948	-3.3	-
Slovenia	(Tolar)	227.520	-1.0700	380 - 660	228.720	227.060	-	-	-	-	-	-	-
Sweden	(SKr)	8.9871	-0.0425	840 - 901	9.0147	8.9600	9.0075	-2.7	9.0474	-2.7	9.2006	-2.4	78.0
Switzerland	(SFr)	1.4552	-0.0012	545 - 558	1.4587	1.4488	1.4544	0.7	1.4526	0.7	1.4431	0.8	114.6
Turkey	(Lira)	1577200	-24300	500 - 900	1599000	1573500	-	-	-	-	-	-	-
UK (0.6324)*	(£)	1.5813	+0.0024	812 - 813	1.5827	1.5777	1.578	2.5	1.5713	2.5	1.5441	2.4	105.2
Euro (0.9914)*	(€)	1.0087	+0.0022	085 - 089	1.0120	1.0058	1.0071	1.9	1.0044	1.7	0.9955	1.3	-
SDR	-	0.74870	-	-	-	-	-	-	-	-	-	-	-
Americas													
Argentina‡	(Peso)	3.5550	-0.0200	500 - 600	3.5600	3.5100	-	-	-	-	-	-	-
Brazil	(R$)	3.5690	-0.1210	660 - 720	3.6660	3.5350	-	-	-	-	-	-	-
Canada	(C$)	1.5870	+0.0065	869 - 871	1.5917	1.5796	1.5889	-1.4	1.5927	-1.4	1.6087	-1.4	75.0
Mexico	(New Peso)	10.1730	-0.0690	720 - 740	10.1800	10.1720	10.2312	-6.9	10.3565	-7.2	11.006	-8.2	-
Peru	(New Sol)	3.5930	-0.0085	925 - 935	3.5975	3.5885	-	-	-	-	-	-	-
USA	($)	-	-	-	-	-	-	-	-	-	-	-	114.1
Pacific/Middle East/Africa													
Australia	(A$)	1.7757	-0.0033	756 - 759	1.7803	1.7699	-	-	-	-	-	-	74.2
Hong Kong	(HK$)	7.7996	+0.0001	993 - 998	7.7998	7.7993	7.8011	-0.2	7.8049	-0.3	7.8331	-0.4	-
India	(Rs)	48.1800	-	300 - 300	48.2300	48.1300	48.3265	-3.7	48.6353	-3.8	50.01	-3.8	-
Indonesia	(Rupiah)	8995.00	-32.00	000 - 000	9018.00	8990.00	-	-	-	-	-	-	-
Iran	(Rial)	7985.00	-	500 - 500	-	-	-	-	-	-	-	-	-
Israel	(Shk)	4.6750	+0.0114	700 - 800	4.6800	4.6660	-	-	-	-	-	-	-
Japan	(Y)	121.115	+0.6300	080 - 150	121.300	120.310	120.975	1.4	120.67	1.5	119.2	1.6	135.1
Kuwait	(Kuwaiti D)	0.3011	-0.0001	009 - 013	0.3013	0.3006	0.3012	-0.6	0.3014	-0.5	0.3027	-0.5	-
Malaysia†	(M$)	3.8000	-	000 - 000	3.8000	3.8000	-	-	-	-	-	-	-
New Zealand	(NZ$)	2.0092	+0.0072	084 - 101	2.0125	2.0048	-	-	-	-	-	-	-
Philippines	(Peso)	53.4050	+0.0300	900 - 200	53.4500	53.3000	53.579	-3.9	54.034	-4.7	56.3075	-5.4	-
Saudi Arabia	(SR)	3.7503	-0.0002	501 - 505	3.7505	3.7501	3.7523	-0.6	3.7574	-0.8	3.7915	-1.1	-
Singapore	(S$)	1.7642	+0.0007	639 - 645	1.7653	1.7625	1.7631	0.7	1.7614	0.6	1.7523	0.7	-
South Africa	(R)	9.5638	-0.0712	600 - 675	9.6287	9.5400	9.6591	-12.0	9.8541	-12.1	10.6788	-11.7	-
South Korea	(Won)	1209.40	+0.9000	930 - 950	1210.00	1204.10	1212.55	-3.1	1219.05	-3.2	1244.05	-2.9	-
Taiwan	(T$)	34.7550	+0.0500	500 - 600	34.7600	34.7100	34.76	-0.2	34.75	0.1	34.6725	0.2	-
Thailand	(Bt)	43.3850	-0.1300	700 - 000	43.5500	43.3300	43.42	-1.0	43.49	-1.0	43.815	-1.0	-
U A E	(Dirham)	3.6730	-	720 - 740	3.6766	3.6720	3.6731	0.0	3.6735	-0.1	3.6761	-0.1	-

*The closing mid-point rates for the Euro and £ are shown in brackets. The other figures in both rows are in the reciprocal form in line with market convention. †Floating rate now shown for Argentina. ‡ Official rate set by Malaysian government. The WM/Reuters rate for the valuation of capital assets is 3.80 MYR/USD. Bid/offer spreads in the Dollar Spot table show only the last three decimal places. J.P. Morgan nominal indices Nov 8: Base average 1990 = 100. Bid, offer, mid spot rates and forward rates in both this and the pound table are derived from the WM/REUTERS 4pm (London time) CLOSING SPOT and FORWARD RATE services. Some values are rounded by the F.T. The exchange rates printed in this table are also available on the internet at http://www.FT.com

Source: Extract from the *Financial Times*, 19 November 2002

Tip	*If you are ever unsure how many figures are required after the decimal point check how many appear in the standard spot quotation.*

The reason information is so very important relates back to one of the favourite sayings in the market: 'every single piece of known information is already discounted in the price'.

So why do markets and prices move?

It all comes down to what we don't know. Therefore the bank with access to faster market information will have the opportunity to change its prices ahead of other market players, assimilating the new information, and will have a competitive advantage, assuming, of course, that it has moved its price the right way!

PROCEDURES AND PRACTICES – BANKS

As already mentioned it is market practice to quote only the last two figures of a price. If the exchange rate at a particular point in time is GBP/USD 1.5850–55, we can expand out the price to form GBP/USD 1.5850–1.5855. A spot trader is likely to quote only 50–55, the client is expected to know the rest. This represents the bid–offer spread on the two currencies in question: basically, how the bank buys and sells pounds against dollars (the base currency against the 'foreign' currency). In a perfect world, the bank trader would deal simultaneously with two different parties on their prices, and would see the 5-pip differential as their profit. Each 0.0001 is known as a 'pip'. Interbank rates can be quoted with a 2- to 5-pip spread, corporate transactions will have a wider spread, sometimes as much as 10 pips, to reflect the different credit risks of the two parties. See Figure 7.3 which illustrates an information page used by many corporate clients.

Let us examine the following rate for 'cable'. This refers to the original way in which banks dealt with one another thirty or so years ago. Then, the only way to ask for and receive prices in GBP/USD was to send messages down the transatlantic submarine cable, and the term 'cable' has stuck.

Telerate Channel page showing major currencies quoted against the dollar, spot and forward

Figure 7.3

	15:46			[BARCLAYS BANK PLC - LONDON]		
[ ]	SPOT	1 MONTH	2 MONTH	3 MONTH	6 MONTH	12 MONTH
GBP	1.5306/12	29.7/27.7	57.9/53.8	87.4/82.3	179/173	352/342
EUR	0.9885/89	15.4/13.3	28.8/25.3	41.4/38.4	80.9/76.9	146/134
JPY	119.84/90	22.5/17.5	40/35	58.5/51.5	121/112	270/250
CHF	1.4864/70	11.5/6.5	19.3/12.2	28.3/18.2	50/40	96.5/76.5
AUD	0.5614/19	17.5/15.5	32/29	57/54	119/113	266/253
CAD	1.5183/89	9/12	22/27	36/42	77/92	157/178
ZAR	10.010/61	90/110	175/205	260/310	540/610	1000/1100
NZD	0.4854/60	19/16	35/32	52.5/48.5	104/97	201/181
SEK	9.1892/52	191/241	370/430	574/644	1165/1265	2140/2440
NOK	7.4907/37	294/364	637/707	945/1035	1912/2038	3615/3815
DKK	7.5123/53	91/151	190/270	295/395	645/795	1140/1440
SAR	3.7500/10	5/13	10/20	15/35	40/60	110/140
HKD	7.7995/05	-22/+19	-28/+23	-27/+24	-49/+52	-58/+92
SGD	1.7662/72	-66/+34	-80/+20	-94/+6	167/17	303/103
THB	41.47/62	-15/+16	-19/+22	-23/+28	-33/+43	-62/+89

Source: Moneyline Telerate Channel T2F (courtesy Barclays Bank)

True story   I found out a little while ago that the use of the cable did not come free. One of the UK merchant banks remarked to me that they had the use of the cable for, I think, thirty or so minutes each afternoon, at a yearly cost of £30,000! That was a lot of money in those days.

Spot rate: GBP/USD   1.5306–12

Alternatively this can be written:

£/$ 1.5306–12, or GBP   1.5306–12

The bank will always quote their price, bid first and offer second. The bid being '06' for the base currency, which is sterling, and the offer being '12'. This can be termed as how the bank buys sterling and sells dollars @ 1.5306; or how the bank sells sterling and buys dollars @ 1.5312.

It is obviously important to establish which of the two currencies is the base currency, in the case above it is sterling. The other currency is referred to as the 'quoted' or the 'foreign' currency. Back to our example: as this is a direct quotation, the bank will sell the foreign currency (the dollar) on the left and buy it on the right. It is worth noting that many users of foreign exchange (clients) ask for their prices in 'foreign currency' terms rather than base currency terms. A UK corporate which wishes to sell dollars receivables against sterling will almost certainly ask for a price to sell the dollars, rather than a price where they can buy sterling (see Figure 7.4).

The same 'rules' apply when dealing with currencies quoted on an indirect basis, for example USD/CHF at a spot rate of 1.4860–65 (see Figure 7.5). By following these simple rules, dealing on the wrong side of the price should be avoided. Another way to reinforce this technical point is to remember that dealers wants to make money out of their trading, in that, they will wish to buy the base currency as cheaply as possible, for as few dollars as possible, and when selling their pounds on to the next player they want to sell them as expensively as possible. The difference will be their profit. A bank will always deal at the most advantageous rate to itself.

Figure 7.4

Spot quotations GBP/USD

Spot rate: GBP/USD 1.5306–12		
Base currency is sterling Foreign/quoted currency is US dollar		
1.5306 (bid)	–	1.5312 (offer)
Bank bids for £ against $ Client buys $ and sells £		Bank offers £ against $ Client sells $ and buys £

Spot quotations USD/CHF

Figure 7.5

Spot rate: USD/CHF   1.4860–65

Base currency is US dollar
Foreign/quoted currency is Swiss Francs

1.4860	–	1.4865
(bid)		(offer)

Bank bids for $ against CHF	Bank offers $ against CHF
Client buys CHF and sells $	Client sells CHF and buys $

Regular dealing amounts in major currencies

Table 7.1

GBP/USD	GBP 5 million
USD/JPY, USD/CHF, etc.	USD 5–10 million
EUR/JPY	EUR 5–10 million

Traders, when dealing interbank, may transact a deal with simply one word, 'Mine' or 'Yours': this is in relation to the base currency. So if the spot rate was EUR/JPY: 118.60–118.65, and a trader shouted 'Mine, 10', they would have bought 10 million euro against yen at 118.65 (dealing on the counterparties' 'offer' rate). The problems arise when inexperienced dealers shout 'Mine', with no amount given. Each currency pair has a market accepted amount for a regular trade. These are shown in Table 7.1. Our inexperienced dealer may shout 'Mine' and be told, 'OK you got 20' 'But I only wanted 5!'

> It is vital to establish what your dealing amount is. This will vary from bank to bank, and from trader to trader. If you agree to make prices in 10 million, and someone tries to deal with you in 20 million, you are only committed to deal in 10, but you may want to do the full amount. Quotations are assumed to be for 'regular' amounts, unless otherwise specified.

Tip

Now we know which side of the price we are on we must consider another market convention where banks, for simplicity, run their trading room positions in US dollars. And although they may be trading USD/CHF, they will generally say they are long of US dollars rather than short of Swiss francs. This allows positions across many currencies to be traded, with the US dollar as the common denominator for running the positions. This is still the case even if the foreign exchange bank itself is not dollar based. A bank's position across many different currencies can then be valued in dollars and may look something like Table 7.2.

This can help the banks to monitor their exposure, by seeing at a glance whether they are long or short in dollar terms.

Table 7.2	Potential dealing room position			
Currency	Long	Short	Rate
GBP/USD	USD 4,546,500	GBP 3,000,000	1.5155
USD/CHF	USD 5,000,000	CHF 7,450,000	1.4900
USD/SGD	SGD 5,298,600	USD 3,000,000	1.7662
USD/NOK	USD 2,500,000	NOK 18,726,750	7.4907
USD/JPY	JPY 1,198,000,000	USD 10,000,000	119.80
Overall US dollar position = short USD 953,500				

PROCEDURES AND PRACTICES – CLIENTS

The bank's clients will always be trying to get the best deal for themselves and, naturally enough, their aims are totally opposite to those of the banks. Few corporate customers can deal on the finest terms. A client may want to deal for an uneven amount, possibly below the minimum amount for which competitive rates are available. This may leave the bank with an amount to cover on less favourable terms unless it has other customer business to go against it.

The bank may also have to add together a series of smaller deals and cover the aggregate amount, leaving itself exposed to changes in the exchange rate. In addition, the bank must also take into account the credit risk: that the client will fail to fulfil its side of the bargain. This may leave the bank with an unbalanced position and exposed to market movements. It also begs the question, is there a credit risk or a settlement risk? Banks seem to be equally divided on this point.

Let us go back to the cable rate – spot rate: GBP/USD 1.5306–12. A client who needs to purchase dollars will be trying to buy as many dollars as they can with their pounds, and will be trying to get as numerically high a rate as possible. The client will be buying the dollars where the bank is selling the dollars, yet the bank will be trying to quote as numerically low as possible.

Larger amounts can generate more attractive rates, but not always. Obviously the rate quoted to a client will reflect the transaction amount, in that a rate to sell USD 75,700 may not be too competitive – it is too small for a pure interbank quotation. On the other hand, a rate to sell USD 5,000,000 will get a very good rate. But what if the sale amount was USD 1,000,000,000? It could then be argued that this is too large for a one-off deal, and for safety the bank may quote a less competitive rate, to give it time to cover the entire transaction in the market.

A young trainee had joined the treasury of a large Middle Eastern multi-national company. He had joined as the 'tea boy' and was working his way up. He hadn't been with the company that long when they gave him the opportunity to place his first deal. He had watched how the dealers worked, and his job was to place a deposit in Deutschmarks over the weekend. It was late in the afternoon on a Friday, he carefully checked the screen rates, and chose the bank with the best price. He called them up and asked if the price on the screen was still good, it was – so he took a deep breath and said 'Yours, 800 million marks'. He was rather hurt to get the reply, 'Thanks, now **** ***!' I thought they'd be pleased he said rather naively.

Note: Normal dealing amount was then DEM 10 million.

Example

Using the data in Table 7.3, we can see which rates are applicable for specific transactions.

Major currency spot rates against the US dollar

Table 7.3

Currency	Bid	Offer
GBP/USD	1.5892	1.5898
USD/JPY	121.21	121.27
USD/CHF	1.4494	1.4500
EUR/USD	1.0124	1.0130

1. A German manufacturer of heavy equipment sells their goods into the US and invoices in USD; they need to convert the dollars to their own domestic currency of euro.

     Client buys EUR, bank sells EUR, quotation is 1.0130.

2. A Swiss importer of American 'off-road' vehicles pays for the goods in US dollars, as part of their contract.

     Client buys dollars, bank sells dollars, quotation is 1.4500.

3. UK client sells USD 2,500,000, for pounds. How much do they get?

     Rate quoted 1.5898, making a total of £1,572,524.85.

4. A Japanese exporter sells goods to America, and invoices in US dollars.

     Client sells dollars, bank buys dollars, quotation 121.21.

5. Client purchases GBP 10,000,000, how many dollars are required for payment?

     Rate quoted 1.5898, making a total of USD 15,898,000.

Quick fix exercise 1

1. A client is trying to buy dollars and sell UK sterling, they have contacted three different banks for prices. They have been quoted:

   Bank A: GBP/USD   1.5892–98
   Bank B: GBP/USD   1.5890–95
   Bank C: GBP/USD   1.5899–04

   At what rate should they deal?

   Using Table 7.3:

2. Where does the bank sell Swiss francs to a client against US dollars?

3. Bank buys 1,000,000,000 yen, from a client against dollars, at which rate and how many dollars will they receive?

4. A client wishes to buy USD 5 million with pounds, what rate will they be quoted and how much sterling will they need?

For answers, refer to the end of the chapter.

CALCULATING CROSS CURRENCY RATES

As mentioned earlier, it is market practice for most currencies to be quoted against the dollar in terms of the number of units of the currency for each single US dollar. This is the indirect method of quotation. Rates quoted the other way round, such as GBP/USD, are direct quotations. A 'cross rate' is a rate of exchange between two currencies where neither is the dollar. There are three different ways of calculating cross rates, dependent upon whether you have two indirect quotations, two direct quotations, or one of each.

Two indirect quotations

Example

The two exchange rates must be cross divided.

Spot: USD/CHF   1.4864–1.4870
Spot: USD/JPY   119.84–119.90

$119.90 \div 1.4864 = 80.66$: how the client can sell JPY, and buy CHF.
$119.84 \div 1.4870 = 80.59$: how the client can buy JPY, and sell CHF.

The bank, of course, will be on the other side of the price:

Spot: CHF/JPY   80.59–80.66

Two direct quotations

The two exchange rates must be cross divided.

Example

Spot: GBP/USD   1.5400–1.5405
Spot: AUD/USD   0.5614–0.5619

1.5400 ÷ 0.5619 = 2.7407: how the client can buy AUD and sell GBP.
1.5405 ÷ 0.5614 = 2.7440: how the client can sell AUD and buy GBP.

The bank, of course, will be on the other side of the price:

Spot: GBP/AUD   2.7407–2.7440

An indirect quotation and a direct quotation

The same side of each exchange rate must be multiplied.

Example

Spot: GBP/USD   1.5400–1.5405
Spot: USD/CHF   1.4864–1.4870

1.5400 × 1.4864 = 2.2891: how the client can buy CHF and sell GBP.
1.5405 × 1.4870 = 2.2907: how the client can sell CHF and buy GBP.

The bank will, as in the previous examples, be on the other side of the price:

Spot: GBP/CHF   2.2891–2.2907

Quick fix exercise 2

1. Given the following rates calculate where a UK exporter would sell Swiss francs receivables for sterling.
   Spot: GBP/USD   1.5892–98
   Spot: USD/CHF   1.4454–1.4500

2. A bank has quoted the following spot rate:
   EUR/JPY   71.13–15
   Where will the client buy yen?

3. Calculate the CHF/JPY cross from the following rates:
   Spot: USD/CHF   1.4494–1.4500
   Spot: USD/JPY   121.21–121.27

For answers, refer to the end of the chapter.

CONCLUSION

To recap, spot foreign exchange is driven totally by supply and demand; this can be influenced by any number of factors acting individually, on either one or both of the currencies, or multiple factors acting in concert upon one or both currencies. Some factors will be more or less important depending upon the time of year, a political agenda, or other third party influences. Major currencies can become minor currencies, weak currencies can become strong and vice versa. In times of crisis there may often be a 'flight to quality' into currencies such as the US dollar or the yen. The currency markets are ever changing and participants with access to state-of-the-art information systems are arguably better placed to profit from market movements than those with the less up-to-date inputs (see Chapter 6 Technology and the Markets).

Answers to quick fix exercises

Exercise 1

1. From Bank C.

2. 1.4494.

3. 121.27, USD 8,246,062.51.

4. 1.5892, £ 3,146,237.10.

Exercise 2

1. $1.5898 \times 1.4500 = 2.30521$: how the client can sell CHF buy GBP.

2. 71.13.

3. $121.27 \div 1.4494 = 83.67$: how the bank can offer CHF.
   $121.21 \div 1.4500 = 83.59$: how the bank can buy CHF.
   Spot: CHF/JPY: 83.59–83.67

The mechanics of forward foreign exchange

Francesca Taylor, Taylor Associates

Forward foreign exchange is naturally more complex than spot FX, as the extra dimension of relative interest rates comes into play in the pricing.

■ ■ ■

INTRODUCTION

Foreign exchange can be bought or sold by many different market participants using many different currencies in most countries around the world. It can be bought or sold value spot, which, as we saw in the previous chapter, generally means a two-business-day value period, or it can be transacted for delivery on a future date, in which case it is a forward transaction. As Continuous Linked Settlement (CLS) continues to make inroads into the FX market, the two-business day settlement period may soon become shorter.

Forward foreign exchange has been available at commercial banks for many years, but the explosive growth occurred in the late 1970s and early 1980s. Before the Second World War it was possible to get forward prices, but the market was quite small and volumes did not increase until some years later. It could also be argued that the development of the pocket calculator in the mid-1970s made forward pricing that much easier and that in turn helped the interbank market to progress rapidly. Unusually, the latest BIS survey (as at 2001) showed a growth in outright forward FX transactions, whilst almost everything else related to FX declined during that period, (1998–2001). Perhaps this can be explained by the corporate market becoming more familiar with the need to hedge their currency risks.

BACKGROUND

There are two distinct types of forward transaction: the forward outright (or outright forward) transaction and the FX swap – not to be confused with currency swaps which are one of the range of derivative currency products. Outright forward deals are used mostly by corporate customers to hedge their currency risk, whereas the professional interbank market will trade 'swap points' or 'differentials' among themselves.

Theoretically, the spot price and the forward price of a currency could be the same, but it is highly unlikely. Ordinarily, the forward rate is either higher or lower than the spot rate, indicating that something has been added or subtracted from the underlying spot exchange rate – these are known as the differentials or the 'points'. Quoting forward differentials, called premiums and discounts, rather than quoting an all-in forward price has advantages. Firstly, forward differentials can remain unchanged for longish periods, even though the spot rate may be very volatile. Secondly, the outright forward rate is not of much interest to the interbank dealer who is quoting only the points.

Question: *Just what are these differentials and why are they so important?*

Answer: Let us consider a trade where a bank has agreed to sell sterling to a customer in 12 months' time, and buy Swiss francs in return. For those readers of the corporate persuasion, this is the same as the client selling Swiss francs and buying sterling, forward for 12 months.

The bank could fix the rate now based on the current spot rate, but that may well move in the next 12 months. The bank, however, is committed to hand over the sterling in 12 months' time, but may end up receiving fewer Swiss francs than it needs to buy the sterling at the then prevailing rates. This could lead to a foreign exchange loss on the Swiss francs.

Question: *How does the bank protect itself against this loss?*

Answer: The FX risk on the forward sale of sterling can be offset by a spot purchase of sterling now. This ensures that the bank has the sterling available and has fixed the exchange rate with which to buy them. But what should they do with this sterling, as it is not required for 12 months?

First, the resulting sterling must be put on deposit in the money markets for 12 months, yielding an interest income. Second, with what do we fund the purchase of the sterling? The bank must borrow Swiss francs from the money markets for 12 months, to buy the sterling spot. The Swiss francs

| Figure 8.1 | **Group of transactions that make up the bank's forward hedge** |

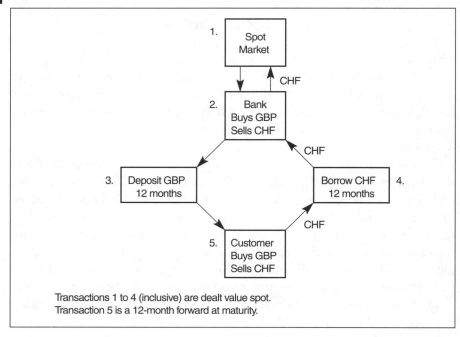

Transactions 1 to 4 (inclusive) are dealt value spot.
Transaction 5 is a 12-month forward at maturity.

Components of a foreign exchange forward transaction

Figure 8.2

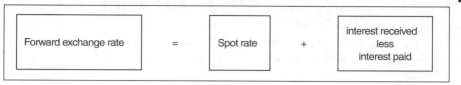

will be repaid by the customer's funds in 12 months' time. There will be a funding cost for this position.

Figure 8.1 shows the bank's transactions.

If we group the transactions in Figure 8.1 together: the forward rate consists of a combination of the current spot rate plus or minus the appropriate differential for the maturity (see Figure 8.2). This will be examined in more detail later in the chapter.

PREMIUMS AND DISCOUNTS

These refer to the forward points, which need to be added or subtracted from the spot rate. There can be an element of confusion when using these terms. One school of thought is that if the forward exchange rate is numerically higher than the spot rate the currency is at a premium, so the points must be added; the other school of thought states that where the forward exchange rate is numerically lower, and points must have been subtracted from the spot rate, then that is a premium currency. In fact it does not matter what terminology is used as long as it is explained. Most of the confusion arises as the interbank market refers to the dollar (or whatever is the base currency) as being at a premium or a discount, whereas other participants are likely to refer to how the foreign or quoted currency compares to the base currency.

Example

Consider the following market data:

Spot rate: GBP/USD	1.5892–1.5898
3-month points	103 97
Forward outright	1.5789–1.5801

In this example you could say that the dollar is at a premium to sterling, so the points must be subtracted, or that sterling is at a discount to the dollar so the points must be subtracted. It ends up at the same thing.

How does the dealer, or the client for that matter, know whether the forward points should be added or subtracted? Outright forward rates are quoted as all-in rates, in a similar way to spot rates, with the smaller number on the left-hand side of the quoted price. The market-making bank will always buy the base currency as cheaply as possible, and sell the foreign or 'quoted' currency as expensively as possible to achieve the best deal for itself (in this example the base currency is sterling and the quoted currency is the US dollar).

This is achieved by having the larger points figure on the left in the case of premium 'quoted' currencies, and the larger figure on the right in the case of discount 'quoted' currencies. Using our example to re-state the position, the dollar is at a premium to sterling so the points must therefore be subtracted; this gives the forward outright rate as GBP/USD 1.5789–1.5801.

Forward prices will always exhibit a larger bid–offer spread than spot prices. The example above illustrates a bid–offer spread on the spot rate of 6 pips, but a 12-pip spread on the forward. The same is true even if we use a currency pair where the dollar or another currency is the base, as shown below.

Example

Consider the following market data:

Spot rate: EUR/USD	1.0124	–1.0130
3-month points	43	41
Forward outright	1.0081	–1.0089

In this example the base currency is the euro and the quoted currency is US dollar. The larger points figure is on the left, as is the case of discount currencies. The dollar is at a premium to the euro so the points must be subtracted, giving a forward outright rate of EUR/USD 1.0081–1.0089. Alternatively, we could have said that the euro is at a discount to the dollar. On both occasions the points are subtracted. This shows a bid–offer spread on the spot rate of 6 pips, yet an 8-pip spread on the forward.

Tip

A 'quick and dirty' way of remembering whether to add or subtract the points relates to the sequence of the numbers when you look at the bid–offer spread on the differentials:

- *If the points sequence is high/low (145–135) subtract the points.*
- *If the points sequence is low/high (20–23) add the points.*

CALCULATING DIFFERENTIALS

The outright forward rate is not a dealer's assessment or forecast of what the spot rate will be on a predetermined future date. It is a simple calculation involving the current spot rate plus or minus the current interest rate differentials at that same moment in time. The forward rate is not a predictor of what the spot rate will be in the future.

As mentioned in Chapter 7, page 96, the market has a saying: 'that every single piece of known information is in the price'. If there were no changes in the data available, and every item of data had been assimilated in the price, and all we experienced was the passage of time, and nothing whatsoever changed, then the current spot rate may well turn out to be the actual spot rate on a specific date in the future. But, as we know, life is not like that; every change, however minute, is reflected in the price, making exchange rates very volatile.

It must also be borne in mind that when pricing any financial instrument the market will always consider the cost of the hedge as the minimum price for the deal.

As stated previously, the interbank market will quote exchange rate forwards not in terms of an outright rate but, rather, in terms of spot rates and differentials (or swap points). The differential or forward swap is an exchange of one currency for another currency on one date to be reversed on a given future date. This can also be achieved by borrowing one currency for a given period while lending the other currency for the same period.

The swap rate will reflect the interest rate differential between the two currencies, converted into foreign exchange terms, using a calculation based on Eurocurrency interest rates (unless otherwise stated).

The logical extension of this is that it is the perceived change in a country's inflation rate that will increase or decrease the number of forward points. The argument is that, when a country experiences inflation, there is a natural tendency by the authorities to increase domestic interest rates to try to combat it, so rates overall increase.

Let us consider the facts. Do we agree that a parallel transaction to calculate the forward differential of a currency pair could also be achieved by borrowing one currency for a given period while lending the other currency for the same period? The rationale for this close association is that a trader should not be able to make a profit by 'round-tripping', i.e. by borrowing and lending currencies for the appropriate period, then reconverting through the exchange rate the principal plus interest and ending up with more money than they started with.

Consider the following simultaneous transactions:

(a) borrow CHF for three months from spot value date;

(b) sell CHF and buy USD value spot;

(c) invest the dollars just purchased for three months from spot value date;

(d) sell forward now the USD principal and interest maturing in three months' time, into CHF.

Basically, the market will adjust for the price of (d) so that there will be no profits or losses. It can be argued that interest differentials, or forward points or swap points, whatever you wish to call them, are merely a 'balancing item' to ensure that arbitrage does not take place. If the four rates are not in line, then round-tripping or arbitrage will occur, when for a short period of time the four transactions above may generate a profit, until such time as market forces bring the rates back into line.

The four transactions (a) to (d) above are more meaningful if we convert them to a formula:

(a) Borrow CHF 100 at a rate of A% per annum. The total amount of principal and interest, (repayable in three months) will be:

$$100 \times \left(1 + \frac{A}{100} \times \frac{days}{360}\right)$$

(b) Sell CHF 100 for USD at the spot rate to give USD (100/spot).

(c) Invest USD (100/spot) at B%. The principal and interest returned (in three months' time) will be:

$$(100/spot) \times \left(1 + \frac{B}{100} \times \frac{days}{360}\right)$$

(d) Sell forward this last amount at the forward rate to give:

$$(100/spot) \times \left(1 + \frac{B}{100} \times \frac{days}{360}\right) \times \textbf{forward outright}$$

Equating the principal and interest in (a) and (d) we get:

$$100 \times \left(1 + \frac{A}{100} \times \frac{days}{360}\right) = (100/spot) \times \left(1 + \frac{B}{100} \times \frac{days}{360}\right) \times \textbf{forward outright}$$

making:

$$\textbf{Forward outright} = (spot) \times \frac{\left(1 + \dfrac{A}{100} \times \dfrac{days}{360}\right)}{\left(1 + \dfrac{B}{100} \times \dfrac{days}{360}\right)}$$

also:

$$\textbf{Forward differential} = (\textbf{Forward outright} - \textbf{spot})$$

$$\textbf{(Forward swap)} = \frac{(spot) \times \left(\dfrac{A - B}{100}\right) \times \left(\dfrac{days}{360}\right)}{\left(1 + \dfrac{B}{100} \times \dfrac{days}{360}\right)} \qquad [8.1]$$

NB: If the interest rate at B% and the number of days are sufficiently small, the following approximation can be made, which I shall call Equation 8.2.

$$\text{Forward swap} \approx (\text{spot}) \times \left(\frac{\text{Interest rate differential}}{100} \right) \times \left(\frac{\text{days}}{360} \right) \quad [8.2]$$

This formula can be reversed as follows:

$$\text{Interest rate differential} \approx \frac{(\text{Forward swap} \times 100 \times 360)}{\text{spot} \times \text{days}}$$

Worked example 1

Consider the following market data:

30-day CHF interest rate	0.65%	(A)
30-day USD interest rate	1.65%	(B)
Spot: USD/CHF	1.48	

Using Equation 8.1:

$$\text{Forward swap} = \frac{1.48 \times \left(\dfrac{-1}{100} \right) \times \left(\dfrac{30}{360} \right)}{1 + \left(\dfrac{1.65}{100} \right) \times \left(\dfrac{30}{360} \right)} = 0.00123 \text{ or } 12.3 \text{ points}$$

Using Equation 8.2:

$$(\text{Approximate swap}) \approx 1.48 \times \frac{-1}{100} \times \frac{30}{360} = 0.00123 \text{ or } 12.3 \text{ points}$$

But if we extend the maturity of the forward transaction the relationship breaks down as shown below.

Worked example 2

Consider the following market data:

1-year CHF interest rate	0.7%	(A)
1-year USD interest rate	1.7%	(B)
Spot: USD/CHF	1.48	

Using Equation 8.1:

$$\text{Forward swap} = \frac{1.48 \times \left(\dfrac{-1}{100} \right) \times \left(\dfrac{365}{360} \right)}{1 + \left(\dfrac{1.65}{100} \right) \times \left(\dfrac{365}{360} \right)} = 0.014759 \text{ or } 147.6 \text{ points}$$

Using Equation 8.2:

$$(\text{Approximate swap}) \approx 1.48 \times \frac{-1}{100} \times \frac{365}{360}$$

$$= 0.015005 \text{ or } 150 \text{ points}$$

Note The day count convention is 360 days as this is market practice for both Euroswiss and Eurodollars, so we are using the Actual/360 calculation. It should also be borne in mind that the interest differentials must be calculated using gross (not net) interest rates, otherwise the costs/receipts are exaggerated.

PROCEDURES AND PRACTICES

FX swaps or differential prices are quoted as two-way prices in the same way as other rates, but technically we should use the correct side of the underlying foreign exchange rate and relevant money market prices for the calculations. It is, however, far easier to use mid-prices throughout to calculate the mid-price of the swap and then to spread the two-way price around this middle rate. When a deal is done, only one price is dealt (the swap price); the actual transaction will be written out as two deals because there will be two separate settlements:

- a settlement on the spot value date;
- a settlement on the forward value date.

Consider the following three-month forward swap quote:

USD/CHF   133–128

133	128
Client buys CHF spot	Client sells CHF spot
Client sells CHF forward	Client buys CHF forward
Bank buys USD spot	Bank sells USD spot
Bank sells USD forward	Bank buys USD forward

A specific spot rate will be needed to complete the calculation to arrive at the settlement rates. The exact spot rate that is used is not that important as long as the near and far sides of the swap preserve the differential.

When you consider where the forward foreign exchange rates are derived from, it is easy to see how close the relationship is between money market interest rates and foreign exchange rates.

CALCULATING OUTRIGHT FORWARDS

The technology that the banks use for quoting forward and spot rates is becoming increasingly sophisticated, and will vary from bank to bank.

As with all fast moving markets it is vital for the traders to have access to completely up-to-date current market information, in order for them to maintain their competitiveness. The Moneyline Telerate network and Reuters offer both information services and dealing technology. It is also market practice for the market making banks to exhibit their current rates on screens for distribution around the market. A sample of the information is shown in Figure 8.3.

Figure 8.3 is a composite FX spot and forward page published through the Moneyline Telerate network and available to most market participants. Some pages and screens, however, will be available only on a selective access basis. This gives contributors the chance to ensure that their information does not go directly to their competitors.

The page quotes major currencies spot and forward against the USD and uses the SWIFT codes to identify them. The page is divided into four quarters with each currency being quoted against the USD.

In practice these are the currencies in question being quoted using the market convention of BASE/TERM currency.

GBP/USD:	Spot rate	1.5680/90
EUR/USD:	Spot rate	0.9863/68
USD/JPY:	Spot rate	122.83/122.85
USD/CHF:	Spot rate	1.4801/20

Composite FX spot and forward screen showing currencies quoted against the US dollar

Figure 8.3

```
10/04    11:55 GMT   [GBP]    [TELERATE FORWARD RATES]        [JPY]        P27B
RBC         TOR   1.5680/ 1.5690 11:40 SPT MIZUHO CB   TOK   122.83/ 122.85 11:35
MIZUHO CB   TOK    -2.45/  -1.95 00:30 O/N MIZUHO CB   TOK    -2.13/  -1.53 06:45
SOC GEN     PAR    -0.94/  -0.84 11:48 T/N SOC GEN     PAR    -0.66/  -0.61 11:48
SOC GEN     PAR    -6.43/  -6.32 11:45 1WK SOC GEN     PAR    -4.38/  -4.28 11:45
SOC GEN     PAR   -27.87/ -27.58 11:29 1MO SOC GEN     PAR   -19.05/ -18.75 11:29
SOC GEN     PAR   -83.90/ -83.40 11:54 3MO SOC GEN     PAR   -52.95/ -52.45 11:54
SOC GEN     PAR  -170.50/-169.50 11:54 6MO SOC GEN     PAR   -98.00/ -97.00 11:54
SOC GEN     PAR  -339.00/-336.00 11:54 1YR SOC GEN     PAR  -199.50/-196.50 11:54
                   [EUR]                                      [CHF]
OHV         AMS   0.9863/ 0.9868 11:54 SPT ABN AMRO    AMS   1.4801/ 1.4820 11:53
BROKER      LDN   -1.290/  -1.28 10:13 O/N MIZUHO CB   TOK    -1.48/  -0.98 00:39
SOC GEN     PAR    -0.48/  -0.38 11:48 T/N SOC GEN     PAR    -0.43/  -0.38 11:48
SOC GEN     PAR    -3.00/  -2.85 11:45 1WK SOC GEN     PAR    -3.15/  -2.85 11:45
NBG         GRC   -13.06/ -12.06 11:54 1MO SOC GEN     PAR   -13.85/ -13.35 11:29
NBG         GRC   -37.64/ -36.64 11:54 3MO SOC GEN     PAR   -37.30/ -36.20 11:54
NBG         GRC   -72.10/ -70.60 11:54 6MO SOC GEN     PAR   -69.50/ -67.50 11:54
SOC GEN     PAR  -130.10/-127.10 11:54 1YR SOC GEN     PAR  -133.75/-128.75 11:54
```

Source: Moneyline Telerate

Example

Using Figure 8.3 we can calculate outright forward rates:

1. Calculate the three-month forward for cable:

Spot rate: GBP/USD	1.5680–1.5690
3-month points	83.9–83.4
Outright	1.55961–1.56066

Note: The points sequence goes high/low, so the points are subtracted. The dollar is at a premium to sterling.

2. Calculate the three-month forward for USD/CHF:

Spot rate: USD/CHF	1.4801–1.4820
3-month points	37.3–36.20
Outright	1.47637–1.47838

Note: The points sequence goes high/low, so the points are subtracted. The Swiss franc is at a premium to the US dollar.

Tip *Remember to incorporate the correct amount of zeros into the differential before adding or subtracting the points from the spot rate. Market information screens are notorious for leaving off the zeros. If the sequence is 145/135 for GBP/USD, check the number of significant figures after the decimal point when the spot rate is quoted – it is four. So the forward points are actually 0.0145/0.0135.*

3. Calculate the six-month forward for USD/JPY:

Spot rate: USD/JPY	122.83–122.85
6-month points	98–97
Outright	121.85–121.88

Note: The points sequence goes high/low, so the points are subtracted. The yen is at a premium to the US dollar.

Figure 8.3 gives the forward differentials for specific monthly periods. These are known as 'straight' dates or 'calendar' dates. Sometimes it may be necessary to transact a deal for a date that is in between these dates; these are known as 'broken' dates. A forward foreign exchange transaction can be arranged for any day in the future as long as it is a business day in both currencies. The forward swap points or differentials are then calculated by interpolating between the given dates on either side, as shown later in the section.

CALCULATING 'STRAIGHT DATE' FORWARDS (AGAINST STERLING)

A client wishes to buy USD 3 million forward for six months against sterling. Consider the following market information:

Spot rate: GBP/CHF	1.5680–90
Transaction date	Friday, 4 October 2002
Spot value date	Tuesday, 8 October 2002
Forward value date	Tuesday, 8 April 2003
6-month points	83.9–83.4

The USD is at a premium to sterling so the points will need to be subtracted, this can be seen as the number sequence is high/low. When calculating rates for outright forward transactions, if you use the right-hand side of the spot rate you also use the right-hand side of the forward differential, and vice versa.

First, we must decide on the correct side of the spot rate. As our client is buying the USD they are on the left-hand side of the rate at GBP/USD at 1.5680.

Second, we need to use the left-hand side of the forward differential, which is 83.9 points or 0.00839.

Third, we need to put all the components together:

Spot rate: GBP/CHF	1.5680
6-month points:	0.00839
Outright	1.55961

The USD will cost GBP 1,923,557.81 (3,000,000 divided by 1.55961).

Quick fix exercise 1

Using the data in Figure 8.3:

1. Calculate the one-month outright forward rate for a client who wishes to sell US dollars and buy sterling.

2. A client wishes to buy forward EUR 10 million with USD for a period of six months. How much will they be charged?

3. A client wants to sell forward CHF 2 million against USD for three months. How much will they receive?

For answers, refer to the end of the chapter.

CALCULATING 'BROKEN DATE' FORWARDS
(AGAINST STERLING)

A customer of the bank needs to sell forward USD 5 million for value 29 May 2003.

Consider the following market information:

Spot rate: GBP/USD	1.5680–1.5690
Transaction date	Friday, 4 October 2002
Spot value date	Tuesday, 8 October 2002
Forward value date	Thursday, 29 May 2003
6-month points	170.5–169.5
12-month points	339–336
Day count – 6 months forward	182 days (8 April 2002)
Day count – 12 months forward	365 days (8 October 2003)
Day count – 29 May 2003	233 days

It is possible to work out the straight date forwards for either 6 or 12 whole months, but our date falls between them both. It is necessary to interpolate between month 6 and month 12 and calculate the number of points per day and add or subtract as required. The dollar is at a premium to sterling so the points will need to be subtracted – this can be seen as the number sequence is high/low. When calculating rates for outright forward transactions, if you use the right-hand side of the spot rate remember to use the right-hand side of the forward differential.

First, we must decide on the correct side of the spot rate. As our client is selling dollars they are on the right-hand side of the rate at GBP/USD 1.5690.

Second, we need to calculate the number of points between month 6 and month 12, and then calculate the number of points per day, using the formula: 12-month points less 6-month points, divided by the number of days (8 April–8 October). This gives:

$$\frac{(0.0336 - 0.01695)}{(365 \text{ days} - 182 \text{ days})} = \frac{0.01665}{183} = 0.000091 \text{ points per day}$$

Third, we need to calculate how many extra points for an additional 51 days between the six-month forward value date and 29 May 2003:

$$(0.000091 \times 51 \text{ days} = 0.004641)$$

Fourth, we need to put all the components together:

Spot rate: GBP/USD	1.5690
6-month points	0.01695
Extra 51 days' points	0.004641
Outright	1.54741

> When calculating currency amounts or currency equivalents using either **Tip** forward or spot exchange rates it is important to calculate down to the final pence and cents. Market participants can get a little crabby if they do not receive, say, the odd 46 pence on their original five million dollar transaction. The USD 5 million will generate GBP 3,231,205.69 (5,000,000 divided by 1.54741).

Quick fix exercise 2

Using the data in Figure 8.3: a UK company director needs to pay a bill of USD 2.2 million, due on 10 December. She wishes to lock in the rate now as she is concerned about the weakness of the pound. Assume the transaction date is 18 March 2003. How much sterling will the dollars cost?

For answer refer to the end of the chapter.

CALCULATING 'STRAIGHT DATE' FORWARDS (AGAINST THE US DOLLAR)

For those readers who feel uncomfortable with using sterling as a base currency, this and the next section provide similar examples using the US dollar as the base – as is more normal in the international markets.

A client wishes to buy CHF 3 million forward for six months against US dollars.

Consider the following market information:

Spot rate: USD/CHF	1.4801–1.4820
Transaction date	Friday, 4 October 2002
Spot value date	Tuesday, 8 October 2002
Forward value date	Tuesday, 8 April 2003
6-month points	69.50–67.50

The CHF is at a premium to the dollar so the points will need to be subtracted. This can be seen, as the number sequence on the forward differential is high/low.

First, we must decide on the correct side of the spot rate. As our client is buying the CHF they are on the left-hand side of the rate at USD/CHF 1.4801. When calculating the number of points per day, do not round the significant figures to the final number of decimal places required until the last calculation has been concluded. Do not round after each stage.

Second, we need to use the left-hand side of the forward differential, which is 69.5 points or 0.00695.

Third, we need to put all the components together:

Spot rate: USD/CHF	1.4801
6-month points:	0.00695
Outright	1.47315

The Swiss francs will cost USD 2,036,452.50 (3,000,000 divided by 1.47315).

Quick fix exercise 3

Using the data in Figure 8.3:

1. What rate will the bank quote to a client who wishes to sell forward for one month CHF 5 million against dollars and how many dollars will the company receive?

2. A client needs to buy GBP 875,000 one month forward. How many dollars will they need, and when will they pay for the sterling?

3. A UK corporate wishes to sell forward for nine months JPY 222,250,000 against US dollars. How many dollars will it receive?

For answers refer to the end of the chapter.

CALCULATING 'BROKEN DATE' FORWARDS (AGAINST THE US DOLLAR)

A customer of the bank needs to sell forward EUR 10 million against the US dollar for value 15 January 2003.

Consider the following market information:

Spot rate: EUR/USD	0.9863–0.9868
Transaction date	Friday, 4 October 2002
Spot value date	Tuesday, 8 October 2002
Forward value date	Wednesday, 15 January 2003
3-month points	37.64–36.64
6-month points	72.10–70.60
Day count – 3 months forward	92 days (8 January 2003)
Day count – 6 months forward	182 days (8 April 2003)
Day count – 15 January 2003	99 days

Our date falls between the three- and six-month rates. It is therefore necessary to interpolate between month 3 and month 6 and then to calculate the number of points per day, multiplied by the number of days, and then to add or subtract as required. The dollar is at a premium to the euro so the points will need to be subtracted – this is evidenced by the high/low number sequence. When calculating rates for outright forward transactions, if you use the right-hand side of the spot rate you also need to use the right-hand side of the forward differential.

First, we must decide on the correct side of the spot rate. As our client is selling euro they are on the left-hand side of the rate at EUR/USD 0.9863.

Second, we need to calculate the number of points between month 3 and month 6, and then calculate the number of points per day, using the formula: 6-month points less 3-month points, divided by the number of days (4 June–4 September).

This gives:

$$\frac{(0.003764 - 0.007210)}{(182 \text{ days} - 92 \text{ days})} = \frac{0.003446}{90} = 0.0000383 \text{ points per day}$$

Third, we need these extra points for an additional seven days between the three-month forward value date and 15 January 2003:

$$0.0000383 \times 7 \text{ days} = 0.000268$$

Fourth, we need to put all the components together:

Spot rate: EUR/USD	0.9863
3-month points	0.003764
Extra 7 days' points	0.000268
Outright	0.98227

The EUR 10 million will generate USD 9,822,700 (10,000,000 multiplied by 0.98227).

PROBLEMS WITH INTERPOLATION

This method of interpolation also assumes that the relationship is linear between the two end dates, when it may not be, but in the absence of further information this is the obvious assumption. When interpolating I have always found it easier to start with the full number of figures after the decimal point. In the example above the two-month forward differential was quoted as 24–21. If you do the calculation first and then add the zeros afterwards you can sometimes trip yourself up. I would always add the zeros first to make the points 0.0024–0.0021, and then commence the calculation.

SHORT DATE FORWARDS

The spot exchange rate for the particular pair of currencies is used as the base from which to calculate the forward rates. Forward foreign exchange is technically anything more than two days forward, although value dates up to

Figure 8.4

Short date foreign exchange

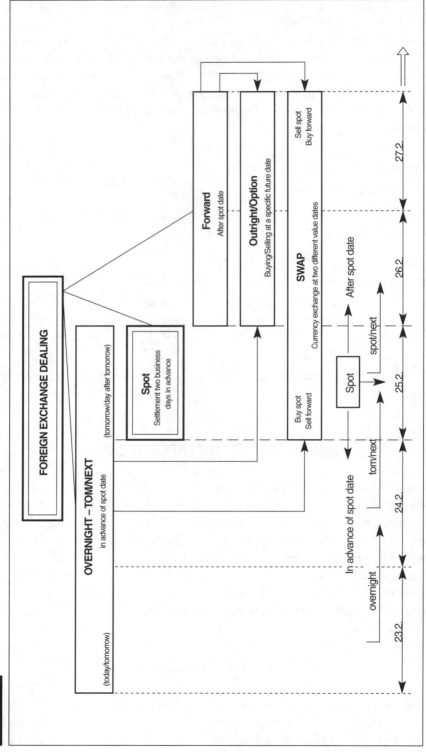

Source: Swiss Bank Corporation – now UBS

one month in the future are known as 'short-dates'. An illustration of some short-dated transactions is shown in Figure 8.4 courtesy of Swiss Bank Corporation.

The terminology used in the short date foreign exchange forward market is based on the deposit market, as forward swaps are quoted on the basis of the relevant deposit/loan rates. In the deposit market the following abbreviations are used:

Overnight	A loan or deposit from today until 'tomorrow'
Tom-next	A loan or deposit from tomorrow to the 'next' day (spot)
Spot-next	A loan or deposit from spot until the 'next' day
Spot-a-week	A loan or deposit from spot until a week later

In the deposit market 'tomorrow' means the 'next working day after today', and 'next' means the 'next working day following'.

In the foreign exchange market the swaps are calculated:

Overnight	A swap today against 'tomorrow'
Tom-next	A swap 'tomorrow' against the 'next' day
Spot-next	A swap spot against the 'next' day
Spot-a-week	A swap spot against a week later

When referring to outright forwards rather than swaps, we usually mention things such as 'value today', 'value tomorrow', 'value spot-next', etc. When discussing swaps and outright forwards for short dates longer than spot, the same guidelines apply as those that are used to calculate longer dates.

It is, however, easy to become confused when trying to calculate rates for forward dates that are shorter than spot (e.g. 'value today' and 'value tomorrow'). The bank will still buy the base currency (sell the variable or quoted currency) on the left-hand side for the far date, and sell the base currency (buy the variable or quoted currency) on the right for the far date. But the spot value date is the far date, and the outright date is the near date.

Value one week

Example 1

A customer of the bank wishes to transact a forward outright purchase of CHF for USD, value one week after spot.

Consider the following market information:

Spot rate: USD/CHF	1.4801–1.4820
Overnight swap	1.48–0.98
Tom-next swap	0.43–0.38
1-week swap	3.15–2.85

The bank will sell the CHF for value spot, on the left at 1.4801. The bank will also sell CHF for value one week after spot (the far date), at a differential of 3.15 pips. So the bank will sell CHF outright one week forward at a rate of 1.4801 less 0.000315 making 1.479785.

Example 2 | **Value tomorrow**

Another client also wishes to purchase CHF outright, but for value tomorrow, using the market data above. This is the same as buying CHF value spot and simultaneously entering into a swap to buy CHF for value tomorrow, and then sell back the CHF value spot.

In this case, the bank sells CHF for value spot on the left at 1.4801. But will also buy CHF value spot (the far date) on the right-hand side of the price at a differential of 0.38 of a pip. The CHF interest rates are lower than those for USD, so the CHF is at a premium to the USD, the points will be subtracted and the dollar will be worth less on the far date and more on the near date. The swap difference must therefore be added to the spot rate to give the outright rate for value tomorrow:

$$1.4801 + 0.000038 = 1.480138$$

The other side of the calculation is $1.4820 + 0.000043 = 1.482043$.

Example 3 | **Value today**

The next customer wishes to buy CHF value today, using the same market data shown above. This will involve three separate transactions:

- buying CHF for value spot, entering into a swap to buy CHF value tomorrow;
- sell CHF back for value spot (tom-next), and entering into a swap to buy CHF value today;
- sell CHF back for value tomorrow (overnight).

The price is therefore calculated at: $1.4801 + 0.000038 + 0.000098 = 1.480236$.

> **Tip**
>
> *When calculating forward dates with value shorter than spot, remember to reverse the swap points and proceed exactly as for the longer dated transaction. In Example (2) above, this would mean points of 0.000038–0.000043; the outright rate is then 1.4801 + 0.000038 on the left, and on the right it is 1.4820 + 0.000048, giving a bid–offer price of 1.480138–1.482048.*

CROSS RATE FORWARD OUTRIGHTS

Just as in spot foreign exchange some currencies are quoted on a direct basis and others on an indirect basis, so the same applies to forward rates. When calculating cross rate outright forwards, the method used will depend upon whether the two particular rates are both direct, both indirect, or one of each.

Two indirect quotations

The two exchange rates must be cross divided.

Spot rate: USD/CHF	1.4801–1.4820
6-month swap	69–67
6-month outright	1.4732–1.4753

Spot rate: USD/JPY	122.83–122.85
6-month swap	98–97
6-month outright	121.85–121.88

$121.85 \div 1.4753 = 82.59$: how the bank buys CHF and sells yen.
$121.88 \div 1.4732 = 82.73$: how the bank sells CHF and buys yen.

6-month forward cross rate CHF/JPY   82.59–82.73.

Two direct quotations

The two exchange rates must be cross divided.

Spot rate: GBP/USD	1.5075–1.5083
1-month swap	12–10
1-month outright	1.5063–1.5073

Spot rate: AUD/USD	0.7397–0.7402
1-month swap	20–15
1-month outright	0.7377–0.7387

$1.5063 \div 0.7387 = 2.0391$: how the bank can buy GBP, and sell AUD.
$1.5073 \div 0.7377 = 2.0432$: how the bank can sell GBP, and buy AUD.

1-month forward cross rate GBP/AUD   2.0391–2.0432.

An indirect quotation and a direct quotation

The same side of each exchange rate must be multiplied.

Spot rate: GBP/USD	1.5680–1.5690
3-month swap	83–82
3-month outright	1.5597–1.5608

Spot rate: USD/CHF	1.4801–1.4820
3-month swap	53–52
3-month outright	1.4748–1.4768

$1.5597 \times 1.4748 = 2.3003$: how the bank buys GBP, and sells CHF.
$1.5608 \times 1.4768 = 2.3050$: how the bank sells GBP, and buys CHF.

Forward cross rate GBP/CHF   2.3003–2.3050.

1. Calculate the cross rate forward outright given the following information:

Spot rate: GBP/USD	1.5075–1.5083
3-month swap	33–31
Spot rate: USD/NZD	1.4968–1.4983
3-month swap	90–100

2. Calculate the cross rate forward outright given the following information:

Spot rate: USD/CHF	1.2090–1.2100
3-month swap	111–106
Spot rate: USD/NZD	1.4968–1.4983
3-month swap	90–100

For answers refer to the end of the chapter.

CROSS RATE FORWARD SWAPS

This becomes a little more complicated. When calculating cross rate forward swaps or differentials, the method used will also depend upon whether the two particular rates are both direct, both indirect, or one of each, and now we need to use a mid-rate spot.

Two indirect quotations

Example

To calculate the forward differentials between two indirect rates, it is necessary to cross divide the mid-spot rate, and also cross divide the forward rates (based on the mid-spot rate), and then subtract one from the other.

Spot rate: USD/CHF	1.4800–1.4820
1-month swap	13–14
Spot rate: USD/JPY	122.83–122.85
1-month swap	19–18

USD/CHF		USD/JPY
1.4810	[Mid-spot]	122.84
13–14	[Swap]	19–18
1.4797–1.4796	[Outright]	122.65–122.66

Cross spot rate: $\dfrac{122.84}{1.4810} = 82.94$

Cross forward outright: $\dfrac{122.65}{1.4796} = 82.89$

$\dfrac{122.66}{1.4797} = 82.90$

Subtract one from the other: 82.94 − 82.89 = 0.05
82.94 − 82.90 = 0.04

1-month CHF/JPY swap: 5–4.

For two direct quotations, and one direct/one indirect quotations follow the example above but multiply or divide using the general rules under Cross rate forward outrights.

OPTION DATED FORWARDS

So far we have examined foreign exchange forward transactions with a single maturity date. These comprise by far the majority. Occasionally, however, a client may be unsure of the exact timing of a currency receipt, although they are sure it will arrive by the end date. In this case they will request from their bank an 'option dated forward', not to be confused with a currency option. A currency option allows the client to walk away from the deal, an option dated forward must be fulfilled by the end date.

Option dated forward

10 November

Example

A client knows they must sell sterling and buy US dollars some time between 12 December and 12 February, and asks for a quote on an option dated forward contract.

Current market data GBP/USD		
Spot rate:	1.5310–1.5320	value 12 November
1-month	1.5272–1.5284	value 12 December
3-month	1.5200–1.5215	value 12 February

In this example it is the three-month bid rate that exchanges the smallest number of US dollars for sterling.

Simultaneously, the bank dealer will enter into an offsetting contract to match their position and lock in a spread. In this case the one-month bid rate gives the maximum amount of US dollars and locks in a spread of 72 points (1.5272–1.5200).

Advantages and disadvantages

The client in our example has locked in an exchange rate, good for the period, and is now no longer concerned about the timing of the delivery, as they have no exchange rate or interest rate risk. Unfortunately, the size of the spread on the deal is massive.

The bank has taken on the client's risk and has charged a wide spread to do it. The bank's total income may be eroded if the company delivers the sterling after 12 December, as the bank will have to cover the shortfall in sterling by a series of overnight swap transactions. The bank is also exposed to adverse interest rate movements and will have additional transaction costs.

CONCLUSION

Forward foreign exchange is naturally more complex than spot FX, as the extra dimension of relative interest rates comes into play in the pricing. The maths itself is not particularly complex but there are many ways you can trip yourself up. In modern dealing rooms both in banks and corporations there are likely to be PCs or add-ons to the main information providers that will calculate forward rates on request. All you need to do is input the far date and the near date, the two currencies in question, and the machine will do the rest. There is a danger here. It is easy to become too reliant on the PC. Understanding the background to the calculation and being able to reproduce screen forward rates will strengthen an individual's knowledge base. Should the pricing model go down, which is always an outside possibility, you will not be 'blind' until it is fixed. To confirm that the rates can be calculated longhand have a try at the exercises throughout the chapter, the answers to which are below.

A final note on forward foreign exchange: things are moving very rapidly in this market and increasingly banks are looking at different ways to hedge their books, other than using loans and deposits which are very 'heavy' on the banks' balance sheets. This is leading the banks to use interest rate derivatives such as FRAs and futures, to cover their risk 'off-balance sheet'.

Answers to quick fix exercises

Exercise 1

1. The spot rate is 1.5690, then subtract the 27.58 forward points (number sequence goes high/low), making 1.5690 − 0.002758 = 1.566242.

2. The spot rate is 0.9868, then subtract the 70.6 forward points (number sequence goes high/low), making 0.9868 − 0.00706 = 0.979740. This makes a cost of EUR 10,000,000 multiplied by 0.979740 = USD 9,797,400.

3. The spot rate is 1.4820, then subtract the 36.2 forward points (number sequence goes high/low), making 1.4820 − 0.00362 = 1.47838. This makes a receipt of CHF 2,000,000 divided by 1.47838 = USD 1,352,832.15.

Exercise 2

Spot rate: GBP/USD	1.5680–90
Transaction date	Tuesday, 18 March 2003
Spot value date	Thursday, 20 March 2003
Forward value date	Wednesday, 10 December 2003
6-month points	170.5–169.5
12-month points	339–336
Day count–6 months forward	184 days (20 September 2003)
Day count–12 months forward	365 days (20 March 2004)
Day count–10 December 2003	265 days

The US dollar is at a premium to sterling, so the points must be subtracted, from the left-hand side of the spot rate (as the client wishes to purchase the dollars).

Spot rate: GBP/USD   1.5680

Number of points (per day) between month 6 and month 12:

$$\frac{(0.0339 - 0.0170.5)}{(365 \text{ days} - 184 \text{ days})} = \frac{0.01685}{181} = 0.00009309 \text{ points per day}$$

We need these extra points for a total of 81 days, making $0.00009309 \times 81 = 0.00754061$.

We now need to put all the components together:

Spot rate: GBP/USD	1.5680
6-month points	0.01705
Extra 81 days' points	0.00754061
Outright	1.54340939

The USD 2.2 million will require GBP 1,425,415.72 (2,200,000 divided by 1.54340939).

Exercise 3

1. The correct spot rate is 1.4820, then subtract the 13.35 forward points (number sequence goes high/low), making $1.4820 - 0.001335 = 1.480665$, making a receipt of USD 3,376,861.07.

2. The correct spot rate is 1.5690, then subtract the 27.58 forward points (number sequence goes high/low), making $1.5690 - 0.002758 = 1.566242$, making a cost of USD 1,370,461.75.

3. The correct spot rate is 122.85, then subtract the 9-month forward points (number sequence goes high/low). To do this, interpolate between the six- and twelve-month points (196.5 and 97), making 99.5 for the 6 month period, this makes 49.75 points for the extra three-month period, add on the points for the initial six-month period at 97, making a total points differential of 146.75, and subtract the total from the spot rate, making 121.3825. A total receipt of JPY 222,250,000 ÷ 121.3825 = USD 1,830,988.82.

Exercise 4

Calculate the following cross rate forward outrights:

1.
Spot rate: GBP/USD	1.5075–1.5083
3-month swap	33–31
3-month outright	1.5042–1.5052

Spot rate: USD/NZD	1.4968–1.4983
3-month swap	90–100
3-month outright	1.5058–1.5083

We need to multiply the same sides of the outright:

1.5042 × 1.5058 = 2.2650: how the client can sell GBP, and buy NZD.
1.5052 × 1.5083 = 2.2703: how the client can buy GBP, and sell NZD.

The bank of course will be on the other side of the price, i.e.
   Forward cross rate GBP/NZD   2.2650–2.2703.

2. Spot rate: USD/NZD   1.4968–1.4983
   3-month swap   90–100
   3-month outright   1.5058–1.5083

   Spot rate: USD/CHF   1.2090–1.2100
   3-month swap   111–106
   3-month outright   1.1979–1.1994

1.5058 ÷ 1.1994 = 1.2555: how the client can buy NZD, and sell CHF.
1.5083 ÷ 1.1979 = 1.2591: how the client can sell NZD, and buy CHF.

The bank of course will be on the other side of the price, i.e.
   Forward cross rate CHF/NZD   1.2555–1.2591.

Emerging market foreign exchange*

Andrew Medhurst, HSBC

Introduction
Non-deliverable forwards and non-deliverable options
Third party payments
Regional and country descriptions
Emerging markets and e-commerce

* Due to the complications in local regulations and variation of limitations and/or restrictions for different entities, the following should be taken as a reference guide only. FX Regulations are subject to change, sometimes at very short notice. Whilst efforts have been made to ensure that information contained in this chapter is accurate, users of this handbook are strongly recommended to consult their bankers for full and up-to-date information regarding domestic regulations governing foreign exchange transactions before dealing. Information shown for individual countries is based on the situation in December 2002. Before dealing in any of these markets please consult your advisers.

INTRODUCTION

Transacting in and risk managing foreign exchange exposures in developing or emerging market currencies requires a much more detailed knowledge of the individual markets than is often appreciated. For a multinational corporation looking to hedge an exposure to the Japanese yen it can be assumed an extensive range of treasury products exists (spot and forward FX, currency options, etc.) and that no regulations imposed by the Japanese authorities prevent anyone from executing their chosen hedging strategy. However, when dealing in emerging market currencies it becomes necessary to establish what FX products are available, whether they are accessible by non-residents of the country concerned and, if so, is this access unconditional or are local approvals or the presentation of supporting documentation required?

Most of the FX products available in emerging market currencies are the same as those encountered in the developed markets in US dollars, sterling, Japanese yen and the euro. Spot and forward foreign exchange and currency options have been covered in other chapters in this book and so the reader is assumed to know the meaning of these terms. What is unique to emerging markets though is the concept of non-deliverable products specifically the non-deliverable forward and the non-deliverable option. Both these products are explained in this chapter.

NON-DELIVERABLE FORWARDS AND NON-DELIVERABLE OPTIONS

The concept of non-deliverable products is particularly appropriate in emerging markets where onshore markets may be illiquid or inaccessible to non-residents. The market mainly consists of non-deliverable forwards (NDFs) which differ from the more conventional FX forward product by the fact that no settlement occurs in the emerging market currency. Since all settlements relating to the transaction are in freely convertible or 'hard' currencies, predominantly US dollars, they can be traded internationally under English or New York law according to internationally agreed standards laid down by the International Swaps and Derivatives Association, Inc. (ISDA).

The market is constantly evolving and trade organizations such as EMTA (http://www.emta.org) have been instrumental in promoting the orderly development of trading markets in such products, particularly in times of market disruption.

NDFs may be useful to both non-resident importers who need to protect their foreign exchange obligations or non-resident exporters wishing to hedge their foreign exchange receivables both in currencies where convertibility is regulated to some degree.

In a conventional forward foreign exchange contract (explained fully in earlier chapters) one party agrees a binding obligation, to buy or sell, an agreed amount of foreign currency, at a pre-agreed rate of exchange on a specified future date. An NDF has the same attributes as a forward but can be thought of as a forward contract which is closed out at maturity with an offsetting spot contract.

The final settlement amount can be determined from the following formula:

$$\text{Settlement amount} = \frac{(\text{Contract forward rate} - \text{Settlement rate}) \times \text{USD amount}}{\text{Settlement rate}}$$

The amount can be positive (in which case the forward seller of US dollars will receive the settlement) or negative (where the forward seller of US dollars pays the settlement).

The NDF is best described with an example.

Example

An importer has agreed to source goods from South Korea for which the company has agreed to be invoiced by the supplier in Korean won (KRW). Concerned about an appreciation of the KRW before the goods are to be paid for the importer enters into an NDF agreeing to purchase the contract value equivalent of KRW versus US dollars.

The importer buys KRW 5 billion at a forward rate of KRW 1250 per US dollar for six months forward value (i.e. bank buys USD 4 million). Let's assume that six months later and two days prior to maturity of the NDF the spot rate is now KRW 1175 (the settlement rate). Using the formula given previously the settlement amount can be calculated as follows:

$$\text{Settlement amount} = \frac{(1250 - 1175) \times \text{USD 4 mn}}{1175}$$

$$\text{Settlement amount} = \text{USD } 255,319.15$$

The positive result means that the importer (as the forward seller of US dollars receives USD 255,319.15) which compensates the importer for the increased USD cost of purchasing the required KRW 5 billion.

The settlement rate used to calculate the settlement amount is agreed in advance between the two counterparties. To ensure transparency, market standards defined by ISDA, are widely used. In the case of KRW this is the rate reported by the Korea Financial Telecommunications and Clearing Corporation which appears on Reuters screen KFTC18. This is an average rate of spot trades carried out onshore in South Korea for that day.

The importer still needs to purchase the required KRW in order to pay his supplier. This trade is separate from the NDF and needs to be executed with a bank capable of making such payments (see the following section). It is important that the importer carefully considers the timing and execution of this spot trade to ensure that the rate achieved is as close to the settlement rate of his NDF hedge as possible. The risk of a difference between these two rates is referred to as basis risk.

In the same way that currency options can be used as an alternative to forwards, non-deliverable options (NDOs) may offer an alternative to NDFs.

THIRD PARTY PAYMENTS

Companies and individuals wishing to remit funds to emerging market beneficiaries often assume that payments must be made in hard currencies such as US dollars or euros. This is not necessarily the case and for most emerging market currencies it is possible to purchase the local currency for payment to an onshore beneficiary even though the currency is illiquid or highly regulated.

Some banks, such as HSBC Bank plc, have developed the infrastructure to make local currency payments in a large number of emerging market currencies on behalf of its customers. This helps customers to transact in currencies without associated administrative costs of maintaining currency accounts in each. The banks will assume the costs of maintaining currency accounts on its customers' behalf or, where non-residents are not allowed to hold such accounts, will work closely with affiliates or correspondent banks to provide such a service.

In this way, we can offer instant dealing rates and settlement in over 120 emerging market currencies including amongst others, the Fiji dollar, the Pakistan rupee, the Russian rouble, the Tanzanian shilling and the Chilean peso. For the importer described in the previous section, having hedged his forward exposure using NDFs, they can subsequently purchase the required KRW necessary to pay the invoice which is settled directly to the beneficiary's account.

REGIONAL AND COUNTRY DESCRIPTIONS

The following sections attempt to summarize the more significant countries in each geographical region enabling the reader to understand something about the currency regimes employed, the sophistication of the local currency markets and the regulatory environment of which participants need to be aware. The factual information provided is the latest data available.

Asia

With one or two exceptions, the main Asian economies have emerged relatively unscathed from the 1997/1998 economic crisis which witnessed the imposition of exchange controls in Malaysia in September 1998 and widespread corporate collapse and debt restructuring in Indonesia. The more economically stable countries like Singapore survived virtually intact. Whilst the impact of the crisis is still being felt in some countries, the region as a whole through its dynamism, resilience and the export-orientated bias of its economies has staged a remarkable recovery. Foreign exchange regimes, which were tightened up during the crisis, have gradually been relaxed although in some cases – notably Malaysia – controls to guard against currency speculation remain the order of the day.

China

Currency: Chinese renminbi (CNY)

Population:	1,284 mn
Nominal GDP:	USD 1,161 bn
Nominal GDP per capita:	USD 905
Total external debt (% GDP):	14.6
International reserves:	USD 212.2 bn

The CNY is convertible for current account items such as import payments and export proceeds based upon documentary evidence. Only dividend payments are allowed to be converted for capital account transactions. Those relating to equity investment or repatriation and shareholders' loans are subject to approval by the State Administration for Foreign Exchange (SAFE) of The Peoples' Bank of China (PBOC). PBOC manages the CNY in an extremely narrow band at about 8.27–8.28 per US dollar and domestic banks are limited in the spreads (17 bps from the daily mid-rate) they can quote in the local spot market.

An experimental CNY forward market up to six months, which can be extended for maximum of another six months, has existed onshore since 1998 and remains highly regulated. It is offered exclusively by three state-owned banks. No foreign-owned bank is currently allowed to offer this product. Any forward trades require supporting documentation evidencing an underlying trade agreement. Currency options in CNY do not exist onshore.

While financial hedging may not be possible for corporates, they may, however, make use of non-deliverable forward (NDF) and non-deliverable options, which exist offshore, allowing overseas offices of corporates to hedge exposures in CNY. Maturities up to ten years are possible for NDFs and two years for NDOs although average transactions are in relatively small amounts (USD 1–3 mn).

Hong Kong Special Administrative Region

Currency: Hong Kong dollar (HKD)

Population:	7.3 mn
Nominal GDP:	USD 162 bn
Nominal GDP per capita:	USD 22,178
Total external debt (% GDP):	N/a
International reserves:	USD 111 bn

Hong Kong SAR can claim to possess one of the most sophisticated and dynamic financial centres in the Far East. The currency peg to the US dollar was established in October 1983 at HKD 7.80 and has survived a number of speculative attempts to dislodge it. The HKD is freely tradable and convertible. Spot FX, forward and currency options in HKD are accessible to both resident and non-resident entities.

The spot and forward markets are relatively liquid and forward currency hedging can easily be transacted for tenors up to ten years and beyond. Currency options are available for periods up to two years. The Hong Kong Monetary Authority intervenes in the FX market by varying liquidity via open market operations and through direct intervention.

India

Currency: Indian rupee (INR). See Figure 9.1.

Population:	1,045 million
Nominal GDP:	USD 484 bn
Nominal GDP per capita:	USD 483
Total external debt (% GDP):	20.7
International reserves:	USD 54.1 bn

The INR is subject to a managed floating exchange rate regime. It is convertible for current account transactions. Although foreign direct investment and foreign institutional investment is permitted, there are restrictions on the capital account. The FX market is open only to resident entities, primarily commercial banks, corporates and other financial institutions. Non-resident entities can only purchase INR from local banks. Selling INR by non-residents is subject to prior approval from the Reserve Bank of India

Figure 9.1

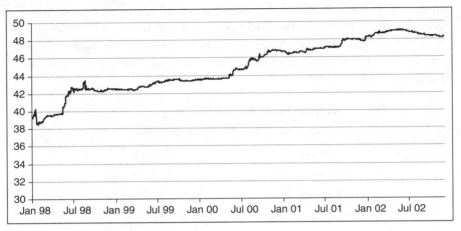

USD–INR

Source: Bloomberg L.P.

(RBI). The RBI can intervene in the FX market during periods of high volatility.

Local corporates can hedge forward exposures onshore to cover actual currency exposures only. Non-residents may access the local forward market but require RBI approval. The RBI permits corporates and institutions to manage their foreign currency and INR exposures through derivatives such as interest rate and currency swaps. Foreign institutional investors may enter into a forward contract with an authorized resident dealer to sell INR to hedge their exposure, but are not yet permitted to use INR derivatives. All trades must be for hedging purposes and only for transactions in accordance with Indian Exchange Control regulations.

An active NDF market in INR exists offshore and it is possible to transact tenors as far as five years.

Indonesia

Currency: Indonesian rupiah (IDR). See Figure 9.2.

Population:	208 mn
Nominal GDP:	USD 145 bn
Nominal GDP per capita:	USD 690
Total external debt (% GDP):	91.7
International reserves:	USD 28.0 bn

The Bank of Indonesia announced new FX regulations in January 2001. Under these regulations, which are restrictive, non-residents are permitted to buy and sell IDR for spot value. Forward sales of US dollars by a non-resident are permitted. Forward purchases of US dollars by non-residents are permitted with documentation where the underlying transaction relates to

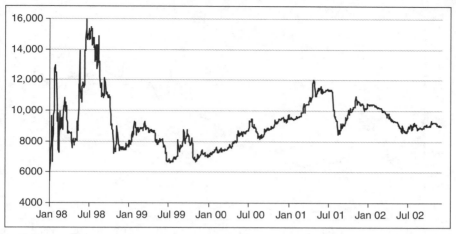

USD–IDR

Figure 9.2

Source: Bloomberg L.P.

'economic activity' like equity investment or an intercompany loan. The new regulations, which also restrict transfers of IDR between non-residents, have effectively transferred IDR onshore thereby facilitating economic activity in IDR but preventing currency speculation.

Malaysia

Currency: Malaysian ringgit (MYR)

Population:	23.3 mn
Nominal GDP:	USD 87.5 bn
Nominal GDP per capita:	USD 3,760
Total external debt (% GDP):	51.0
International reserves:	USD 30.8 bn

Capital controls were imposed in September 1998 to insulate Malaysia from the financial crisis affecting most of South East Asia at that time and the MYR has not been tradable offshore since that time. Bank Negara Malaysia fixed the exchange rate against the USD at MYR 3.80 with local banks permitted to quote up to a maximum MYR 0.03 from this central rate.

An onshore forward FX market exists but currency options for USD/MYR are not available. However, the use of currency options for hedging purposes can be considered for non-MYR currency pairs such as USD/JPY and EUR/USD as long the exposure is supported by documentary evidence.

Non-residents can only access the onshore forward MYR market for the sole purpose of purchasing MYR-denominated securities listed on the Kuala Lumpur Stock Exchange. Payments for visible trade and most services are required to be settled in hard currency.

Figure 9.3

USD–PHP

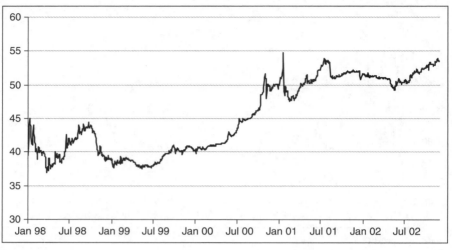

Source: Bloomberg L.P.

Philippines

Currency: Philippine peso (PHP). See Figure 9.3.

Population:	75.6 mn
Nominal GDP:	USD 71.4 bn
Nominal GDP per capita:	USD 944
Total external debt (% GDP):	73.9
International reserves:	USD 15.5 bn

The Philippines operates a free floating exchange rate policy but the PHP is not fully convertible. While PHP can be purchased freely by non-residents it is important to obtain documentary evidence of the original inward remittance of hard currency (referred to as a 'BSRD' or 'Bangko Sentral Registration Document') in order subsequently to purchase hard currency for PHP and repatriate the funds offshore. An onshore forward market exists and periods predominantly up to three years may be hedged although this market is predominantly for resident banks and companies.

For non-residents an active NDF market exists and NDOs are available for periods up to one year.

Singapore

Currency: Singapore dollar (SGD). See Figure 9.4.

Population:	4 mn
Nominal GDP:	USD 85.6 bn
Nominal GDP per capita:	USD 21,400
Total external debt:	14.0
International reserves:	USD 75.8 bn

USD–SGD

Figure 9.4

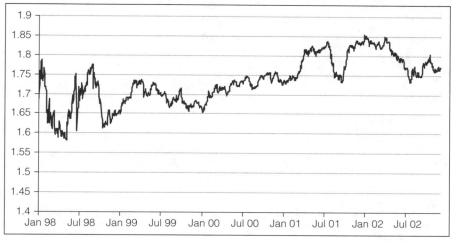

Source: Bloomberg L.P.

The SGD floats freely but is linked to a trade-weighted basket of major currencies and so currency intervention by the authorities is occasionally seen. The SGD is internationally convertible and so spot and forward transactions can be executed with both resident and non-resident banks. Singapore has one of the most developed financial markets in the region and offers good liquidity in spot, forward and currency option products. Long-dated forward exposures can be hedged with transactions beyond ten years possible if required.

Restrictions concerning the ability of non-resident corporations to borrow SGD using the FX forward markets were relaxed in 2002 therefore removing restrictions on the amounts that non-residents can trade with onshore banks.

South Korea

Currency: Korean won (KRW). See Figure 9.5.

Population:	48.3 mn
Nominal GDP:	USD 422.5 bn
Nominal GDP per capita:	USD 8,747
Total external debt (% GDP):	28.4
International reserves:	USD 102.8 bn

South Korea has liberalized its FX regulations since the Asian crisis of 1997/98 and despite the fact that the currency remains internationally non-convertible the ability of non-residents to hedge underlying exposures to the KRW is good.

Figure 9.5

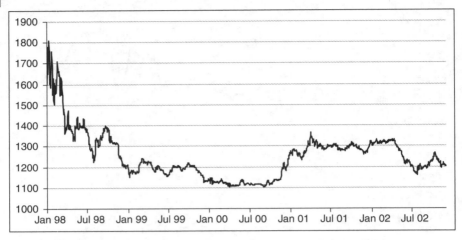

USD–KRW

Source: Bloomberg L.P.

Foreign entities can access the liquid onshore spot market provided that FX transactions are linked to an underlying investment, or to the purchase or sale of securities or bonds. FX transactions for purely speculative purposes are not permitted. Offshore investors may also access the local forward market which is relatively liquid, offering tenors up to ten years. Non-residents selling KRW must provide to the counterparty bank documentary evidence of the underlying asset or trade contract being hedged before hard currency receipts can be remitted offshore. Currency options are available in the onshore market.

In the offshore markets the KRW NDF and NDO markets allow non-residents to hedge exposures which may be impossible or not practical to hedge with onshore banks.

Taiwan

Currency: Taiwanese dollar (TWD). See Figure 9.6.

Population:	22.4 mn
Nominal GDP:	USD 281 bn
Nominal GDP per capita:	USD 12,522
Total external debt (% GDP):	N/A
International reserves:	USD 157.6 bn

The TWD is freely floating but only available for physical delivery in Taiwan. Non-residents may buy and sell TWD in the spot market through local banks possessing an FX licence granted by the Ministry of Finance and the Central Bank in Taiwan. However, they would require approval from the central bank and documentary proof to specify the hedging purpose.

USD–TWD

Figure 9.6

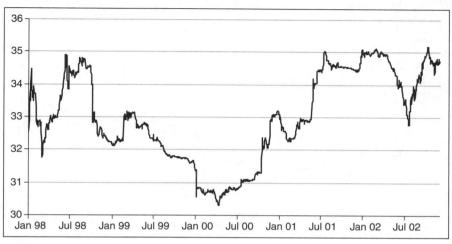

Source: Bloomberg L.P.

Forwards, which are generally not available to non-residents, are available up to seven years but liquidity declines for periods beyond one year. Options priced off NDFs are actively used among hedgers onshore.

An active NDF market exists offshore for maturities up to five years and there is some NDO activity thereby allowing non-residents to hedge forward exposures to the TWD.

Thailand

Currency: Thai baht (THB). See Figure 9.7.

Population:	62.4 mn
Nominal GDP:	USD 115 bn
Nominal GDP per capita:	USD 1,837
Total external debt (% GDP):	58.7
International reserves:	USD 32.9 bn

All restrictions imposed on the THB spot market as a result of the 1997 crisis were removed from 30 January 1998. The THB is internationally convertible and traded by both non-resident and resident banks. Thailand operates a floating exchange rate although intervention is used to limit excess volatility.

The onshore forward market is restricted to non-residents although legitimate exposures may be hedged by non-resident companies with onshore banks. Evidence of underlying transactions may be required by the local banks, and in some cases the Bank of Thailand may need to be approached for specific approval. An offshore forward market exists but the available liquidity may be limited, particularly when the local authorities perceive that

USD–THB

Figure 9.7

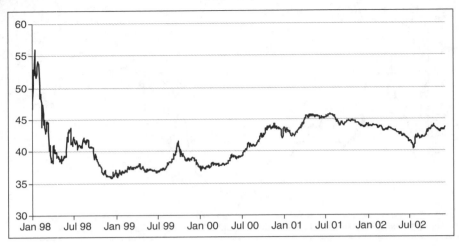

Source: Bloomberg L.P.

currency speculation is increasing. In order to limit international speculation against the THB various restrictions, such as the inability of non-
residents to overdraw THB accounts, are in force.

Central and eastern Europe, Middle East and Africa

Central and eastern Europe, Middle East and Africa (CEEMEA) can be
divided into two sub-regions. One is central and eastern Europe, of which
three countries are covered in this section: Poland, the Czech Republic and
Hungary. These three countries are expected to join the EU in 2004. The
EU has compelled them to adopt the entire body of EU law ahead of
membership, which has involved a number of measures to improve the
overall business environment. For instance, they all made their currencies
convertible for current account purposes in the mid-1990s, and they have
also been compelled to remove almost all capital controls. That has paved
the way for the development of relatively sophisticated money and derivatives markets. Since these countries hope to join EMU soon after joining the
EU, they have also switched the anchor for monetary policy to inflation
targeting and allowed their currencies to float freely. The drive towards EU
membership has had a number of broader implications. The resulting
improvement in political risk as well as the quality of business environment
has spurred capital inflows, putting sustained upward pressure on the
region's currencies. All of this also means that central and eastern Europe
is increasingly perceived as a hybrid asset class, with features not just of
emerging markets, but also of more developed markets.

The remainder of the CEEMEA region has lacked external forces compelling them to liberalize foreign exchange markets as rapidly as has been the

case in central and eastern Europe, Egypt and South Africa, for instance, retain substantial capital controls. While Turkey and Israel do not have capital controls, their currencies retain some of the features of emerging markets.

Poland

Currency: Polish zloty (PLN). See Figure 9.8.

Population:	38.6 mn
Nominal GDP:	USD 176 bn
Nominal GDP per capita:	USD 4,560
Total external debt (% GDP):	40.2
International reserves:	USD 25.7 bn

The Polish zloty (PLN) was governed by a crawling peg for much of the 1990s, an arrangement whereby the exchange rate depreciated based on inflation differentials so as to maintain competitiveness. In April 2000, however, the National Bank of Poland (NBP) allowed the PLN to float freely. Although the NBP reserves the right to intervene, its policy so far has been to set interest rates only, and allow market forces to determine the exchange rate. As the EUR–PLN cross rate is an important indicator of manufacturing competitiveness, the market assesses the strength of the zloty relative to the central parity of its former basket (comprising 55% EUR/45% USD).

The PLN has been fully convertible for current account transactions since July 1995. The NBP has also gradually removed capital controls. For instance, the new Foreign Exchange Law that came into force in October

USD–PLN

Figure 9.8

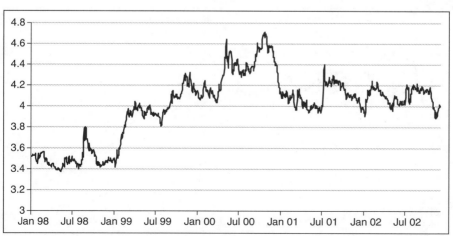

Source: Bloomberg L.P.

2002 removed all outstanding restrictions on short-term loans, deposits and FX transactions. However, banking legislation still bars foreign banks from marketing such products to non-bank institutions in Poland.

The Polish FX market is relatively liquid. Normal spot transaction size is EUR 3 mn equivalent and EUR 20 mn equivalent for forwards. Spot FX and forward FX (up to ten years) can be transacted both onshore and off-shore. FX options are available up to two years.

Czech Republic

Currency: Czech koruna (CZK). See Figure 9.9.

Population:	10.3 mn
Nominal GDP:	USD 56.7 bn
Nominal GDP per capita:	USD 5,511
Total external debt (% GDP):	38.3
International reserves:	USD 14.4 bn

The Czech National Bank (CNB) floated the Czech Koruna (CZK) in mid-1997, making this the first of the central European currencies to be freely floated. The exchange rate is determined by the market, although in practice the CNB has intervened repeatedly to slow down what it views as excessive appreciation.

The Czech Republic has also progressed the fastest in eastern Europe in terms of liberalizing its domestic FX and money markets. The CZK has been fully convertible for all current account and most capital account transactions since October 1995. There are no restrictions on the repatriation of profits whether income or capital gains. Czech residents may borrow freely

Figure 9.9

EUR–CZK

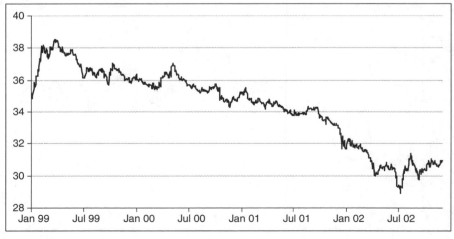

Source: Bloomberg L.P.

from non-residents and derivatives transactions may be entered into without restriction between residents and non-residents including forward FX, swaps and currency options. Non-residents may borrow freely in CZK.

Forward rates both onshore and offshore are very liquid in the one year market, but also available up to ten years. CZK currency options are available up to two years.

Hungary

Currency: Hungarian forint (HUF). See Figure 9.10.

Population:	10.2 mn
Nominal GDP:	USD 51.9 bn
Nominal GDP per capita:	USD 5,103
Total external debt (% GDP):	34.5
International reserves:	USD 10.9 bn

The Hungarian forint (HUF) was governed by a crawling peg mechanism until 2001, when the National Bank of Hungary (NBH) fixed its central parity at 276.1 parity versus the euro. The NBH also widened the bands within which the currency can trade to 15% either side of the central parity, so that the currency now resembles a free float.

The HUF became fully convertible for current account transactions in January 1996. However, the Hungarian authorities have been slower to liberalize capital account transactions, waiting until mid-2001 to liberalize money market transactions. There are no restrictions governing the opening of HUF accounts offshore by either residents or non-residents. Hungarian banks may borrow freely from non-residents and derivatives transactions

EUR–HUF

Figure 9.10

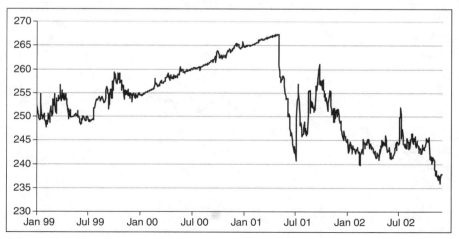

Source: Bloomberg L.P.

(including forward FX, swaps, options and futures) are permitted without prior approval from the NBH. However, onshore non-bank clients still require NBH permission to use FX products from offshore banks.

Spot FX can be carried out onshore and offshore. Forward FX is possible up to ten years, although its greatest depth is up to one year. Normal market size for spot is EUR 3 mn equivalent with EUR 10–20 mn equivalent for forwards. FX options are available for up to one year.

Israel

Currency: Israeli shekel (ILS). See Figure 9.11.

Population:	6.4 mn
Nominal GDP:	USD 112 bn
Nominal GDP per capita:	USD 17,467
Total external debt (% GDP):	57.4
International reserves:	USD 23.4 bn

The ILS is a free-floating currency fluctuating within a wide band fixed by the Bank of Israel. The band was last changed in December 2001. Its floor, limiting the currency's ability to strengthen has been fixed at ILS 4.10 for 2002, while the 'ceiling' has been fixed at ILS 6.60 at the beginning of 2002 with the flexibility to depreciate by up to 6% by the end of the year. The market often judges the ILS's strength relative to a trade-weighted basket, called SAL, comprising USD (66%), EUR (22%), GBP (6.5%) and JPY (5.5%).

The ILS is fully convertible on both current and capital account with no restrictions on capital repatriation, dividend or profit remittances. Normal

Figure 9.11

USD–ILS

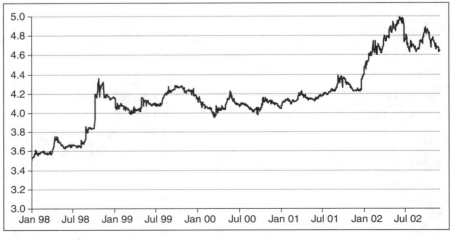

Source: Bloomberg L.P.

market size for spot transactions is USD 5–10 mn and USD 10–20 mn for forwards. Forwards are most liquid up to one year but contracts can be done for up to two years. FX options are freely available OTC or exchange-listed with the majority of transactions carried out OTC.

Egypt

Currency: Egyptian pound (EGP). See Figure 9.12.

Population:	66.6 mn
Nominal GDP:	USD 87.3 bn
Nominal GDP per capita:	USD 1,311
Total external debt (% GDP):	32.0
International reserves:	USD 13.0 bn

The EGP was pegged for many years at 3.4 versus the USD. Since mid-2000, however, there have been periodic devaluations, and the Central Bank of Egypt (CBE) has permitted banks to sell USD within a 3% band either side of the central parity.

Since mid-January 2002, the EGP/USD central rate has been 4.51. Given the continuing USD shortages, however, the currency has remained at or close to the top of the band at 4.65 for most of this year. The offshore or NDF rate is consistently quoted at around a 10% premium (higher rate).

To maintain its reserve levels, the CBE has imposed import restrictions and rationed USD, which has restricted liquidity. Only a spot FX market exists in Egypt today, where it is extremely difficult to purchase hard currency. The authorities have tended to discourage the development of a forward FX market or derivatives market.

USD–EGP

Figure 9.12

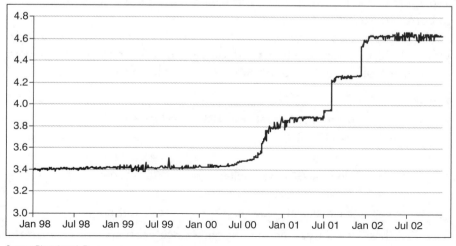

Source: Bloomberg L.P.

Figure 9.13

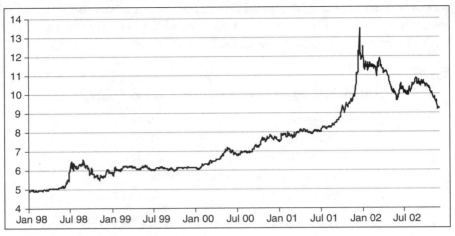

USD–ZAR

Source: Bloomberg L.P.

South Africa

Currency: South African rand (ZAR). See Figure 9.13.

Population:	44.6 mn
Nominal GDP:	USD 113 bn
Nominal GDP per capita:	USD 2,536
Total external debt (% GDP):	27.8
International reserves:	USD 6.1 bn

The ZAR is a free floating currency, which is fully convertible for current-account purposes. However, the South African Reserve Bank has taken a gradualist approach to relaxing capital controls. The SARB has maintained severe restrictions on residents' ability to move funds offshore. Regulations also apply to the FX forward market, which restrict offshore entities' ability to borrow onshore.

Normal spot transaction size is USD 3 mn. For forwards it amounts to USD 10–20 mn, for which periods can go out as far as ten years both onshore and offshore. FX options are also available up to two years.

Turkey

Currency: Turkish lira (TRL). See Figure 9.14.

Population:	67.7 mn
Nominal GDP:	USD 147 bn
Nominal GDP per capita:	USD 2,170
Total external debt (% GDP):	78.4
International reserves:	USD 18.7 bn

The TRL has been a free-floating currency since February 2001, when the Central Bank (Türkiye Cumhuriyet Merkez Bankasi) abandoned a crawling

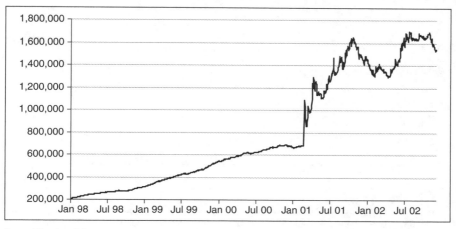

USD–TRL

| Figure 9.14 |

Source: Bloomberg L.P.

peg mechanism under which the currency depreciated in line with the inflation differential.

The currency, while remaining fully convertible on both current and capital account, is freely floating with minimal central bank intervention. Spot and forward FX markets are open, both onshore and offshore. The normal transaction size for both spot and forward is USD 1 mn. However, lack of liquidity and lines in the forward market restricts tenors to one year maximum. FX options are available out to one year.

Latin America

The past few years have seen rapid development of currency markets in Latin America. This is primarily the result of the successive collapses of fixed or managed FX regimes, which has led to a sharp increase in the number of floating exchange rate regimes. In turn, this has created an increase in the currencies' volatility, forcing the introduction of new products ranging from simple FX forward contracts to more advanced FX options in the most liberal and liquid markets. Having said that, in many cases the currencies' 'free-float' would be more accurately described as a 'dirty-float', since central banks continue to play a major role in the market by intervening heavily to minimize exchange rate volatility.

Argentina

Currency: Argentine peso (ARS). See Figure 9.15.

Population:	36 mn
Nominal GDP:	USD 75 bn (2002)
Nominal per capita GDP:	USD 2,083
Total external debt (% GDP):	162
International reserves:	USD 10.0 bn

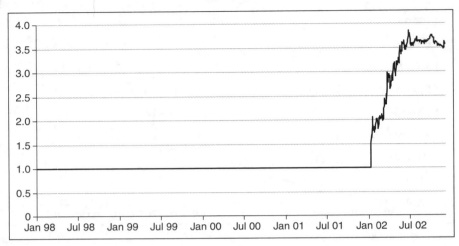

USD–ARS

Source: Bloomberg L.P.

On 6 January 2002, the Argentine authorities abandoned a nine-year old currency board, which ensured international convertibility of the ARS at a fixed rate of 1 : 1 against the US dollar. This coincided with a default on the Republic of Argentina's external and internal obligations as a result of a significant fall in the central bank's (Banco Central de la Republica Argentina) foreign currency reserves due to strong USD outflows.

Following the devaluation, the Argentine government imposed a freeze on deposits and tight restrictions on currency transactions to protect its USD reserves from falling further. Though the peso is officially a free-floating currency, the central bank has been aggressively intervening in the FX market to ensure the currency's stability and try to rebuild its USD reserves. At this stage, offshore NDF contracts remain the only form of FX forwards available with maturities of up to one year and an extremely tight liquidity. The typical transaction size ranges between USD 0.5–1 mn.

Brazil

Currency: Brazilian real (BRL). See Figure 9.16.

Population:	169 mn
Nominal GDP:	USD 338.3 bn
Nominal per capita GDP:	USD 2,001
Total external debt (% GDP):	65
International reserves:	USD 36 bn

The Brazilian real has been a free-floating currency since January 1999. An increase in the political uncertainty in the country ahead of the 2002 presidential election has resulted in a severe depreciation in the currency,

USD–BRL

Figure 9.16

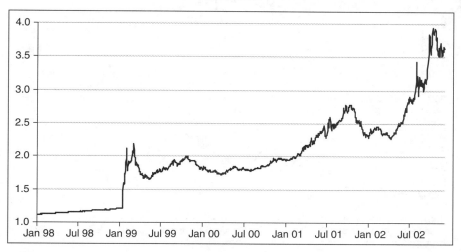

Source: Bloomberg L.P.

underlining its vulnerability to a deterioration in investor sentiment. This led the Banco Central do Brasil to play a major role in the FX market by intervening either in the spot or the repo market to reduce the BRL's volatility.

While it is possible to transact spot FX onshore, forward FX is only traded in an NDF form with maturities ranging from one month to up to one year and in sizes of USD 1–2 mn. An FX futures market is also available providing maturities of up to one year. The FX option market remains extremely illiquid with maturities hardly extending beyond one year.

Chile

Currency: Chilean peso (CLP). See Figure 9.17.

Population:	15.4 mn
Nominal GDP:	USD 60 bn
Nominal per capita GDP:	USD 3,896
Total external debt (% GDP):	57
International reserves:	USD 15 bn

The Chilean peso has recently shown its vulnerability to the increasing pressure on the Brazilian real. This trend is likely to continue going forward, as Chile will remain vulnerable to risks of contagion in the region despite its investment grade rating.

The Chilean FX market offers a wide range of products with FX spot and forward traded onshore and up to five years maturity for forward contracts. There is also an NDF and an FX options markets for maturities ranging from one week to one year. Spot and forward transaction sizes can reach USD 5–10 mn.

Figure 9.17

USD–CLP

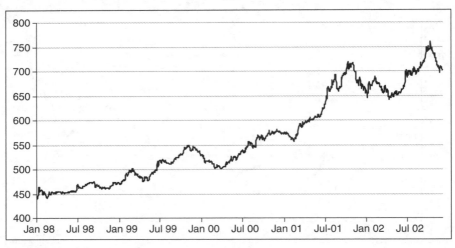

Source: Bloomberg L.P.

Mexico

Currency: Mexican peso (MXN). See Figure 9.18.

Population:	105 mn
Nominal GDP:	USD 600 bn
Nominal GDP per capita:	USD 5,714
Total external debt (% GDP):	26
International reserves:	USD 46 bn

Mexico is the only major Latin American country with a fully convertible currency, which floats freely against the US dollar. Mexico's participation in

Figure 9.18

USD–MXN

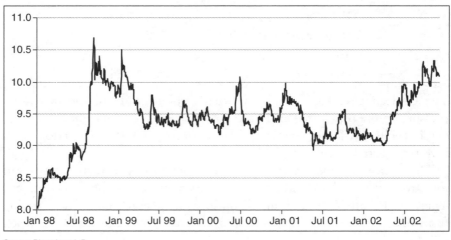

Source: Bloomberg L.P.

the North America Free Trade Association (NAFTA) and the currency's convertibility has resulted in the demand and ability of international banks to develop and offer a complete range of MXN FX products.

Spot and forward foreign exchange and currency options are all available in MXN and while liquidity is highest for the short-dated maturities of less than one year, longer tenor forwards and options are relatively easy to arrange. These products are available from both onshore and offshore banks.

EMERGING MARKETS AND E-COMMERCE

This section raises several interesting areas of discussion, from the benefits of e-trading in general to the particular issues facing the emerging markets themselves. While e-trading undoubtedly offers advantages in efficiency, it is inextricably linked to the 'bricks and mortar' that stands behind the e-channel, and the degree to which services are extended through the 'e' medium.

E-commerce efficiencies

E-commerce offers several clear advantages over the more traditional methods of trading. Faster price discovery and trade execution are certainly advantageous, but probably the biggest gains lie in the area of straight-through processing (STP). By enabling the deal flow to be transacted with minimal human intervention, the trade process can be managed on an exception management basis, rather than requiring every trade to be checked. The efficiencies are immediately clear with both lower resourcing costs and a vastly reduced error rate. It is these errors that can cause missed or inaccurate payments, with the resultant cost implications.

The automation of the pricing, which allows sub-3 second delivery of the price, is reliant on a homogenous and liquid market in the instrument concerned. While spot FX pricing of euros against USD falls into this category, the challenge increases as one moves further away from an established market. Considering a forward price of 73 days outright for Czech Koruna against Moroccan Dhiram for instance, it is intuitively evident that a running price will not be available and that particular skills will be required in order to generate the correct price.

The pricing issues described above certainly do not preclude e-trading in emerging markets. The efficiencies to be gained from e-trading are to an extent related to the settlement and confirmation process, which can now take place automatically. The manual intervention required for the less liquid currencies nonetheless allows the efficiencies of e-trading to be enjoyed, with price delivery through the e-channel taking, perhaps 30 seconds, rather than the three seconds for the automatically generated price.

Underlying service

Before evaluating the online offerings available it is important to understand the extent to which the underlying service will support your company's needs. Dealing in certain emerging market currencies can pose particular problems and it is prudent to consider the requirements first, before exploring how they may apply to an online platform.

Regulations and restrictions in emerging markets can manifest themselves in many ways, of which the following are examples:

- Different pricing in a currency from an onshore, local bank compared with offshore banks.
- Inability of a non-resident company to deal in the local currency markets (e.g. Malaysia) or only in exceptional circumstances and with permission from the authorities.
- Inability of resident companies to transact with non-resident banks without a permit from the authorities to do so (e.g. Taiwan).
- Ability of offshore banks to offer a service to non-resident companies in a particular currency but only for specific purposes (e.g. a third party payment in local currency to a local beneficiary).

The choice of online platform is therefore not limited to an assessment of functionality within a particular offering, but is linked also to the service that already exists within the more traditional channels and how they can be made available.

An online approach

Having established a normal business relationship, and knowing that your bank can fulfil your expectations in the normal way, the ability of your bank to provide an online solution to this area can be considered.

Following on from the above variations it is necessary for your chosen bank platform to ensure that:

- The appropriate price (i.e. distinguishing between an onshore or offshore price) is quoted.
- Any price originates from the appropriate office of the banking organization.
- A price is quoted only if regulations or the law allows it.

Each emerging market currency has its own particular set of requirements and HSBC has years of experience in meeting these responsibilities. Some can be handled with a simple online transaction. Others may need documentary evidence or are more complex structured transactions that can necessitate detailed conversations between bank and customer over a period of days and weeks. Obviously in such circumstances the execution is but a small part of the overall transaction and it is unlikely that an online platform would replace the need for substantive verbal dialogue. Once again this is not simply a question of efficient trade execution, but rather taking advantage of the underlying bank relationship that is so important in ensuring a successful outcome to the overall deal.

Foreign exchange trading for the individual investor

John Austin, IG Markets

'Traditional' margin FX

FX spread betting

FX as a Contract for Difference (CFD)

In recent years a number of factors have conspired to make it increasingly easy for a private individual to speculate on the FX market. Over-capacity in the industry has led to bitter spread competition between market makers and an increased willingness by companies to take private client business as seriously as institutional trading. In addition to this the range of FX products available to the individual has increased dramatically, as has the sophistication of most online dealing systems and technical analysis software. Taken together this means that the choice of ways into the market, the trading tools available and the terms on which one can deal have never been better.

There are three main ways for a private individual to trade in the FX markets: 'traditional' margin FX, FX spread betting and FX as a Contract for Difference (CFD).

'TRADITIONAL' MARGIN FX

Here the individual investor trades almost exactly as an institution would. There are a number of small companies offering the service to individuals and all work in the same way. The client puts down a small margin (typically 1–3%) and deals on spot rates. Daily 'tom-next' rollovers are used to correct for the interest rate differential between the currencies in each rate, and the client will typically manage his position by leaving a series of stop, limit, 'OCO' (one cancels the other) and contingent orders with the market maker. All of this – the dealing and the order leaving process – tends to be done online. Examples of managing exposures using orders follow in the next section.

Orders

An order is an instruction to deal if the market reaches a certain level. Two main types of order are commonly used in the foreign exchange market, the stop order and the limit order.

Stop orders

An instruction to deal if a market moves to a less favourable level (i.e. an instruction to buy if a market goes up to a specified level, or to sell if a market goes down to a specified level) is called a stop order. A stop order is often placed to put a cap on the potential loss on an existing position; that is why stop orders are sometimes called 'stop-loss orders'. However, a stop order can also be used to establish a new position.

Stop orders can usually be left on the basis of one of three methods.

The three types of stop order

Method 1 Let us assume that a trader is long USD/JPY and wishes to place a stop order on this position:

Sell at 130.00 'stop bid'.

The order will be filled based on the current market price plus the spread which the trader normally receives. The tabulation below shows where the market has to trade before the stop is hit, based on the spread:

Spread	Market price	Executed rate
05 pips	130. 01/04	130.00
Market spread	130. 00/03	130.00

Method 2 Again, assume a trader is long USD/JPY and wishes to place a stop order on the position:

Sell at 130.00 'on stop'.

This order will only be filled when the market actually trades at 130.00. At this point and, as before, based on the trader's spread, the order will be filled at a rate, subject to slippage of course, no worse than that indicated below:

Spread	Executed rate
05 pips	129.97
Market spread	129.98

Method 3 The trader has a long position in USD/JPY and wishes to place a stop order:

Sell at 130.00 'stop offer'.

This order will only be filled when the market is 130.00 offered. At this point the fill will again be subject to spread as follows:

Spread	Executed rate
05 pips	129.95
Market spread	129.97

In each of the above methods, if the trader's order was to buy, the same principle would apply. These procedures do not in any way prevent the trader from achieving what they want when they give the order and have the additional advantage of giving them the opportunity to check an independent record of market prices. If at the time of giving the order the trader fails to specify how they want the stop to be treated, most market makers will automatically apply Method 2.

Limit orders

An instruction to deal if a market moves to a more favourable level (i.e. an instruction to buy if a market goes down to a specified level, or to sell if a market goes up to a specified level) is called a limit order. A limit order is often used to take profit on an existing position but can also be used to establish a new one. It is important to understand that the normal dealing spread one pays will be taken into account when determining whether a limit order has been triggered.

Example

Assume a trader is normally quoted a 5-pip dealing spread. €/$ is trading at 0.9010. The trader believes the dollar is going to strengthen, but thinks that €/$ will fall back to below 0.8960 before it goes higher. They put on a limit order to buy €1,000,000 against the dollar at 0.8960. The limit order is triggered when €/$ is offered in the interbank market at 0.8959, reflecting the difference between the 3-pip spread in the interbank market and the 5-pip spread which they are normally quoted. They buy €1,000,000 against the dollar at 0.8960.

'OCO' orders

An 'OCO' ('one cancels the other') order is a special type of order where a stop and a limit order, or sometimes two stop orders, in the same market are linked together. With an OCO order, the triggering of one of the two linked orders results in the automatic cancellation of the other order.

Example

A trader sells $500,000 against the Swiss franc at 1.7030, looking for a short-term move to 1.6950. However, they decide that if $/CHF moves above 1.7060 they want to cut out their position. They put on a limit order to buy $500,000 against the Swiss franc at 1.6950, and a stop order to buy $500,000 against the Swiss franc at 1.7060 on an OCO basis.

'GTC' orders

When placing an order, one must specify for how long the order is to be worked. A trader might, for example, specify that a particular order is 'good until 4 p.m. today'. If they do not specify how long the order is to be worked, it will be treated as a GTC (good until cancelled) order. The GTC is a very common type of order; it remains valid, 24 hours a day, until cancelled by the trader. Such an order is not automatically cancelled at the close of business on Friday evening either; it is reinstated on Monday morning unless the trader specifies otherwise.

'Day' orders

Day orders are good until 22:00 London time or any other earlier specified time.

The transaction charge faced by an individual on any one deal is the bid–offer spread. These days this spread is not materially wider than that seen between institutions, provided the client deals in at least USD 1,000,000 at a time. In smaller sizes (say, USD 100,000) the spread on a major pair like EUR/USD will tend to be wider – perhaps closer to 5–7 pips than 2–3 pips.

FX SPREAD BETTING

Spread betting is as old as the City itself, but was first offered as an organized service in 1974 by IG Index, a company that today remains the largest spread betting bookmaker. The idea is simple: the client asks for a price in the relevant spot rate, and then chooses to buy or sell a specified amount, expressed in GBP per pip movement.

For example, if quoted a spot EUR/USD rate of '9950–58', a client might choose to go long the euro by buying £10 per point at 9958. If the deal is subsequently closed by the client selling 10 points higher, at 9968, he will show a profit of £10 × 10 = £100. If the client had held the position overnight the trade would have been closed and then reopened at a slightly different level, with the difference in the levels representing the difference in overnight interest rates between the two currencies concerned.

As in all FX trading, the only cost to the client is the bid–offer spread. This tends to be wider for a spread bet than for a 'genuine' trade, for a number of reasons:

1. The spread bet allows access to the market for individual clients who would not be considered 'expert', and thus would not be permitted to open a conventional FX trading account.

2. Clients can use this method to deal in a size very much below the minima seen in other areas of the industry. The smallest marketable amount seen between institutions is typically USD 1,000,000. Even small, private client FX market makers tend to demand a minimum ticket size of at least USD 100,000. A spread bet can be for as little as USD 10,000.

3. Spread betting clients can use 'guaranteed' (i.e. slippage-free) stops to trade on much lower margin. Some of the larger bookmakers will even allow a trusted client to deal on zero margin, without any kind of stop (so long as the client is a UK resident).

4. Profits from spread betting are free of Capital Gains Tax (so long as the client is not using spread betting activity as his main source of income. The transaction is considered to fall under gambling legislation, rather than the legislation covering investment activity; there is a small Gross Profits Tax that the bookmaker absorbs as part of their costs).

Increasing numbers of people are taking the view that these benefits outweigh the slightly larger headline transaction costs involved. The number of people using spread bets has increased dramatically over the last five years, in marked contrast to the significant decline in volumes seen recently over much of the rest of the retail financial services sector.

FX AS A CONTRACT FOR DIFFERENCE (CFD)

This is the newest route to the FX market for the retail investor. Contracts for difference (CFDs) became popular in the late 1990s as a vehicle to allow individuals to margin-trade on individual equities without having to pay stamp duty. The concept is simple. For example, an investor wishing to speculate on BP would open a CFD with a broker, put down a 10% margin and then pay or receive funding for as long as the position remained open. When he came to close the position, he would pay or receive the difference between his opening and closing levels. Thus an investor going short of 100,000 shares in BP at 450p, later buying them back at 400p, would receive a payment for the difference from the broker (in this case the difference would come to 50p × 100,000 = £50,000). During the period he would receive funding from the broker of, perhaps, LIBOR minus 1%, and would be expected to pay the broker for any dividends paid out by BP.

The system works equally well for FX. Simply substitute the 'funding charge' for the interest rate on the second-named currency and the 'dividend' for the first-named currency's interest rate. Thus a client buying USD against the JPY would pay a funding charge to the market maker to compensate that market maker for the JPY the investor is effectively borrowing. Meanwhile, the market maker would pay the investor for the interest he should be receiving on his long USD position. This exchange of cash flows is netted out to give a daily payment to the client in JPY.

This all sounds rather complicated. However, from the client's side it is not. The broker makes all the necessary calculations (using pre-agreed interest rates) and the client escapes the tiresome and unnecessary complexities of value dates and 'tom-next' rollovers. All that is left is an undated open position with a constant opening level, together with a separate stream of small daily credits/debits reflecting the difference in interest rates between the two currencies involved.

This makes it far simpler to keep track of one's open positions; occasional mistakes are spotted sooner and are easier to put right, and many speculators prefer the psychological aspect of having a fixed 'reference point' where they are long/short of a market. In addition to this, organizing and monitoring one's orders is also made straightforward; the fact that rollovers do not occur means that stop or limit orders can be left against a specific deal, automatically being cancelled when that deal is closed.

Another key feature of the CFD is its flexibility. Once an individual has submitted the paperwork necessary to open an account they can use that account for far more than FX. CFD clients will typically use their accounts for trading a combination of spot FX, FX options (see below), individual equities, index futures, and even commodity and interest rate contracts. The choice of instruments on which one can trade a CFD is limited only by the imagination, and the attitude to risk, of the broker. These 'one stop shop' CFD brokerages (often subdepartments of the major spread betting companies) allow truly active traders significant economies of scale in terms of the margin that must be put down to support a portfolio.

Flexibility of CFDs: over-the-counter FX options

The CFD approach lends itself naturally to FX options. Instead of trading on a call or put that is exercisable into the underlying currency the individual trades a contract for difference that is not, technically, an option, but is priced in such a way as to mimic the price of a 'true' option exactly.

An example makes this a little clearer. Consider the case of a call option on EUR/USD, with a strike of 1.0000, a maturity of one month and a current spot rate of 0.9900. The CFD on this will be priced exactly as a 'real' call would be, maybe as '55–60 USD pips'. The investor can go long or short of this quote just as though he were buying or writing a genuine option. From his point of view the only difference between the CFD and the 'real' call is that the instrument is never exercised into cash euros, even at expiry. The P&L on the deal is worked out on a cash-settled basis; if the instrument is held until expiry, when the spot EUR/USD rate is, say, 1.0100, then the CFD will close automatically at 100 USD pips and a buyer on the original quote books a profit of 100–60 = 40 USD pips (equivalent to USD 4,000 per million euro's dealt). Note that in this case there is no exchange of cash flows over the life of the instrument – the difference in interest rates between the two currencies is already implicit in the CFD's initial price.

This kind of flexibility and clarity is allowing CFD brokerages to draw in increasing amounts of business from traditional FX houses, just as over the previous few years they took market share from conventional shares and futures brokers. Expect this trend to continue, driven by:

1. the increasing expertise and marketing skill of the CFD houses;

2. the strength of the underlying product on offer; and

3. the increasing demand from investors for a counterparty that can offer every imaginable speculative instrument for the price of a single set of account-opening forms.

The development of this kind of service is a sign of the times, and a clear signal about the future of the retail industry – there has never been a better time to be a private speculator, and things are only going to get better.

Currency risk management

Francesca Taylor, Taylor Associates

Foreign exchange risk is
dangerous; it is expensive and
should not be ignored.

■ ■ ■

INTRODUCTION

The management of foreign exchange risk is critical in today's ever changing financial markets. But what is currency risk? In terms of volumes, with something in excess of USD 1.2 trillion changing hands every day on the foreign exchanges, only a small percentage is accounted for by corporates hedging their positions – between 5% and 10% of the total figure. The balance consists of global interbank and institutional business. Currency risk can initially be subdivided by the two groups of people who are most active in the markets: hedgers and traders.

A hedger is a company or individual who has an actual exposure to a particular currency: they need to pay away a foreign currency or receive a foreign currency, and wish to manage (avoid) the risk of an adverse exchange rate movement. The risk to a hedger is either of receiving a smaller amount of the base (or domestic) currency than expected, or of paying out more of the base currency to purchase a required amount of foreign currency.

A trader, on the other hand, has no requirement to pay or receive the currency but simply wants to speculate on the future direction of the currency movement for profit. It can be argued however, that most interbank foreign exchange trading is hedging, as each bank seeks to get out of positions that it has just received as a result of business from customers or other banks. The risk to a trader is that their view on the market is wrong, it may lose them money, or not make them as much as they thought, or the timing is wrong.

EXAMPLE OF CURRENCY RISK

19 November

Example

A UK company, Brain Tools plc, has sold some machine parts to the US. The company's base currency is sterling, but it has agreed to receive payment in US dollars in three months' time, on 19 February. Brain needs to recover the sterling price (including profit margin) of GBP 250,000; it will then convert this amount to US dollars for invoicing purposes. Let us assume that Brain chooses to use today's spot exchange rate – which is, say, GBP/USD: 1.60.

When Brain sends its invoice to the US buyer, it will state that the buyer is due to pay the seller USD 400,000 (1.60 × 250,000) in three months' time. If Brain does not hedge its currency exposure on this invoice it could make an exchange rate profit or a loss on the transaction, i.e. the rate could go in Brain's favour or may move against it. A profit is unlikely to cause a problem (but in some companies it may), but a loss will certainly be unwelcome.

If Brain decides not to hedge its position on the foreign exchanges, it is running a risk. It is impossible to predict the direction of an exchange rate with confidence, so we must assume one of two things can happen: the rate can increase or decrease (weaken or strengthen) against the base currency. In a three-month period it is not impossible for the FX rate to move 5 cents in either direction.

19 February

The original spot rate of exchange (the rate quoted on 19 November) could have moved by the end of this three-month period as shown below:

- USD increases (strengthens) to: GBP/USD 1.5500.
- USD decreases (weakens) to: GBP/USD 1.6500.

The treasurer of Brain has already calculated that she needs to receive GBP 250,000 for the transaction. If she does not hedge her position, she will be compelled to accept the exchange rate on the day the dollars actually arrive, i.e.:

- If the dollar has strengthened to GBP/USD 1.5500, the company will receive GBP 258,064.
- If the dollar has weakened to GBP/USD 1.6500, the company will receive only GBP 242,424.

In the first instance the company has made a windfall profit, in the second it has not received what it requires for the manufacture of the goods. Brain may end up selling the machine parts at a loss. Yet the client has paid the amount asked, and the company quoted the dollar equivalent on the day. No one is to blame, but worldwide events have changed either the value of sterling or the value of the US dollar. This is why currency risk is accepted as a way of life for companies who both export and import goods.

In the case of an importer, they may need to buy euro to pay a supplier, and budgets on the piece of equipment costing, say, GBP 175,000. But when it comes to the payment date, if they have taken out no hedging transactions, when they buy euros on the foreign exchanges they may cost as much as GBP 195,000.

COMPANY ATTITUDES TO RISK

The corporate culture inherent in a company will influence the way that foreign exchange hedging is taken out. Different companies view foreign exchange risk in different ways. There are two extreme views. First, the company whose view is: 'we make widgets, we do not speculate on the foreign exchanges'. This company would almost certainly hedge every single transaction denominated in foreign currency, usually by using traditional forward foreign exchange contracts.

Second, there is the company that believes that the flows of currency through the treasury department should be 'managed' and the return maximized. Inevitably, this will involve decisions where a view on a particular currency is taken in anticipation of a receipt or payment. In some cases it may actually entail opening up currency positions for gain. Naturally enough – and especially with imperfect information – the trades that are undertaken to maximize profit may end up as loss-making positions.

Although there are some companies which do hold these extreme positions, most corporations will generally fall somewhere in between, although there will be a greater concentration towards the conservative end.

HEDGING GUIDELINES

There are a number of steps to be taken after the original currency risk has been identified.

Step 1 – Identify

The identification of the currency risk is vital. Currency risk can vary from the 'staring you in the face risk' to the 'I feel uncomfortable about this price risk'. Once the risk has been identified there are other steps to follow before leaping on the phone to call your bank's dealers. Ideally, the whole process should look like Figure 11.1.

Hedging comes last although most clients will readily admit that they often skip the middle steps. We will arrive at the hedging soon, but I've always found it important to set the terms of reference. We know now that we have the exposure, so what should we do next?

The hedging process

Figure 11.1

```
IDENTIFY
   ↓
QUANTIFY
   ↓
CLASSIFY
   ↓
HEDGE
either forward FX
or OTC currency options
```

Step 2 – Quantify

This is where we must quantify the risk. Each company and client will have a different threshold where they begin to feel pain. For a small company it may be USD 20,000, for a larger multinational institution it may be USD 100,000. There comes a point where the exposure may well exist but was regarded as not material enough to worry about. Ideally, the board of directors will have decided the level of cover and what constitutes a material exposure. If it is a material exposure we will need to ascertain the exact size as far as is possible.

Step 3 – Classify

Now we must classify the type of risk to give us the best chance of hedging correctly. There are a range of currency risks that look similar but are, in fact, quite different. The terms relating to currency exposure that many readers, especially corporates, will recognize are:

- transaction
- translation
- economic.

Unfortunately, these terms lead to a certain amount of confusion. Transaction and translation risk are not so hard to understand. But what is economic exposure? Does it mean that if it isn't transaction or translation it must be economic? This was usually cited as a reason for not covering the exposure. It is now possible to subdivide currency risks still further, and I suggest a classification as follows.

Transaction exposures

1. **Standard**: the risk that exchange rates will move between the time an invoice is raised and payment is made.

2. **Recurring**: the exposure to movements in currency rates that the company knows it will enter into at some time in the future, but cannot be certain as to the exact value or timing. Most exports and imports fall into this category.

3. **Contingent**: tender to contract (TTC) exposure. Where the company has tendered or bid for business in a foreign currency, and must keep the currency rate fixed, but where there is no certainty that the company will win the business and it may well be three to six months before the result of the bid is known.

Trading exposures

1. **Liquidity exposure**: arising from deliberate treasury management action to change the currency of debt or cash with the specific aim of optimizing interest levels.

2. **Speculative exposures**: deliberate management action to open foreign exchange positions which are not to manage commercial exposures but instead to take speculative positions.

Competitive exposures

1. **Direct**: as a result of the company's home currency strengthening, its competitors, because production costs will reduce in lower terms, will be able to undercut the sales price in both the domestic and the export markets.

2. **Indirect**: adverse currency movements will change a company's competitive position even though the currency may not be one that the company trades in directly, e.g. a UK company trading wood pulp in USD is at risk to Scandinavian currencies, because of the location of the world wood pulp manufacturers.

Translation exposures

1. **Balance sheet**: when an asset is translated at year end, due to an exchange rate move, the asset value will fluctuate with the FX markets, giving rise to possible profits or losses later, e.g. Dutch company, EUR balance sheet, with a US subsidiary to be revalued.

2. **Consolidated P/L**: the risk that currency movements during the year will adversely impact on the profits of the group, and thus on the earnings per share of an international group of companies. This could be due to a fall in the value of the currency in which one or more of the subsidiary's accounts are prepared, relative to the parent company.

Step 4 – Hedge

The last step is to hedge the position. Some companies will use forward contracts and others will benefit from currency options. Essentially, the main choices facing a hedger are:

- do nothing;
- fix the FX rate by means of an option type product, where a premium is due;
- fix the FX rate by means of a zero premium product, such as a traditional forward FX deal.

Table 11.1

Quantifying and hedging foreign exchange risk

Exposure	Method of quantification	Cover method
Transaction exposures		
Standard	Books of account	Forwards or currency options
Recurring	Estimate turnover for a given period	Include with standard exposures – use forwards or currency options
Contingent	Avoid – or forecast likelihood	Include with standard exposures or use currency options
Trading exposures		
Liquidity	Books of account adjusted for positions	Forward market
Speculative	Dealing positions	Spot or forward market
Competitive exposures		
Direct	Competitor analysis	None in short term – relevant to new investments
Indirect	Project analysis	None in short term – relevant to new investments
Translation exposures		
Balance sheet	Books of account	Match fund assets
Profit and loss	Profit forecasts	Forwards or currency options

Table 11.1 shows the suggested methods of quantifying and covering these risks.

There is a complication with managing currency risks: not only can both sides of the equation move (both currencies in the pair can strengthen or weaken) but to cover longer-term foreign exchange exposures (over, say, five years) a different product is required – the currency swap. In simple terms a currency swap has a closer relationship with long-term forward foreign exchange than with other types of swaps. However, conventional classification places it firmly in the derivative category and outside the scope of this book, but further details can be found in *Mastering Derivatives Markets*, second edition, by Francesca Taylor (Financial Times Prentice Hall, 2000).

COMPARE AND CONTRAST TRADITIONAL FX FORWARDS AND OTC OPTIONS

If the client chooses to use traditional forward FX for his hedge he will achieve a zero cost transaction, but may forgo profit opportunities later. An

Comparison of OTC currency options and forward contracts

Table 11.2

Currency options	Forward contracts
Right to buy or sell	Obligation to buy or sell, or pay away the currency
No obligation to deliver or pay the underlying currency	Must deliver on/before maturity
No loss possible excluding the option premium	Unlimited opportunity loss possible, with respect to the forward rate
Eliminates downside risk and retains unlimited profit potential	Eliminates downside risk and upside potential
Perfect hedge for variable exposures	Imperfect currency hedge for variable exposures

option will cost the client a premium but may in the end achieve a more favourable outcome (see Table 11.2).

The real deal breaker as far as most companies are concerned is the cost of the option. If options were available free of charge then, almost without exception, every single piece of forward hedging would be taken out using options. It is clear they are a far superior product, but they have to be paid for, and it has to be admitted that sometimes they are expensive. Forward foreign exchange contracts are available free of charge as long as the client has sufficient room on an available credit line.

The real choice for many companies will be finely balanced, taking into account the extra benefits available under the option – but where a premium is payable for the product – against a foreign exchange deal, which costs nothing but which allows no chance of profit at all as it obligates both parties to convert the currency at the predetermined rate.

Some companies will wish to profit from their currency transactions and may well deliberately not hedge existing currency exposures. Some companies, as we have discussed, may also actively seek foreign exchange risk as a means of enhancing their income. The danger here is that the commercial side of the business, which may be profitable in its own right, could be overshadowed by foreign exchange losses if some irresponsible or unlucky decisions on currency are taken.

The corporate culture of the company can be situated at either end of the decision bracket in Figure 11.2.

True hedgers in the corporate world are comparatively rare. Let me explain what I mean by a true hedger – a company or individual who sells forward even if they believe that the currency may move in their favour.

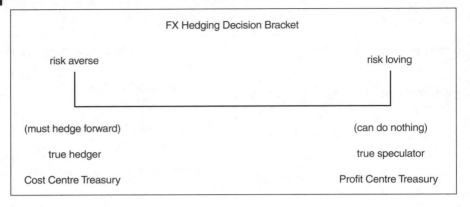

Figure 11.2

Hedging decisions

FX Hedging Decision Bracket

risk averse · risk loving

(must hedge forward) · (can do nothing)

true hedger · true speculator

Cost Centre Treasury · Profit Centre Treasury

They wish to make no windfall profits or windfall losses, all they require of their hedging transaction is the ability to know in advance what the rate of exchange will be for their transaction. Typically, this type of company is risk averse, and no conscious thought is required of their dealers: they know they must sell or buy the currency forward, all that remains is to get the best deal on the day at the best rate. This generally is known as a cost centre treasury.

Corporate speculators do exist: companies such as the big multinationals which have their own treasury functions where they can actively open up speculative positions for profit. This is classified as a profit centre treasury. They will be allowed to run unhedged positions as part of their mandate.

DECISION RULES

Are there any guidelines as to when a particular product should be used?

Once the risk identification/hedging process has been followed, and the risk has been classified, some risks can still be hedged with either an option or a forward. Assuming the company has the mandate to use either product, the final decision should come down to the circumstances on the day. Some days a traditional forward will be the right choice, on others the option. The decision will entail the company taking a 'view on the market'. This is nothing to be frightened of.

Example

Consider a receiver of dollars in three months' time: the company is not allowed to do nothing because that could be speculative.

1. If the company felt the value of the dollar was going to weaken. In this case the traditional forward contract would be the right choice – it costs nothing and covers the downside.

2. If the company felt the value of the dollar was going to strengthen then it would hope to realize more sterling. Here a traditional forward would be a questionable choice. (By selling the currency forward the client would be saying he does not want to realize the extra sterling.) The correct choice would be an OTC currency option. It will cost a premium but this can be more than offset by the sterling gain (you hope).

3. If the company felt the dollar was going nowhere, the traditional forward would again be the right choice – it costs nothing and covers the downside, and no upside is expected.

4. If the company felt the GBP/USD exchange rate would be volatile, the option would be the right choice because with a volatile market there is always the chance that the currency will suddenly improve, realizing more sterling. The danger here is that if the market is already volatile the option will be expensive.

Hedging guidelines

Table 11.3

View on the target currency	Risk management instrument
Weakens	Forward contract
Strengthens	Currency option
Goes nowhere	Forward contract
Highly volatile	Currency option

These rules can be summarized as in Table 11.3.

One cautionary note: it is easy for a company with a risk management policy to feel 'smug' – especially if it sells or buys all its currency forward. But ask yourself a question: if no one knows in which direction the US dollar (or any other currency for that matter) is going to move tomorrow or the next day, and if you believe every single piece of known information is in the exchange rate already, what is the probability of that hedge being successful? Answer: 50 : 50. So every company which hedges its exposures using forwards will be right half the time, and the companies which have a rather more cavalier attitude to risk and don't hedge because they think it is all a 'mug's game' will also be right half the time. A sobering thought!

TRADING RISK

A true speculator will be a bank. But any institution that makes some or all of its profits by taking 'views' on currency or other commodities for profit is trading. These speculative positions may be live for a matter of a few minutes or a few months. There is rarely any underlying transaction.

Trading example

Example

A foreign exchange trader in a bank or in a large corporate wishes to take risk by buying and selling currency for a profit. They may have a short-term view on the direction of the US dollar, or a long-term view on some other currency. They will position themselves accordingly, by either buying or selling the currency now, in order to reverse out of the deal at a later date – hopefully, making money in the process.

10 May

A proprietary trader in a financial institution feels that the dollar is showing signs of strength and wishes to take a position that will make them money in the near future. They decide to hold dollars for a week.

Action – 10 May

First they must choose which currency pair to trade in. Let us assume it is USD/JPY. They will buy the dollars on the market, either spot – in which case they must fund the position from two days' time – or they can swap them forward for, say, a week. They decide to buy the dollars forward (value 19 May) and are able to buy in at a rate of USD/JPY 123.50.

Action – 17 May

In a week's time the dollar has strengthened to USD/JPY 125.50, so they sell the dollars (value 19 May) without taking delivery of them, and make a profit. If the position had been taken in USD 10 million the profit would be:

Dollars USD/JPY		Yen	Transaction
10,000,000 × 123.5	=	1,235,000,000	(Sell yen and buy dollars)
10,000,000 × 125.5	=	1,255,000,000	(Sell dollars and buy yen)
Profit	=	20,000,000 yen	

At the current spot rate the profit in dollars is USD 159,362.55.

If the view had been wrong it would have been just as easy to lose the same amount of money.

CONCLUSION

I have addressed the concept of foreign exchange risk management in isolation. I have deliberately not tried to imply that if you hedge your foreign exchange risk you must be achieving a better deal for the company than if you weren't hedging the risks. Foreign exchange risk is dangerous; it is expensive and should not be ignored. The 'do nothing' alternative is an option only if it is a conscious decision, rather than 'I thought someone else was going to do it' or the regular dealer was off sick that day. There are many and various techniques to use and a working knowledge of these will always be beneficial, even if the company has not yet got a mandate to use them. Remember the saying: 'time spent in reconnaissance is never lost'.

Background and development of the currency option market

Francesca Taylor, Taylor Associates

If options were available free of charge they would be used all the time, however they are not free of charge. It is the premium payment that needs to be considered in the light of possible market movements – and very often the premium appears high.

■ ■ ■

INTRODUCTION

Currency option market activity goes hand in hand with global foreign exchange market activity and the BIS survey covering the period up to end June 2002 shows a 16% surge in business. Not really surprising; volatility has increased and traders have been quick to seize the opportunities. When you consider the many bank consolidations in the last few years and the slow down in the global financial markets this is quite remarkable growth.

Options belong to a group of products known as derivative instruments (the others being futures and swaps), but for those readers unfamiliar with options, let me explain what a derivative is. The expression 'derivative' covers any transaction where:

- There is (normally) no movement of principal – the majority of the transactions are 'cash-settled'.
- The price of the derivative itself is driven by the price of an underlying 'asset'.
- Over the counter (OTC) markets exist alongside exchange traded markets.

BASIC DERIVATIVE MARKET BACKGROUND

A **derivative instrument** is one whose performance is based on (or derived from) the behaviour of the price of an underlying asset (often known simply as the 'underlying'). The underlying itself does not need to be bought or sold. A premium may be due.   **Definition**

A true derivative instrument requires no movement of principal funds. It is this characteristic that makes them such useful tools both to hedge and to take risk, and why, until comparatively recently, these same instruments were known as 'off-balance sheet' instruments. Off-balance sheet signified that as no movement of principal occurred, there was no requirement for the transaction to appear on the company balance sheet. However, with the introduction of the new accounting regulations (FAS 133 and IAS 39) I'm not sure we can really say this anymore.

There are many types of derivative product, but specifically the term includes three key products:

- options

- futures
- swaps.

Different types of derivatives

Exchange-traded vs over the counter (OTC) instruments

A derivative product can be transacted either by exchange-traded means, where a fixed and pre-specified contract is bought or sold on a recognized exchange, or it can be transacted over the counter (OTC). An OTC instrument is written or created by a bank (or sometimes corporate and other financial institutions) and tailored to suit the exact requirements of the client, i.e. dates, amounts, currencies, etc.

An exchange-traded instrument

This is an instrument that is bought or sold directly on an exchange such as LIFFE – the London International Financial Futures Exchange, now owned by Euronext – or the CBOT (the Chicago Board of Trade) or the Philadelphia Stock Exchange.

Each exchange-traded product has a 'contract specification', which details precisely the characteristics of the 'underlying' and the obligations of the seller and buyer at maturity. Typical exchange-traded instruments include financial futures, listed options and traded currency options. These contracts are mostly traded electronically, but some 'open outcry' exchanges remain. The clearing house of each exchange will take the credit risk of each member, so there is no requirement to check if credit lines are clear in advance of a trade. For further details on how the clearing house operates refer to *Mastering Derivatives Markets*, second edition, by Francesca Taylor (Financial Times Prentice Hall, 2000).

An over the counter (OTC) instrument

An OTC instrument is one that is sold (written) by a bank (usually) to a client (usually) and tailored to fit a specific set of requirements. Sometimes, banks will purchase these products from companies or other non-banks, but each buyer and each seller must take the credit risk of their counterparty. An OTC product allows for much greater flexibility in terms of expiry date, strike, amount, underlying commodity, and vast amounts of these transactions are executed every day. An OTC instrument can be very simple in which case it is known as a 'vanilla' product (named after the simplest variety of ice cream), or it can be exceedingly complex. The price of the trade will be agreed upon between the parties, is confidential, and will involve many factors.

Single and multiple settlement products

Table 12.1

Single settlement	Multiple settlement
Financial futures/FRAs	Interest rate swaps
Interest rate options	Interest rate caps, collars, floors
Currency options	Currency swaps
Energy CFDs	Energy swaps

Single vs multiple settlement

Derivatives also divide neatly into products where there is a single settlement at or during maturity, and those where there are multiple settlements throughout the life of transaction (see Table 12.1). Derivative products with multiple settlements, such as swaps and caps, typically cover interest rates and fall outside the scope of this book.

Premium or non-premium based

Some derivatives require the payment of a premium, others do not. Options require the payment of a premium – in fact any product, where the buyer (client or bank) has paid a premium, is an option, even if the premium is disguised. The option product allows the buyer themselves to decide the course of action to take at or during the maturity. The purchaser (holder) of the product can 'abandon' the instrument if it offers an unfavourable or worse rate than that available elsewhere in the market. The client will always choose the alternative that offers the best outcome, either the rate on the derivative instrument or the current underlying market rate.

Any premium based instrument will guarantee for the client (holder) a worst or best case outcome, whereas a non-premium based instrument, such as a swap offers an absolute rate which cannot be improved upon.

Liquidity

Liquidity is an important concept in any tradable instrument, especially in derivatives. It is an indicator of how likely one is to be able to sell or to buy the instrument at a particular point in time.

There is an important saying in the market: '**there is a price for buying, a price for selling and a price for selling quickly**'.

Liquidity in interest rate derivatives is far greater with the exchange-traded products, and hundreds of thousands of contracts are bought and sold each day on the major exchanges. The chance therefore of finding willing buyers and willing sellers at a particular time and price is very good.

The scale tips the other way with currency options and currency derivatives generally, showing a major shift towards OTC currency products rather than those that are exchange based. Liquidity in the vanilla OTC instruments is also very good, but will be spread among many types of similar but non-identical transactions. As a result of this, as deals become more complex, liquidity will start to dry up, resulting in some deals being so complex and so 'structured' that there is in effect zero liquidity.

> **Tip** *Liquidity needs to be monitored on a regular basis. It is affected ultimately by supply and demand, but this in turn can be driven by changing credit quality, currency weakness or strength, volatility, etc.*

Credit risk

Credit risk is another important factor. It is the risk that the counterparty to the deal may go bankrupt or enter into liquidation before the contract matures, thus rendering them unable to fulfil their obligations. Credit risk is much lower with exchange-traded products as the clearing house (which is an affiliate of the regulated exchange) becomes counterparty to every trade, reducing exposure to individual clients. The risk on OTC products such as options is high as each party to the transaction takes the credit risk of the other. If you do not like the risk, you do not deal.

GROWTH OF THE CURRENCY OPTION MARKET

Currency options are foreign exchange derivatives and they exhibit similar trends to those shown in the underlying foreign exchange markets. The most recent survey is the half yearly survey conducted by the Bank for International Settlements (BIS), Basel, where figures are available for the six-month period finishing end of June 2002. Currency options had shown a small decline of 1% (as at the end December 2001), however, activity in currency options surged by over 39% from end December to show a notional amount of USD 3.4 trillion. This activity is due to the increase in volatility of major currency pairs – especially EUR/USD. In the same period, interest rate derivatives showed a 16% rise. For more information please view the BIS website, www.bis.org.

Table 12.2 shows data from the most recent survey.

Spot and forward foreign exchange are both traditionally OTC markets exhibiting continuous trading, 24 hours a day around the world. The FX volumes far outstrip the size of the actual trade flows. It follows therefore

The global OTC derivatives market

Table 12.2

(amounts outstanding in billions of US dollars)

	Notional amounts				Gross market values			
	End Dec 2000	End Jun 2001	End Dec 2001	End Jun 2002	End Dec 2000	End Jun 2001	End Dec 2001	End Jun 2002
GRAND TOTAL	95,199	99,755	111,115	127,564	3,183	3,045	3,788	4,450
Foreign exchange contracts	15,666	16,910	16,748	18,075	849	773	779	1,052
Outright forwards and forex swaps	10,134	10,582	10,336	10,427	469	395	374	615
Currency swaps	3,194	3,832	3,942	4,220	313	314	335	340
Options	2,338	2,496	2,470	3,427	67	63	70	97
Interest rate contracts	64,668	67,465	77,513	89,995	1,426	1,573	2,210	2,468
FRAs	6,423	6,537	7,737	9,146	12	15	19	19
Swaps	48,768	51,407	58,897	68,274	1,260	1,404	1,969	2,214
Options	9,476	9,521	10,879	12,575	154	154	222	235
Equity-linked contracts	1,891	1,884	1,881	2,214	289	199	205	243
Forwards and swaps	335	329	320	386	61	49	58	62
Options	1,555	1,556	1,561	1,828	229	150	147	181
Commodity contracts	662	590	598	777	133	83	75	78
Gold	218	203	231	279	17	21	20	28
Other	445	387	367	498	116	62	55	51
Forwards and swaps	248	229	217	290	–	–	–	–
Options	196	158	150	208	–	–	–	–
Other	12,313	12,906	14,375	16,503	485	417	519	609
Gross credit exposure					1,080	1,019	1,171	1,316
Memorandum item: Exchange-traded contracts	14,270	19,521	23,798	24,085				

Source: BIS, Basel.

that if the 'underlying foreign exchange asset' trades most efficiently in an OTC manner, then its derivative will also trade best in that medium.

OTC currency options continue to be very successful as more and more banks and corporations seek to hedge their currency exposures with derivative products as well as traditional spot and forward foreign exchange transactions. The disciplines of currency options and foreign exchange are very close and each complements the other.

WHAT IS A CURRENCY OPTION?

Definition A **currency option** gives the buyer (holder) the right, but not the obligation, to buy or sell a specific amount of currency at a specific exchange rate (the strike), on or before a specific future date. A premium is due.

Definition discussed

A currency option gives the client (or the bank) the chance to fix the rate of exchange that will apply to a forthcoming transaction. Everything is described from the client's, or holder's, perspective. The holder of the option need not proceed with the deal if he can find a more advantageous exchange rate elsewhere. The option instrument will let the holder choose the rate of exchange (the strike), and then the writing (or selling) bank must guarantee that rate if and when required. Because this option provides a type of optional guarantee, rather than an obligation, a premium is due. This is normally paid within two business days in either of the currencies of the option. Some banks may take the premium payment in a third currency but it is at their discretion.

In the above circumstances the client is the buyer (holder) of the option and must pay the premium. The holder has all the rights with the sole obligation to pay the premium by the due date. In contrast, the bank is the seller or writer of the option, it has all the obligations and no rights at all under the option: all it can receive is the premium paid by the purchaser yet the bank's obligations are onerous. It is the bank which must have the 'underlying' foreign exchange ready in case the holder requires it. It is the bank which must also hedge the risks on the option position. The underlying in this case is the receipt or payment of one currency against another currency.

Options can be cash settled at expiry or they can be sold back at any time during the life of the transaction for residual or 'fair value' (see under Currency option terminology, pp. 192–3). Alternatively, the currency can be physically delivered or paid to the writing bank (this is known as 'exercise'). The client will then receive the counter currency at the exchange rate previously agreed under the option. It is also possible to elect for cash settlement on exercise of the option, rather than physical delivery.

It should be noted that there may not always be a positive benefit on the option, some options will expire worthless.

The currency option is a more flexible hedging instrument than traditional forward foreign exchange and gives the buyer (holder) of the option four alternatives. The choice of:

- when to exercise
- whether to exercise
- how much to exercise
- the strike (or exercise) price.

When?

There are a range of currency option types: the two most popular are American options and European options. Under an American-style currency option a greater flexibility is offered. Consider an American-style option to sell US dollars and buy sterling; on exercise, the dollars can be delivered by the option holder to the bank, on any business day until expiry, for value two business days later. By comparison, under a European-style option, the holder can deliver the dollars against exercise only on the actual expiry date (for value two business days later), as specified at the beginning of the option contract. A European-style option operates in a similar fashion to a traditional forward foreign exchange contract. But with the forward contract the currency must be delivered on the maturity date – whereas the European option may be abandoned. More recently, the simpler exotic structures have become popular, such as the Bermudan – which can be exercised on selected dates. For more information on exotic options see Chapter 14 by Yuval Levy of SuperDerivatives.

With a traditional forward contract

If a client has sold forward some dollars for two months against sterling, and the dollars do not arrive in time, then the forward contract must still be honoured. This may lead to the client having the expense of buying the required amount of currency from the spot market, possibly at a worse rate, and then delivering it under the forward contract.

With the European-style currency option

If a client has transacted an option contract, should the dollars not arrive the option is simply abandoned, or if there is value remaining it can be sold back to the writing bank and the residual (fair) value realized (see the section 'Terminology', below).

Occasionally the underlying exposure that the option is covering may be shortened, or for some reason the option may no longer be required: then, as above, the option can be sold back to the writing bank for fair value. But if the underlying exposure is lengthened it is not possible to extend the option at the same strike, or to roll it over into a new deal, as these practices are open to fraud. If the time period on the option needs to be lengthened the most effective way to bring about this is to sell the original option back to the bank for fair value, and take out a new transaction covering the fresh maturity date at the current prevailing market conditions.

Whether?

An option will be exercised by the holder, only if it is profitable for him/her to do so. Where the spot exchange rate on maturity remains more favourable than the option strike price, the option will be allowed to lapse, and the underlying deal will be transacted in the spot market. This is known as 'abandoning the option'.

Note that with exotic options the reference rate may be a combination of more than one rate, see Chapter 14 by Yuval Levy of SuperDerivatives.

How much?

When the currency option is originally established, it is for a specific amount of a reference currency, and it is upon this figure that the option premium is based. This is a notional maximum amount of currency. If the resulting currency receipt or payment turns out to be for a lesser figure, it may be possible (in some cases) for the excess cover provided by the option to be sold back for fair value to the writing bank. Should an excess amount of currency arrive there is no provision for additional cover under the original option.

Strike

The strike price of the option is chosen by the client or holder at the outset – it is sometimes known as the exercise price. The premium that is due for the option will be a function of how the strike price relates to the current market price and various other inputs into the pricing model (see the section 'Premium determinants', below).

TERMINOLOGY

The growth in currency option volumes can be traced to the beginnings of the 1970s. The first commonly used option pricing model was written in the early 1970s by Fisher Black and Myron Scholes and was published in the *Journal of Political Economy* in 1973. Their treatise contained many new descriptive words, that are now in every day usage – at least among options users and providers. This jargon can need translating and before we go any further I have detailed some of the terminology opposite.

Terminology discussed

It is very important to specify whether you are the buyer or seller of the option and whether you are selling or buying the underlying currencies. Potentially there could be a four-way price, which is why we need the additional terms, **puts** and **calls**. There are also a number of different ways that people describe options. Some talk about 'calling' or 'putting' the foreign currency, others about calling or putting the dollar. There is added confusion when you consider cross currencies, for example, if the currencies are

Currency option terminology

Call option	The right (not the obligation) to buy foreign currency.
Put option	The right (not the obligation) to sell foreign currency.
Exercise	Conversion of the option into the underlying physical transaction or alternatively elect for cash settlement.
Strike price	Exchange rate chosen by the holder. Prices can be described as: – at the money (ATM) – in the money (ITM) – out of the money (OTM).
Expiry date	Last day on which the option may be exercised. Up to 10.00 New York time (usually), two business days before the value date.
Value date	The day on which the currency is delivered.
Premium	The price of the option.
American option	An option which can be exercised on any business day up to and including the expiry date.
European option	An option which can be exercised on the expiry date only.
Bermudan option	An option which can be exercised on selected business days and the expiry date.
Asian option	A European-style option linked to the average currency rate over a pre-set period.
Intrinsic value	Difference between the strike price and the current market exchange rate.
Time value	Difference between the option premium and intrinsic value; including the time left until expiry, volatility, forward differentials, market expectations.
Fair value	Combination of intrinsic value and time value, as calculated by an option pricing model.
Volatility	Normalized annualized standard deviation of the returns of the daily underlying spot exchange rate for the rate concerned.

EUR/NOK, which one is foreign? It is always safer to specify both sides, not just to call the euro, but to call the euro and put the Norwegian krone; then there is no possibility of confusion.

Exercise is how to convert the option, which at inception is simply a piece of paper, into the 'underlying asset'. The term is also used to denote the physical movement of the underlying (the respective currencies), unless the option is to be cash settled and bought back by the writing bank or sold for its intrinsic value (see below).

The **strike price** or exercise price is the exchange rate chosen by the client. This can be at the same rate as the underlying commodity (often the forward rate) or it may be better or worse. The terms that we use are at the money (ATM), in the money (ITM), and out of the money (OTM). The pricing model itself will compare the strike with the current underlying currency rates.

The **expiry date** is the last date on which the option can be utilized for value two business days later. This will be the last day for both European-, American-, Bermudan- and Asian-style options. There are also cut-off times on the expiry date, they could be either:

- 10.00 hours New York time (15.00 hours London time).
- 10.00 hours Tokyo time (01.00 hours London time, therefore hard to exercise in the European time zone).

This allows the option writers to be exercised by their clients and then they can in turn exercise their option with, perhaps, other interbank players.

The **premium** is the figure calculated by the option pricing model for the particular transaction. It is normally quoted in:

- cents per pound (sterling or other currency)
- pence per dollar (US or other currency)
- percentage of transaction amount.

The pricing model will calculate a break-even price and it will be up to the trader to spread the premium to create the bid–offer price.

An **American option** offers more flexibility to a holder who needs to deliver his dollars or his pounds physically, can be more expensive, and can be exercised on any business day up to and including the expiry date. In contrast, a **European option** can be exercised only on the expiry date for value two business days later. A **Bermudan option** allows exercise on selected dates, each of these types of option can be sold back to the writing bank at any time. An average rate option (often known as an **Asian option**) is, in fact, a simple exotic structure, linking the value of the option at expiry to average currency rates over a pre-set period.

The option premium calculated by the pricing model can be divided into two parts, **intrinsic value** and **time value**. The intrinsic value is measured by the present value of the amount by which it is in the money, e.g. for a European-style US dollar put, sterling call, used to cover a dollar receivable against sterling in three months' time:

- Forward outright rate for three months is $1.47
- Option strike rate is $1.44
- Intrinsic value is present value (PV) of $1.47 − $1.44 = PV of 3 cents.

Intrinsic value provides the minimum premium level at which the option will trade. Intrinsic value can only ever be zero or a positive number.

The **time value** component of the option expresses the risk premium in the option and is a function of several variables:

- the relationship between the strike rate and the spot rate
- the time to maturity
- the interest rate differential between the two currencies
- the volatility of the currency pair.

The pricing model will calculate the **fair value** of an option: this is a break-even premium level. It will then be up to the trader to spread the premium to create the bid–offer price for the option.

Volatility is a measure of the degree of 'scatter' of the range of possible future outcomes for the underlying commodity. A volatility input is only required for option products. If you wish to speculate on the level of volatility you will need to trade options. Its importance lies in the basic maths of the option pricing model. Volatility is quoted as a percentage with a bid–offer spread.

KEY FEATURES OF CURRENCY OPTIONS

Insurance protection

A premium is paid by the buyer or holder of the option to the writing (selling) bank, which in turn guarantees a fixed exchange rate if/when required by the option holder.

Profit potential

When hedging with an option any chance of currency loss is eliminated. The only outflow of funds relates to the premium payment. If the underlying market movement is in the holder's favour, upside potential is available, as the option will be abandoned, allowing the holder the chance to enter into a spot deal. If the underlying market movement is against the holder, the option will be 'exercised' at the previously agreed rate. An option profile describes 'asymmetry of risk'. The most that a holder can lose is the option premium, the most he can profit is limited only by how far the market moves.

When trading with options, the initial up-front premium can be regarded as a stop-loss. If the market does not move in the expected direction, the option will expire worthless and the only downside will be the premium paid. Should the market move in a profitable direction, the option can be exercised or sold back to the writing bank for fair value, which will hopefully recoup more than the original premium payment.

Sell back

The option can be sold back in whole or in part, for fair value to the writing bank. The writing bank will not require an explanation for the sell back – it may be that the client has merely changed his mind. This is not a negotiable piece of paper; it can only be sold back to the writing (selling) bank, it cannot be on-sold to a third party and is not transferable.

Premium

A premium is due which is based on a series of variables that are input into an option pricing model, many of which are derived from the original Black and Scholes model. Many traders use different models for the more exotic structures, for more information in pricing see Chapter 14 by Yuval Levy of SuperDerivatives. The premium figure will comprise intrinsic value and time value.

PREMIUM DETERMINANTS

There are a number of important factors that affect the premium due on an option. Each of the following inputs is entered into the pricing model, which then calculates the option premium:

- strike price
- underlying price
- maturity
- volatility
- interest rate differentials
- American/European/Bermudan/Asian
- Call/put.

Strike price vs underlying price

The underlying benchmark against which the strike price on the currency option is measured is the appropriate foreign exchange rate. European options are measured against the outright forward rate, whilst American options – as they can be exercised at any time, are usually compared with the current spot rate.

Strike prices are referred to as follows (see Table 12.3):

Terminology

At the money (ATM)	Where the strike price is equal to the current benchmark rate.
In the money (ITM)	Where the strike price is more favourable than the current benchmark rate, the option premium is higher than that for an ATM option.
Out of the money (OTM)	Where the strike rate is less favourable than the benchmark rate and the option premium is lower than that for an ATM or ITM option.

In, at, and out of the money

Table 12.3

Assume the current forward rate of dollars against sterling is £1 = $1.50.

Client purchases option to sell dollars against sterling		Client purchases option to buy dollars against sterling
$1.40	IN THE MONEY	$1.60
$1.50	AT THE MONEY	$1.50
$1.60	OUT OF THE MONEY	$1.40

Maturity

The longer the time to expiry or maturity, the higher the probability of large exchange rate movements, and the higher the chance of profitable exercise by the buyer. The buyer should be prepared to pay a higher premium for a longer dated option than a short-dated option. The relationship between the premium due on an option and the maturity of the transaction is not a linear relationship. As shown in Figure 12.1, the premium due for a six-month option is not double that of a three-month option, and is never likely to be.

Volatility

It is the volatility input into the pricing model that differentiates one banks' price from another. All other premium determinants are matters of fact that

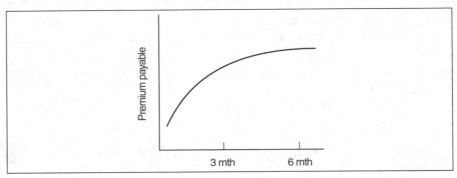

Figure 12.1

The non-linear relationship between maturity and premium

are available to market participants simultaneously either from current trading conditions or direct from the client. If a client purchases an option with high volatility, he has purchased an asset with a good chance of very profitable exercise.

Interest rate differentials

Forward foreign exchange rates are calculated using the interest rate differentials of the two currencies concerned. Currencies are at a premium or discount to each other, reflecting whether the forward points are added to or subtracted from the spot rate. This differential will affect the premium due on an option.

Interest rates affect option pricing in two ways:

1. By affecting the forward price of the asset and hence the intrinsic value.
2. By affecting the present value (PV) calculations within the option pricing model, and ultimately the (PV) of the option premium.

American or European or Bermudan or Asian?

Generally, an American-style option gives the holder greater flexibility. If the client wishes to buy or call a currency with a higher interest rate (discount currency), the American-style option will be more expensive. If the client wants to call a premium currency the price of the American and the European option will be the same. Alternatively one of the less standard structures may be chosen

Call or put?

The client needs to specify whether they wish to buy or sell the foreign currency.

THE IMPORTANCE OF VOLATILITY

A volatility input is required for option pricing. The 'grandfather' option pricing model was written by Black and Scholes in 1972. This assumes that the underlying financial asset, in this case forward foreign exchange rates, behaves in a similar fashion to a log-normal distribution. Normal distributions are typically found in nature, for example the height of trees, the weight of children, the length of snakes, etc. The volatility input into the option pricing model generates a prediction of how a particular exchange rate will move in the future. It will not necessarily predict what the exchange rate will be as a rate on a specific date in the future, but just how the exchange rate will behave; will there be a large degree of scatter around a theoretical average, with exchange rates all over the place, or will there be very little movement as the currency stays within a narrow range? The best way to explain this is by using an example from nature.

You have been given the job of statistically sampling a penguin population in **Example**
Antarctica.

Height data is being collected from a sample representation of king penguins in Antarctica. One hundred penguins will be measured and then the data analyzed. Once we have the data we can calculate the average height of the penguins – this is known as the mean.

Many years ago a German scientist called Gauss undertook some research. He showed that if you sampled data from any population with a normal distribution, once you had calculated the mean you could calculate certain 'confidence limits'. He calculated that if you took the mean (which you have already calculated) plus or minus something called a standard deviation you could ensure that 66% of all the data readings would fall between these limits. He then further predicted that if you took the mean plus or minus two standard deviations you could then guarantee that 95% of all the data would fall within these wider limits.

Let's assume the penguins have been measured, the mean has been calculated at 1 metre, and the standard deviation computed from the data, giving a figure of 10%. This would give us a normal distribution as shown in Figure 12.2.

Once the data has been collected it is not too difficult to carry out the calculations – anyone who has studied statistics will recognize the shape of the normal distribution. But how does all this fit in with options and option pricing? Well, standard deviation and volatility are the same thing.

The statistical definition of volatility is 'the normalized annualized

Figure 12.2

The projected analysis of the height of king penguins

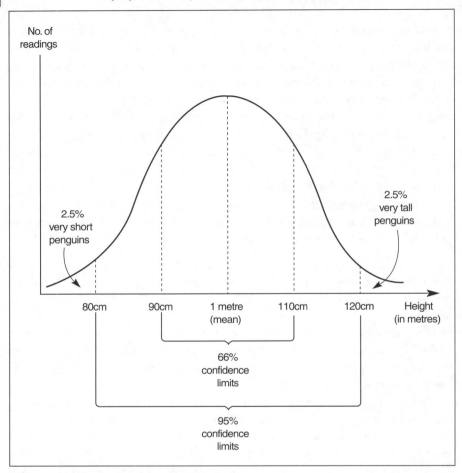

standard deviation of the returns of the underlying commodity'. The biggest problem in using volatility is trying to establish what volatility will be in the future, before there is any data to back it up.

There are two different types of volatility: historic and implied.

Example

Consider a trader trying to price a currency option in three-month USD/JPY. They have to guess the shape of the normal curve: will it be steep with low volatility, and most readings about the mean, or will it be very flat, with high volatility and many readings widely scattered? In fact, the trader is trying to guess how volatile the exchange rate will be in advance. Not an easy thing to do (see Figure 12.3).

The effect of different volatility levels on the shape of the normal curve

Figure 12.3

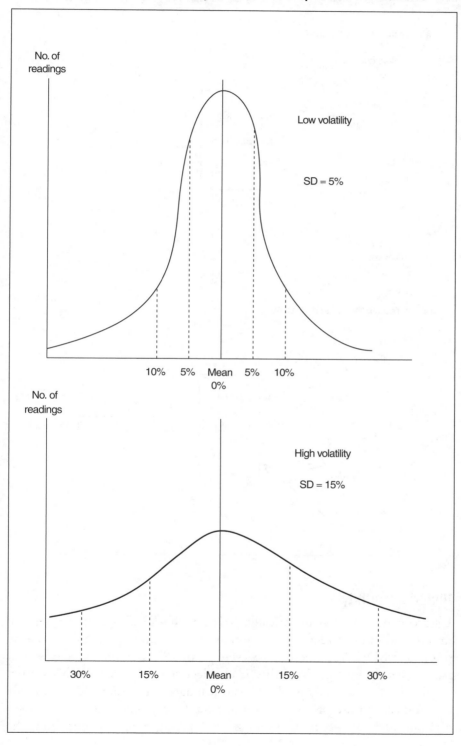

Figure 12.4   **Variable inputs for option premium calculation**

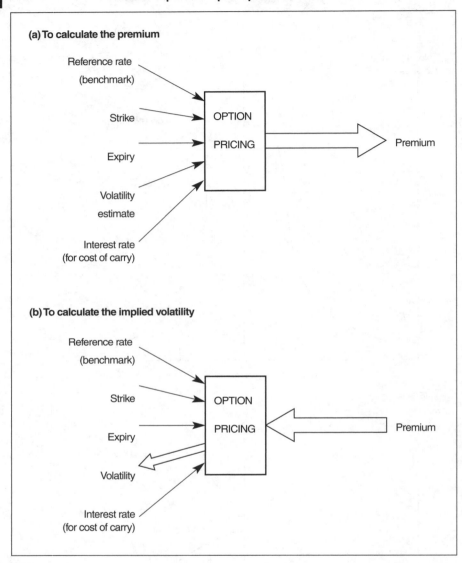

(a) To calculate the premium

Reference rate
(benchmark)

Strike

OPTION

PRICING

Expiry

Premium

Volatility
estimate

Interest rate
(for cost of carry)

(b) To calculate the implied volatility

Reference rate
(benchmark)

Strike

OPTION

PRICING

Expiry

Premium

Volatility

Interest rate
(for cost of carry)

Historic volatility

Data can be collected historically; it is possible to analyze the spread of movements of the underlying commodity by recording, for example, closing prices of USD/JPY. If these prices were plotted on a graph a type of scatter pattern would emerge. Volatility is in effect the definition of this scatter. Whilst this type of analysis allows historical data to be examined, it can only ever indicate future prices, it will not be able to predict them but, rather, give an idea of where they might be, taking into account how the

The linear relationship between premium and volatility

Figure 12.5

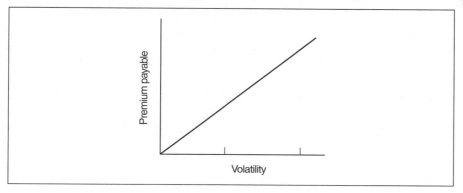

commodity has moved in the past. This is assuming you believe that history repeats itself.

Implied volatility

What the trader will actually input into his option pricing model is implied volatility. This is the current volatility level implicit in today's option prices. It can be derived from prices in both exchange-traded and OTC options – you may wonder how. First, find a currency option with a premium that is already quoted and trading in the market, hopefully with a similar expiry date and the same currency pair, and then get the model to work backwards to deduce the volatility. This is illustrated in Figure 12.4.

Volatility itself has a spread. It is quoted as an annual percentage. For example, it may be quoted as 10.6–11.1%. If the client wants to buy the option, use 11.1%; if he is trying to sell it to you, use 10.6%.

There are now many different option pricing models; a number of inputs are requested by the model, which then calculates the premium. Whichever single input you do not give the model it will take the data from the other inputs and work backwards.

In conclusion, we saw earlier in the section that the premium/maturity profile was non-linear, but the profile of premium/volatility is linear, as shown in Figure 12.5, i.e. the higher the perceived volatility, the higher the premium. Higher volatility implies a greater possible dispersion of prices at expiry, and logically the option holder has an asset with a greater chance of more profitable exercise.

COMPARISONS BETWEEN OTC CURRENCY OPTIONS AND FORWARD FOREIGN EXCHANGE

Both traders and hedgers can use currency options and forward foreign exchange. The easiest way to compare the two products is to consider

Table 12.4 **Comparisons between OTC currency options and forward foreign exchange**

Currency options	Forward contracts
Right to buy or sell	Obligation to buy or sell
No obligation to deliver or receive currency	Must deliver currency on/before maturity date
No loss possible except the premium, which can be considerable	Unlimited opportunity loss possible, as the forward ties the client into a fixed rate
Eliminates downside risk whilst retaining unlimited profit potential	Eliminates all downside risk but allows no upside potential at all
Perfect hedge for variable exposures, but can be expensive	Rigid hedge for variable exposures

the similarities and differences from the user's or holder's point of view.

Table 12.4 summarizes the main differences between OTC currency options and traditional forward foreign exchange. A forward contract is fine as a hedging product if complete information is available; the amount is known, the currencies, and when – to the day – the currency will be paid/received ('the end of the month' is not acceptable, it is too vague). In everyday business the luxury of complete information is not always available, dates and amounts have to be estimated, and some clients simply pay late. In those circumstances an option is the perfect alternative. It is not a zero cost alternative like a forward transaction but it is immensely flexible, and some options can be designed to have very low or even zero premiums.

USING A CURRENCY OPTION TO HEDGE A CURRENCY RECEIVABLE

Example **2 October**

A major British company has won an export order in the Far East. Delivery and payment will be in six months' time and will be in dollars. The treasurer is unsure on which day the money will be available in their account, and is worried that the value of the dollar may fall (depreciate) before they receive the invoice amount of USD 2,250,000. If he does nothing and the value of the dollar falls, they will not realize sufficient sterling from the resulting foreign exchange conversion to cover their costs and the profit margin. But if the value of the dollar increases they will be very happy. The treasurer is not sure in which direction the dollar will move, but under company policy is not allowed to do nothing, because of the possible risk of losing money. If he transacts a forward contract with one of their bankers, they must give up any windfall profits should the currency move in their favour, but if he transacts an option he has insurance if things go wrong and profit opportunities if things go right.

Action – 2 October

The treasurer will ask for an indication level on a dollar put, sterling call option, American-style, strike = at the money, and an expiry date in three months (2 January) for value two business days later.

The current financial information available is:

	GBP/USD
Spot rate:	1.5100
Six-month outright forward rate:	1.5050

The option strike will be at the money forward (ATMF), at USD $1.5050. The premium due for this option is, say, 1.9% of the dollar amount. The total premium is 1.9% of USD 2,250,000, which is USD 42,750, and must be paid to the option writer two business days after the deal is struck. The option can now be filed or put in a drawer for six months until expiry, or until the dollars arrive, whichever is earlier.

Action – 2 April

The dollars arrive by the due date. The treasurer calls the bank to check the current level of the spot rate. If the dollar has strengthened (appreciated) to, say, USD 1.4550 = GBP 1, then the option will be worthless and will be abandoned and the transaction will be effected in the spot market. If the dollar has depreciated to, say, USD 1.5550 = GBP 1, the treasurer will exercise the option at the agreed rate of USD 1.5050. The company will need to call the bank to confirm that it wishes to exercise its option, as exercise is not automatic. It is the holder's responsibility to exercise the option. The bank has no obligation to remind the client to exercise. If the company exercises the option, the treasurer must deliver USD 2,250,000 and will receive sterling at USD 1.5050, giving a sterling out-turn of GBP 1,495,016.61. Technically the option premium should be deducted to work out the break-even rate (to be absolutely correct the NPV of the premium). This would give a net sterling out-turn of GBP 1,495,016.61 less the amount of the option premium in sterling (for premium conversion purposes the spot rate is always used, USD 42,750 divided by 1.5100 = GBP 28,311.26): a total figure of GBP 1,466,705.35.

Under the terms of this currency option it does not matter when the dollars arrive as the treasurer has purchased an American-style option,

Figure 12.6   **Best and worst case outcomes for the example**

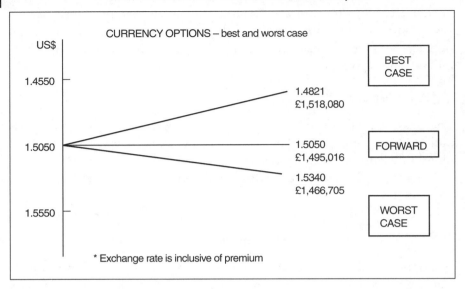

allowing delivery of the currency on any business day in the period (for value two business days later). If originally the company had purchased a European-style option, there would be a restriction and the dollars would need to be placed on deposit until the expiry date, when they could be delivered under the option.

As Figure 12.6 shows, there is always a best and worst case – indeed the nature of FX means that no one knows how far or how fast a currency will move. A 5 cent move in the six-month period has been used for the purposes of illustration.

If the client had chosen a traditional forward contract and been lucky with the receipt of the dollars on the correct date, he would have achieved at best and at worst, a rate of USD 1.5100 – an out-turn of GBP 1,495,016.61.

The other figures in the diagram are arrived at by calculating the sterling proceeds of USD 2,250,000 (net of the premium) and then working backwards to establish the effective exchange rate.

The option will always be the second best alternative. If the client knew with 100% certainty that the dollar was going to depreciate, he would sell forward, a hedging alternative that would cost nothing and allow no profit. But if he was not expecting to profit he has given up nothing. If the client had known with 100% certainty that the dollar would appreciate, he would do nothing and simply sell the dollars at the better rate when they arrived in three month's time. The option allows you to get the best possible outcome, the 'insured' rate when required, or the profit when the market moves favourably, but a premium is required. In effect, the option allows you to be wrong without it costing the holder too much money. The interesting point is a client would be more than happy to abandon an option – it implies the underlying transaction is showing a profit.

USING CURRENCY OPTIONS TO SPECULATE

A private client believes that the Japanese yen will appreciate against the dollar over the next two weeks. He is prepared to put on a position equivalent to USD 10 million. He has no desire physically to hold either currency and no requirement for flexibility on the date, so he will purchase a two-week European-style option that he can sell back, but will not need to exercise. By selling the option back to the option writer the currency gain, if there is one, will be factored into the sell-back price. This negates the need for physical foreign exchange transactions.

Current financial information:

	USD/JPY
Spot rate:	123.00
Outright forward rate:	122.50

Strategy

The client will purchase a European-style yen call, US dollar put in USD 10 million for expiry in two weeks. The option premium is calculated at 0.6%, which is USD 60,000 or yen 7.38 million, payable within two business days of the transaction date. This option will run for two weeks. The client must decide when he believes he has the maximum profit on the deal. Let us assume that, ten days after inception, the option trade is showing a healthy profit. The strike on the ATMF option was originally set at USD/JPY 122.50, the spot rate is now 118.50 and the client does not think there will be much more movement, so he wants to close out his position and take his profit. As this is a European option, he must contact the writing bank and ask them to 'buy-back' the option. They will calculate the buy-back premium (fair value) through the option pricing model. The buy-back premium will incorporate the foreign exchange gain (intrinsic value) and will also incorporate any residual time value.

Early exercise

If the private client had purchased a more expensive American-style option, he could still have sold it back at any time. But why pay for exercise flexibility if you never want to exercise? In this case the client had no requirement for either of the currencies, so the ability to exercise the option into its underlying currencies is superfluous. This client simply wants to profit from his view on exchange rates.

The other problem with exercising an option early is that all the client or trader would receive is the intrinsic value; that is, the amount by which the option is in the money, the amount by which the option is better than the underlying market rate. If there was any time value left it would be lost. Instead of early exercise it is always better to sell back an option. This ensures that the time value component is always included in the sell back premium.

Another consideration for using European options and selling them back, is that if the client chose to exercise the option it would be necessary for him to take delivery of the physical yen and pay for them with physical dollars, simultaneously needing to sell the yen back into the market to crystallize the profit. In that case the transaction costs on the foreign exchange deals may be significant on their own.

BASIC WORKINGS OF CURRENCY OPTIONS

Whether the market participants use American or European options, whether they buy them or sell them, will depend upon a number of factors acting either in isolation or simultaneously, but the following rules apply:

1. The option is exercised only when it is advantageous for the holder.

2. If the ruling spot rate is more favourable, the option will be abandoned.

3. The downside risk is protected, with a one-for-one gain if the market moves favourably.

4. The writer of the option is obliged to deliver the 'underlying' if the option is exercised.

The mechanics of currency options

Francesca Taylor, Taylor Associates

The fair value of an option at expiry is the sum of every possible value it could achieve, multiplied by the probability of that value occurring.

■ ■ ■

INTRODUCTION

Most option pricing models in use today have evolved from the model written by Professors Fisher Black and Myron Scholes in the early 1970s. Although there has been a fair amount of tinkering with the basic Black and Scholes formula to make it work with interest rates and currency and to a certain extent more exotic structures, the essential element within the model confirms that exchange rates move in the same way as nature, and that a normal distribution is a fair way of considering the data. Option pricing is actually based on a log-normal distribution, which is very different from a straight normal distribution to a statistician, but for our purposes it is close enough to be viewed similarly. It would be dangerous to assume that exchange rates moved in a normal fashion, but while the prices are not normally distributed, the returns mostly are. An investor holding dollars is just as likely to see the value of the dollar increase as decrease.

THE BLACK AND SCHOLES OPTION PRICING MODEL

In 1973 Fisher Black and Myron Scholes published their paper on option pricing. The mathematics needed to derive the complete formula are awesome, and I do not intend to develop them in this book.

But, generally speaking, Black and Scholes proved that the fair price for any financial asset is its expected value. If the gold price had a 35% chance of achieving USD 319, and a 65% chance of achieving USD 350, the fair value of gold at that time would be:

$$(0.35 \times \$319) + (0.65 \times \$350) = \$339.15 \text{ per ounce}$$

The same principle applies to options: the fair value of an option at expiry is the sum of every possible value it could achieve, multiplied by the probability of that value occurring. In the example above there were only two discrete outcomes, but options can take on almost any value, so continuous rather than discrete probability distributions are required.

The discussion of the Black and Scholes formula that I find most helpful is that developed by Lawrence Galitz in his book *Financial Engineering* (Financial Times Prentice Hall, 1994). For those readers who wish to follow the math a little more closely this is reproduced in Appendix 2.

It is important to bear in mind that pricing models are exactly that, *models* of reality, rather than reality itself. The Black and Scholes model makes other assumptions apart from normally distributed returns. These are shown below in Table 13.1.

Table 13.1	**Basic assumptions of the Black and Scholes model**

- The option is European-style, and cannot be exercised before expiry
- There are no taxes, transaction costs, or margin requirements
- Lending and borrowing are possible at the same riskless rate, which accrues continuously in time
- The underlying asset can be bought or sold freely, even in fractional units
- The underlying asset can be sold short, and the proceeds are available to the short seller
- The underlying asset pays no dividends or other distributions before maturity
- The underlying price is continuous in time, with no jumps or discontinuities
- The variability of underlying asset prices and interest rates remains constant

Source: L. Galitz, *Financial Engineering*, Financial Times Prentice Hall

Whilst many of the assumptions are not strictly true, the basic model can be adjusted. For example, in a currency option, the foreign currency does pay a distribution because when the currency is placed on deposit it will accrue interest; when this is factored into the formula you have the Garman–Kohlhagen model for currency options.

The reason the Black and Scholes model (and its derivatives) has been so successful is due to its reliability, robustness, and consistent pricing. In the last few years there have been many modifications made to the models, especially with reference to exotic options.

EXPIRY OR PROFIT AND LOSS PROFILES

Options can be *puts* and *calls*, both of which can be bought or sold. These four basic structures are long call, short call, long put, short put. In fact, the right to buy or sell the underlying and the right to buy or sell the option itself. Each type of option has a particular 'signature'. The easiest way to understand how options work is to construct the profit and loss (P/L) profile of the transaction at expiry. Some people know these as expiry profiles.

Consider the currency pair USD/CHF: if a trader bought cash CHF today in the expectation of the CHF strengthening, the P/L profile would be as shown in Figure 13.1.

The trader buys the CHF at 1.50 and then, as the Swiss franc appreciates, and the dollar weakens (towards 1.40), the position will start moving into profit. In contrast, if the CHF depreciates and the dollar strengthens (towards 1.60), the same position would move into loss. This is equivalent to an unhedged position, with an equal probability of profit or loss.

Instead of running a spot risk with an equal chance of gain or loss the

Expiry profile of an unhedged position

Figure 13.1

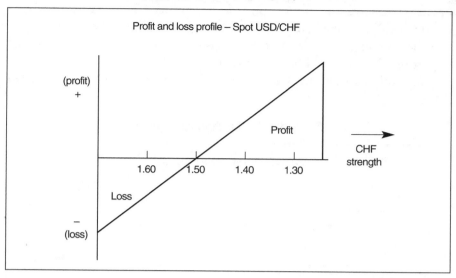

trader could purchase an option with the same strike of 1.5000. This would allow a similar 1 : 1 profit opportunity, but where the potential downside is now limited to the premium paid. The upside is limited only by the extent of the positive market movement. The trader will buy a CHF call, USD put option, they would be 'long' the call. This P/L profile is shown in Figure 13.2.

The profile of the CHF call option mirrors that of the unhedged position, except that it starts from a negative position reflecting the premium paid.

Expiry profile of a long call option

Figure 13.2

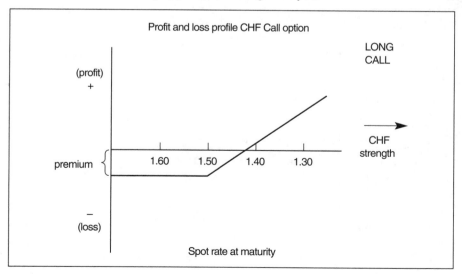

One must take into account the premium on the option and any associated interest rate costs. An option purchaser may need to fund (borrow) the option premium, or if the trader does not need to fund the position they may be forgoing extra interest on a potential deposit. Other associated opportunity costs should be also recognized.

The bank writing the CHF call option against USD, as shown in

Figure 13.3

Expiry profile of a short call option

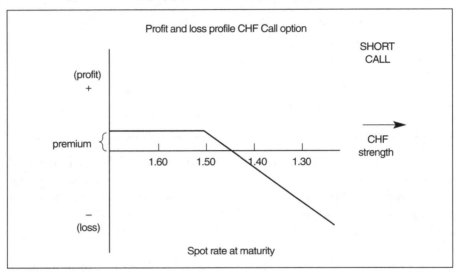

Figure 13.4

Expiry profile of a long put option

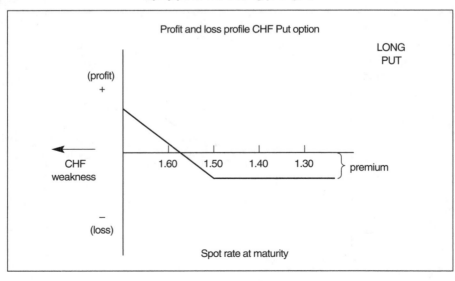

Expiry profile of a short put option

Figure 13.5

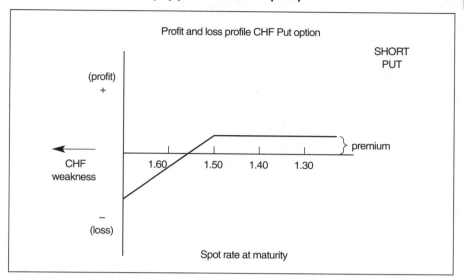

Figure 13.2, would have a mirror image of the position. It will receive the premium, yet its potential for losses is high, unless the position is hedged. This is shown in Figure 13.3. In this case, the bank that has written the option is 'short' the call option.

Assume that the trader has now changed their mind about the direction of the Swiss franc. They feel the CHF is about to weaken, so with their new trade they need to buy a CHF put, USD call option, (see Figure 13.4). The trader is hoping to profit from a fall in the value of the CHF so wishes to profit towards the right-hand side of Figure 13.4 – this is why the diagram appears the other way around.

This P/L profile shows that the holder of this option can lose only their premium, should the exchange rate remain above 1.50, but can profit as long as the market moves in their favour (towards 1.60). In comparison the writer of this option, who is 'short' the CHF put option, could lose a considerable amount, as shown in Figure 13.5.

The four key strategies – the long call, long put, short call, short put – are shown together in Figure 13.6.

PUT–CALL PARITY

You may have noticed in our discussion on the Black and Scholes model for option pricing that we have concentrated on calculating the value of a call option. Well, what about put options – surely, they are equally important?

Figure 13.6

The four basic option strategies

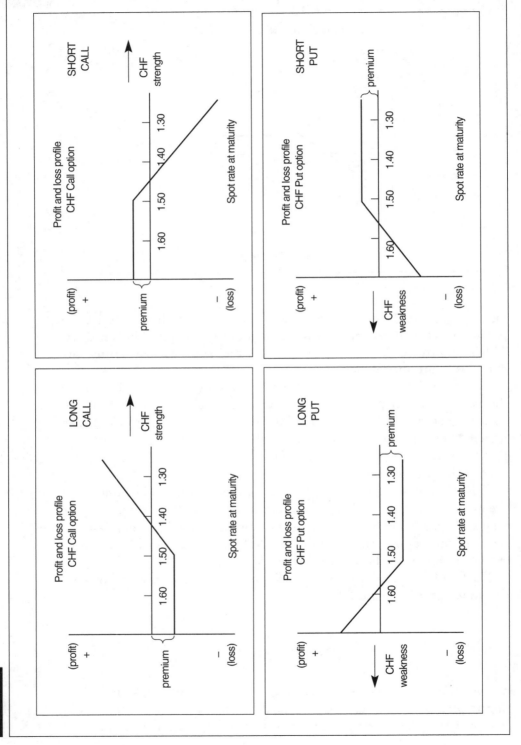

Luckily the price of a call option and the price of a put option are linked through a relationship known as the put–call parity theorem.

Imagine you had to transact the following deals simultaneously:

- sell a call option, with strike ATM and expiry three months;
- buy a put option, with strike ATM and expiry three months;
- buy the underlying asset;
- borrow money to fund the purchase of the asset for three months.

Outcome

In three months' time the borrowing will need to be repaid. The call option will either be in the money (ITM), at the money (ATM), or out of the money (OTM) at expiry:

1. If the call option is in the money at expiry it will be exercised against the seller, who must deliver the asset at the agreed strike price, and this will repay the borrowing. The put will expire worthless. Net cash flow zero.

2. If the call option is out of the money at expiry, the put can be exercised, giving the buyer the right to sell the underlying at the agreed strike price, and this can then repay the borrowing. Net cash flow zero.

3. If the call option is exactly at the money at expiry, both options are worthless, and the underlying asset can be sold at the market price, and can repay the original borrowing.

Put–call parity

Figure 13.7

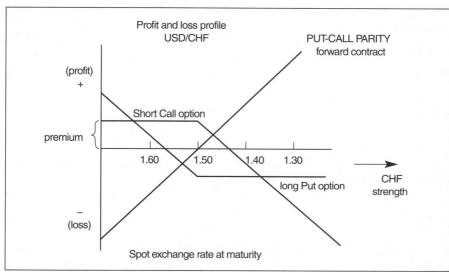

This set of transactions will always produce a zero cash flow, and allows for pricing a put option from the price of a call option. For those readers who prefer to think in diagrammatic form, Figure 13.7 describes the profit and loss profile of an unhedged forward contract. It superimposes the profiles of a European-style long put option and European-style short call option upon the forward purchase of the CHF. Creating forward positions through the simultaneous purchase and sale of options gives rise to synthetic forward positions.

OPTION GREEKS

When a traditional option reaches maturity its value is determined solely by the price of the underlying asset and the strike price of the option, in effect its intrinsic value. But prior to maturity the value of the option will depend upon a number of factors:

- strike price
- underlying price
- maturity
- expected currency volatility
- interest rates.

The option pricing model needs the above inputs in order to calculate the option premium. Only the strike price will remain fixed; all the other variables will change with the market or with the passage of time. Each variable changes the option premium in a distinct way. The manner of the change in movement is described by the 'option Greeks'. They define how the single variable changes while the others remain the same. The most important option Greeks are:

- delta
- gamma
- theta
- vega
- phi/rho.

Those of you with a classical education may recognize that vega is not a Greek letter. It probably came from *Star Trek*!

Delta

The definition of delta is 'The change in the option premium for a unit change in the underlying exchange rate'. This is an important measure as it shows how the price of the option will change as the underlying market moves. The value of delta can range from zero to one. An option which is deeply out of the money (OTM), with no chance of profitable exercise, will have a delta of 0.00. An option which is deeply in the money (ITM) will behave like the underlying cash market because there is a 100% certainty that the option will be exercised – in this case the delta will be 1.00. An option which is at the money (ATM) will have a delta of 0.5. The deltas of ITM options increase as expiry nears and exercise becomes more certain. Deltas of OTM options decrease as expiry nears and the option looks like being abandoned. There are two interpretations of delta: firstly, that delta describes the slope of the premium/underlying asset curve: and, secondly, that delta is the hedge ratio. Using delta as a hedge ratio means that the delta on a particular option can meaningfully help hedge the position.

Consider a trader who has bought an ATM CHF call, USD put option in CHF 10 million, with one month to expiry. As the underlying spot rate moves so the option will become worth more or less, it will not stay ATM. If the option goes into the money the trader will exercise the option, and the writing bank must have the CHF 10 million ready for them. If the option at expiry is OTM the trader will not exercise the option and the writing bank needs to hold zero CHF.

On the day of purchase when the option is ATM the chance of profitable exercise is deemed to be in the region of 50%, i.e. there is an equal chance that the currency could strengthen or weaken and the delta is 0.5. The option writer therefore needs to hold 50% of the underlying CHF ready for the buyer, should they require it at expiry. The option writer will buy in 50% of CHF 10 million. A week later the spot market has moved in the option's favour and the delta on the position is now 60% or 0.6; the option writer needs to buy in another 10% of cover. The next day the market moves back to 55% or 0.55, the option writer needs to sell 5% of the cover, and so on. Every time the position is re-hedged the trader will pay away the bid–offer spread, and will incur a loss.

This procedure is known as delta hedging: it is time consuming and costly. If the position is delta neutral, or delta hedged, the spot component has been locked in, at that point. Option portfolios that are not exposed to small movements in the underlying exchange rate are said to be delta hedged or delta neutral (see Figure 13.8).

Gamma

This is the only option Greek that does not measure the sensitivity of the option premium. Instead gamma measures how the option's delta changes when the underlying asset moves. The definition of gamma is 'The rate of change of delta for a unit change in the underlying exchange rate'. The more

Figure 13.8

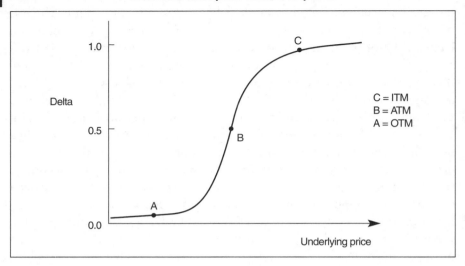

Delta of a call option at various points

C = ITM
B = ATM
A = OTM

frequently an option portfolio needs to be re-hedged the higher will be the gamma, for a given movement in the underlying asset. It reflects how much and how fast the hedge ratio changes. Options with a small gamma are relatively easy to hedge, because the hedge ratio will not change much as the spot rate moves. Options with a high gamma such as short dated ATM options can be treacherous to manage and very costly.

Imagine the last day of an option's maturity; it is still ATM, a very small move in the underlying spot rate, say +0.0005, may swing the option ITM. In that case the option writer needs to have 100% of the underlying ready for the option holder not if, but *when*, they exercise. Twenty minutes later the spot rate has moved back – 0.0007, the option is now OTM. The option writer now needs to hold 0% cover. Every time the market moves, even in very small amounts, the delta may swing from zero to one; with nothing in between, this is the classic high gamma position (see Figure 13.9).

Theta

The definition of theta is 'The change in the option premium for a given change in the period to expiry (usually the passage of a day)'.

The time value component of the option expresses the risk premium in the option and is a function of several variables:

- the relationship between the strike rate and the spot rate;
- the time to maturity;
- the interest rate differential between the two currencies;
- the volatility of the currency pair.

Gamma of a call option

Figure 13.9

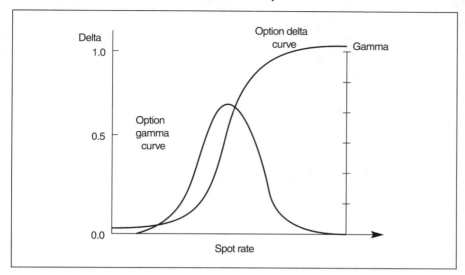

To the option writer this risk premium is highest when the option is at the money, because at this point there is the greatest uncertainty over whether the option will expire worthless or have some value at maturity.

If the option moves into the money, the writer can be more sure the option will be exercised, if it moves out of the money the opposite applies. The more deeply in or out of the money the option moves the greater the confidence of the option writer in the final outcome: will it or won't it be exercised?

In simple terms the longer the time to expiry the more an option is worth. As time passes, the option writer can define the risk more accurately, and in the last few days before expiry the time value diminishes rapidly. The time value of an option decays as expiry approaches.

Long-dated options have more time value than short-dated options; as an option ages, so its time value will decay. Theta describes exactly how much time value is lost from day to day, and is a precise measure of time decay. At inception an option will have 100% of its time value. Consider a 90-day ATM option. How much time value has been lost after one day? Answer: one-ninetieth. The next day the option loses one-eighty-ninth, and so on. So in the early part of an option's maturity it retains most of its time value. Time decay is almost constant for the first two thirds of the option's life, and 70% through the life of an option it still retains around half of its original value. The decay increases in the last third, and in the last week it loses progressively one-seventh, then one-sixth, then one-fifth, etc. of the time value that is left. Theta is highest in ATM options close to expiry. Time decay is highest with ATM options and is shown in Figure 13.10.

Figure 13.10

Graph of time value decay

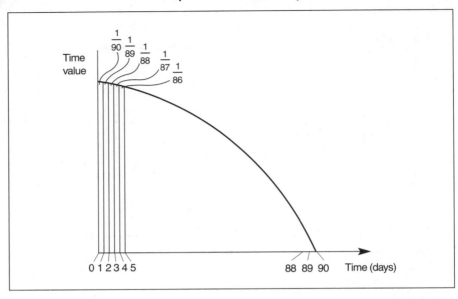

Vega

The definition of vega is 'The change in the option premium for a 1% change in volatility'. This is a straight-line relationship. As volatility increases so does uncertainty and so does the premium. An option with a high volatility gives the holder a greater chance of more profitable exercise than an option with low volatility (see Figure 13.11).

Figure 13.11

Volatility of an ATM call option

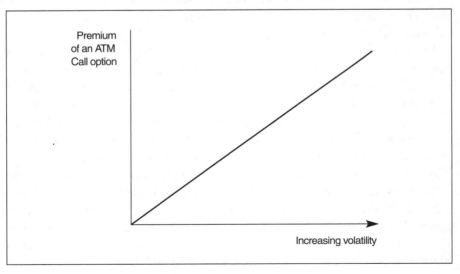

Phi/rho

This is one of the lesser-used sensitivity ratios, but for completeness I will define it here. Phi is the change in premium for a unit change in interest rates. In the case of a USD/CHF option, phi is the change in premium for a unit change in the US dollar interest rate (the base currency). Rho is the change in the CHF interest rate (the 'foreign' or 'quoted' currency). In effect the sensitivity of the option to a change in the 'cost of carry'.

COMBINING OPTIONS TO CREATE MORE COMPLEX STRATEGIES

Trading volatility

Options are the only product, derivative or otherwise, where volatility is an input. We have discussed volatility at some length, and we have looked at how a hedger and a trader may use options, either to risk manage a currency position or to speculate on the direction of a currency. It is also possible to trade or speculate on volatility. This does not mean we are trying to forecast the direction on an exchange rate; rather, we are trying to forecast a 'slow-down' or a 'speed up', or an increase or decrease in uncertainty. Mostly it is banks who trade volatility, corporates would need very clear mandates from their board of directors to allow them to trade in this way.

Volatility strategies

The long straddle

A trader takes the view that volatility will increase; it often does at the begin-ning of a new financial year when everyone is back in the market 'bright eyed and bushy tailed'. The direction of the market is unknown, but they feel definitely that it will move. If they thought the currency would strengthen they would buy a call option, if they thought the currency were going to weaken they would buy a put option. In fact, they will buy both the call option and the put option. This will entail paying two premiums. But if the market moves far enough, one of the options will be heavily in the money (ITM), and when it is sold back it will more than cover the cost of the two original option premiums, and allow for some profit (see Figure 13.12).

If the market strengthens the call option goes ITM. If the market weakens the put option goes ITM. Whichever option goes in the money you sell it back, hoping that the profit on the one option will cover the cost of the two

Figure 13.12

The long straddle

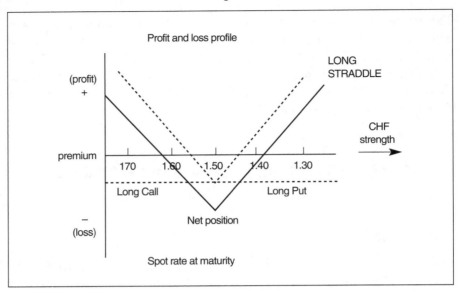

premiums. As long as the market moves you make profits with this strategy. You will make most money if there is a big swing in one direction quickly – then when you sell the option back you can recover some time value. You will lose most money – both your premiums – if the market does not move at all.

The short straddle

It is early December. In the run up to Christmas and New Year many banks' trading operations tend to calm down, staff go on holiday, and it is rare for big trading positions to be put on at this time. If a speculative position goes wrong, it may be hard to trade out of as liquidity will be lower. A bad position may even affect the dealer's bonus, which he or she has hopefully earned, and which is mostly paid annually, based on profits up to 31 December; the last thing he or she wants to do is something risky that may lose money. Bearing this in mind you would expect volatility to decrease: fewer players in the market, smaller positions. But should you sell the call or a put? Your view on volatility will not give you a guide as to the direction of the currency. The answer is that you sell both the call and the put, ATM, receiving two option premiums (see Figure 13.13).

This is a high risk strategy. In this example you have taken in two expensive premiums, but if the view on the market is wrong and volatility increases not decreases, there is a possibility of serious loss. In effect you will have sold options at, say, a volatility of 9% and may have to buy them back to close out the positions at 12%, making a loss. You will make most profit

The short straddle

Figure 13.13

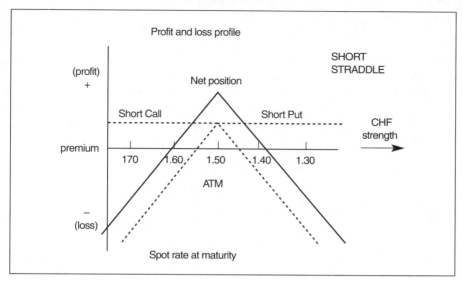

Profit and loss profile

SHORT STRADDLE

(profit) +

Net position

Short Call   Short Put

CHF strength

premium

170   1.60   1.50   1.40   1.30

ATM

−

(loss)

Spot rate at maturity

if the volatility decreases or remains the same, and you will lose if the market exchange rate moves by even a small amount in either direction. The amount of the loss will be realized only at expiry or sell back – potentially it could be very big indeed; it will be limited only by how far the market moves (in either direction).

AVAILABILITY

The OTC currency option is very liquid and most commercial banks will have an option service that they offer to clients. The large international banks will offer a service in many currencies, whilst some smaller banks will concentrate on niche markets. The minimum transaction size for a currency option will vary from bank to bank, but is likely to be in the region of USD 250,000 or equivalent. To be assured of a competitive price the size of the transaction will ideally be in excess of USD 1,000,000.

Exotic options: the way to transparency

Yuval Levy, SuperDerivatives

INTRODUCTION

An exotic option can simply be described as one that is non-standard, or in other words an option that is not vanilla. Exotic options, as is indicated by the name, are more complex than vanillas. For vanillas, the payout depends only where the price of the underlying instrument stands at expiry. Exotic options possess additional features resulting in a payout profile that depends on additional factors, such as the path of the underlying until the expiry date. The feature that most often distinguishes exotic options normally involves a barrier or some type of averaging procedure.

As a separate class of product, exotics probably account for less than 20% of the notional amount traded. However, this statistic should be treated with caution, as exotics have a far greater impact than the figure suggests and account for a much larger proportion of the risk in the market. Consequently, exotics can have a significant impact on both the vanilla option and the underlying spot markets. There are several reasons for this, including the fact that exotics can facilitate leveraging.

Quantitive analysts (quants), academics and financial marketers have been pushing the boundaries of standard options pricing for many years. This has resulted in a huge array of products. However, many of these are dependent on beautiful mathematical works which are simply too theoretical in nature. Many have been left to gather dust, locked away in an Excel spreadsheet and never used in practice.

Over the last decade, a number of exotic products have emerged to become accepted as a mainstream part of the FX options business. The creation of exotic products that are actually used has proved not just a matter of tweaking a model, putting a name to it and hoping that someone will buy it. Just like anything, from cars to chocolate bars, the best products tend to be those that are actually required or wanted and which perform a useful role.

BLACK–SCHOLES AND ITS LIMITATIONS

As a product, options first became widely used after the publication of the Black–Scholes model in 1973 for vanilla options. This significantly introduced transparency and it became the benchmark method of pricing all options. Despite the model's limitations, and there are many, it has remained at the core of most option pricing systems and it is often used to price exotic options as well.

At the heart of Black–Scholes is the assumption that the underlying product adopts a random walk movement, known as Brownian motion. However, Brownian motion is characterized by a constant level of fluctuation (volatility). This prevents the model from providing a realistic pricing for the many options whose volatility changes constantly over their lifetime.

Because the Black–Scholes model ignores the factor of volatility fluctuation, it provides a distorted probability distribution for the underlying movement. The market has tried to overcome this major and fundamental problem of the model by 'adjusting' its prices. This has led to the development of the volatility smile, which acknowledges that different volatility prices exist for each option of different strike price and maturity (see Figure 14.1).

The main issue remains that users of the entire options market, but particularly for those trading and hedging through exotics, have had to address the fact that the theoretical value derived from Black–Scholes-based models often deviates substantially from the actual price that the option trades at. This poses problems. How can anyone trust an instrument that they may not be able to price correctly (Figure 14.2)? However, many practitioners

| Figure 14.1 | **Premium in basis points for smile corrected volatility over ATM volatility for EUR/USD** |

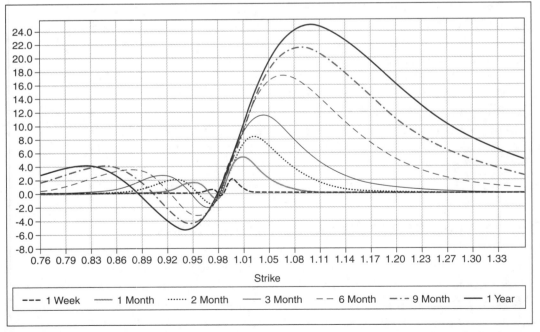

The X-axis shows the strike rate, while the Y-axis shows the basis point correction. The charts display the correction over a range of strikes and for different periods. A correction of up to 25 basis points can be seen, obtained at 14 delta call for a strike of 1.10

An example for a difference between the real market price and the calculated theoretical value (based on Black–Scholes approach) for an exotic option

Figure 14.2

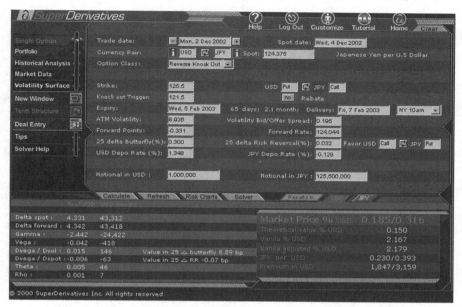

The option in this example is a USD put/JPY call reverse knock-out with strike of 125.50 and a trigger 121.50. The theoretical value is 0.15% of the USD notional; this option is actually traded in the market at a mid-price of 0.25%, around 10 basis points over the theoretical value. So, for every $10 million traded, the option will be priced incorrectly by $10,000. Clearly the impact on large portfolios could be significant

have continued to use these inadequate models based on the Black–Scholes approach, since its mechanism enables the generation of some simulation processes, notably the Monte-Carlo method, to derive the price of almost any option.

Despite these obvious issues, exotics have proved popular. This is because they are extremely effective instruments. For corporates, they can be used to hedge more efficiently than vanillas and certainly more so than the broadsword approach of using outright forwards. Speculators and others can make use of them to achieve great leverage. In other words they can significantly increase their exposure to the market place, often more cheaply than if they used other tools.

But it remains a fact that, despite their obvious attractions, many potential users of exotics have been deterred because of the market's opacity, caused primarily by the accepted limitations of pricing. The calculations of exotic valuations have involved many financial market experts. Teams of quants, traders and salespeople have spent immeasurable time discussing, testing and analyzing how well the new models fit the practical world to try and resolve this major issue.

NEW PRODUCTS, GREATER MARGINS; MORE MATURE PRODUCTS, SLIMMER MARGINS BUT GREATER VOLUME

Typically, in the early part of the life cycle of product development, the margins available to the banks that quoted these new options have been quite large. In part, this was because the banks selling such options to their customers were taking considerable risks. They needed the extra spread to compensate for potential errors or deviation from the price provided using the Black–Scholes approach. However, as they have become more familiar with the risks associated with the new products, and as competition intensified between the banks for this customer business, prices have tightened.

Another interesting development was that many banks were comfortable to accept huge risk in the belief that their models were right and others were wrong. For a while, activity in certain classes was effectively driven by a 'battle of models', also known as model arbitrage.

While this led to a short-term increase in turnover, in the long term it could never have been good for the market. In reality, would end users accept a product that could have a very different value, depending on who was asked for a price? The answer is obviously negative and for the market to mature, it has sought to introduce greater transparency.

The turning point in exotic options pricing was when they started to trade through interbank dealers. All market makers could compare their prices. Over a period of four to five years, the market makers gained more experience in the risk of managing exotic options. At the same time, the market started to reach some consensus of the prices of exotic options, as well as on how much the theoretical value derived from Black–Scholes-based models should be corrected. Obtaining this correction was often no more than the gut feeling of experienced traders.

Clearly, the mathematical side of pricing exotic options accurately is extremely complex. Interestingly, and as mentioned above, the market itself evolved to produce the most accurate estimate of where the price should be for these exotic products. This is a feature of financial markets; they find equilibrium points on their own, regardless of which tools individual institutions use.

Throughout this period, several institutions have tried to develop models to price exotic options accurately by making adjustments to the Black–Scholes model. Usually, this approach entails trying to adjust the probability behaviour of the underlying. The main problem has been that reaching a universally accurate model has been an extremely difficult task.

TOWARDS TRANSPARENCY

The most successful models to evolve are those, such as SuperDerivatives', which have been built around the way the market behaves and not merely by adjusting the probability function of the underlying. The combination of practical and theoretical experience has led to the creation of systems that should be able to produce the market price for all options.

By providing models over the internet, SuperDerivatives has been able to provide everybody with the ability to price exotic options as accurately as the most experienced traders. The models even generate bid–offer prices, indicating the fair spread for each option. Until the recent advent of such readily available systems, there is little doubt that the exotic options market has been held back because of a lack of transparency.

SuperDerivatives is not the only company to make its models available over the web. A few banks have also made use of internet technology to provide their customers with a version of their proprietary pricing systems. This, of course, helps to increase transparency, but it still excludes many end users as banks typically only provide access to their clients.

Another potential problem is that banks' prices are not neutral. If neutral price providers are squeezed out, it could lead to the exotics market becoming overly concentrated. It also raises the issue of whether it is right for users to be totally reliant on just one or two institutions for their pricing, and just as importantly, for their revaluation needs.

The introduction of transparency by a neutral and independent system means that margins should tighten, while liquidity increases. Being able to access easily the all-important market price for over 70 different classes of options on just a single platform, rather than from numerous ad hoc spreadsheets from numerous different banks will open up the world of exotics to a far wider user base. The belief is that the loss of margin should be compensated for by the increase in volume.

Ultimately, what is important to remember is that although the pricing of exotics is undoubtedly complex, most practitioners do not need to question how exactly the models have been derived. This is the same as the fact that people do not need to know how a car works to be able to drive one. As long as there is confidence that the models are accurate, then the important issue is to understand how the products can be applied to real hedging problems, or how they can be utilized efficiently for trading and risk management.

There are numerous types of exotic options but activity has tended to concentrate on just a few classes of options. Below is a description of the most popular exotics being used at the moment.

OPTIONS WITH BARRIERS

Barrier options are the largest and most popular group of exotic options that have wide practical application. They are also known as path dependent options because the payout at expiry is dependent not only on the underlying (spot) rate at expiry but also on where the rate has travelled during the option's life.

The principle is simple. The underlying option or a payment becomes activated (knocked in) or deactivated (knocked out) if at some time during the life of the option the price of the underlying hits the barrier, also known as a trigger. The barrier is determined at the time of the initial exotic option trade. If, for example a USD/JPY option has a barrier at the rate of 123.50, the barrier is hit when the spot price trades at this level.

In liquid markets, such as those of the major currencies, this will usually mean that the spot rate has been hit on one of the electronic trading platforms, such as EBS. In illiquid currencies, such as some cross and emerging markets' currencies, then it is usual that the two counterparties will have to agree the point of reference. This may entail checking prices with an inter-dealer broker or calling several banks.

This class of exotics are known by several names, including barrier options, knock-out (in) options, down-and-out (in) when the barrier is below the current spot rate, and up-and-out (in) options when the barrier is above the current spot.

Barriers can be triggered in a number of ways:

1. **American-style barrier** – this barrier is active during the whole life of the option. As a result the option can be knocked in or knocked out at any time from inception to maturity. These are the most common type of barrier options.

2. **European-style barrier** – this barrier is only effective at expiry. The criteria is that spot at expiration is above or below the trigger.

3. **Partial or window barrier** – this is an American-style barrier only effective during a particular time window during the option's life. This may be at the beginning, middle or end of the option's life.

Regular barrier options

Regular barrier options, known also as simple or normal barrier options, are similar to vanilla options; there is an expiry and a strike price, but they also have an American-style barrier known as an out-strike or in-strike. For a knock-out option, if the price of the underlying asset hits the barrier, the option is extinguished. If the barrier has not been hit by expiration the option will have the same payout as that of a vanilla European option. The barrier must be below spot for a call option, also known as a down-and-out call. For a put option, also known as an up-and-out put, the barrier must be above spot.

The main characteristic of regular barrier options is that when the underlying approaches the trigger the corresponding vanilla option is losing value and if the barrier is not touched the payout is unlimited.

There are two types of regular knock-out options. The first is a normal knock out or out-of-the-money knock out. In this case the strike will be above spot for a call option and below for a put option. This means that when the barrier is reached, the underlying European option has no intrinsic value and a relatively low price.

The second is an in-the-money knock out that will have a strike below the barrier (which is below the spot) for a call option and above the barrier for a put option. This means that when the barrier is reached the corresponding European vanilla option has intrinsic value and a relatively high price. This is still classed as a regular knock out because the corresponding European option is losing value when approaching the knocked-out trigger. These should not be confused with the reverse knock out, where the option is knocked out as it is moving in the money or gaining value.

For a knock-in option, a vanilla European option becomes activated if the underlying asset price hits the barrier. The payout then becomes identical to that of a vanilla European option. If the barrier has not been hit by expiration then the option will not be activated. For a call option, or down-and-in call, the barrier must be below spot. For a put option, or up-and-in put, the barrier must be above spot. This means that the option becomes activated as the corresponding vanilla option is moving out of the money. Notice that a combination of a knock-in and a knock-out option with the same strike and barrier forms a vanilla option.

As in the case of knock-out options, there are two types of regular knock-in option. The first is a normal knock-in or out-of-the-money knock-in option. In this case the strike will be above the spot for a call and below the spot for a put.

In this case, the underlying European option has no intrinsic value and a relatively low price when the barrier is reached. The second is an in-the-money knock in that will have a strike below the barrier for a call option and above the barrier for a put option. This means that when the barrier is reached the corresponding European vanilla option is in the money.

Example 1

A US exporter receives euros and needs to sell these to buy US dollars. They buy a euro put, dollar call option with a strike price the same as the forward rate and with a knock out at 0.9900.

Currency:	EUR/USD
Spot:	0.9750
Outright Fwd:	0.9687
Strike:	0.9687
Type:	Euro put/USD call
Knock-out trigger:	0.9900
Expiry:	Six months
Price:	1.28%
Price of equivalent vanilla option:	2.5%

The exporter has the advantage of being protected at the forward rate providing the barrier of 0.9900 is not hit. At expiry, as long as the spot rate has not reached 0.9900, they will have a vanilla option but will have paid considerably less premium for it. If the barrier is hit at some point during the option's life they can take advantage of the underlying rate moving in their favour either to lock in a forward deal at the improved rate or to buy another option, again at an improved rate.

The main benefit of buying this type of option is the reduced cost. In addition it provides the flexibility to improve the rate at which the underlying deal is executed.

Reverse-barrier options

Reverse-barrier options are those with an American-style barrier, which is in effect when the corresponding vanilla option is in the money (has intrinsic value) and at the same time the corresponding vanilla option becomes more expensive as spot approaches the barrier. These include the reverse knock out and reverse knock in.

Reverse knock out

A reverse knock out differs from a vanilla by the addition of a knock-out barrier. If the underlying asset price hits the barrier, the option is extinguished. If the barrier has not been hit by expiration then the payout is the same as that of a vanilla European option. The maximum payout though is limited by the barrier, whereas a regular vanilla European option has unlimited potential payout.

For a call option, or an up-and-out call, the barrier will be above the spot and strike rate; the strike can be anywhere under the barrier. For a put option, or down-and-out put, the barrier will be below the spot and strike rate.

		Example 2
Currency:	USD/JPY	
Spot:	123.00	
Strike:	120.00	
Knock in trigger:	125.00	
Expiry:	Three months	
Price:	0.2%	
Price of equivalent vanilla option:	3.06%	

The buyer of this option has the advantage of paying considerably less premium than for the equivalent vanilla option. But for this reduced premium, they have to accept the considerable risk that the option will be knocked out and have no value at all.

Figures 14.3(a) and (b) compare the change in value of the option across a number of time spectrums. The potential value of the vanilla option is unlimited. The potential payout of the reverse knock out is limited by the barrier at 125 to only 5 yen per $1 notional.

Charts of the theoretical value (in % of USD notional) for reverse knock-out **Figure 14.3a**

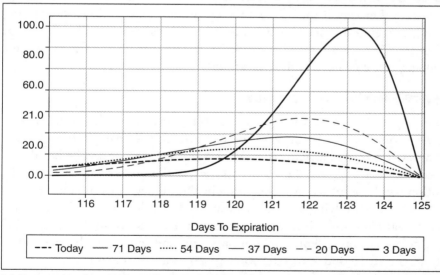

(a) Reverse knock out option strike 120.00 USD call/JPY put with trigger at 125.00 and expiration of three months. As the spot goes up, the price of the option initially goes up, but as it get closer to the trigger it goes down to zero. The maximum payout is therefore limited by the barrier. For example, at a spot of 121.00 theoretical value is 0.2%. For this spot, the probability to touch the trigger (using Black–Scholes method) is 46%.

Figure 14.13b **Vanilla options for spot in the range 115–125, charted for various times from now until option expiration**

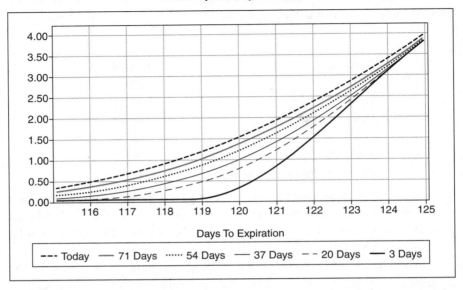

Days To Expiration

- - - Today —— 71 Days ······ 54 Days —— 37 Days – – 20 Days —— 3 Days

(b) Vanilla option with same strike and expiration as the option in (a). As seen from the chart the option has unlimited potential payout. For this option, the theoretical value at a spot of 121.00 is 2.0%.

These options are most likely to be used by speculators who can take advantage of the leverage that can be gained. For a relatively small initial premium they can, if they choose the optimum moment to sell the option, multiply their initial stake many times. Professional traders will use this type of option because of the characteristics it has, which may fit the specific hedging risk they have in their portfolio.

Reverse knock in and forward extra

Similarly to the reverse knock out, there is the reverse knock-in option. This differs from a vanilla by the addition of an in-strike or barrier. If the underlying asset hits the barrier this activates a European option. The key difference between a regular knock in and an in-the-money knock in is that option will be activated as it is moving in-the-money or gaining value.

Once the underlying option has been activated, the payout will be identical to that of a vanilla European option. If the barrier is not hit, the option will not be activated. For a call option, or up-and-in call, the barrier will be above the strike and spot rate; for a put option, or down-and-in put, the barrier will be below the strike and spot rate. Notice that a combination of reverse knock in and reverse knock out with the same strike and barrier is a vanilla option.

Many hedgers like to sell reverse knock-in options in order to finance buying vanillas they need for hedging. The most common application of the reverse knock in is in combination with a vanilla option with the same strike and is known as a forward extra (or forward plus).

Example 3

A UK exporter will receive US dollars in six months' time and will need to sell them to buy sterling.

They could enter a forward contract at a rate of 1.5304 but instead they enter a forward extra where they buy a vanilla sterling call/dollar put option with a strike of 1.5330; at the same time they sell a sterling put/dollar call, with a strike of 1.5330 and a reverse knock in at 1.4933, both expiring in six months. There is no premium to pay, so it is a zero cost strategy (see Figure 14.4).

The 1.5530 sterling put/dollar call option will knock in only if the spot rate hits the 1.4933 barrier at some point during the life of the option. The possible outcomes at expiry will be:

1. If the GBP/USD rate remains above the barrier and above the strike of 1.5330, they will exercise the option and buy GBP at 1.5330.

2. If GBP/USD rate remains above the barrier but below the 1.5330, they will buy their GBP/USD in the spot market at the prevailing rate.

Theoretical value (in % of GBP notional) for the forward extra option described in the text

Figure 14.4

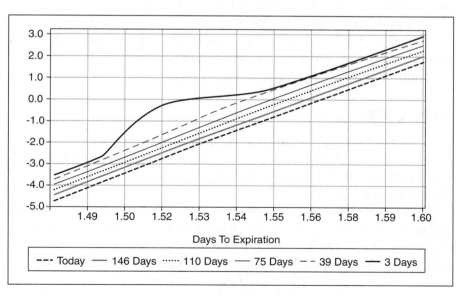

The X-axis represents the GBP/USD spot rate and the Y-axis is the cost of the structure. At the current spot rate of 1.551 the total value of this structure is zero.

3. If the GBP/USD rate has hit the barrier of 1.4933 at any point during the life of the option, they will buy GBP at 1.5330 through their obligation to the option they have sold.

Their worst case is that they buy their sterling at a rate slightly worse than they would have done had they entered a forward contract (1.5330 instead of 1.5304).

Their best case is that they benefit from sterling being below 1.5330 but above 1.4933 at expiry.

For corporations, this is a conservative way of potentially gaining from a hedging transaction and is very close in structure to a forward deal, something which nearly all end users are totally comfortable with.

Double barriers

The double barrier is an option that differs from a vanilla by the addition of two triggers; one is above and one is below the initial spot rate. One will be an in-the-money barrier and one will be an out-of-the-money barrier. If the underlying asset price hits either of the barriers, the option will be extinguished (or activated).

If neither of the barriers has been hit by expiration then the payout will be, in the case of a double knock out, the same as that of an equivalent European option. In the case of a double knock in, the vanilla option will be activated only if one of the barriers has been hit before expiry.

The users of double-barrier options are most often speculators or investors whose view is that the asset price (spot rate) will remain within a range for a chosen time period. These types of option are best executed when volatility is considered too high and expected to go lower.

Binary options

Binary options are also barriers, but the payout is either zero or a predetermined fixed amount. For the buyer of the binary, breaching the barrier activates or extinguishes a fixed payout. The payout can be in either currency of the chosen currency pair.

The amount of the payout is not dependent on how far in-the-money the option moves. If hitting the barrier activates a payout, this will be made at expiration. The barrier is in effect during the whole life of the option and as such is an American-style barrier. These options are also known as American-style digitals or all-or-nothing options.

Binary options are one of the most widely used exotic options in foreign exchange. They are popular with speculators and investors as hedges for other assets dependent on foreign exchange rates. They have also been packaged with vanillas and with other barrier and binary options to create structures with names such as cascade options, step premium options and many others. In addition they can be packaged with knock-out options so that when the trigger is hit the buyer receives the premium back (known as rebate). Their main use is by option traders as part of their portfolio management and to hedge the risks of other exotic options such as reverse knock outs.

There are four basic types of binary option.

1. One touch. The buyer of a one touch option will pay an up front premium and receive a fixed payout at expiration if the one touch trigger is hit at any time before expiration. If the one touch trigger is not hit before expiration there will be no payout.

Example 4

A US corporation predicts it will lose a sales contract of USD 1 million once the USD/JPY rate moves below 115.00 during the next three months. It does not need to sell dollars and buy yen, but needs compensation for the potential loss of revenue. It buys a three-month one touch with a trigger of 115.00 to give a payout of USD 1 million. The option costs 14% of the nominal amount, or USD 140,000. If at any time during the three months the USD/JPY rate reaches 115.00, the payout of USD 1 million will be triggered. This will then be paid at expiry.

---

2. No touch. This is similar to a one touch but the buyer receives the payout if the barrier is not touched.

3. Double no touch. This has two triggers and is also known as a range binary. A fixed payout will be made if the spot remains within the set range during the life of the option. The buyer of the double no touch will pay an up front premium and receive a fixed payout at expiration if neither of the triggers has been hit by expiration. If either of the two triggers is hit at any time before expiration there will be no payout.

Example 5

A brokerage firm generates revenue from its FX business. When markets are volatile, it typically generates higher revenues. It is forecasting that if EUR/USD will remain in a range there will be less activity by its customers and wants to protect against the potential loss of revenue.

It buys a EUR/USD 0.9700/1.0200 double no touch for two months with a payout of USD 2 million. The option costs 24%, or USD 480,000. Provided the spot rate does not hit either of the barriers during the two-month period, the brokerage will receive the USD 2 million payout.

Figure 14.5 **Change of the theoretical value (in % of EUR payout) for a double no touch option over time and with spot**

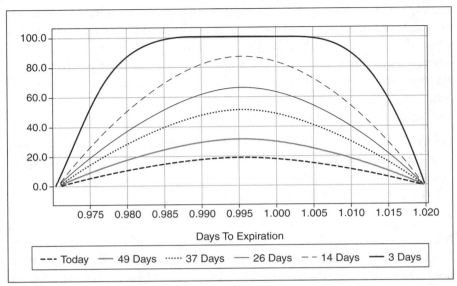

Days To Expiration

--- Today   — 49 Days   ⋯⋯ 37 Days   — 26 Days   – – 14 Days   — 3 Days

The option in this example is EUR/USD double no touch with triggers at 0.9700 and 1.0200, expiring in two months. At a spot of 0.9950, the theoretical value is 17%. However, the corrected market value at this spot would be 24%. The value is increasing with time as the probability to hit the triggers in the remaining time until expiration is going down. Similarly, as the spot gets closer to any of the triggers the value of the option drops to zero with the increasing probability of hitting it

Figure 14.5 shows how the value of such an option will change over time and with spot. In contrast to the previous examples, where the option strategies have been designed to hedge a particular cash flow and are often left to run until they expire or knock out (or in), typically the users of binary options are more likely to actively manage them. This means they will continuously be assessing the risk/reward of the option and will consider closing the position before expiry. This also contributes to the liquidity in these products.

4. Double one touch. This is similar to the double no touch but the buyer receives the payout if either one of the barriers is touched.

European digital options

European digitals are a class of option where the payout is fixed, but in contrast to binary options where the payout is triggered if the barrier is hit at any time during the options life, the payout of a European digital is dependent on where spot is at expiration only.

There are principally two types of these options, a European digital and a European range bet. The buyer of a European digital will pay an up front premium and receive a fixed payout if, at expiration, the underlying asset price is above the strike for a call or below the strike for a put. The payout can be in either currency of the chosen currency pair.

A European range bet has two strikes and a fixed payout. The option can be structured so that the payout can be made if the underlying asset price at expiry time is inside the two-strike range at expiration or in the other option class if the underlying asset price is outside the two-strike range. In both cases the strike prices act as European-style barriers that activate or extinguish the payout at expiration only. The payout can be in either currency of the chosen currency pair.

Partial/window barriers

Many of the barrier-style options described above are now also available where the chosen barrier/barriers is/are only in effect during a particular time window during the option's life. This means that hedgers, risk managers and speculators can tailor the risk profile of the option even more precisely. Figure 14.6 shows the value of a partial barrier knock-out option with same strike, trigger where appropriate and expiration of the reverse knock out (RKO) and vanilla options shown in Figures 14.3(a) and 14.3(b). Notice the very different profile of the option's value.

Example 6

A corporation needs to hedge with a euro call USD put (see Example 1). It buys a euro put for six months, strike 0.9687 with a knock-out trigger at 0.9900. However, it is worried that during the last two months of the option the market may be jittery because of elections in Germany.

So it buys a partial barrier option where the trigger is in effect only during the first four months. If the 0.9900 trigger has not been touched during this period, the option will become a regular vanilla option for the last two months of its life. This provides the corporation with added security at only a marginally higher cost (1.53% instead of 1.28%).

Average options

Average options were one of the first types of exotic option to be widely used and they are still very popular, particularly for corporations. The reason for this is that they enable those with regular cash flows to hedge them efficiently and at a lower cost than by using vanilla options.

There are a number of types of these options, with the most popular being

Figure 14.6 Theoretical value (in % of USD notional) of a partial barrier knock-out option with same strike, trigger and expiration of the reverse knock out (RKO) shown in Figure 14.3(a): strike 120.00 USD call/JPY put, trigger at 125.00 and expiration of three months

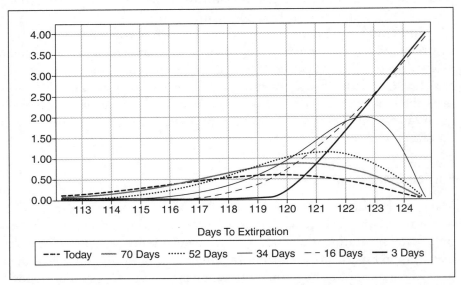

The trigger is active only during the time window of the first two months. If the trigger is not hit in the first two months, the option becomes a vanilla and the charts of the last periods have the same characteristics of the vanilla option of Figure 3(b).

For the spot of 121.00 the theoretical value is 0.5%, higher than the value of the RKO option, but still much cheaper than the vanilla

the average rate option. The key feature of the average rate option is that the payout is determined by the mean spot rate observed in different predetermined dates over the life of the option, whereas the payout of a vanilla option is determined by the underlying (spot) rate at expiration.

Example 7   A Japanese corporation expects revenue of USD 1 million at the end of every month in the next 12 months. It therefore has a requirement to buy yen and sell USD 1 million every month for a year. It could cover with a strip of outright forwards, which would give it an average rate of 121.39 fixed. Alternatively it can buy a USD 12 million dollar put/yen call average rate option with a strike price of 121.39, expiry one year, for a cost of USD 295,000.

At each month end, which will be the chosen fixing dates, the corporation will sell its dollars in the spot market. At the same time there will be a 'fixing' on its average rate option. After 12 months the corporation will have executed all the required deals to buy its yen and sell its dollars. At the same time the average rate option will be protecting it from any adverse movements.

If at expiration the average rate observed over the 12 fixings is above 121.39 then the corporation will receive nothing, as it will have dealt at rates better than the strike price. If the average rate is below 121.39 it will receive a cash settlement for the difference between the strike price and the observed average.

These options are extremely flexible: fixings can be tailored to suit the actual dates and amounts of the cash flow. They are also cheaper than hedging with a strip of vanilla options and require no management of the hedge until the end of the period.

Compound options

A compound option is one that gives the buyer the right but not the obligation to buy or sell another option at an agreed price on an agreed date. The right to buy an option is a compound call and the right to sell an option is a compound put. There are four possible variations. A call on a call, a call on a put, a put on a call and a put on a put.

The buyer of the compound chooses the option he wants to buy or sell and the premium he wants to pay. He also chooses the expiry for the compound option itself. At expiration of the compound option, the buyer can then choose to exercise his right to buy or sell the underlying option. If he chooses to exercise this he will then hold a standard vanilla European option until expiry. If he can buy the underlying option cheaper in the market he will allow the compound option to expire.

The most common application of compound options is where the need for the underlying vanilla option is contingent on an event, such as a takeover. The customer knows that if the event does take place he will need the option, so he prefers to secure the price of the option now. This also enables him to factor in the hedging costs into his tender or takeover costs. The customer will find that buying the compound provides a cheaper and more flexible hedge than by buying the underlying vanilla option and then selling it if it is not required.

Chooser

The main feature of a chooser is that the option type (put or call) is not decided until a predetermined date. On the 'choose date', the buyer of the option decides if it is going to be a put or a call at the predetermined strike rate and expiry. From the choose date the option will become a standard vanilla European until expiration. The benefit of the chooser is that it gives the buyer the same 'at expiration' benefit as buying a straddle (a put and call at the same strike price), but at a cheaper cost.

Accrual/floater

This class of option is a modified binary option where a fixed payout is made on the basis of the underlying asset price remaining above, or below a pre-agreed rate or within a pre-agreed range on some predetermined dates (fixings) during a certain time period.

Example 8

A fund manager wants to hedge against losses that will be incurred if USD/JPY trades above 124.00 over the next three months. She buys a one-sided accrual, which will payout USD 100,000 per each predetermined fixing date if USD/JPY is above 124. She chooses weekly fixings. The cost is USD 266,000. At the end of three months she will receive USD 100,000 for each fixing date where the spot rate was above 124.00. So of the 12 fixings her maximum potential payout will be USD 1,200,000. Her worst case is she gets no payouts and loses the premium.

A variation of this is the range accrual where upper and lower strikes are set.

Fader

The fader is like a vanilla option. However, the notional of the option at expiration is dependent on the rate of the spot at some predetermined fixing dates. The buyer will choose if the notional will increase or decrease as the spot is above or below the trigger, or inside/outside the range set by two triggers. At expiration the notional will be calculated based on the ratio of the number of fixings in which the condition was met over the total number of fixings.

Faders have several uses. First of all, they help in the hedging of predetermined cash flows, since the user can decide that if on a date the spot rate is above a certain level that it needs no hedge (fade out). It is obviously cheaper than buying the vanilla option for the whole amount. Faders are also good tools to speculate with as they can also pay out for partially successful bets, while at the same time its risk/reward profile is relatively cheap.

There can be four variations.

1. **Fade out one sided.** The buyer has to select fixing dates, set a trigger and determine if the notional decreases (fades out) when the fixing is above or

below the trigger. If the condition is that the notional fades out below the trigger and that there are n fixings in which spot rate is above the trigger out of the N fixings. Then the notional at expiration will be n/N times the agreed upon notional.

2. **Fade in one sided.** Here the notional will be zero unless the conditions set by the trigger (above or below) are met on at least one occasion. Then the notional at expiration will be n/N times the agreed upon notional.

3. **Fade out range.** The buyer has to select fixing dates and set a range and determine if the notional decreases (fades out) when the fixing is inside or outside the range. If the condition is that it fades out outside the range and that there are n fixings in which the spot rate is inside the range out of the total number of fixings N. Then the notional at expiration will be n/N times the agreed upon notional.

4. **Fade in range.** Here the notional will be zero unless the conditions set by the two triggers (inside or outside) are met on at least one occasion. Then the notional at expiration will be n/N times the agreed upon notional.

CONCLUSION

This chapter has provided a brief review of the development of exotic options from the invention of the Black–Scholes model to the introduction of more accurate models such as SuperDerivatives. Some of the most common types of exotic structures have been described.

The options market is now significantly more advanced than in the days when it could only offer simple strategies to hedge a rate going up or down, using simple vanilla options. In particular, it shows the enormous flexibility of the product range and how banks have responded to the exacting demands of their customers for precise hedging tools. Advances in modelling, as well as technology, have significantly opened up this area to the benefit of all option users.

Transparency is now the way ahead. Readily available systems, such as SuperDerivatives, mean that exotic options no longer need to be the preserve of just expert or experienced traders. They are now available to all options users and, in particular, to those requiring bespoke and efficient hedging.

The recent technological advances, including the internet, enable access to real time price transparency to anyone who has a computer and telephone line. A new level of openness and sophistication has been introduced to what was even only a few years ago an extremely opaque market. The benefits to anyone with currency exposure are enormous. Clearly the way is paved for increase in liquidity and hedging efficiencies.

e-Foreign exchange

Francesca Taylor, Taylor Associates

One way for banks to gain more
profitable business involved
profitable business involved
linking FX with fund management
■ ■ ■

INTRODUCTION

Many new terms are creeping into finance, for example, what exactly is meant by the term e-fx? You may well ask! Although (we are told) this is the shape of the brave new world, the advances in FX, both technologically and financially can sometimes leave one feeling adrift and perhaps believing that these new goodies are only for the very sophisticated, very large customers. Not so. The banks have developed a range of initiatives for both large and small clients and this chapter will review some of the progress to date. However, due to the size of most transactions in this market, any development will tend to be focused towards the company/bank rather than the small user.

In practice, the developments of the last ten years have mostly come about as a result of the new set of linkages between the traditional IT and FX marketplaces. You may be forgiven for feeling that the end-user is participating in a real-time case study – a challenge to the IT markets.

BACKGROUND

The first steps were taken about ten years ago when Reuters and EBS launched an interbank trading system. This was followed a little later by banks offering single bank dealing systems – allowing the client to obtain FX rates via a system rather than having to pick up a telephone. But you were still tied to that particular bank and their rates. In the late 1990s multi-bank platforms arrived, allowing a client to ask for multiple quotes across the same system, thus receiving quotations from a number of pre-set banks.

A word on the terminology before we proceed. The buy-side of the market, is generally assumed to be the user of the services which are provided by the sell-side who are the organizations providing the services. The buy-side consists of smaller banks, small and large corporations, funds, governments and even some fabulously wealthy private individuals. The sell-side are mostly the larger banks and financial organizations who create the platforms and portals through which users can access the products. In effect the sell-side are the price makers and the buy-side are the price takers.

FX markets are perhaps the most decentralized of all the capital market instruments with hundreds if not thousands of sellers and buyers spread across the globe. Although volumes in FX have declined recently, when you compare the size of the market in the mid-1980s and then compare it to

Figure 15.1

FX sector growth

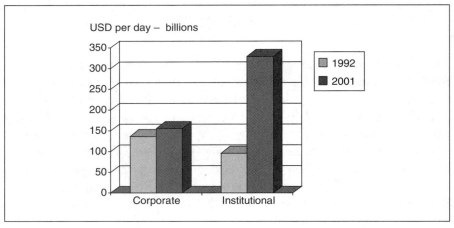

USD per day – billions

Source: BIS

now, it has shown phenomenal growth. However, this growth has not been uniform across all sectors of the market (see Figure 15.1):

- Corporate FX – USD 137 bn *per day* in 1992 increased to USD 156 bn in 2001.

- Institutional FX – USD 96 bn *per day* in 1992 increased to USD 329 bn in 2001.

The rapid expansion in institutional FX stems from investment growth and cross-border diversification coupled with funds taking a dynamic view to hedging and trading their portfolios.

FOUNDATION

The Reuters/EBS platform became the backbone of the whole industry. The interbank FX market all but disappeared as bank traders seemed to prefer dealing on machines, rather than with each other. Bid–offer spreads were pared down to the bare minimum and many peripheral players in the market were driven out of business. At the same time, banks were still having to maintain high levels of administrative staff to handle the telephone/fax dealing of their corporate clients. It was therefore only a matter of time before the banks began to try and use their existing experience to effect cost savings across their non-bank clients.

One way for the banks to gain more profitable business, involved linking FX with fund management, or custody-style business. Volumes linked with the fund management industry grew whilst the equity markets surged. At the same time, as price transparency grew so profit margins came under extreme pressure as FX bid–offer spreads were cut down to an absolute minimum.

STRAIGHT-THROUGH PROCESSING

This surge in institutional buy-side clients, coupled with the squeezing of FX margins, meant that the sell-side banks had to do something. If they could reduce the amount of administration involved with these funds, thereby reducing costs then profitability would be enhanced and new client business attracted. By developing their own in-house electronic trading systems to reduce manual intervention they commenced 'Straight-through processing', known now, simply as STP.

As expectations amongst the institutional investors grew, so the buy-side became much stronger. In the bond and equity divisions of the major banks, some even spoke of 'buy-side empowerment' as players shifted a major portion of their traditional business away from the broker dealers towards the electronic computer networks (ECNs).

The FX markets until this point had been dominated by a small number of banks. The onset of the new technology meant that FX was now just a part of a much wider, more balanced market with sell-side providers needing to offer services over a multitude of asset classes, not just FX. They also needed to offer services in, equity, fixed income, derivatives, energy and credit (to name but a few). Buy-side clients needed easy access to these markets, coupled with pricing, netting, clearing, custody and risk management as well as real-time information and data feeds. But, after all this outlay, would the end-user:

(a) see the extra benefit?

(b) be asked/prepared to pay more?

SINGLE BANK PLATFORMS

Customer demands amongst the big players led to the first banking platforms. But, to some market participants this just made things more complicated. If a fund manager wanted to phone three banks, he could get rates from each one, and then deal, or not, according to the price. The first platforms, however, would only support one bank, so the fund manager would have needed three different platforms, each with their unique protocols. These three platforms would then need to be linked to the back and middle office for management and accounting functions.

Imagine the scene: the fund manager needs to decide – do I telephone three banks or do I enter my request into three different computer systems each requiring the information in a different format? Needless to say, the telephone service was chosen most of the time!

MULTIPLE BANK PLATFORMS

As you would expect, by this time a vast number of dollars, pounds, euro and yen had been gobbled up, yet the banks were still not quite delivering what the client wanted. FX customers felt that they would be better served by online dealing platforms that brought together the currency offerings of multiple banks. A few brave major FX banks decided to move forward and stick with the institutional investor market. Thus the bank-owned, multi-dealer platforms and independent dealing platforms were born.

Yet to date, only an estimated 15–25% of top tier corporate, financial and public treasury officials go online to purchase FX, according to research consultancy Greenwich Associates. Even though they enjoy a general understanding of the benefits of online trading – easy access to research and multiple prices, rapid executions, reduced administrative risk and simplified post-trade confirmation and clearing – institutional/corporate users and investors have been reluctant to take the plunge. They prefer to wait until an online platform emerges with high levels of efficiency and liquidity. The problem is that they are the ones who ultimately supply the necessary liquidity, a classic dilemma.

Ironically, the proliferation of multi-bank FX platforms may actually have complicated the problem. With many users, still smarting from the labour of linking to the many single-dealer platforms, why integrate to multi-bank systems without knowing in advance which of the multi-bank platforms would attain critical mass and prevail in an eventual industry shake-out.

Over the last year the number of multi-bank FX platforms has substantially consolidated and this should make the next step easy. For FX dealers though, the situation may not be so simple. Participation in a multi-bank platform is essential for any FX bank wanting to service the institutional investment industry. But it is no guarantee of success. In fact, multi-dealer platforms may make it more difficult for FX dealers to distinguish themselves in the marketplace. If every bank on a multi-dealer platform offers virtually identical prices – to within a basis point or two – and identical operational efficiencies, how do they distinguish themselves in the marketplace?

WHERE NEXT?

It seems apparent that it will be the value-added services offered by the banks which will make them distinctive and attractive. A range of these services, an electronic trading 'wish list', might include the following:

- Pricing, refer for quotations (RFQs), single bank, multi-bank
- Real-time streaming prices
- Custody
- Settlement, STP
- Clearing, RTGS, netting
- Fully or partially outsourced risk management
- Risk, cost and performance management
- Liquidity management
- Multi-asset classes, integrated platforms
- Real time information and data
- Research, analytics
- Trade order management systems
- Intelligent platforms
- Multi-market, multi-counterparty, multi-asset class.

Multi-bank electronic trading: a brief history and current use

Ted Sanborn, Currenex

INTRODUCTION

The traditional categories of participants in the FX marketplaces are multi-national corporations, international fund managers and government agencies in the role of customers who need to receive foreign currencies or convert foreign currencies to meet obligations. The customers initiate requests for FX price quotes from large international banks and execute (agree to) trades totalling USD 485 billion per day.[1] The banks act as market makers, ready to make prices to buy or sell FX from their customers and trade among themselves in order to redistribute currencies.

Currently, the majority of customers execute their FX trades by phone, but they are rapidly evolving their modus operandi as shown in Figure 16.1.

Due to the extensive benefits that customers can gain, electronic trading will soon replace the phone as the primary means for these trades. One market analyst, the TowerGroup forecasts that by the end of 2003, three out of four customers will be trading FX electronically.[2]

A significant percentage of customers who trade FX electronically use a multi-bank FX trading service, or more succinctly, a multi-bank e-fx service. Some participants refer to these services as portals, because they provide access to a number of banks. Others may call them platforms, products or exchanges.

Service is an apt description, because a multi-bank e-fx service provides

Percentage of customers trading FX electronically[3]　　　　**Figure 16.1**

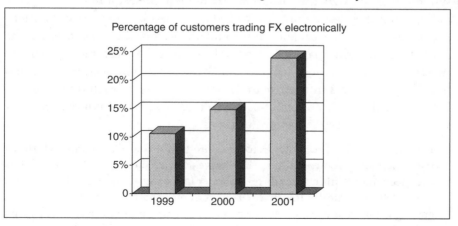

Percentage of customers trading FX electronically

---

[1] 'Central Bank Survey of Foreign Exchange and Derivatives Market Activity', Bank for International Settlements, March 2002.
[2] 'Electronic FX Systems, an Update', TowerGroup, September 2001, Bob Iati.
[3] 'Electronic Trading Shows Gains Among FX Users', Greenwich Associates 2002 Report.

more than just an electronic means by which participants can trade. The successful services also provide a network of banks with whom the customers can trade, and provides additional support such as trading related features, connectivity to other systems, and customer service personnel who pro-actively advise its members.

This chapter describes the origination of these services, focuses on the background of one multi-bank e-fx service as an example, and describes how customers use these types of services to reduce costs, add efficiencies and minimize errors in their FX trading and related activities.

EVOLUTION OF CUSTOMER DEMAND FOR MULTI-BANK eFX

Electronic trading of FX between banks (interbank trading) began in the 1980s and expanded relatively quickly so that by the end of the 1990s the majority of interbank FX trading occurred on electronic trading services.

Meanwhile, banks continued to trade with their customers via the phone, a ubiquitous tool that allows the customers to receive price quotes from any bank in the world. However, a phone-based trading process limits the number of simultaneous quotes, requires a significant amount of effort for even the most routine trades, and exposes the customers to numerous ineffi-ciencies and inaccuracies.

Customers and banks recognized the digital divide between the interbank world and the bank-to-customer world but opinions varied on how to address this gap. Some banks responded by offering proprietary trading systems that allowed the customers to request price quotes and execute online – but they could only deal with that one bank. Single-bank solutions had appeal in certain situations, but could not address the broad needs of the market because the majority of actively trading FX customers distribute their trades among a list of ten to twenty banks. The typical customer would like to request prices from three to six of those banks for each transaction to help ensure they get a fair price – a difficult task by phone in the fast-moving FX market, as the extract below illustrates.

> It's 9 a.m. ... and three Intel executives are huddled around a table cluttered with telephones and computers. The first executive shouts, 'Go!' and each hits the speed dial. Within seconds the room erupts with shouted numbers – '14!', '16!', '18!'. Frantically the first person scribbles the numbers down between getting his own quotes. When the room quiets, he points to caller No. 3, who yells 'Done!' into the receiver. Intel is now the owner of $5 million worth of Japanese yen.[4]

---

[4] 'Currency Buying comes of Age – e-company', Margaret Boitano, *Fortune Magazine*, 2 October 2000.

Even in those circumstances where customers wish to negotiate with just one bank, they would prefer a multi-bank service that allows them to choose to deal with any one of their banks through one access point. From this single point of entry they can access all of their trade records and summaries of trade activities for viewing, printing, or downloading.

Authoritative research from Greenwich Associates confirms the importance of a multi-bank service, noting that in the year 2000, 84% of customers who trade electronically or are considering trading electronically indicated a preference of multi-bank over single-bank e-fx services.[5] By 2002, that percentage had increased to 87%, as participants witnessed the success of services such as the one from Currenex.[6]

Regardless of strong demand, some sceptics believed that the customer-to-bank trading process relied on relationship-based nuances that electronic trading could not effectively replicate. Others claimed that the demand was ahead of the technology. Yet some people had a vision of a service that could add value for both customers and banks and found that the web-based technology that emerged in the 1990s created an opportunity, if properly harnessed, to create and deliver such a service in a secure and high-performing fashion to a global audience.

CURRENEX BRINGS TOGETHER THE BUY-SIDE AND THEIR BANKS

A group of investors formed Currenex in December 1999 in order to purchase Waldron Management, a company that had already delivered a multi-bank service, but needed to develop and expand the business further. These investors brought together a diverse team with experience in the FX markets, information services and technology who rebuilt the service and delivered the first web-based multi-bank e-fx service. Currenex announced its presence in the market in April 2000 as the first and only multi-bank e-fx service, as shown in Figure 16.2.

Excerpt from the *Financial Times News Digest*, 27 April 2000   **Figure 16.2**

Currenex offers forex service

Currenex, a US web service company, today launches an online foreign exchange service hosting quotes from more than 20 banks. Banks have long been able to trade currencies electronically on an interbank system but Currenex's service is intended to give companies, investment fund managers and agencies more direct access to the foreign exchange market. **Christopher Swann**

---

[5] 'Electronic Trading and Internet Use by Foreign Exchange Professionals', Greenwich Associates, 2000.
[6] 'Next Generation FX Trading, Chairman's Overview', Presentation by Peter B. D'Amario, Greenwich Associates, 12 September 2002.

The Currenex team established a highly focused mission to 'Provide the most efficient and effective Independent Exchange for foreign exchange and money market asset classes, linking institutional buyers and sellers worldwide'. Very quickly, a number of early adopters excitedly joined the service to experience these efficiencies.

One of the early adopters, Dimitry Mastrosov, Treasury Manager of Mastercard International shared his excitement in an interview with *FX Week* in August 2000. Mastrosov, who was already executing 97% of his FX business through Currenex, noted that

> ... competitive bidding for every single trade is possible only through an online system like Currenex. Additionally, automation processes made possible by the online environment have drastically reduced the number of possible errors and allowed for a closer integration of a company's business applications with the FX functions.[7]

Figure 16.3 shows a customer setting up a simultaneous request for quotes (RFQs) to multiple banks. In this example, the customer requests a spot transaction to buy USD 10 million in exchange for euros. Spot means that the parties will settle (deliver to each other) the currencies in two business days (except in the case of the Canadian dollar, which settles in one day).

There is no minimum or maximum on the amount traded, but the typical range is between the equivalent of USD 1–20 million.

The customer selects a single bank or specific banks that will receive the request, adds any other relevant details, and clicks the 'send' button to send this request to those banks.

Figure 16.4 shows the response of live (executable) price quotes from the selected banks. Executable means that the bank will honour this price if the customer selects it. These prices are only available for a short interval, typically five seconds, but could be longer depending on the type of request, and in most cases, can be updated by the quoting banks.

---

[7] 'What e-fx means to Mastercard International', *FX Week*, 14 August 2000.

Defining a request for quote

Figure 16.3

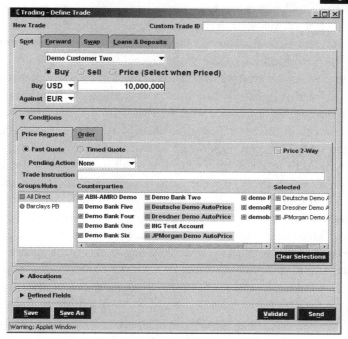

Receiving live bank quotes

Figure 16.4

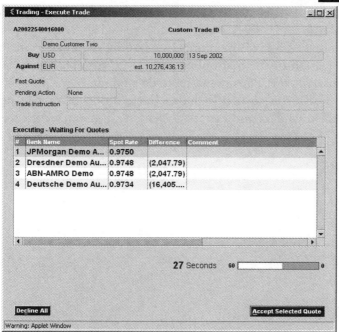

In any case, the customer can accept a price by clicking on it when it is displayed and will immediately receive a 'trade complete' message as shown in Figure 16.5. When a customer completes a trade, the service automatically creates an electronic record that is available to both parties for viewing, printing or downloading, as shown in Figure 16.6.

In addition to its trading capability, the first version of the Currenex service provided support for pre- and post-trade activities with upload and downloading of trades, stored settlement instructions and a variety of reports, such as an activity report that breaks out the number of requests and completed trades by counterparty or instrument type. Customers also have access to an audit report with a snapshot of all live quotes from the time of execution, allowing them to record and demonstrate their best practices for auditors and other parties.

Contrary to what many banks and customers had feared, the Currenex customers have found that the use of this service has actually enhanced their relationships with the banks. Since they began executing trades online the customers found that their phone time with the banks was more productive, focusing on strategies and complicated trades instead of wasting time discussing routine trades and resolving mistakes. In addition, both the banks and customers now have accurate independent records of the number of requested and completed trades to help them evaluate the value of their trading relationships.

Following its initial release, Currenex worked closely with both customers and banks such as Royal Dutch Shell and Compaq on the customer side of the market, and ABN Amro and Barclays on the bank side to identify additional needs and added many trading-related enhancements. Examples include an expansion of the number of trading methods to include orders and the creation of the first online process for negotiating the rolling of a spot to forward dates and amending trade amounts.

Other areas of expansion included the addition of market information such as real-time data and historical charts and integrated chat capabilities between counterparties.

Trade complete message

Figure 16.5

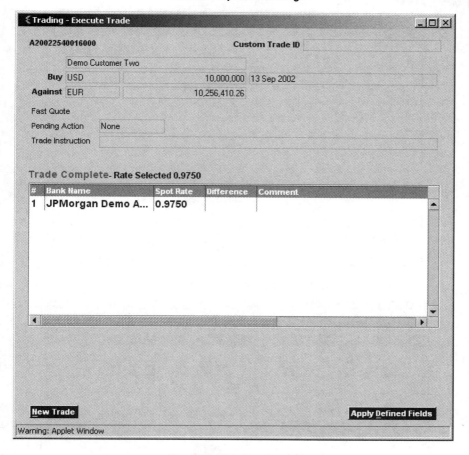

Completed trade record

Figure 16.6

Figure 16.7

Currenex main view – (a) circa 2000

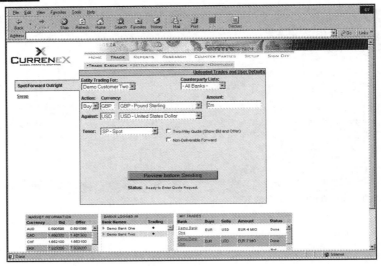

Currenex main view – (b) circa 2002

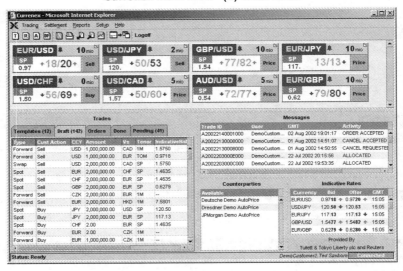

Currenex even changed the user interface of its service to allow for a more intuitive and flexible display, all built around the workflow of its members, as shown in Figure 16.7.

By the end of 2002, Currenex had hundreds of customers and over 50 of the largest FX banks as trading members on its service. By this time other entities had created similar systems in recognition of the value of multi-bank e-fx. Collectively these services contributed to an acceleration of electronic trading of FX that added value for all participants.

CUSTOMERS MEASURE UP MULTI-BANK eFX

Customers use electronic trading as an effective management tool by establishing clear objectives and evolving their processes to take advantage of all possible areas of improvement. The typical trade cycle, as shown in Figure 16.8, has many steps, each of which can be examined for inefficiencies that might be enhanced through the use of electronic trading.

Illustration of trade and settlement cycle   **Figure 16.8**

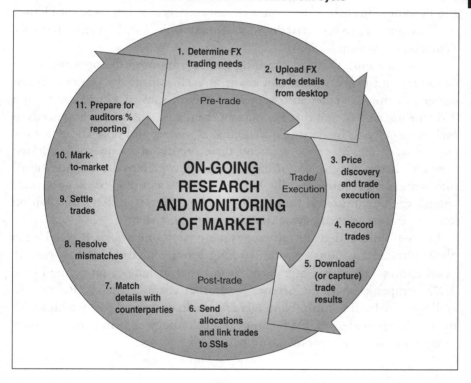

Customers measure their success within a number of areas touched by this cycle, including external trading, internal operations and back-office processing. In some situations, they measure direct savings on the FX prices received through a multi-bank e-fx service in comparison to prices received on the phone. In other situations, the cost savings are more indirect. For example, one European Corporate Treasurer reported to Currenex that by using a multi-bank e-fx Service, he has reduced headcounts for the middle office by 38%, back office by 50% and front office traders by 66%.

Back- and middle-office savings may result from the ability to eliminate the traditional confirmation and matching by phone and other systems because both parties already have a shared electronic record from an independent party and can even agree to pre-approve all standard settlement instructions.

In a 2002 survey of power users of multi-bank e-fx services, Greenwich Associates noted that 78% of its participants experienced a reduction in errors, 76% reduced their time and effort for trading and related processes and 67% of its survey participants found that its existing resources were much more likely to be adding value to the department than before.[8]

For many companies, the biggest advantage of online trading is the straight-through processing (STP) capability whereby trades can be passed from one system to another without the risk of human intervention. Joerg Raichle of the German group Henkel emphasizes that, 'We want good prices and liquidity, but just as important is connectivity'.[9] A key issue for Henkel in choosing a (e-fx) system was compatibility with their Treasury Workstation System (TWS).

The ideal connectivity to a trading service minimizes the opportunity to introduce and propagate human errors at each step in the process. A customer can upload trades into a trading service, such as Currenex, from a TWS or internal system that has already calculated specific trading needs in each currency pair by netting out various exposures and obligations. At the appropriate time, he or she can send these pre-defined requests to selected banks with the click of a button and pick the preferred rate. Additional information can automatically be sent to the winning bank and trade records can be captured automatically into both parties' systems for position keeping and transfer to payment and accounting systems.

To help ensure that all relevant systems are compatible, Royal Dutch Shell initiated an industry-wide working group called TWIST (Treasury Workstation Integration Standards Team) that includes a set of the major TWS companies, banks, Currenex, and other vendors, such as Reuters. In addition, the leading multi-bank e-fx services have formed partnerships with the leading providers of TWS and other technology to help ensure smooth integration for their customers and banks.

CONCLUSION

The four-stage process of new technology adoption described by Geoffrey Moore in *Crossing the Chasm*[10] is a useful model for studying the evolution of multi-bank e-fx services. Moore describes Phase 1 as the introduction of an innovative technology that brings new efficiencies but is met with scepti-

---

[8] 'EFX On the Rise, Findings in Greenwich Associates Report Confirms Growing Trend', Currenex 2002
[9] 'Henkel goes independent for FX', *German Corporate Finance*, July 2001.
[10] Moore, Geoffrey A., *Crossing the Chasm: Marketing and Selling High-Tech Products to Mainstream Customers*, Harpers Business Press, 1991.

Entry, exit and growth of multi-bank e-fx services

Figure 16.9

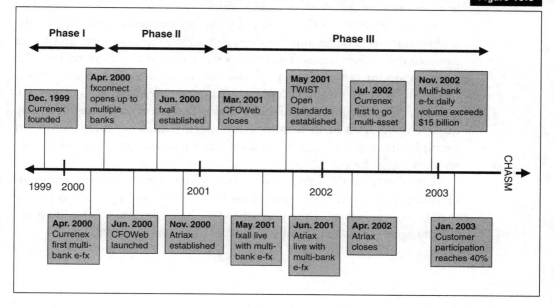

cism and Phase 2 as the 'me too' phase when other companies join the party. In Phase 3, the market leaders continue moving forward and defining new standards as the innovation builds up critical mass.

The multi-bank e-fx services quickly moved through Phases 1–3 from 1999 to 2002, as described in this chapter and as illustrated in Figure 16.9.

Initially, many customers and banks were sceptical, but soon multiple providers emerged, some on a global basis, some regionally, some focused on the top tier of the market and others on the lower tiers. Some survived, and some quickly failed: on 5 April 2002, for example, Atriax, a multi-bank e-fx service backed by a consortia of banks, announced that it would cease its business after just 17 months of operation.[11]

In the final phase of Moore's adoption model, one or more surviving players 'crosses the chasm' by expanding the market to a point where the new innovation is broadly used. This phase may occur in the years 2003–2004 for multi-bank e-fx services. The providers of these services will continue to fuel demand by enhancing connectivity to other systems, adding trading methods and expanding into related asset classes. For example, in 2002, in response to its members, Currenex expanded its service to include the Money Market Asset Class with the introduction of electronic trading of loans and deposits.

Complete access to bank liquidity on any service represents one of the key factors for reaching the final phase. Currently, some banks provide prices on

---

[11] 'Atriax to Cease Operations', Press Release, 5 April 2002.

any major service, while others only provide prices on selected services, or just services in which they have ownership.

Another key factor is the number of connectivity points provided by the multi-bank e-fx services and the degree to which the customers and banks embrace these connections. The services that can provide connectivity to the most important systems and accelerate the use of these connection points will be more likely to survive and establish market leadership. For example, many banks have connected to multi-bank e-fx services using the underlying quote engines used in their proprietary systems, allowing them to support multiple channels with one internal infrastructure and providing added liquidity to each channel.

Regardless of which service providers survive to leap the chasm, it appears inevitable that multi-bank e-fx will be the primary trading method for the majority of customers in the years ahead as the critical mass is building up, already exceeding USD 15 billion per day by the end of 2002.

Innovations in e-fx

Anneliese Widdows, Citigroup

E-COMMERCE TODAY

As internet users become increasingly sophisticated and accustomed to using the web as a source of wide-ranging information and transactional services, one of the challenges for leading financial service providers is to respond more innovatively to their clients' needs.

In the early 1990s pioneer financial institutions introduced the first electronic dealing platforms, when expectations of the features and benefits of such a product range were limited, namely, book small ticket deals at a good rate. Small tickets over the phone were not well received, centralized corporate treasuries and the fund management industry (as we know it today) were in their infancy, and rate information services (such as Reuters, Bloomberg and Telerate), with the exception of banks and FX brokers were not widely available.

Today FX participants have high expectations for the online products and services that institutions supply. The key market players have dedicated vast capital outlays toward e-fx and offer an array of online tools. In an increasingly competitive marketplace with consolidation set to continue, e-commerce is a precursor for success.

The advent of the euro and the growth of online trading has resulted in a greater focus on the client within the majority of sell-side institutions. The infrastructure cost of this focus can be high though, and this has prompted many to look at their business plans, specifically how they deliver their FX services to their clients. This changing landscape of the FX market means that it is harder to make money as volumes, volatility and spreads are all much reduced. At the same time as many of the traditional sources of revenue have contracted, many financial institutions have discovered the tremendous cost of creating an efficient infrastructure to deliver products to their clients in the best possible fashion. Following initial pan-industry enthusiasm for e-trading, many have decided that it is not such a long-term proposition as it first sounded due to the costs associated with developing and more importantly enhancing an offering.

WHITE LABELLING

One of the latest products to be launched in the market as a result of this shift, is designed to provide a solution for this. Known as outsourcing or white labelling in the FX market. It is where software providers or banks package a complete trading system for delivery to other banks or financial institutions. For example, Citigroup's CitiFX White Label trading system.

White labelling avoids re-inventing the wheel, and affords lower tier banks access to the leading technology that might ensure their long term survival. They can deliver a complete trading solution to their clients, without making their own independent investment in building and enhancing what are increasingly complex platforms. The banks can utilize state-of-the-art technology necessary to offer robust, scalable platforms while minimizing costs and time to market. White Label platforms provide client solutions, increase bank efficiencies, and ensure that their institution is positioned to compete in an evolving market.

Successful e-fx has cultivated institutions which implement strategies that service every element of the client relationship cycle. It is crucial that foreign exchange providers understand their customers' business and that e-commerce works alongside sales professionals, traders and analysts to enhance the value-added services their institution offers. Trusted advisors must adopt a thorough understanding of why their clients transact foreign exchange and what factors affect their decisions now and in the future. Once institutions have an accurate understanding of their clients' needs they can then respond through innovative FX portals that achieve optimum efficiencies in their clients' workflow, thus satisfying their evolving requirements for information, communication and risk management.

VALUE-ADDED SERVICES

The FX market moves rapidly and is influenced by a vast array of factors; participants have an ever-increasing appetite for market information and intelligence. The internet facilitates instantaneous dissemination of market commentary. A plethora of currency experts and analysts convey currency views, strategies, outlook, forecasts and analysis online, real time and in direct response to market movements. Foreign exchange participants can also support their decisions and policies through extensive web libraries which host in-depth research, views, analysis and historical forecasts.

Flow analysis

E-fx has also facilitated the increasing interest in flow analysis, through the introduction of e-fx products that aim to target influential flow. At Citigroup the CitiFX Flows team presents unique analysis from the currency markets to provide information about future price movement. Analysis of transactional data has been gathered from 35 dealing floors for almost a decade, and has allowed a unique insight into the momentum within the market. Clients accessing the decision-aiding tool are provided with data that estimates the outstanding positions in the global market.

Currency risk analysis

Analysis and decision support is extended further through web-based tools that offer detailed analysis of currency risk. Participants are increasingly looking for sophisticated hedging strategies and face a variety of important FX issues. Foreign exchange providers have responded through a range of analytical tools that help quantify currency risk. Select, top tier FX providers now offer configurable web tools that allow clients to see almost instantaneously what sort of risks result from a decision to hedge (or not).

Portfolio optimizers/dynamic hedging

Investors can, for example, decide upon the optimal mix of currency hedging instruments for international equity and bond portfolios. Online portfolio optimizers have been designed to tailor hedging strategies according to their institutions risk/return criteria or overall return target. Analytical tools are also being developed to allow customers to choose dynamic hedging strategies. Chosen strategies can be weighted and recommended trades can be obtained, with the ability to backtest historical spot, forward and volatility data. The tool will allow portfolio managers to analyze different ways of maximizing profits and reducing risks.

VaR

Corporate treasuries benefit through tools that analyze their value-at-risk. Calculation of FX exposure, hedging constraints and market view through Monte Carlo simulation[1] can achieve an optimal hedging mix with respect for their risk tolerance, and offer a rational approach to implementing hedging strategies in uncertain situations.

TRANSACTIONAL INNOVATION

With transactional tools at the heart of the e-fx revolution, institutions have continuously reviewed and upgraded existing systems, many have evolved considerably from their early form in the mid- to late 1990s. A major development has been the emergence of the multi-bank space. Multi-bank

---

[1] Monte Carlo simulation is one of several methodologies to calculate VaR of an exposure. It is particularly appropriate for cross-asset and asymmetrical exposures. We use Monte Carlo to define rational approaches to these kinds of risks, and to achieve optimal hedge mixes in uncertain and complex currency situations.

portals occupy an important role in the marketplace. Major portals such as FXall have gained dominance after market consolidation. FXall offers pricing from 35 + liquidity providers and has become extremely popular among participants focused on price transparency.

Benchmarking

Proprietary trading systems have evolved exponentially. E-fx pioneers have offered electronic FX trading for over a decade, accumulating operational experience, technological knowledge and extensive client feedback. One of the resulting innovations delivered from one of the major market participants is a benchmark trading system, offering transparent and reliable pricing of global currencies. This product operates using a proprietary computer algorithm to poll the wholesale FX market and fix FX rates. The system is independently audited and takes a mid-rate snap shot eleven times a day including all major time zones.

Benchmarking can be an attractive offering for both corporates and fund managers. Pricing is completely transparent, rates can be used to revalue positions and trade in conjunction with the reference rate produced. The system also addresses price slippage for sizeable trades, there are no execution limits and all trades are executed at a verifiable reference rate. The system is also very versatile, and is fully scalable. Clients can choose to implement the benchmark trading system as a complete order management system for their central treasury and its internal subsidiaries, or adopt the system on an ad hoc transactional basis.

Currency crossing

Another new product launched in mid-December 2002 to expand transactional services offerings to customers is a revolutionary currency-crossing tool to cater for the execution of large currency transactions. Foreign exchange participants are increasingly considering the impact of price slippage when the market is alerted to a large order, and allocating importance to absolute returns in addition to relative returns. This new product allows all participants to execute large currency orders anonymously at a transparent market price with minimal slippage.

Live rate trading

In addition to price fixing processes and new crossing tools there have been numerous advances to live rate trading and request for quote systems (RFQ). Systems are constantly evolving, with faster more intuitive interfaces that support 24/6 trading (excluding Saturday: from 8 p.m. GMT Sunday to

10 p.m. Friday) swaps, forward and spot in 90+ currencies. Trades can be netted, merged or split according to client needs. Platforms have also introduced the ability to deal via real time, streaming FX rates. Clients click and book direct on a live, streaming spot rate, ensuring absolute price transparency.

CONFIRMATION, SETTLEMENT AND STP

As stated earlier, successful e-commerce strategies do not stop at pricing systems. Confirmation, settlement and reporting processes are also developing rapidly. Institutions work toward systems that enhance straight-through processing (STP). STP provides automatic trade import for position keeping systems, trade processing occurs with little or no manual intervention, and ensures both counterparties receive identical data for trades, with instant and accurate position updates. STP vastly improves efficiencies whilst reducing operational risk and operational cost.

E-commerce processes aim to reduce settlement cycles through automated matching of trades at the back end. Clients can confirm trades with one click, advances link bank confirmation systems automatically to client systems with the facility to confirm all systems automatically without client intervention. Clients can view and download all trade details, with the ability to actively manage their positions daily to obtain real time mark-to-market spot, forward and option positions. Positions can be downloaded and routed back to transactional platforms to maintain hedging, reducing the need to re-key trade details, limiting errors.

STP is also supported through moves to create a single standard for XML messaging. For example, Citigroup put forward FXML for acceptance as a standard protocol for the market along with UBS. A single standard of communication is viewed as important for communication and development and as a result, software companies such as Microsoft and IBM are now concentrating efforts on allowing different trading systems to 'talk to each other'.

Further innovations in FX settlement include continuous linked settlement, CLS™ services. Launched in Q402 consisting of 66 banks, broker dealers and shareholders, CLS aims to receive the majority of global FX transactions for reconciliation and remove settlement risk. All trades are settled simultaneously and therefore there is no resulting time gap or Herstatt risk,[2] as the principal can never be lost.

---

[2] Herstatt risk or settlement risk. This arises when payments are not exchanged simultaneously. The counterparty that settles first is exposed to settlement risk until they are recompensed. Settlement risk is particularly pronounced for foreign exchange transactions, as settlement can be sent from counterparties in different time zones, and therefore up to an eighteen hour difference. Bank Herstatt declared bankruptcy in 1974 before payment on foreign exchange contracts.

CONTROL

Online trading also strengthens audit capacity, allowing forex transactors to retain the high level of accounting detail needed for their internal and external regulatory requirements such as FAS133. Customisable reports with intelligent filters have been created and they can be downloaded or delivered via e-mail, depending on user preferences.

THE FUTURE

The next frontier in e-forex is increasingly expected to be online options trading. Several institutions offer tools that allow clients to analyze and price very complex option structures. However, client feedback indicates an increased desire for online options trading tools. FX transactors are attracted to price transparency, the ability to remove labour-intensive practices that arise from the pursuit of price discovery, and to process efficiencies that reduce costly errors and inaccurate position keeping. In some cases online options trading may allow new participants to enter the market as a result of comprehensive audit trails, and the ability to monitor options positions online with continuous revaluation.

However, at present financial institutions appear to have split opinions, and it is uncertain how the market will progress. Most support and offer online risk management tools for structuring and pricing an idea and for risk management post execution. Yet those holding back from implementing online derivatives transactions believe that the majority of options are tailor made to suit the user's risk appetite or hedging need, and that it would be extremely difficult to replicate this online. Online trading requires automated pricing from a fixed set of parameters and therefore more complex structures may require manual intervention, it may therefore be limited perhaps to plain vanilla options and some barrier exotics.

Options market excluded, e-fx covers almost every facet of foreign exchange. Market participants are equipped with sophisticated transactional tools, risk management solutions, market analysis and forecasts. These innovations, in combination with the relationships and advice sales professionals and risk advisors offer, create a marketplace that offers a comprehensive package that enables transactors to conduct their business in the most efficient way possible.

Electronic procurement of foreign exchange: the corporate perspective

Neil Cotter, LogicaCMG

INTRODUCTION

There have been many attempts by third parties to create internet-based marketplaces for the buying and selling of goods and services. Invariably such attempts to bring marketplaces online has been met with an initial wave of enthusiasm particularly from the customer base, shortly followed by disappointment in the quality of the internet service. Disappointment stems from three areas:

1. The inability to replicate the cut and thrust of the existing marketplace.

2. The difficulty in integrating the marketplace so it feeds directly and seamlessly into supplier and customer systems.

3. The resistance of suppliers (e.g. banks for the FX market) to invest time and money in integrating with an unproven marketplace.

The latter factor is often the most crucial since it creates a chicken and egg situation. That is, customers will not use the system unless most of their suppliers have signed up and suppliers will only spend money to interface to a central system once the majority of their customers are using it. The result is that the company running the portal runs out of money taking suppliers out to dinner and closes down.

However, the same scenario has not happened in buying foreign exchange online. Some FX portals have indeed gone out of business (notably, Atriax) but this is largely a consolidation factor. More and more FX is now being traded online and this trend will continue.

Buying and selling FX has unusual attributes compared with many other marketplaces. Notably, the very high values involved, the crucial importance of a good control environment and the rapidly changing prices of the 'goods'. Let us take a look at the control issues ...

BARINGS SCENARIOS – THE CONTINUING RISK

Periodically 'Barings'-type scenarios arise in corporate treasury departments (and banks, of course) and for each one in the public domain, no doubt there are another dozen which are quietly brushed under the financial reporting carpet. A number of reasons cause these disasters including:

- the 'black box' nature of the treasury department making it difficult to oversee what is happening in sufficient detail;

- the small number of staff involved and the resultant difficulty in satisfactory duty segregation (even for a FTSE 100 company it may be only three people) and control environment;
- the relatively low investment in technology spend – some large corporate treasuries still operate mainly from spreadsheets which are prone to error;
- the ease with which incorrect position reporting can occur – say by data input error – resulting in incorrect transactions being executed in the future.

These problems are exacerbated by the fact that corporate treasury transactions are nearly always executed via telephonic instruction (Figure 18.1(a)). No doubt many readers personally use the internet for executing their own share transactions or for paying bills. However, treasury is not there yet: typically a corporate dealer will call two banks for a quote, agree a deal verbally with the selected bank; then the bank, and possibly the corporate, will follow up with a written confirmation of what they believe was agreed; signed confirmations will then be returned agreeing the transaction.

There are many opportunities for error with the plurality of manual processes. But the problem does not just end there – transactions need to be settled and payments often go astray. This requires staff to chase up and agree details, with the possibility of incurring large overdraft costs. To put it bluntly it is a mess which can be suitably mitigated if you are as large as BP, say, with the resource to remove much of the manual intervention, but for a FTSE 250 company the administrative overhead and the recording

Figure 18.1

Evolution of online treasury dealing

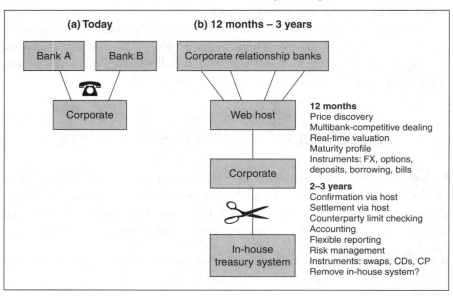

complexity often precludes them from using the best instruments to manage the company's treasury risk at the most competitive prices.

Audit committees recognize the huge risks of a misguided, neglectful or incompetent treasury department and for those poor committee members the e-revolution may help them sleep easier sooner than they think.

MOVING OUT OF THE DARK AGES

Why are treasury transactions still in the dark ages? The complicating factor is that the treasury transactions are not quoted on an exchange. They are bilateral agreements between the corporate and the bank to deliver, in the case of FX, one currency for another on a specific date at a specific exchange rate for a specific amount. They are too customized to enable them to be exchange traded. So there are no market makers, as such, to ensure the corporate obtains a market rate or any form of system to centralize settlements. Consequently the corporate must call two or more banks at the same time and choose the bank which gives them the best rate then modify the payment instructions based on who is chosen. Herein lies the problem: if the corporate is happy to execute all their transactions with one bank then, yes, they can easily have an electronic interface with that bank and develop straight-through processing (STP) from transaction execution to settlement. Nearly all major banks have developed such interfaces which are ideal for their captive customers. Unfortunately FX is like any commoditized product and if one purchases from the same place each time then one will not get the best rates – this is human nature! It is essential to have a choice of banks to deal with (in Logica's case we deal with six). However, treasurers are not going to spend time operating through six different software systems and STP solutions – they do not have the time or resource. And anyway, it is very difficult to replicate the market efficiency of the telephone by using different systems at the same time – it is simply impractical.

For the banks it is not much better – they require large back offices to chase up confirmations, agree settlement instructions, follow up on errors, etc. They often have expensive dealers tied up on small transactions from corporate customers. There has to be a better way for all but banks have been happy with the status quo since, as it is a level playing field, it is the customer who pays for the inefficiencies in the final analysis.

CORPORATIVE IMPERATIVE FOR A SINGLE WINDOW TO THE FINANCIAL MARKETS

The obvious way forward is for the banks to develop a collaborative system for offering and auctioning their financial instruments through a *single window* to the customer (see Figure 18.1(b). Effectively, each bank will have a shop window in the electronic high street to advertise its wares together with the current prices. The challenge for these windows or portals will be to replicate the cut and thrust of the voice-driven market. Banks now recognize that this will become the primary customer interface and a number have invested in joint ventures to develop the technology. These portals are sponsored and financed by separate groups of banks although there are many non-founding banks who are operating from both platforms. Another portal, Currenex, is independently financed by venture capital and a minority share holding from a major FX customer, Shell.

At the moment these platforms are focusing on a narrow range of instruments (i.e. FX) in particular, none of them currently provide a capability to execute money market transactions, which many single bank systems can do. Additionally they are heavily focused on the execution element of the transaction, but they are starting to recognize the value of providing features such as a comprehensive reporting capability to the corporate customer. If the customer chooses to execute all their transactions through the one platform then the platform has a complete record of all their transactions. If there is then an automatic link to the corporate treasury system then re-keying errors are removed. Many treasuries only require basic treasury reporting so once these platforms include money market instruments they will be sufficient to use it as an online treasury system without any outlay in internal systems. The existing treasury system can then be discarded. The savings in internal IT support and software outlay and maintenance will be very substantial.

Since the transaction is being executed *through* the platform it can also act as a real-time policeman. It has visibility of the overall position and volume of transactions and can therefore prevent dealers from breaching limits accidentally or deliberately – such a structure could have avoided the Barings or Showa Shell fiasco (Figure 18.2). When fully implemented it can also provide up-to-date market values on the transactions – again another indicator of when things may be going wrong.

Treasury systems are often unable to record unusual transactions which then have to be recorded separately on a spreadsheet. This is highly unsatisfactory. As the platforms develop they should be able to record such complex transactions (as they are the conduit for executing the deal there should be little room for error).

For companies that have treasury operations in different offices it is possible to use these platforms to make the treasury centre the *bank* to the regional treasury operation and for all internal treasury transactions to be aggregated and netted at the centre for external execution. This generates real cost savings since costs can be saved on netting and the skill and time required of external execution can be concentrated at the centre. Effectively

Showa Shell foreign exchange losses

Figure 18.2

On 20 February 1993, Showa Shell Sekiyu, a Japanese oil refiner and distributor that was 50% owned by Royal Dutch/Shell, reported that it had lost JPY 125 bn (USD 1.05 bn) in 1992. The firm's losses, equal to 82% of its shareholders' equity, stemmed from USD 6.4 bn worth of speculative foreign exchange contracts. These were accumulated by the firm's treasury department, apparently without authorization. The contracts, taken out in 1989 and subsequently rolled over, bought the dollar forward at an average exchange rate of JPY 145, to which level the yen had briefly weakened that year. At the end of 1992, the yen was trading at JPY 125 per dollar.

In Showa Shell's case, because the losses were 'unrealized,' i.e. not closed out, they did not have to be reported in company accounts. Banks in Japan routinely allowed their counterparties to defer settlement of loss making contracts by rolling them over until they were advised by their ministry of finance to desist.

treasuries now have a sophisticated intercompany FX trading system at little or no cost. A side benefit is its use in supporting transfer pricing on internal FX.

One possible alternative to the above solution is to use a product by Citibank called Chief Dealer – FX Benchmark. This allows a number of customers to have their deals aggregated and netted. Citibank transacts in the market at predetermined times in the day and the price of the transaction is independently benchmarked against the mid-market rate. For many who do not need to execute FX to particular rates or immediately this can be a useful means of obtaining a competitive rate with minimum fuss. Since it is directly linked to the Citibank systems it can provide far more functionality than the current multi-bank systems.

PRICING ENGINE – A CORPORATE HIDDEN BENEFIT

A recent estimate suggested the total cost of a London dealer (office space, IT systems, back office, salary, etc.) is close to USD 1 mn yet many dealers are often tied up doing small FX deals for customers which they cannot refuse as they have to be seen to provide a complete service. Many of the banks now have pricing engines whereby a request for quote via the platform can be automatically calculated by computer and returned to the customer. Again this efficiency should be passed on to the customer over time with finer pricing since banks will be able to reduce headcount. If the pricing engine feeds through to the multi-bank portal (as can be done by Fxall) then this should provide better service quality to the customer since the bank can continually update and 'stream' quotes to the customer since there is no manual intervention at the bank end. Arguably it also fits better with the realities of the FX market since it allows continuous price updating. It also removes re-keying errors when banks return quotes to customers. Buying and selling shares through the internet is cheaper than ringing up a broker – it is likely that similar price differentials will occur with FX trading over time.

FUTURE IMPACT ON CASH MANAGEMENT

Eventually these systems should have a significant impact on day-to-day cash management. However, this is some way off since it will be necessary for the platform to act as a conduit for settling transactions with the bank. To do this it will need to operate via a clearing mechanism since, ideally, corporates will want to pay to one place and have the platform deal with the transmission of the payment to the relevant bank. Possibly the main corporate currency accounts could be maintained by the platform making it unnecessary for physical cash transfers to take place. There seems no reason, given time and sufficient imagination, that the platform could not become the treasurer's clearing bank.

This will be a real step forward for mid-size corporates since it could enable competitive dealing but without an increased administrative headache of multi-bank dealing.

THE DOWNSIDES

If these platforms are used as corporate treasury systems they do have drawbacks. First, transacting electronically can make the treasurer more distant from the market since he or she has reduced contacts with dealers on market conditions. Second, if the platform fails it has catastrophic implications. As well as being unable to trade it may prevent the treasurer from accessing the system for basic treasury reports. It will be a brave treasurer who switches fully online until there are well established market-leading platforms

CONCLUSION

The rapid approach of multi-bank dealing platforms should generate another level of efficiency for procuring FX and other financial instruments for both bank and customers (see Figure 18.3). There are compelling

Competitive advantages of online treasury versus telephonic transactions

Figure 18.3

Metric	Advantages
Price discovery	Corporates will have access to extensive live pricing from all its key central relationship banks.
Auction	Bids can be solicited and managed from many counterparties without additional staff overhead or transaction complexity.
Execution	Counterparties will be forced to quote against strict timelines ensuring transparency of best price. Corporate dealer time will be reduced via price engines. Activity will become almost clerical.
Validation	Platform can identify and prevent real-time breach of deal limits by counterparty and in aggregate.
Netting/settling	Platform can act as 'clearing agent' for all parties with all funds flowing through web host. No requirement to make payments direct to counterparties.
Confirmation	Confirmations instantly sent by web host electronically to both parties in standardised format.
Record	Simultaneous recording of transaction on online treasury system avoiding risk of re-keying error or data manipulation. Particularly helpful for complex products.
Account	High volume of customers will enable investment in significant accounting/reporting capability.
Monitor/value	Platform will have real-time data feeds to value MTM positions with no risk of re-keying errors. No bespoke datafeeds required. Price targets can be set-up to initiate action.
Risk management	Real-time VAR datafeeds will be available. Real-time sensitivity analysis likely to be built in.
Accessibility	Full system access from mobile phones, palm held devices, TV, etc.

reasons for corporates to embrace this technology. Apart from the eventual finer pricing which will occur, it dramatically improves all aspects of the transaction versus the traditional telephonic method. It is incumbent upon corporate treasurers to investigate these opportunities to ensure that best practice is adopted when it becomes available.

Improving the business process

Corporates and their banks dealing with FX: effective execution and efficient processing.

Tom Buschman, Shell International and TWIST

Buy-side: foreign exchange as an instrument for liquidity management

The importance of centralized liquidity management for corporates

Sell-side (banks): foreign exchange as a service for clients and as a trading instrument

Price formation of foreign exchange transactions

The case for automation in foreign exchange processing

Effective straight-through processing

Bottlenecks in the realisation of operational benefits

Technological advancement in corporates and banks

The role of electronic trading platforms

Standardization within and across organizations

TWIST standards for integration

The Foreign Exchange markets are the worlds largest markets. Over a trillion dollars' worth of currencies are reported by the Bank of International Settlements (BIS) to be changing hands every day in the registered FX markets. It is estimated that around 25% of this volume is transacted between fund managers and banks and some 10% between corporates and banks. Banks transact the remainder between themselves – twice as much as they transact with their corporate and fund manager clients. However, concluding that foreign exchange, in fact, is an interbank activity would give insufficient emphasis to the nature of foreign exchange as an effective instrument used worldwide to cover liquidity needs.

In this chapter we explain the role FX has for the buy-side and the rapid developments shown in those companies that improve their liquidity management and can thus improve their market interaction. We will consider the role of FX execution for banks and their resulting transaction behaviour, as well as the consequential pressure by the buy-side to standardize FX processing and improve FX execution. The barriers to achieving this and the resolution of these problems are also described. The chapter closes with an explanation of the TWIST integration standards initiative, which is a widely supported effort by influential market players including banks and their clients to achieve marketwide straight-through processing of financial instruments, including FX.

BUY-SIDE: FOREIGN EXCHANGE AS AN INSTRUMENT FOR LIQUIDITY MANAGEMENT

Foreign exchange is transacted daily on a massive scale by millions of individuals and businesses worldwide. Anyone who is involved in international business or travels outside his or her country regularly engages in foreign exchange transactions. Companies that sell or purchase goods or services overseas are faced with the decision at each individual commercial transaction to receive or pay the funds in the currency of its own preference or in the currency required by the foreign client or supplier. The expected cost of such currency conversion will implicitly or explicitly be embedded in the agreed price of the related commercial transaction. The company could retain the exposure and aggregate the funds with other required or provided funds in the same foreign currency. It may also decide to cover the liquidity need and offload the currency risk by entering into a currency transaction, transferring the currency risk and liquidity impact to another, more preferred currency. In particular, when there is a time lag between the commercial transaction and the payment or receipt of funds, companies tend to hedge currency exposures in 'foreign' currencies at the moment they arise, avoiding any negative impact on the profitability of the foreign commercial transactions by currency movements.

In larger organizations, these currency transactions are often executed between subsidiaries and a central treasury that operates an internal bank structure. These internal banks in turn offload netted and aggregated undesired positions to the banking sector. Such an internal bank structure allows for netting and aggregating positions on a global scale and keeping tight liquidity pools in one or just a few preferred ('home') currencies. This also minimizes the leakage of spreads between buying and selling currencies and brings benefits of scale when ultimately dealing with banks. Quite often these internal bank structures consist of a number of legal entities in several countries that are used for routing the transactions executed with subsidiaries.

The result is that many corporate foreign exchange transactions with the financial markets have been preceded by one or more internal transactions that are linked to the original liquidity and hedging requirements. Likewise, transactions executed by fund managers with banks relate to the coverage of liquidity needs and the necessity to 'lock in' exposures that arise from the acquisition and disposal of investments and their monetary returns like dividends, interest payments and rental income. When fund managers operate multiple portfolios, they may also operate a structure that allows for internal netting and aggregation between these portfolios.

This means that the one third of total transactions in foreign exchange markets that are executed between banks and their clients, in fact, represent a much higher volume of transactions that do not pass through the official FX markets. Where FX markets are already considered to be by far the largest markets, the total amount of foreign exchange transactions processed worldwide is even higher.

THE IMPORTANCE OF CENTRALIZED LIQUIDITY MANAGEMENT FOR CORPORATES

The availability of cash for any organization generally is not a given and tends to come at a considerable price. Money flows in and out of every organization on a daily basis in various currencies. A lack of coordination of these flows and their consequential funding requirements in the respective currencies would lead to leakage of value and could even jeopardize the underlying business activities. To avoid this, a company first needs to ensure committed planning of activities, prudent spending of cash as well as disciplined collection of receivables.

Irrespective of this planning and prudent management of cash by the business, a corporate will spend considerable effort in operating an integrated and standardized infrastructure that allows for internal offsetting of cash shortages by surpluses elsewhere in the organization. With an integrated infrastructure, standardized processing of numerous payments and receipts creates significant scale efficiencies and enhances the centralized control of cash. Such offsetting needs to be done across currencies, to avoid the expensive maintenance of surpluses in certain currencies and shortages in other currencies, and their related risks of adverse currency movements. The result is a complex network of internal foreign exchange transactions between subsidiaries and the central treasury.

A centralized and standardized treasury function can be expected to add significant value to the bottom line of the company by making good use of this infrastructure and the available information. If set up properly this infrastructure provides the corporate with the following benefits:

- Avoidance of unnecessary credit limitations and spread leakage that may result from simultaneous funding and investing in different parts of the organization.

- Strengthened negotiating position versus banks worldwide by centralized arrangement of FX transactions, funding and investments.

- Leverage on the consolidated creditworthiness of the portfolio of businesses.

- Facilitated communication with banks about the performance of those business activities being funded.

- Enablement of coordinated fiscal optimization across the organization on a daily basis.

- Adequate reporting on exposures and provision of specialized support to the businesses for the management of those currency, interest rate and counterparty risk exposures, allowing for appropriate risk management strategies to be designed and implemented.

A company's or fund manager's centralized treasury function that has established efficient liquidity management of the cash flows in the organization provides significant positive results to the company or fund. This is enhanced by effective management of its service providers, such as banks and software suppliers, as well as the knowledgeable use of the available information.

SELL-SIDE (BANKS): FOREIGN EXCHANGE AS A SERVICE FOR CLIENTS AND AS A TRADING INSTRUMENT

Banks have fundamentally different needs and interests in transacting foreign exchange transactions than do their clients. Foreign exchange transactions executed by corporates as well as fund managers with banks are originated in instantaneous liquidity and hedging requirements. Unlike their clients who often need to offload their positions as soon as they arise as the result of underlying commercial activities, banks can decide whether or not they accept transactions of clients and can also choose whether they like to incorporate the transaction in a position or pass the exposure to others. A bank can keep active positions in certain currencies in its books for a limited or longer period of time or offload exposures to other banks or clients. The positions that are kept by banks relate to the following:

- the natural liquidity position of the bank;
- the liquidity position of the bank's customers;
- the credit standing of the bank;
- the risk appetite of the bank;
- the size of the bank;
- the access by the bank to market information about, for instance, supply and demand.

As in most marketplaces, the capability for banks to operate in FX markets in a profitable manner depends very much on their risk appetite, influence in the marketplace based on size as well as reputation and ultimately depends on the access to information and their trading strategies. Size, access to information and influence tend to be interrelated. Therefore the size of the banks tends to be used to generalize the expected behaviour of banks in FX markets. There is a distinction between top tier, middle tier and small tier banks.

- **Top tier banks (large banks).** These banks generally have a high credit rating, which facilitates the development of a strong customer base. They offer customers a wide selection of financially traded products with the ability to cross-subsidize individual transactions within the objective to maintain the relationship with their key customers. These banks tend to have natural liquidity positions in a range of currencies which allows them to take positions vis-à-vis other banks and their customers, whilst influencing the pricing as market makers in these currencies. These banks tend to be well informed about supply and demand in currencies based on their clients' commercial activities. They have little need to speculate in the foreign exchange market but need to be actively engaged to provide the liquidity required to service their customers. In turn they have an interest to capture as much buy-side flow as possible to service their customers, remain informed and use the customers' liquidity. Large banks can build portfolios of customers with opposing liquidity needs, which allows them to service these customers with limited risks.

- **Middle tier banks (medium-size banks).** The credit ratings of these banks are from mid to top level, which allows them the facility of capturing a mixture of corporate transactions predominantly from middle tier corporates. They also offer a certain level of economic and technical analysis, but within specialist groups of currencies or instruments given the limited number of traders employed. Subsequently they can only capture a limited amount of corporate transactions. For their profitability in FX markets, these banks tend to rely more on the traders' capabilities to make money from speculative/proprietary transactions.

- **Lower tier banks (small banks).** The credit rating of most of these banks is low, making it virtually impossible for these banks to trade with the corporate sector. These banks may have a small customer base and usually have only small trading desks. These banks depend heavily on speculative/proprietary trading for making profits in FX markets.

The trading rooms of the banks tend to have the same basic set up, primarily consisting of sales staff who deal with clients and traders who deal with the exposures. Sales and traders are supported by a number of functions like middle office, back office, controlling/accounting, risk management and IT development. Sales staff have the role to maintain a relationship with customers, capture as much client deal flows as possible and obtain information about existing or upcoming exposures of clients. Traders tend to have an explicit objective to make money out of the flows of transactions that stem from customer liquidity needs. Depending on the profile of the bank, these traders generally are instructed to show one of the following three behaviour patterns:

- pro-actively take positions before liquidity needs arise;
- make as much money at the back of the transactions with customers;
- offload any exposures that arise to other, market making banks.

The position of a bank and the mandate given to its traders normally differs per currency. The size of EUR and USD liquidity needs has resulted in an active EUR/USD market with most banks keeping positions in these currencies and limited scope for speculation by individual players. Other currencies can be highly influenced by a limited group of market makers. Who these market makers are varies with each currency. In some currencies the dominant players are still central banks that have a high influence on the prices set by commercial banks. In other currencies those banks that are the main cash clearing banks of that currency – and which effectively dominate the collection and redistribution of the currency flows – have become market-making banks, influencing short-term interest rates and exchange rates of the currency concerned. In other currencies large pension funds play a determining role in setting price levels for the home currency they operate in. In some circumstances it is also possible for large investors or large corporates effectively to dictate the price of the currency for a period of time by indicating an acceptable price level for a large currency transaction.

PRICE FORMATION OF FOREIGN EXCHANGE TRANSACTIONS

The different interests of banks and their clients play a role in the pricing of foreign exchange transactions. This pricing is indirectly related to economic indicators. But, in particular, where these indicators tend to be conflicting, volatility in prices can be sustained. With several banks keeping positions in currencies for a limited period of time, short-term influence over the market price becomes key. This role is increasingly played by market making banks, who can afford to build up large positions, have broad access to information and can dictate the market price. The volatility of market prices suits these banks since they are in a position to influence the direction and level of the price and consequently 'play the market'.

With currency markets not being regulated and the right pricing of currencies being difficult to assess, the large volumes of transactions in foreign exchange markets have made it the most volatile of marketplaces. This in turn has affected the transparency of markets for corporates and funds. With no access to relevant market information or detailed information about transactions executed, smaller banks as well as the corporates and fund managers normally are not in a position to 'play the market'. Generally the only way they can act is either purely to speculate or to offload any positions directly to others.

As a result, in particular top tier and market making banks have an interest to preserve a situation of high price volatility and limited access to timely information about market drivers or even more importantly prices and values of executed transactions. This has led to agreements between banks and the interbank trading platforms they contracted (Reuters and EBS) that do not allow interbank trading information to be shared with others than member banks. The banks further restricted the membership of these platforms to banks. In addition, banks successfully tried to demotivate so-called voice brokers (interdealer brokers) in the FX markets to provide services to any other market players than the banking community. As a result, corporates and fund managers did not have any access to trading facilities that were common in interbank FX markets nor were given access to relevant information about executed transactions. They had to do with amalgamated rate information and rate feeds collected by data vendors from bank traders that not necessarily is timely or an indication of committed prices.

The banks not only have access to these same rate feeds and hence have access to the price information seen by their clients, but also have the ability to influence directly these rate feeds. The rate feeds used by corporates and fund managers are produced by a limited group of data vendors. The information obtained by these vendors is generally supplied directly by bank traders via a multi-contributor page. As the price data is for information only and do not directly relate to transactions executed nor require execution commitments from these bank traders, the prices informed by these traders via the data vendors do not necessarily have a direct bearing to market levels. Banks can use the medium of data vendors in various ways, such as:

- Advertising and marketing of the bank's presence within a particular currency pair.

- Stimulating a certain market direction, which can assist the bank trader that provides the rate feeds in offloading his or her position in a profitable manner.

- Attempting to reflect to potential clients with an identified liquidity interest market levels that do not necessarily reflect the market prices or their real direction.

The fact that corporates and funds need to cover their FX needs means that banks are in a favourable position vis-à-vis their clients. Banks are well aware that their clients often need to execute the foreign exchange transaction on the day they make their request. Clients tend to transact with a limited group of banks, normally comprising their relationship banks. These banks know their clients and their underlying business well, which allows them easily to identify patterns in their clients' liquidity needs. For example, a corporate that tends to buy its base products in US dollars and sells its end products in various countries, will regularly need to buy US dollars and sell the other currencies. Therefore banks can anticipate the need of these clients and the resulting currency exposures that are likely to arise. It then takes a good sales person to 'sound out' the level of market awareness and skills of the client's trader to ensure that the right price for the bank is executed, irrespective of the market price. Corporates and fund managers tend to respond by putting banks in direct competition. This is limited though by the physical inability of corporate traders to speak via the telephone with more than two banks at the time. Direct competition is further hampered by the market volatility, which makes prices at different points in time incomparable.

Over the years a process has been established through which banks can make use of an advantageous situation in dealing with their clients. This relates in the first instance to their ability to execute trades based purely on commercial considerations, whereas their clients are much more restricted to the liquidity requirements they need to cover. Further banks have a benefit stemming from their market position, their ability to influence the markets, their access to proper trade supporting tools and, last but not least, their better access to market information and prices of executed trades.

This situation benefits from a lack of automation around trade execution by corporate and fund clients. The banks noticed that automation of trade execution and settlement in the interbank market in the 1990s provided considerable processing efficiencies but also significantly increased the market transparency and lowered margins for interbank trades. This experience added to the reluctance of banks to introduce automated FX execution between themselves and their clients. Hence, the initiative had to come from the corporate and fund community. They needed a sufficiently large case for automation and accessibility of the required technology to push their banks into a more pro-active approach towards automation of the FX transaction processing between the banks and themselves.

THE CASE FOR AUTOMATION IN FOREIGN EXCHANGE PROCESSING

In the financial markets, in particular foreign exchange and cash market instruments are considered to be commodity products that are transacted by the banks in fragmented markets with a need to connect many liquidity providing banks at various locations with their clients. Further, considerable human intervention is involved in the initiation, execution, confirmation, netting and settlement of millions of such transactions per day. Where transacted amounts can be high and urgent processing is often required, controls need to be very strict around transaction execution and settlement. Such controls can be very time consuming and error prone when performed manually. The following types of error are frequently made when FX transactions are processed manually:

- incorrect principal amount mentioned to counterparty;
- sale instead of purchase of foreign currency;
- incorrect exchange rates quoted on deals by bank;
- non-valid settlement date agreed or registered;
- incorrect registration of counterparty name in back-office systems;
- omission or double registration of transactions in back-office systems.

As mentioned before, the liquidity requirements of corporate subsidiaries and fund managers portfolios are transformed into strings of foreign exchange and money market transactions between corporate entities or between portfolios and then via the treasury function with banks. For accounting and process control purposes, the internal transactions need to be linked to external transactions:

- The FAS 133 accounting rules have led to the requirement to relate external transactions to underlying business exposures. Such direct links avoid the unnecessary reporting of currency results in the P&L statement of the central treasury that could arise from the external transactions when viewed in isolation.

- Process controls and efficiency are served by a close link of internal and external transactions as well. It ensures executing the right transactions and the direct allocation of prices obtained externally to subsidiaries, minimizing costly errors or currency results in the central treasury.

Automating the processing of such strings of commodity transactions like FX, inside clients and between clients and banks, provides a large potential for improved efficiency, controls and speed in execution.

EFFECTIVE STRAIGHT-THROUGH PROCESSING

Rightly or wrongly, many service providers and system vendors lay claim on providing tools that allow for straight-through processing. This has led to confusion as to what straight-through processing entails. In the context of this chapter, we therefore define *effective* full straight-through processing of FX transactions as an end-to-end process with a minimum of manual intervention, within organizations and between market participants. With effective straight-through processing, any piece of information needs to be registered only once throughout the process, irrespective of the amount of systems and organizations involved. Applied to a single FX transaction between two entities, this means that throughout its trade life cycle of identification, initiation, execution, confirmation, netting, settlement, reconciliation and reporting, the relevant information about, for instance, credit restrictions, execution limitations, negotiation details, settlement details and accounting details are added where and when required. The information can be added manually, like the execution and authorization by the buy-side front office. It can also be added semi-automatically, coming from static data files like the inclusion of settlement instructions. It can also be generated automatically based on certain parameters as is current practice with the auto-pricing systems used by many banks. The transaction and its details then flow from one system to another and from one user to another. Effective straight-through processing of individual transactions between two entities can be extended to strings of transactions discussed previously in this chapter. Transactions in strings are very similar and tend to differ only with respect to counterparty plus respective settlement details and price. So relevant data can be passed to subsequent transactions easily. The result is an end-to-end process with a minimum of manual intervention from the identification of the underlying exposure to the reporting of a resulting transaction executed with financial markets. This avoids errors, improves efficiency and speeds up the chain of events.

With effective straight through processing, data flow from one system to another where manual controls around the interfaces between these systems are replaced by secure interfaces with adequate communication protocols. Manual controls still play an important role, but are restricted to where they are required from a process point of view. They tend to be constructed as authorizations at several points in the process and compliance checks that keep track of the correct functioning of the process. With an improvement of the design and functionality of the systems involved in the process, this manual intervention in the process will further shift from authorizations to disciplined compliance checks. The integration of systems poses the challenge of ensuring the overall control framework around the string of transactions is robust and requires confidence in the automated process and systems that are deployed. But it also allows for significant improvements in the control framework, since in a more automated environment controls can be designed to be preventative. Preventative controls can for instance be incorporated in the process by validating transactions automatically at the moment of execution (for example, on available credit, dealer authorizations, maximum amounts, maximum economic exposures, etc.) instead of manually at the moment of confirmation or settlement.

When designed properly, effective straight through processing provides the following benefits for both high volumes of small transactions as well as large transactions that may come in smaller volumes:

- Cost reduction from minimized and focused manual intervention that rationalizes operational activities.

- Error reduction due to the elimination of double data input in different systems and elimination of manual interface and process controls.

- Improved controls arising from enforced limit and authorization checks before transactions are executed, which avoids execution of wrong decisions and avoids fraudulent behaviour.

- Cost reduction from minimized correction of errors related to data input, interfaces and processing mistakes.

- Alignment of settlement activities between corporates, fund managers and their banks, allowing for effective netting of positions and netting of settlements, reducing credit exposures and operational risks.

- Improved transaction execution, liquidity management and exposure management related to improved, unambiguous information and release of treasury staff from operational activities.

- Speeding up of transaction preparation and execution, allowing for more timely and commercially driven coverage of liquidity and hedging requirements.

Effective straight-through processing requires the linking of several systems in an efficient and controlled manner. Systems that are likely to be involved in the trade life cycle of strings of foreign exchange transactions are enterprise resource planning systems (ERP), treasury management systems (TMS), pricing systems, credit systems, risk management systems, trading platforms, transaction registration and accounting systems, settlement and payment systems, confirmation matching systems, and (internal) information broadcast systems.

The implementation of full straight-through processing requires a change management process for the upgrade and sometimes implementation of systems, the improvement of interfaces, the restructuring of controls and the review of activities in front office, back office and middle office/treasury controllers departments.

BOTTLENECKS IN THE REALISATION OF OPERATIONAL BENEFITS

In the second section of this chapter it was explained how a centralized and standardized treasury that coordinates a company's liquidity management can add significant value to the company's bottom line profitability. From a corporate point of view, the realization of a centralized and automated process requires the fulfilment of a few conditions. First of all it requires internal political backing for committed and disciplined cash planning by the businesses. Second, there needs to be internal support for the centralization and standardization of activities. Third, a treasury needs to be enabled to invest in the necessary but readily available technology to create the necessary infrastructure.

For very large multinational companies, the diversity of their business activities, its global scale and its involvement in many projects and joint ventures add to this complexity. Further, various legal and fiscal restrictions in regulated economies provide additional constraints for centralization of liquidity management for all subsidiaries irrespective of their location. However, most companies have been able to pass these hurdles and implemented a centralized treasury in a number of variations. Until recently though it was difficult to fully obtain the benefits of centralization. The remaining major bottlenecks were:

- The absence of standardized technology solutions that could enable cross-organizational electronic communication in an efficient and controlled manner.

- The absence of market infrastructures that would allow corporates and fund managers to perform parts of the transaction process electronically with their banks.

- A lack of market standards for operational processes.

In the remainder of this chapter we cover these three areas and the major developments that provide a solution to each of them: technology advancement, electronic trading and standardization.

TECHNOLOGICAL ADVANCEMENT IN CORPORATES AND BANKS

Significant advances in technology in the last decade have made major improvements now obtainable at low cost, based on a standardization in technical infrastructures across organizations. The internet has simplified communication within and between organizations and allows for efficient rapid deployment of new IT functionality. Data processing and electronic communication has become more available and affordable. These technical developments have accelerated the ability to implement straight-through processing since it involves cross-organizational communication and standardized interfaces between distinct systems in networking environments.

Within corporations, important company-wide implementations of Enterprise Resource Planning systems (ERPs) have been realized that provide significant improvements in their access to information and processing capabilities. In their treasury organizations, treasury management systems (TMS) have provided corporate treasurers with the ability to perform limited forms of straight-through processing for a number of years now. This means that once a deal has been executed and manually keyed into such a TMS, the generation of deal confirmations, settlement instructions, accounting entries and management information reports can be automated without the necessity for further re-keying of data. These systems are now gradually being upgraded to allow for open communication with other systems based on standard interfaces, hence facilitating components of the described, effective straight-through processing.

Within banks, easy access to better technical solutions and the impacts of globalization have created in recent years a drive towards standardizing and connecting their own operations. Interbank electronic trading, confirmation matching facilities via the SWIFT interbank network and Continuous Linked Settlement have provided the banks with highly automated processing of their interbank transactions of foreign exchange.

Independent system providers often provide the technical solutions. These vendors started to explore in the first instance with fund managers and more recently also with corporate treasuries how these could make use of the same systems and services for processes in these organizations that are similar to bank operations. A good example is the recent surge of the use by corporates of bank-independent software for processing commercial payments and internal bank account structures, where previously they were dependent on proprietary tools provided by the banks. Another example is the development of market infrastructure providers like trading platforms, confirmation matching services and netting, clearing and settlement services. These allow banks, corporates and fund managers to make use of the shared services that increasingly are deployed via the internet.

THE ROLE OF ELECTRONIC TRADING PLATFORMS

Where companies can create various forms of straight-through processing in their respective organizations by linking their internal systems, they will not be able to come to effective straight-through processing as described in this chapter without the ability to connect to various systems of other market players involved in their transactions. Electronic trading platforms provide electronically driven transaction execution and supporting services. These platforms can provide an efficient solution for cross-organizational connectivity at the moment of trade preparation, negotiation, execution and, if required, netting and settlement. Trading platforms can provide these solutions by themselves or together with other market infrastructures such as netting and clearing services.

In addition, in particular internet-based electronic trading can allow for significant improvements in deal execution with FX and other financial markets by making these markets more transparent and accessible. They can provide several trade execution mechanisms that allow for price identification and transaction execution for varying sizes of trades and under various circumstances. Examples of trade execution mechanisms are 'request for quote' to several banks, single direct execution based on orders, single quotes or streamed executable quotes, contractual pre-arrangements like benchmark trades, book building, prime brokerage and enhanced market access. Trade execution can still be complemented by conversations via the telephone, whilst registration of executed trades and the authentication of trading parties still takes place electronically.

In FX markets, regulators have restricted their involvement to the settlement and clearing part of the process; an example is the significant pressure from, for instance, the FED on the banks to accept and implement Continuous Linked Settlement (CLS). Other areas like distribution of market information and trade execution practices are not covered by regulatory authorities. As a result, the design of electronic trading platforms and their activities are not subject to tightly defined general rules but are primarily driven by the preferences of their respective owners. This means that trading platforms can differ in the ways in which they allow transactions to be executed and the variety of execution mechanisms. They may also have distinguished policies for acceptance of market participants to become trading members, either via membership agreements or via commercial requirements and or technical requirements. Different trading platforms may also have different policies with regard to the distribution of information about the transactions that are executed as well as those that have not been executed.

In the early 1990s, two electronic trading platforms for FX were set up that since then have dominated the interbank trading of FX. The first platform was created by Reuters, an independent company that also is a large market information provider. In reaction to Reuters' development, a group of major FX banks established a cooperative called EBS (Electronic Brokerage System). Other vendors like Bloomberg have since then attempted to enter the interbank market for electronic FX trading, but without apparent success. The banks, in fact, were able to define between themselves an allocation of trading volumes over Reuters and EBS and were not minded to support additional service offerings. As a result, the Reuters and EBS platforms did not evolve their trade execution models and were also slow in their reaction to the internet boom. Their close dependence for the success of their platforms on interbank trading volumes and the agreements of banks with these platforms mentioned in the fourth section of this chapter limited their appetite to provide trading services for the buy-side of FX markets. The banks themselves did not create multi-bank trading platforms for their clients until the internet allowed independent providers to provide such offerings.

So while banks have been trading electronically with each other for most of the last decade, until recently most trading by banks with corporate clients and fund managers was done over the telephone. But the development of interbank electronic trading and the ability to provide trade

execution to clients via single bank offerings resulted in significant investments by the banks to automate their internal processes of pricing, credit
checking and settlement of executed trades.

In recent years, the following have accelerated the development of
electronic trading:

- Internal pressure at major banks to complete transactions more efficiently
  with clients.
- Recognition by a few banks that electronic trading could be an attractive
  distribution channel allowing for rapid growth of client transactions.
- Development of multi-bank offerings by independents, driven by the
  boom of the internet.
- Expectations by several first tier banks that transaction portals could
  provide a significant commercial success and possibly transfer the transaction margins from transaction execution to transaction delivery via the
  portals.
- Continuous pressure by a few major clients to open up electronic trading
  to the buy-side, enabling straight-through processing, increased market
  transparency and wider market access.

In the first two years of development of multi-bank portals, the focus of
the major banks was on ensuring ownership of this particular market space
and avoiding erosion of margins that could be the result of increased market
transparency. They tried to steer their buy-side customers away from bank-
independent service offerings provided by portals like Currenex and 360T
towards two bank-owned trading platforms, Atriax and FXall. The complexity of electronic trading and the required change management processes
at both banks and their customers were underestimated. With the subsequent slow down of the economy, the collapse of the internet boom and the
inability to attract customers to platforms that only gave them access to
subsets of their liquidity providers, growth was not as high as anticipated.

One-and-a-half years after its inception, the major bank-led trading platform, Atriax, created by Citibank, Deutsche Bank, JP Morgan Chase and
Reuters, ceased its operations. Costs were running too high and revenues were
lagging behind optimistic projections. The bank independent portals mentioned and another bank-owned platform continued their operations, with the
latter trying to attract customers by offering its services free to buy-side users
whilst obtaining revenues exclusively from its bank customers. The existence
for over a year of two competing bank-led platforms has helped competition
between platforms and their development. It also removed concerns about the
ability to transact very large amounts via internet-based platforms.

Where the focus of the banks initially was on the threat of such multi-
bank trading platforms for their FX transaction margins and their negative

perception on enhanced market transparency, the attention only moved to the possible role of these trading platforms in facilitating straight-through processing after the corporate and fund manager users of these platforms indicated their prioritization of processing efficiencies instead of execution benefits.

STANDARDIZATION WITHIN AND ACROSS ORGANIZATIONS

The deployment of bank-independent tools and services like trading platforms comes with a need for standardized connectivity between these systems and the banks that effect the commercial payments. Previously banks had no particular interest in such a standardization due to their strategy of locking in customers with proprietary solutions. Currently, however, banks have an increased understanding that customers desire a level of independence. Furthermore a renewed cost awareness has drawn attention to the high costs of maintaining proprietary solutions as well as the negative implications of inefficient client processes for the banks' own efficiencies and their operational risks levels.

Historically, each electronic trading platform, banking system and treasury management system is built to its own specifications, and connecting them requires costly customized interfaces. The obvious solution is to have a single set of standard interfaces that all parties can implement, simplifying systems integration and allowing corporates greater choice of platforms, treasury management systems and banks. The development of such single standard interfaces requires close cooperation between various market players with different interests.

For a standardization initiative to be successful in obtaining support from all relevant players in the marketplace to design and realize effective straight-through processing throughout the trade life cycle, the following is needed:

- Involvement in the design by market participants (corporates, fund managers and their banks) of different sizes, location and position in the marketplace;

- Involvement in the design of system vendors that build and maintain the systems that need to be linked and updated.

- Involvement of various service providers that play a role in the transaction, like trading platforms, brokers, confirmation matching service providers, clearing and netting services and communication network providers.

- An agnostic approach towards technical solutions, avoiding certain service providers or market players to dominate the design or try to control the implementation for their own benefits.

■ A pragmatic approach, ensuring speed in design and implementation.

A number of initiatives have helped driving the standardization in the financial markets. These services were primarily focused on the settlement of financial transactions. The interbank payments network SWIFT has provided a worldwide standardized settlement process within the banking community, which was extended to other financial institutions in the 1980s. However, no access was provided to its payment network for corporates because of the banks' fear that corporates would disintermediate the banks when settling their commercial transactions. In the 1990s, confirmation matching services emerged that could link corporates to SWIFT interbank confirmation services. However, since confirmation matching forms only a limited part of their operational processes, not all corporates took up these services. The development over a decade of Continuous Linked Settlement (CLS) and its operational launch in 2002 provided another push for standardized processing of foreign exchange transactions. Also, in the case of CLS, its services are primarily focused on the interbank community, but the interest of its membership banks to leverage on the massive investments needed for the realization of CLS have spurred a desire to roll-out its service offering rapidly to non-banks.

Both SWIFT and CLS are service providers that have an interest to subject their standardization efforts to their own technical and commercial capabilities. In the meantime, where the banks have for many years worked on standard solutions for the interbank markets, they focused on propagating and delivering proprietary solutions to their client base in an attempt to lock these clients in and have shown a related lack of interest in working with other banks to promote standardized offerings to corporate and fund customers.

TWIST STANDARDS FOR INTEGRATION

Since banks and software vendors were driving towards proprietary solutions, and existing standardization initiatives were either not sufficiently inclusive or focused on subsets of the transaction life cycle, pro-active action was required at the beginning of 2001. At the time, the Royal Dutch/Shell Group started an initiative called TWIST, which stands for the Treasury Workstation Integration Standards Team. TWIST is a not-for-profit industry group delivering non-proprietary integration standards to facilitate an efficient, controlled and open-dealing marketplace for financial instruments. The aim of TWIST is to create a more open environment where it is easier for all parties to link the systems of their choice together, and to achieve effective straight-through processing of financial transactions, including foreign exchange.

TWIST has rapidly grown into a respected and important standards organization that brings together representatives of leading corporate treasuries, fund managers, banks, system suppliers, electronic trading platforms, market infrastructures (confirmation matching services, clearing and settlement services, communication networks), consultancy firms and learning organizations. TWIST is open to market participants and service providers, irrespective of their size or role in the marketplace.

TWIST develops practical message standards for corporate treasuries and fund managers to communicate with banks, brokers and electronic trading platforms about financial transactions at various stages of their trade life cycle. The messages are based on the XML (eXtensible Markup Language), a general and widely used data standard. For the exchange of information between parties, TWIST has created a set of messages that can relate to a specific individual transaction, or can convey more general information, such as deal statements, lists of trades, settlement agreements and standard instructions. The exchange of messages are structured in specific conversations between market participants, between market participants and service providers or between internal systems. TWIST aims to facilitate communications between parties, but it can also help automate the movement and processing of data within an organization. The standardized electronic messages also provide the means to convey information directly between in-house systems, and can eliminate manual procedures, such as the re-keying of data from one system to another. The market players and their interaction as covered by TWIST is shown in Figure 19.1.

The messages support all of the various processes within the trade life cycle:

 Figure 19.1

TWIST coverage for FX instruments

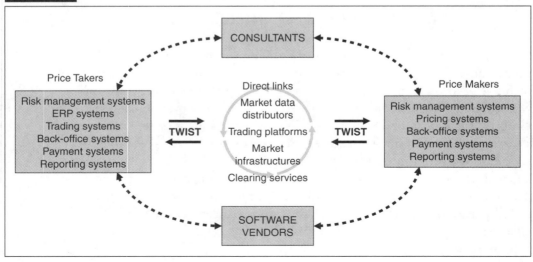

- Relationship set up and management.
- Trade origination.
- Trade execution and confirmation, including pricing and credit as well as modifications.
- Netting and settlement.
- Reconciliation and reporting.

The message sets where necessary include acknowledgements, confirmations and/or rejections to reduce ambiguity and improve certainty. And, in addition to enabling the various parties to specify all the details of a trade or other subject, TWIST includes free form comment messages that allow users to add background information or notes.

Clearly, the introduction of new messaging standards should not compromise the security and reliability of an organization's operations. At the same time, the controls associated with the standards must not entail overheads that make an organization reluctant to adopt them. Recognizing this, TWIST has been careful to strike a balance between providing appropriate controls and making sure the implementation of the messages is practical and cost-effective. Part of this strategy is to avoid overlap with security and reliability measures that already exist in the environment into which the TWIST messages will be introduced, and to make use of protocols and other mechanisms that are already in place, but without assumptions as to what these might be. Furthermore, not all parts of the trading process have the same security requirements. For example, market data does not usually need the same level of controls surrounding it as would the exchange of standing settlement instructions. So controls should be appropriate to the particular activity the messages are supporting.

TWIST recognizes that organizations will be implementing the standards in a range of different situations and within different technology infrastructures. In some cases, organizations will already have communications links in place and will be able to make use of existing security and reliability controls, at least to some degree, whereas for others TWIST will be their starting point in establishing new connections. Also, depending on their business, organizations will not necessarily wish to implement all of the messages. TWIST is designed to be modular, and organizations can choose only the subset that they require, and consequently will need only a subset of the possible controls. It follows therefore that TWIST is not prescriptive in terms of controls, and instead offers guidance on how organizations might achieve their required level of security and readability within a particular environment. TWIST aims to facilitate the controlled implementation of effective straight-through processing, but it remains the responsibility of each individual organization to ensure that the process of automation does

Figure 19.2

TWIST coverage for FX instruments

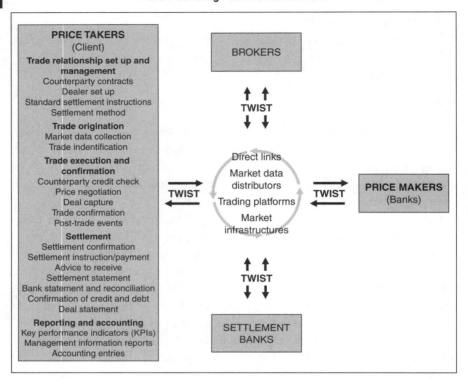

not undermine existing controls, and should identify and address any new risks introduced by the messages (see Figure 19.2).

Shortly after publication of its first complete set of standards in October 2002, many market participants and service providers started with the implementation in their internal processes and external service offerings. With the application of these open standards, banks and their clients ensure the benefits of effective straight through processing, with overall efficiency improvements and more transparent and rapid execution in the FX marketplace. As stated in the beginning of this chapter, such improvements are needed for corprorates to achieve optimisation in their liquidity management and market interaction.

More information about TWIST, detailed descriptions of its standards, a validation tool and simple instructions on how to use the standards as well as how to support TWIST as a member or endorser can be found on its website: www.TWISTstandards.org

Technical analysis

Derek Taylor, Taylor Associates

INTRODUCTION

To the participants in today's markets, the words technical analysis conjure up a mental picture of a studious character poring over mountains of charts in the hope of finding the 'financial holy grail' – the sure fire method of making a profit on a deal. This is, of course, as fanciful as finding the original 'holy grail'. But it doesn't matter whether your interest is in commodities, equities, bonds or foreign exchange, the principles and disciplines practised by technical analysts are of growing importance in the dynamic financial markets of today.

Let us first define the subject.

> **Technical analysis** is the study of market action, primarily through the use of charts, for the purpose of forecasting future price trends. **Definition**

It is this study of market action, which interests us. Traders, whether market followers or market makers, know that the value of having as much information as possible is absolutely crucial to the decision-making process. Making the correct choice of when to trade, and when to enter and exit positions is of vital importance. Even when making the wrong choice, the ability to quickly recognize the mistake and exit the trade cheaply is going to result in substantial savings, and the ability to 'fight again another day'. Even the disbeliever, and there are many, cannot afford to ignore the technical indicators. There are increasing numbers of followers, and indeed computer trading systems using the principles to make trading decisions are becoming commonplace.

THE THREE RULES

1. Market action discounts everything

This is probably the cornerstone of technical analysis. Anything that can affect the market price – fundamental, political, psychological or otherwise – is already reflected in the price of that commodity. The charts do not move by themselves, it is the economic fundamentals (supply and demand) that cause bull and bear markets. The charts simply reflect the bullish or bearish psychology of the marketplace.

2. Prices move in trends

We generally accept the fact that markets do in fact trend, and the purpose of charting the price action is to identify trends in their early stages for the purpose of trading in the direction of those trends.

3. History repeats itself

The key to understanding the future lies in the study of the past. The study of market action has to do with the study of human psychology, which tends not to change. Therefore identifying chart patterns of a bullish and bearish nature will give us an insight as to what might happen in the future, a repetition of the past.

TECHNICAL VERSUS FUNDAMENTAL ANALYSIS

Technical analysis concentrates on the study of market action, while fundamental analysis looks at the economic forces of supply and demand that cause markets to rise, fall or stay the same. Both groups are trying to determine in which direction prices are likely to move. The pure technician believes that effect is all he needs to know and the causes are unnecessary, while the fundamentalist always has to know why. Traders, however, need a working knowledge of both types of analysis in order to make quantified decisions about when to deal and in what direction. But here comes the problem, because usually at the beginning of important market moves the fundamentals do not explain what the market is doing.

'Market price tends to lead the known fundamentals'

Known fundamentals are the key words here. Prices have already discounted the known fundamentals and are reacting to the unknown fundamentals. Don't forget that breaking news has already been seen by some people and by the time it hits the major news networks price action has already begun. By the time it is reported in the newspapers the major part of a market movement may already be over.

DIFFERENT TYPES OF CHART

Line charts

The simplest form of chart constructed by plotting points between the price and time axis and joining them with a line (see Figure 20.1). The advantage

A line chart of the GBP/USD exchange rate, March to November 2002

Figure 20.1

Source: Moneyline Telerate

of this chart is that it is simple to understand but holds only the basic information about price action.

Point and figure charts

Point and figure charts are often said to be one-dimensional charts, because they have no time scale (see Figure 20.2). Constructed with Xs and Os which represent discrete price intervals, all price movements that are less than the assigned price interval are ignored.

Point and figure charts were supposed to have been used by Charles Dow who called them 'the book method'. But the name has been attributed to Victor de Villiers (*The Point and Figure Method of Anticipating Stock Price Movements*, Brightwaters, NY: Windsor Books, 1933). They are believed to have developed in the early part of this century in the USA as floor traders used them as an easy way of tracking prices. Floor traders jotted down stock price movements. This was later refined to plotting price rises as Xs and falling prices as Os, making the direction of the market easy to read.

The point and figure chart is a study of pure price movement, time is not a consideration.

Figure 20.2

Point and figure chart showing the GBP/USD exchange rate, March to November 2002

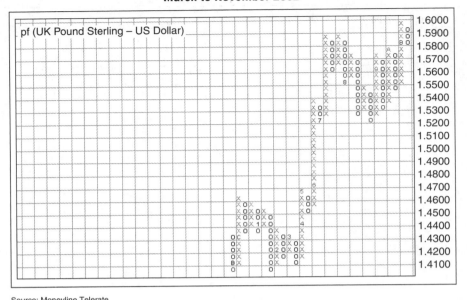

Source: Moneyline Telerate

Figure 20.3

Shows the GBP/USD bar chart, March to November 2002

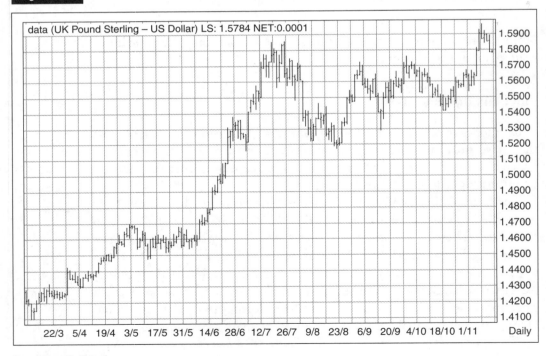

Source: Moneyline Telerate

Bar charts

A commonly used type of chart is the daily bar chart (see Figure 20.3). Note that the price action is the same as for the line chart, but with more detail. The reason that it is called a bar chart is that a vertical bar represents each day's action. The vertical bar shows the range on the day and a tick to the left of the bar shows the opening price with a tick to the right showing the closing price. So each day's price action can be taken in at a glance, high, low, open and close.

A bar chart can be constructed for any time period. Intra-day bar charts showing high, low and last prices for periods as short as five minutes can be made. Weekly and monthly trend analysis bar charts can be constructed, or for any time period, even for many years.

Japanese candlesticks

The Japanese had been evolving their own form of technical analysis for the two centuries preceding Charles Dow and the early western 'point and figure' charting. The method is referred to as 'Japanese candlesticks' and at first glance is similar to western 'bar charts' (see Figure 20.4).

A Japanese candlestick chart of GBP/USD commencing April 2002   **Figure 20.4**

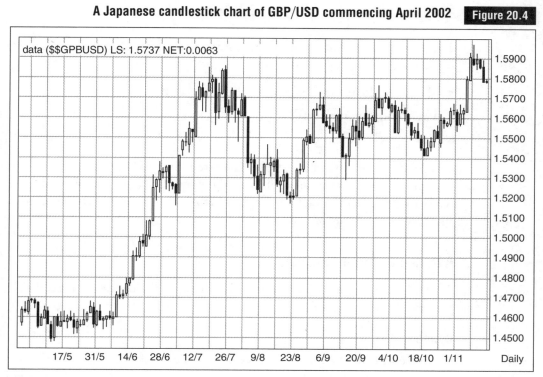

Source: Moneyline Telerate

Figure 20.5

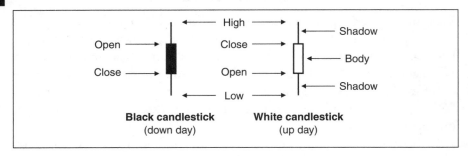

Japanese candlesticks

Black candlestick
(down day)

White candlestick
(up day)

In fact there is a lot more to this ancient form of technical analysis. It is worth noting that we have the same detail of price action, open, close, high and low, but it is represented in a much more graphical manner, and is therefore easier to read. The white candlesticks are 'updays', and the black candlesticks are 'downdays' (see Figure 20.5).

The technique uses patterns of candlesticks to determine entry and exit points for trades, as well as measuring the bullish or bearish market tendencies.

TREND

The concept of *trend* is absolutely essential to the technical approach to market analysis. You have probably heard the following:

- **Always trade in the direction of the trend.**
- **The trend is your friend.**
- **Never buck the trend.**

It is good advice, but what is trend? The trend is simply the direction of the market. Markets never move in a straight line but are characterized by a series of peaks and troughs or zigzags. *It is the direction of the peaks and troughs that constitute market trend.*

A trend has three directions

A trend has three directions, uptrend, downtrend and sideways trend (see Figure 20.6).

Uptrend

An uptrend is defined as a succession of higher peaks and troughs (higher highs and higher lows). Relative safety in being 'long', using a buy strategy.

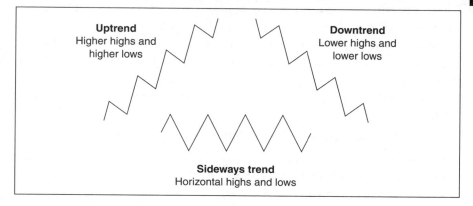

The three directions of trend

Figure 20.6

Uptrend
Higher highs and
higher lows

Downtrend
Lower highs and
lower lows

Sideways trend
Horizontal highs and lows

Downtrend

The opposite is true for a downtrend, when the successive peaks and troughs are lower (lower highs and lower lows). Relatively safe to go 'short'.

Sideways trend

But for approximately a third of the time markets tend to move sideways or in a 'trading range', where the peaks and troughs are horizontal. This can result in paying away spreads or 'tops and bottoms' as we try to discover whether to be long, short, do nothing or indeed to look elsewhere.

A trend has three classifications

- **Major (primary) trend** – six months and beyond.
- **Intermediate (secondary) trend** – three weeks to six months.
- **Near term (minor) trend** – up to three weeks.

If you are a pension fund manager, then your investment strategy is based upon many concepts, one of which is time. Pension funds invest over the long-term, twenty or thirty years or more. On the other hand, futures traders, FX dealers and internet daytraders have a trading time frame, which runs to days or even hours and seconds. In either case the ability to recognize trend and the use of technical analysis, can be a major advantage.

Different markets work with different time frames, and the classifications mentioned here are guidelines. Trends can cover periods from seconds to over 100 years.

Support and resistance

In a trend we will see peaks and troughs. Troughs are where the buying interest is sufficiently strong enough to overcome selling pressure, where the market experiences support. Peaks are the opposite, where selling pressure overcomes buying pressure and a price advance is turned around, the market running into resistance. So for an uptrend to continue each successive low (support) must be higher than the last and each rally (resistance) must be higher than the last. If the sequence is broken then a possible change of trend could occur.

In an uptrend, resistance levels are not sufficient to stop renewed buying demand.

Remember – higher highs and higher lows.

For a downtrend to continue each successive low (support) must be lower than the last and each rally (resistance) must be lower than the last. If the sequence is broken then a possible change of trend could occur.

In a downtrend, support levels are not sufficient to stop selling pressure and the market moves to lower levels.

Remember – lower highs and lower lows.

Resistance becomes support

Whenever a support or resistance level is penetrated by a significant amount, they reverse their roles and become the opposite.

| Figure 20.7 | **Example of trendlines showing support and resistance – USD/CHF October 2001 to April 2002** |

Source: Moneyline Telerate

Figure 20.7 shows the uptrend break of 14 March 2002. Notice that the previous support line now becomes a resistance level. Here comes the psychology – imagine the three types of market participants:

- **The Longs** – have already bought at the old support level they are currently losing money, and are looking for the cheapest exit point, or even to turn around and go short. Therefore their breakeven is at or near to the old support level.

- **The Shorts** – should already be short at higher resistance levels. A break of support levels would give confidence to remain short and even increase the position.

- **The Sideliners** – who have either not traded and are looking for a good level to get on the trend, or those who were long, cut out early and are looking for a new dealing opportunity. Or even those who were short, took profit too soon, and may be looking for a good level to re-instate a short position. They are all looking for a opportunity to sell on the next rally, so we may not see that old support level again, which is now looking like a very good level to sell. In fact creating a new resistance level.

JAPANESE CANDLESTICK TECHNIQUES

Traditionally, most people look at technical analysis from the 'western' perspective. But the Japanese were evolving their own style of technical analysis two centuries before Charles Dow and the early western 'point and figure' charting. The method is referred to as 'Japanese candlesticks' and at first glance is similar to western 'bar charts'. In fact, there is much, much more to this ancient form of technical analysis.

On the other side of the world, two centuries before Charles Dow, lived a man who was already perfecting trading techniques that the West would not grasp for many, many years. His name was Munehisa Homma. From 1500 to 1600 Japan was a country at war, where the daimyo or feudal lords fought for domination. Finally a leader emerged in the form of General Ieyasu Tokugawa who unified Japan and his family ruled from 1615 to 1867. The era is referred to as the Tokugawa Shogunate. The military conditions that endured in Japan over centuries became an integral part of candlestick technology. Traders require many of the skills needed by soldiers to win a battle: strategy, psychology, competition, strategic withdrawals and, of course, luck. In fact, many candlestick terms have battlefield analogies, night and morning attacks, advancing three soldiers, counter-attack lines, etc.

The most important patterns signify a change of direction in the market, known as a trend reversal. Bearish reversal patterns, occurring after a sustained rising or bull market, have names like 'hanging man' and 'dark cloud cover'. It is not difficult to guess what they signify. The bull market reverses sharply as the bears take over.

On the other hand, bullish reversal patterns have names like 'morning star' and 'hammer' (as in hammering out a base), where the candlestick pattern shows a reversal of a bearish trend as the buyers prevail. See Figures 20.8 and 20.9.

Continuation patterns

Most candlestick patterns are trend reversals. However, there are a group of patterns, which are continuation indicators (see Figure 20.10). A continuation pattern tells us that the established trend is likely to carry on. Positions can possibly be increased, with a reasonable degree of safety.

The Japanese say '*there are times to buy, times to sell and times to rest*'. In order to see the practical applications of both reversal and continuation patterns, Figure 20.11 is a real life chart featuring a number of the candlestick patterns discussed.

| Figure 20.8 | **Reversal patterns** |

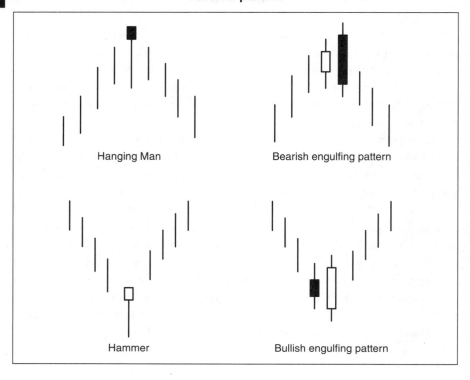

Hanging Man   Bearish engulfing pattern

Hammer   Bullish engulfing pattern

Star formations

Figure 20.9

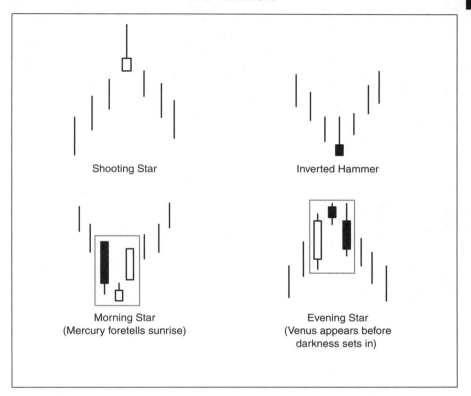

Shooting Star

Inverted Hammer

Morning Star
(Mercury foretells sunrise)

Evening Star
(Venus appears before
darkness sets in)

Example of continuation patterns

Figure 20.10

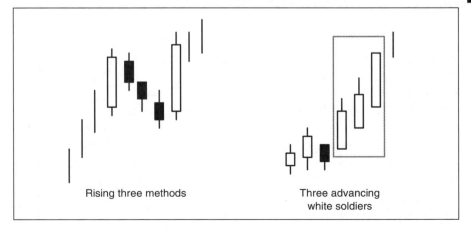

Rising three methods

Three advancing
white soldiers

Figure 20.11   **Examples of candlestick patterns on a GBP/USD chart from May 2002**

Source: Moneyline Telerate

MOVING AVERAGES

A moving average is a trend following device used to signal trend reversals or changes of direction. The signal that a trend has changed is given when the moving average turns from rising to falling (or vice versa).

There are three main ways of calculating moving averages, simple, weighted or smoothed, where the arithmetic mean of a given span is calculated, then either weighted with more recent data or smoothed between the latest price and the average.

Because of the time lag nature of moving averages, they will always follow behind market action, and can never anticipate, only react. The average will smooth the price movement, making it easier to see the underlying trend. It follows that the time lag will be reduced with shorter averages, in comparison to longer averages, but can never be totally eradicated. A five-day average will hug the price action more closely than a 50-day average. Normally, the closing price is used in the calculation of the average.

Single moving average

Using a single simple moving average gives us simple rules:

Buy when rallying prices cross the moving average.
Sell when falling prices cross the moving average.

If the moving average itself turns in the direction of the price crossing, this is considered to be confirmation. Here a simple single moving average is applied which tracks the price closely with multiple crossings. The shorter, more sensitive moving averages will produce many false signals. To remove some of this short-term random price movement or 'noise', a longer moving average can be used. However, the longer average suffers more from price lag. The trick is to use an average that cuts out excess 'noise', but gives reasonably early signals.

Two moving averages

With a single moving average, a lot of noise gives false signals. The use of combinations of two or even three moving averages can improve reliability and results. The first average, normally the longer, is used for trend identification, while the shorter second average is the trigger.

The double crossover method

This method requires a continuous presence in the market. The user is either long or short. Buy when the shorter average (trigger) crosses above the longer (trend). Sell short when the shorter average (trigger) crosses below the longer (trend) (see Figure 20.12).

Moving averages – advantages and disadvantages

Advantages

- Moving averages are trend following.
- They trade in the direction of the trend.
- Used correctly they allow profits to run and cut losses quickly.
- They work well in trending markets.

Disadvantages

- They work poorly in sideways, range trading markets.
- They work poorly in volatile non-trending markets.

Figure 20.12   **Moving averages**

ma(5)=1.5836 ma2(15)=1.5716 data2 (UK Pound Sterling – US Dollar) LS: 1.5781 NET:-0.0002

Notice that in a strongly trending market the buy and sell signals are clear, but in a sideways trending market the moving averages do not work well.

Source: Moneyline Telerate

Sensitivity

As market conditions change the sensitivity of the moving average can be adjusted. For instance, a particular currency pair might be working well with a 10- and 30-day moving average combination. But changing fundamentals could lead to a more volatile, active market. In order not to get caught by 'whipsaws' in the price, the averages might need to be shortened to, say, 5 and 15 days. The more sensitive combination would give sharper, quicker indicators in response to the new market conditions.

If a trader wishes to keep clear of a sideways, range trading market he could employ a much less sensitive, longer average (or combination), maybe coupled with filters, to give him solely an indication of a breakout and possible new trend.

OSCILLATORS – RSI, MACD, STOCHASTICS, MOMENTUM

Oscillators offer a more objective approach to analyzing the market using mathematically derived techniques.

Pattern recognition techniques tend to be subjective, as are the trend following methods so far discussed. However, oscillators use a variety of different mathematical techniques, as a means of recognizing when the market is overextended, commonly referred to as overbought and oversold situations.

Commonly an oscillator is plotted along the bottom of a price chart, with a scale of 0–100. When the oscillator reaches the top end of the scale (near 100) the market is in an overbought situation. If it reaches the bottom end of the scale, then a possible oversold situation is likely.

The three main uses of oscillators are:

1. Recognizing overbought and oversold situations.

2. Used as divergence indicators.

3. Measuring market momentum.

There are many different techniques employed by analysts, covering a variety of situations and applications, we shall explore a few.

Relative strength index

The RSI compares the relative strength of price advances to price declines over a specified period.

The RSI is an oscillator developed by J. Welles Wilder Jr. It is calculated by taking the number of points gained over a period and the number of points lost over a period (the most common periods are 9 or 14 days). The average of the gains is divided by the average of the losses and plotted on a fixed scale of 0–100.

Using the RSI

1. A sell signal generated above 80 and a buy signal below 20, some prefer 70–30, see Figure 20.13.

2. In a strong uptrend: 80 overbought: 40 oversold.
   In a strong downtrend: 60 overbought: 20 oversold.

Moving average convergence/divergence (MACD)

MACD is a popular momentum indicator using two exponential moving averages to produce a crossover system, used to indicate changing trend direction.

Devised by Gerald Appel, MACD is a popular momentum indicator using exponential moving averages to produce a crossover system, used to indicate trend direction. Two exponentially smoothed moving averages, called the

Figure 20.13   **MACD and RSI, GBP/JPY, April 2002 – October 2002**

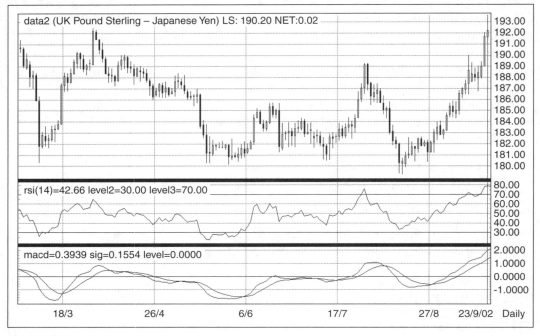

Source: Moneyline Telerate

MACD line and the Trigger or Signal line, revolve above and below a zero line.

Using MACD

1. Simple buy and sell signals are generated when the lines cross.

2. A more reliable signal is generated when both lines cross, and then cross the zero line, as in Figure 20.13.

3. The most reliable signals are those coupled with convergence or divergence. Divergence is where the market trend is in one direction but the oscillator is moving in the opposite direction. For example, a strong signal would be generated by divergence coupled with a crossover and then a move through the zero line.

Stochastics

The stochastic indicator compares the latest closing price with the total range of price action for a specified period.

The stochastic oscillator is based on the concept that in an uptrend, prices will tend to close nearer the upper end of the day's range, and in a downtrend, closing prices tend to be nearer the lower end of the day's range.

From this concept George Lane devised the stochastic formula, using closing prices, lowest lows and highest highs within a given time period. Two lines are plotted, the first called %K or fast stochastic, which is used in conjunction with a second, smoothed line, called %D, or slow stochastic. Once again, the two lines are plotted against a scale of between 0 and 100, generating overbought and oversold indicators but coupled with buy and sell signals triggered by the lines crossing, similar to moving averages.

Using stochastics

1. The overbought zone is usually 80% or higher and oversold zone 20% or lower, as shown in Figure 20.14.

2. The %K and %D lines are used together as an indicator of trend change.

3. Buy and sell signals occur when %K crosses %D, provided that both lines have gone into overbought or oversold territory.

Momentum

Momentum measures the rate of change of prices, as opposed to the actual prices themselves.

Market momentum is measured by continually taking price differences for a set time period, usually 10 days, and plotting the rate of change around a

Momentum and stochastics, GBP/USD, January 2002 – November 2002　　**Figure 20.14**

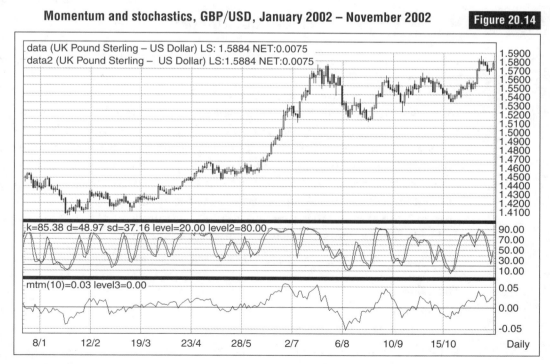

Source: Moneyline Telerate

zero line. So for instance, if positive price differences are continuing to move higher, away from the zero line, then we are seeing increasing positive momentum or velocity. However, if the positive market trend continues but the momentum decreases, then the price trend is slowing down or even possibly reversing.

By plotting price differences over a set period of time, the momentum line is measuring the rate at which the market is accelerating or decelerating in either an advancing or declining price trend. The momentum line tends to lead price movements by a few days making it a very useful early warning indicator.

Uses of momentum

- Overbought and oversold indicator – momentum usually hits a peak before prices turn.
- Momentum employs a zero line – if the zero line is breached then buy and sell signals are generated, see Figure 20.14.
- Oscillators should not be used to trade against market trend. Therefore, if the market trend is up then buy signals should be used on a positive crossing of the zero line. Likewise, sell signals must be used, only in a downtrend after a negative crossing of the zero line.

FIBONACCI NUMBERS

Leonardo Pisano was known as Fibonacci meaning 'blockhead'; he was anything but.

He travelled extensively around the Mediterranean and North Africa, studying with Arab mathematicians an ancient mystical Hindu–Arabic numbering system. In 1202 he competed a book titled *Liber Abaci* (the book of the abacus) which received the endorsement of the Holy Roman Emperor, Frederick II. For the first time in history the counting and calculation systems employed by the Greeks, Romans, Arabs and Hebrews were amalgamated in one system, with practical applications in architecture, bookkeeping, money changing, weights and measures and even the measurement of risk.

The book describes a mathematical number sequence:

$$1, 2, 3, 5, 8, 13, 21, 34, 55, 89, 144, 233 \ldots \text{ to infinity}$$

Key points

- The sum of any two numbers equals the next highest number ($8 + 13 = 21$, $21 + 34 = 55$)
- Divide any number by the next highest number and the answer is always 0.625, and after 89 it is 0.618.

- Divide any number by its preceding number and the ratio is always 1.6, and after 144 always 1.618.

- The ratio of any alternate number is 2.618 or its inverse 0.382

- The ratio of 1.618 or 0.618 was known to the ancient Greeks as the golden ratio, and was used in the construction of the Parthenon.

The Egyptians used the golden ratio in the building of the pyramids. One edge of the Great Pyramid is 783.3 feet long and the height is 484.4 feet (783.3 divided by 484.4 is 1.617). The height of 484.4 feet is 5813 inches (5, 8, 13), from the fibonacci series.

In the human body it is the ratio of height and the position of the naval, as well as finger lengths. There are religious connotations, with the shape and proportions of the Christian cross. The golden ratio appears everywhere, in flower patterns, tree shapes and has applications in art, music, architecture, biology and astronomy.

ELLIOTT WAVE THEORY

The Elliott wave theory gives an overall perspective to market movement, helping to explain why and where chart patterns develop, and what they mean.

R. N. Elliott was an accountant who retired due to ill health in 1927, and during his long period of convalescence he developed his theory of market behaviour. Elliott wave theory gives the analyst more advanced warnings than traditional trend following techniques.

There are three basic aspects to wave theory.

1. **Pattern**. The wave patterns or formations that formulate the most important aspects of the theory.

2. **Ratio**. The ratio analysis measures the relationships between the different waves. This is used to determine price objectives and retracement points.

3. **Time**. Time relationships exist to confirm the wave patterns and ratios. (Considered to be of less value than the other two.)

Basic 8 wave pattern

The basic theory contends that the bull/bear cycle of a market follows a basic 8 wave pattern, which repeats over and over again (see Figure 20.15). The bull phase has 5 waves, followed by the reversal and the bear phase with 3 waves. See the example of a basic 8 wave pattern in Figure 20.16.

Figure 20.15

Elliott's basic 8 wave pattern

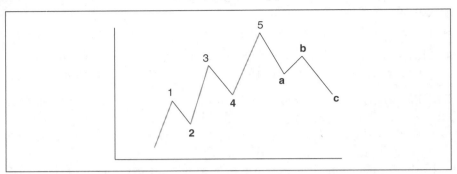

Figure 20.16

Example of Elliott waves: EUR/USD September 2000 to January 2001

Note the basic 8 wave (1–5 and a–c) pattern accompanied by Fibonacci retracement lines

Source: Moneyline Telerate

In the bull phase the 5 waves are made up of 3 rising waves, numbers 1, 3 and 5 called impulse waves. Wave numbers 2 and 4 are against the rising trend and are called corrective waves.

The 5 wave advance is followed by a 3 wave downward correction, waves lettered a, b and c. For convenience, wave practitioners call these waves 5s and 3s. The most important waves to trade are the impulse waves numbers 3 and 5. Wave 3 usually has the most powerful up move, while the top of wave 5 calls for a reversal of positions.

Fibonacci ratios on Elliott waves

Figure 20.17

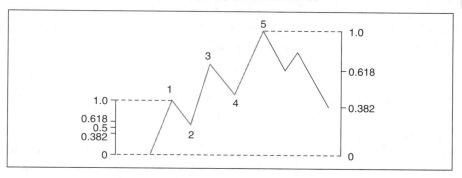

Elliott wave and Fibonacci

- Wave 2 often retraces 50% or 61.8% or wave 1.
- Wave 3 is often 1.618% of wave 2.
- Wave 4 often retraces 38.2% of wave 3.
- The top of wave 5 can be approximated by wave 1 × 2.236 (2 × 1.618) the figure is added to the top and bottom of wave 1 for max./min. price targets.
- In corrections, the tops of waves 2 and 4 provide support levels.
- If one of the 3 impulse waves extends, then the other two should be equal. If wave 5 extends, then 1 and 3 should be equal, and if 3 extends then 1 and 5 should be equal.
- If waves 1 and 3 are equal and wave 5 looks set to extend, then a price target for wave 5 can be measured by taking the distance from the bottom of wave 1 to the top of wave 3. Multiply this by 1.618 and add to the bottom of wave 4.
- In a normal zigzag correction (5–3–5) wave c is often about equal to wave a.
- Percentage retracement levels using Fibonacci numbers, 50% 62% (0.618) and 38% (0.382), as shown in Figure 20.17.

Interestingly, 'time targets' can be found by counting forward from tops and bottoms using Fibonacci numbers 8, 13, 21, 34 days forward, etc.

CONCLUSION

At the start of my career in treasury, many years ago, the term technical analysis was unheard of; in fact, charts and chartists were thought of as a bit of a joke, without any bearing on the real world of buying and selling money. The world moves on, with the advances in technology, especially in terms of high-powered computers and the accessibility of real-time market information. The days of laboriously plotting point and figure charts by hand are long gone, as a wealth of instant data and technical tools are available not just to professional technical analysts and traders, but to anyone with a PC.

The global financial markets have come a long way and now operate using very sophisticated products and trading platforms. Computerized trading is a fact, with machines increasingly involved in making and taking trading decisions. Anyone who wishes to be a part of today's rapidly changing financial markets must have an understanding of technical analysis and the techniques employed. Charts are said to be self-fulfilling prophecies, but the fact remains that many market participants use chart points, support and resistance levels, moving averages and many other technical tools to make real trading decisions. *Ignorance is no excuse*, and, in fact, an absolute disadvantage. The one constant that never changes is human behaviour; markets are driven by greed and fear. The study of technical analysis is the study of price action and market behaviour, and so long as people buy and sell, speculate and accumulate, then the psychological aspect of technical analysis will hold true.

From a personal point of view, I like to take trading decisions based on fundamental analysis, in other words what to buy or sell and why? History is littered with people who make the right choice, but at the wrong time, and end up losing badly. Therefore the timing of entry and exit points to trades is as important as getting the right direction. It must also be remembered that when positions are taken they should *always* be accompanied by stop-loss limits. The use of exit points to prevent loss is essential and a necessary discipline. A more difficult discipline is the use of target levels for profits, most people will either take a profit too quickly or miss the opportunity to maximize a profit by simply being too greedy. The combination of fundamental and technical analysis is still not a sure fire method of always winning, but rather a method of moving the odds in one's favour, and maintaining trading discipline.

I would like to close with a mention of the Society of Technical Analysts. The STA's main objective is to promote greater use and understanding of technical analysis as a vital investment tool. It aims to serve all members of the investment community – from professionals of the investment industry to interested members of the public. (Details can be found at: www.sta-uk.org.)

Further reading

Elliott Wave Principle Applied to the Foreign Exchange Markets, Robert Balan, published by BBS Financial Publications.

Fibonacci Applications and Strategies for Traders, Robert Fischer, published by John Wiley & Sons Inc.

Fundamentals of Technical Analysis, Japanese Candlestick Techniques, www.financial-e-learning.com

Japanese Candlestick Charting Techniques, Steve Nison, published by the New York Institute of Finance.

Technical Analysis of the Financial Markets, John J. Murphy, published by the New York Institute of Finance.

Continuous linked settlement: changing the way the world works

Joseph De Feo, CLS Bank International

INTRODUCTION

The elimination of settlement risk in the world's foreign exchange markets became a reality in September 2002 as CLS Bank International (CLS Bank) launched its Continuous Linked Settlement (CLS™) service – settling live instructions for foreign exchange trades. CLS Bank changes the way the financial services industry operates, linking seven of the world's central banks and many of the world's leading financial institutions in a unique global settlement system. This is the first of its kind – a global banking settlement system.

Continuous Linked Settlement replaces the method of cross-border settlement that has been in place for over 300 years. Even with today's modern technology at our fingertips, the old method of settlement can take two days or more to settle payment instructions associated with FX trading transactions and even longer if reconciliation issues and holidays are involved.

CLS Bank eliminates the 'temporal' (settlement) risk in cross-currency payment instruction settlement, substantially reducing operational risk in the FX markets. Each side of a foreign exchange trade can now be settled simultaneously and irrevocably, in a payment versus payment (PVP) mode that introduces a far higher degree of certainty into the settlement process which will benefit the market as a whole. If the strict settlement criteria for both the payment instructions received into CLS Bank from the parties are not met, the instructions do not settle and no funds are exchanged, protecting the principal of both parties.

Who's involved

The CLS service is only available through the unique and regulated relationship between CLS Bank, the central banks in whose currencies CLS settles, and members of CLS Bank.

The CLS process involves a number of different parties (see Figure 21.1):

- Shareholders;
- Settlement Members;
- User Members;
- Third parties.

Shareholders

CLS Bank is owned by nearly 70 of the world's largest financial groups

Figure 21.1

CLS: who is involved

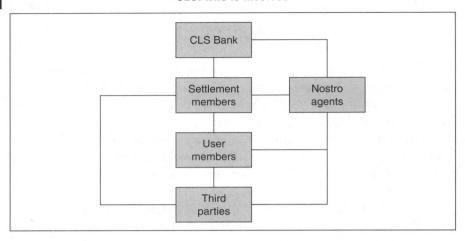

throughout the US, Europe and Asia Pacific. Between them, our shareholders are responsible for more than half the value transferred in the world's FX market. Five CLS shareholders alone represent over 44% of this market. Our shareholders have invested in CLS to develop CLS settlement. Each has purchased an equal shareholding in the CLS Group of companies. Each shareholder has the exclusive right to become a CLS Bank Settlement Member with direct access to the CLS system.

Settlement Members

A Settlement Member must be a shareholder of CLS Group and must show that they have the financial and operational capability and sufficient liquidity to support their financial commitments to CLS. They can each submit settlement instructions directly to CLS Bank and receive information on the status of their instructions. Each Settlement Member has a multi-currency account with CLS Bank, with the ability to move funds. Settlement Members have direct access and input deals on their own behalf and on behalf of their customers. They can provide a branded CLS service to their third-party customers as part of their agreement with CLS Bank.

User Members

User members can submit settlement instructions for themselves and their customers. However, User Members do not have an account with CLS Bank. Instead they are sponsored by a Settlement Member who acts on their behalf. Each instruction submitted by a user member must be authorized by a designated Settlement Member. The instruction is then eligible for settlement through the account Settlement Member's account.

Third parties

Third parties are customers of Settlement and User Members and have no direct access to CLS. Settlement or User Members must handle all instructions and financial flows, which are consolidated in CLS. The terms on which members can act on behalf of third parties are governed by private arrangement. These do not directly involve CLS Bank and third parties do not have any relationship with CLS Bank. Members may provide a trademarked CLS service to their third-party customers.

CLS Bank links the Real Time Gross Settlement (RTGS) systems operated by central banks in seven currencies (US dollar, euro, UK pound, Japanese yen, Swiss franc, Canadian dollar and Australian dollar). Additional currencies will be added over time with three Scandinavian currencies (Swedish krona, Danish krone and Norwegian krone) and the Singapore dollar due to become CLS Bank eligible currencies in 2003. Following this the New Zealand and Hong Kong dollars will become CLS Bank eligible currencies once all the requirements in CLS Bank's rules have been satisfied.

BENEFITS OF CLS

The FX market has grown dramatically in recent years, with the average daily turnover in global FX reaching up to levels as high as USD 3 trillion. Against this backdrop the market requires a robust, reliable cross-currency settlement process, and CLS Bank provides this (Figure 21.2). In addition CLS Bank is an industry creation, rather than an imposed solution, and as such it offers the market a whole range of opportunities and benefits:

- As mentioned, CLS Bank eliminates temporal risk in settlements derived from FX market transactions. CLS Bank will maintain links with the relevant central banks' Real Time Gross Settlement (RTGS) systems that will enable it to provide global settlement with a similar degree of finality

CLS Bank – an ongoing process of submitting instructions, funding and execution　　**Figure 21.2**

and certainty for CLS Bank-settled trades as is provided through a domestic central bank RTGS system.

- At the heart of CLS Bank's unique settlement process is the five-hour operating 'window', during which the participating currency central bank RTGS systems have overlapping operating times, that enable cross-currency transactions to be settled and funded on the same day. In this window eligible settlement instructions for a particular date are settled and funds are requested to be paid in and are paid out by CLS Bank to complete the projected settlement-funding obligation. Each Settlement Member of CLS Bank receives a 'pay-in schedule' that details the Member's net position in each currency and when payments are required in each currency to satisfy the funding obligation derived from the projected settlements. This will enable banks to reduce gross liquidity risk, as payments are required solely on the net position of all settlement instructions made in each currency rather than on an instruction-by-instruction basis, as is the case at present. The coordination of this multilateral netting approach and the structure of the CLS Bank accounting system enables the leveraging of all values in any currency (within limits) to settle other currencies so long as an overall positive multicurrency account balance is maintained.

- Real-time settlement information is available to institutions for the first time, enabling Settlement Members to benefit from a more holistic view of their funds availability. This will lead to improvements in operational efficiency, allowing banks to trace settlements and manage liquidity more efficiently and reduce credit risks associated with the settlement for cross currency business.

- CLS Bank can also assist in the reduction of the cost of settlement. CLS reduces the numbers of instructions needed by as much as 95%, leading to a reduction in payment and receipt and reconciliation errors in settlements.

The benefits of CLS will also be felt in all areas of the banking industry. Reduced settlement risk may enable traders to expand their FX business with CLS participating counter-party banks by making it possible to increase limits due to the reduction in settlement risk. Combined with the ability to monitor and control exposures and shorter and more secure settlement periods, this reduced risk will result in fewer reservations in conducting business in CLS Bank currencies.

Treasury and cash managers benefit from the early notification of a trade's settlement status – leading to greater certainty in respect of intra-day and end-of-day cash positions. CLS also facilitates the rationalization of 'nostro' account relationships and leveraging of multicurrency accounts provided by global settlement agents.

While CLS Bank brings many benefits, the change that it brings is also posing challenges as well. Because of the requirement to 'pay-in', or fund, obligations to CLS Bank during the five-hour window, Settlement Members will need to devise different liquidity management procedures. However, this change may also create an opportunity – many expect a market for intra-day liquidity to emerge as banks find they require liquidity at particular times of the day to facilitate these timed payments.

The pay-in schedule sent to each Settlement Member details the Member's funding obligation to settle its submitted instructions and when payments are required in each currency to satisfy that obligation. This will enable banks to manage liquidity risk in many ways. First, and never possible before, CLS Bank pays out on the basis of value in the Settlement Member account not individual currencies paid in. This enables liquidity managers to leverage funds as a whole. In addition, payments are required solely on the net position of all settlement instructions made in each currency rather than on a trade-by-trade basis, as is the case now.

As indicated above, these multilateral netted positions will reduce gross total individual instructions by around 95%. This provides for vastly improved leveraging of the total liquidity available. And, CLS Bank provides a real-time information system tracking funds through the process in a manner not possible today.

CHALLENGES

Before banks can fully reap the benefits of CLS, they will have to fundamentally change a number of operational practices. This will have an impact beyond their IT infrastructure, extending to the way they do business in terms of liquidity and risk management, correspondent banking, trading and operational management. Building the settlement mechanism is no longer the challenge. The real challenge now is for the banks to move seamlessly away from a value-dated basis to one related to the schedule of 'timed payments'.

They will also have to come to terms with real-time global liquidity management as the focus shifts to intra-day liquidity. Settlement Members will need to establish new processes to enable them to make and receive payments from multiple sources. They will also have to manage multicurrency liquidity in real-time and coordinate liquidity management with the banks' treasury functions in their 'home' currency, as well as in all the CLS eligible currencies.

Critically, the requirement to fund obligations to CLS Bank at specific times means that, intra-day, banks will need to forecast carefully and manage their liquidity requirements to ensure they satisfy these obligations

– this alone will change the way the market works today. But for those banks that can meet the challenge, efficient liquidity management will mean competitive advantage with more cash available for lending, investing and funding operations.

The market benefits that we have been discussing are already becoming a

Continuous linked settlement – how it works

CLS Bank provides its member banks with a continuous linked settlement service that will enable them to settle both sides of a foreign currency trade simultaneously.

CLS Bank will hold accounts in the major central banks of the settling currencies, receive funds and make payments in central bank funds. By using payment versus payment, CLS Bank will provide simultaneously settlement of payment instructions with real-time settlement confirmation. CLS Bank will not, however, guarantee the settlement of every instruction that is submitted for settlement, provide protection against the failure of forward trades or become a counterparty to any currency trade submitted for settlement.

CLS Bank offers two types of membership to qualifying shareholders: settlement membership and user membership. Settlement Members will have accounts with CLS Bank, user members will not and must instead be sponsored by a Settlement Member.

Non-members known as third party customers may also settle their trades in CLS Bank through private arrangements with CLS Bank members.

Each settlement day, Settlement Members with instructions due to settle, will receive a pay-in schedule detailing amounts to be paid to and received from CLS Bank. Members will be required to follow the schedule by making timed payments over the five-hour settlement period to CLS Bank. During the settlement period, instructions will be required by CLS Bank to pass three risk management tests before being settled. CLS Bank in turn will make payouts in rounded amounts to Settlement Members as a result of these settlements.

The settlement process will operate continuously during the settlement period, receiving payments from settlement members, settling instructions and they pay-out funds to those members. At the end of the settlement period, any instructions not settled will be advised to members. They will have the option to settle outside CLS or resubmit to CLS Bank for settlement the next business day.

Initially, the service will settle instructions involving any two of seven eligible currencies: Australian dollar, Canadian dollar, euro, Japanese yen, Swiss franc, UK pound and the US dollar.

Figure 21.3

The CLS Bank settlement process

| 06:30 | 07:00 | 09:00 | 12:00 |

Funding and execution takes place during a five-hour window when the opening times of the relevant RTGS system overlap and are open to send and receive funds

Submitting instructions

▶ Up until 06:30 CET, Settlement Members can submit settlement instructions directly to CLS Bank for processing.

▶ At 06:30 each Settlement Member receives its final pay-in schedule for the day.

Banks can review net pay-in totals at any time before the settlement day, so they have a window on the day's transactions.

Because payments are made on the net positions for each currency (rather than on a gross transaction-by-transaction basis), CLS reduces the funding necessary for the gross total individual instructions by up to 90%.

Settlement and funding

▶ Settlement Members pay in the net funds at the relevant central banks.

▶ Once the first funding is paid in, the settlement execution cycle starts at 07:00 CET.

Banks receive real-time information and manage their own data. Tracking operational errors reduces costly reconciliation delays.

Banks can leverage values in any currency to settle other currencies, as long as they maintain an overall positive account balance.

Execution

▶ Between 07:00 and 09:00 CET, CLS Bank continuously receives funds from Settlement Members, settles instructions across its books, and pays out funds to Settlement Members – until all instructions are settled.

▶ Trades that can't immediately settle are put back in the queue and continually revisited until they settle.

CLS checks that each Settlement Member has a net positive balance across all currencies (after market volatility haircuts) ensuring that CLS Bank and its Settlement Members are protected.

▶ Between 09:00 and 12:00 CET, the pay-ins and pay-outs are finalized.

▶ If there are no problems by 12:00 CET all funds will have been disbursed back to Settlement Members.

If the strict settlement criteria aren't met for one side of a trade, the instructions to CLS Bank are don't settle and no funds are exchanged.

reality. Over USD 50 trillion cumulatively was successfully settled in CLS Bank's first of operation. As CLS Bank develops our aim is to drive out the efficiencies CLS can bring to the inevitable growth of cross-border business and its role in developing new markets. Our Settlement Members are already receiving cost benefits from the liquidity management, straight-through processing (STP) and the reduction of reconciliation errors CLS brings, and in 2003 we look forward to bringing these benefits to the wider market.

Appendices

Central Bank contributors to the Bank for International Settlements 2001 Triennial Central Bank Survey

The following is a list of the official monetary institutions which provided national foreign exchange and derivatives market data, and to which requests for additional copies of this report should be addressed. Queries about the data may also be made to the BIS. The fax number is prefaced by the relevant country and area codes.

Australia:	Reserve Bank of Australia	+61 2 9551 8023
Austria:	Austrian National Bank	+43 1 40420 3199
Bahrain:	Bahrain Monetary Agency	+973 532 274
Belgium:	National Bank of Belgium	+32 2 2213101
Brazil:	Central Bank of Brazil	+55 61 2269513
Canada:	Bank of Canada	+1 613 782 7535
Chile:	Central Bank of Chile	+56 2 670 2106
China:	The People's Bank of China	+86 10 6601 6725
Colombia:	Bank of the Republic	+571 281 3018
Czech Republic:	Czech National Bank	+420 2 2441 3460
Denmark:	National Bank of Denmark	+45 33 63 7103
Finland:	Bank of Finland	+358 9 662 546
France:	Bank of France	+33 142 923 940
Germany:	Deutsche Bundesbank	+49 69 9566 8624
Greece:	Bank of Greece	+30 10 325 5503
Hong Kong SAR:	Hong Kong Monetary Authority	+852 2878 2460
Hungary:	National Bank of Hungary	+36 1 331 3941
India:	Reserve Bank of India	+91 22 261 1427
Indonesia:	Bank Indonesia	+62 21 350 1871
Ireland:	Central Bank of Ireland	+353 1 670 6871
Israel:	Bank of Israel	+972 2 652 2457
Italy:	Bank of Italy	+39 06 4792 2086
	Ufficio Italiano dei Cambi	+39 06 4663 4282
Japan:	Bank of Japan	+81 3 5203 7187
Korea:	Bank of Korea	+82 2 759 5736

Luxembourg:	Central Bank of Luxembourg	+352 4774 4920
Malaysia:	Central Bank of Malaysia	+603 2698 5378
Mexico:	Bank of Mexico	+52 55 5227 8795
Netherlands:	Netherlands Bank	+31 20 524 2512
New Zealand:	Reserve Bank of New Zealand	+64 4 471 3880
Norway:	Central Bank of Norway	+47 22 316542
Peru:	Central Reserve Bank of Peru	+511 427 1100
Philippines:	Central Bank of the Philippines	+632 525 3453
Poland:	National Bank of Poland	+48 22 826 5645
Portugal:	Bank of Portugal	+351 213 12 8478
Russia:	Central Bank of the Russian Federation	+7095 923 8196
Saudi Arabia:	Saudi Arabian Monetary Agency	+966 1 466 2119
Singapore:	Monetary Authority of Singapore	+65 62 299328
Slovak Republic:	National Bank of Slovakia	+421 2 5953 2876
Slovenia:	Bank of Slovenia	+386 1 251 5516
South Africa:	South African Reserve Bank	+27 12 313 3675
Spain:	Bank of Spain	+34 91 338 6102
Sweden:	Sveriges Riksbank	+46 8 787 245348
Switzerland:	Swiss National Bank	+41 1 631 8114
Taiwan, China:	The Central Bank of China	+886 2 2357 1959
Thailand:	Bank of Thailand	+662 283 5400
Turkey:	Central Bank of the Republic of Turkey	+90 312 3127766
United Kingdom:	Bank of England	+44 20 7601 3208
United States:	Federal Reserve Bank of New York	+1 212 720 1216
Bank for International Settlements		+41 61 280 9100

(Source: BIS, Triennial Central Bank Survey 2001. See: www.bis.org/publ/rpfx02t.pdf)

The Black–Scholes Option Pricing Formula

The fair price for any financial asset is its expected value. For example, if a share had a 30% chance of achieving a price of 40, and a 70% chance of achieving a price of 50, the fair value at that time would be:

$$(0.30 \times 40) + (0.70 \times 50) = 47$$

The same principle applies to options. The fair value of an option at expiry is the sum of every possible value it could achieve multiplied by the probability of that value occurring. In the simple example given above, there were just two discrete outcomes. Options, however, can take on almost any value, so it is necessary to use continuous rather than discrete probability distributions. With a discrete distribution, the probability of a particular outcome can be measured directly from the height of the bar. For continuous distributions, the probability of a particular range of outcomes is measured by taking the area beneath that section of the curve.

From the definition of a Call option, the expected value of the option at maturity is:

$$E[C_T] = E[\max(S_T - X, o)] \tag{A}$$

where:

$E[C_T]$ is the expected value of the Call option at maturity
S_T is the price of the underlying asset at maturity
X is the strike price of the option

There are two possible situations that can arise at maturity. If $S_T > X$, the Call option expires in the money, and $\max(S_T - X, o) = S_T - X$. If $S_T < X$, the option expires out of the money, and $\max(S_T - X o) = o$. If p is defined as the probability that $S_T > X$ equation (A) can be rewritten:

$$E[C_T] = p \times (E[S_T 1 S_T > X] - X) + (I - p) \times o$$
$$= p \times (E[S^T 1 S^T > X] - X) \tag{B}$$

where:

p is the probability that $S^T > X$
$E[S^T 1 S^T > X]$ is the expected value of S_T given that $S_T > X$

Equation (B) gives us an expression for the expected value of the Call at maturity. To obtain the fair price at the inception of the contract, the expression must be discounted back to its present value to obtain the following:

$$C = p \times e^{-rt} \times E[S_T 1 S_T > X] - X) \tag{C}$$

where

C is the fair price for the option at inception

r is the continuously compounded riskless rate of interest

t is the length of time until maturity

The problem of pricing an option has been reduced to two slightly simpler problems:

(a) determine p – the probability that the option ends in the money such that $S_T > X$

(b) determine $E[S_T 1 S_T > X]$ – the expected value of the underlying asset given that the option ends in the money

The solution for both of these problems can be found in the lognormal distribution of financial prices. Figure X.1 shows the same lognormal price distribution as that of Figure X.2, but highlights the part of the distribution for which the price exceeds 120. This will be of interest if we wish to price an option whose strike price was set at 120.

The area of the shaded part is 34% of the area under the graph as a whole, so the probability that the final price will exceed 120 is 0.34. The expected value of the shaded part is 137.894. If continuously compounded interest rates are 12%, the fair price for the option struck at 120 is:

$$C = 0.34 \times e^{-0.12} \times (137.894 - 120) = 5.40$$

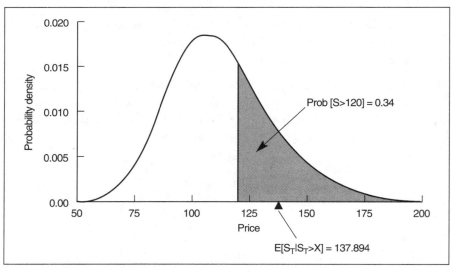

Figure X.1

Lognormal distribution for in the money outcomes

Prob [S>120] = 0.34

$E[S_T|S_T>X]$ = 137.894

Lognormal distribution of prices

Figure X.2

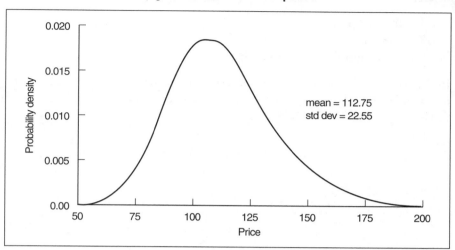

This is, in fact, exactly the value of the option as suggested by the B–S model.

How were the values of 0.34 and 137.894 calculated? It is relatively straight-forward to derive an expression for the probability p, but rather more difficult to do so for the expectation expression $E[S_T | S_T > X]$. We therefore will show here how the probability can be calculated, but not how the expectation can be derived; for the latter we will merely state the end result. Combining the two expressions will give us the formula for the B–S model itself.

Finding the probability p that the underlying price at maturity S_T will exceed some critical price X is the same as finding the probability that the return over the period will exceed some critical value r_x. This is an easier problem to solve, because returns follow a normal distribution, and normal distributions are easier to work with than lognormal distributions. Remembering that returns are defined as the logarithm of the price relatives means that we must find the probability p such that:

$$p = Prob[S_T > X] = Prob\left[\text{return} > \ln\left(\frac{X}{S_0}\right)\right] \qquad \text{(D)}$$

where S_0 is the underlying price at the outset.

In general, the probability that a normally distributed variable x will exceed some critical value x_{crit} is given by:

$$Prob[x > x_{crit}] = I - N\left(\frac{x_{crit} - \mu^*}{\sigma^*}\right) \qquad \text{(E)}$$

where:

μ^* is the mean of x
σ^* is the standard deviation of x
$N(.)$ is the cumulative normal distribution

In the context of equation (D), we need to find expressions for μ^* and σ^*, the mean and standard deviation of returns. We have an expression for the expected value of the price relative S_T/S_O. This is:

$$E\left[\frac{S_t}{S_0}\right] = e^{\mu t} + \frac{\sigma^2 t}{2}$$

If we define r such that:

$$r = \mu + \frac{\sigma^2}{2} \tag{F}$$

we can then rewrite equation 10.7 in a simpler way:

$$E\left[\frac{S_T}{s_0}\right] = e^{et} \tag{G}$$

The new variable r is not only a convenient shorthand for the expression $\mu + \sigma^2/2$, it is actually the continuously compounded riskless rate of interest. It may seem surprising that this is the relevant interest rate to use when valuing risky investments like options, but the answer to this conundrum lies in the risk neutrality argument.

The basis for the risk neutrality argument is the possibility of constructing a riskless portfolio combining an option with some proportion of the underlying asset. In fact, this approach is the foundation of the binomial method for option valuation. A riskless portfolio is one that has the same financial outcome regardless of event, and therefore future cash flows should be discounted at the riskless interest rate. With such a portfolio, investors' risk preferences are irrelevant, and the portfolio should be worth the same whether being valued by risk-averse or by risk-neutral investors. Since it is easier to value the portfolio at the riskless rate used by risk-neutral investors, we may as well choose the riskless rate.

Note that the risk neutrality argument does not imply that all financial assets actually do grow at the riskless rate implied by equation (G). What the argument says is that the same answer for the price of an option will be obtained whether we choose the riskless rate or some higher interest rate. If a higher rate were selected, the underlying asset would grow at a faster rate, but the payoffs from an option on this asset would also have to be discounted back at a higher rate, and the two effects cancel out.

Another way to consider this is to remember that the option price is determined in proportion to the price of the underlying asset; double both the underlying asset price and the strike price, and the option price will also double.

If the underlying asset price happens to be depressed because risk-averse investors are discounting future cash flows at a particularly high rate, the price of the option will also be depressed since it is calculated in proportion, but this is just as it should be. To be consistent, the same investors should discount future cash flows from the option at the same high rate.

We now have:

$$E\left[\ln\left(\frac{S_t}{S_0}\right)\right] = \mu t = \left(r - \frac{\sigma^2}{2}\right)t = \mu^* \tag{H}$$

which gives an expression for μ^*, the mean return. The standard deviation of returns is defined as $\sigma\sqrt{t}$. Combining equations (D) and (E) we now have:

$$Prob[S_T > X] = Prob\left[\text{return} > \ln\left(\frac{X}{S_0}\right)\right]$$

$$= I - N\left(\frac{\ln\left(\frac{X}{S_0}\right) - \left(r - \frac{\sigma^2}{2}\right)t}{\sigma\sqrt{t}}\right) \tag{I}$$

The symmetry of the normal distribution means that $I - N(d) = N(-d)$, so:

$$p = Prob[S_T > X] = N\left(\frac{\ln\left(\frac{S_0}{X}\right) + \left(r - \frac{\sigma^2}{2}\right)t}{\sigma\sqrt{t}}\right)$$

Substituting the values in the previous example, we have:

$$Prob[S_T > X] = N\left(\frac{\ln\left(\frac{100}{120}\right) + \left(0.12 - \frac{0.20^2}{2}\right) \times 1}{0.20\sqrt{I}}\right) = N(-0.4116) = 0.34$$

and this is the value for the probability p obtained before.

Finding a formula for the expression $E[S_T 1 S_T > X]$ involves integrating the normal distribution curve over the range X to ∞. When this is done, the result is:

$$E[S_T 1 S_T > X] = S_0 e^{rt} \frac{N(d_1)}{N(d_2)} \tag{K}$$

where

$$d_1 = \frac{\ln\left(\frac{S_0}{X}\right) + \left(r + \frac{\sigma^2}{2}\right)t}{\sigma\sqrt{t}} \quad \text{and}$$

$$d_2 = \frac{\ln\left(\frac{S_0}{X}\right) + \left(r - \frac{\sigma^2}{2}\right)t}{\sigma\sqrt{t}} = d_1 - s\sqrt{t} \tag{L}$$

Now we have expressions for p (equation (J)) and $E[S_T 1 S_T > X]$ (equation (K)), and can insert these into equation (C) to obtain the complete formula for a Call option:

$$C = N(d_2) \times e - rt \times \left(S_0 e^{rt} \frac{N(d_1)}{N(d_2)} - X \right)$$

$$\therefore \quad C = S_0 N(d_1) - Xe^{-rt} N(d_2) \tag{M}$$

This is the famous Black–Scholes model. It provides a single formula, which enables the fair price for a Call option to be calculated. As the foregoing derivation has demonstrated, the formula can be interpreted as measuring the expected present value of the option based on the key assumption that prices follow a lognormal distribution.

As an illustration of this, Figures X.3 and X.4 show the results of a Monte Carlo simulation. The behavior of a financial asset was simulated by a computer over 10,000 trials. In each trial, the return was sampled at random from a normal distribution with mean $\mu = 10\%$ and standard deviation $\sigma = 20\%$. If the return in a given trial turned out to be p, the price S_t after a period of time t would be given by $S_t = S_0 e^{pt}$, and the present value of the option would be $(S_t - X)/e^{-rt}$ if $S_t > X$, and 0 otherwise.

Starting always with an initial price of 100, this experiment gave rise to the distribution of prices after one year illustrated in Figure X.3. This has a mean equation 112.75 and a standard deviation of 22.77, almost exactly that predicted by equation 10.7 and illustrated in the theoretical distribution of Figure X.2. The probability of the underlying price being below 120 was 0.66, the same as the theoretical figure of 0.66 (1.00 − 0.34) predicted by equation (J).

The corresponding distribution of option prices is illustrated in Figure X.4. The option expired out of the money in 66% of the trials, while in the remainder

Figure X.3

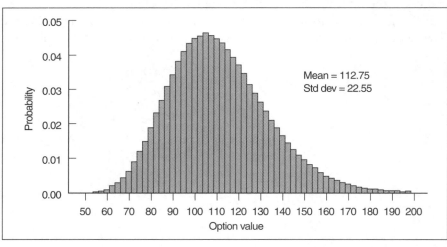

Distribution of underlying asset prices

Mean = 112.75
Std dev = 22.55

Distribution of option values

Figure X.4

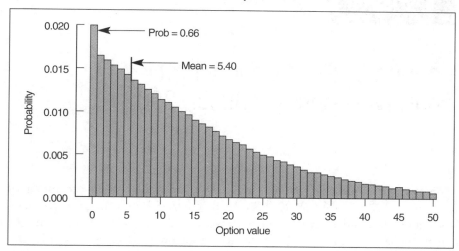

of cases it expired in the money with values ranging from just above zero to as high as 110. The mean of this wide distribution was 5.40, exactly the price calculated using the B–S model in equation (M).

Thus, starting only with an assumption of returns which are normally distributed, and using nothing other than very simple arithmetic, the Monte Carlo simulation arrives at the same answer for the expected value of the option as the B–S model.

This appendix is reproduced with kind permission from *Financial Engineering – Tools and Techniques to Manage Financial Risk*, by Lawrence Galitz (Financial Times Prentice Hall, revised edition 1995) – available from leading bookshops at £90.00.

London Code of Conduct for non-investment products, 2002

The London Code of Conduct (LCC) was superseded when the Financial Services and Markets Act 2000 (FSMA), together with its associated secondary legislation, took effect at the end of November 2001 (N2). At that time the Financial Services Authority (FSA) formally took on its new responsibilities and a new Inter-Professionals Code (IPC) covering investment products succeeded the current London Code of Conduct (LCC) for investment and non-investment products.

However, trading in the wholesale markets in non-investment products (NIPs), that is trading in sterling, foreign exchange and bullion wholesale deposit markets, and the spot and forward foreign exchange and bullion markets, was not covered by the IPC. There was, however, strong market support for a code to cover these markets, and, in November 2001, a draft NIPs Code was published for consultation.

The draft NIPs Code was drawn up by a wide cross-section of market practitioners representing principals and brokers in the foreign exchange, money and bullion markets. The work was carried out by the Foreign Exchange Joint Standing Committee, the Wholesale Sterling Deposits Working Group (a sub-group of the Money Market Liaison Group) and the London Bullion Market Association, and was based on the LCC, while working in tandem with the FSA's work on the IPC.

The NIPs Code will apply to both FSA authorized and non-FSA authorized institutions.

The NIPs code is published by kind permission of The Bank of England.

THE NON-INVESTMENT PRODUCTS CODE

Foreword by the Bank of England

This Code has been drawn up by market practitioners representing principals and brokers in the foreign exchange, money and bullion markets[1] to underpin the professionalism and high standards of these markets. It applies to trading in the wholesale markets in Non-Investment Products (NIPs), that is sterling, foreign exchange and bullion wholesale deposit markets, and the spot and forward foreign exchange and bullion markets. These products were previously covered by the London Code of Conduct, and are not among the investments covered by the Inter-Professionals Conduct (IPC) Chapter of the Financial Services Authority (FSA) Handbook.

In its handbook the FSA is publishing separately codes, rules and guidance relevant to conduct in the wholesale markets in investment products. These FSA publications include the Inter-Professionals Conduct. These provisions in the IPC are applicable to firms which are authorized under the Financial Services and Markets Act (2000) or which transact business in the United Kingdom under the EU passport and are subject to FSA Conduct of Business rules. The IPC will not cover transactions in investments that are deposits as specified in the Regulated Activities Order.

The NIPs Code has been drawn up by a wide cross-section of market participants in the London market, including the Bank of England and the Financial Services Authority, but its provisions are intended only as guidance on what is currently believed to constitute good practice in these markets. The Code has no statutory underpinning except where it refers to existing legal requirements. Those who have prepared the NIPs Code have sought, where appropriate, to make its provisions consistent with the relevant parallel provisions in the FSA Handbook, bearing in mind, in particular, that some firms will operate both in the NIPs and investment product markets.

---

[1] Coordinated by the Foreign Exchange Joint Standing Committee, the Money Markets Liaison Group and the Management Committee of the London Bullion Market Association.

I INTRODUCTION

II GENERAL STANDARDS

III CONTROLS

IV CONFIRMATION AND SETTLEMENT

ANNEXES

Annex 1: Dealing principles and procedures: statements of good practice

I INTRODUCTION

Aims and coverage

1. The London financial markets have a long-established reputation for their high degree of professionalism and the maintenance of the highest standards of business conduct. All those operating in these markets share a common interest in their health and in maintaining the established exacting standards. This code is intended to help underpin these standards.

2. The Code is applicable to wholesale market dealings in non-investment products, namely:

   - sterling wholesale deposits[1]
   - foreign currency wholesale deposits[1]
   - gold and silver bullion wholesale deposits
   - spot and forward foreign exchange[2,3]
   - spot and forward gold and silver bullion.

3. The Code sets out for management and individuals at broking firms and principals, standards of good practice in the market. The spirit of the code applies equally to business transacted via electronic or traditional media. Principals include firms authorised under the Financial Services and Markets Act 2000 and similar firms operating in the United Kingdom under the EU passport arrangements, as well as other companies and institutions, local authorities and other public bodies which operate in the wholesale NIPs markets.

4. The following trade associations have endorsed the Code and commended it to their members: the Association of Corporate Treasurers, British Bankers' Association, Building Societies Association, Chartered Institute of Public Finance and Accountancy, London Bullion Market Association, London Investment Banking Association and the Wholesale Market Brokers' Association.

5. The Code has been developed by market practitioners and co-ordinated through the Foreign Exchange Joint Standing Committee, the Money Markets Liaison Group and the Management Committee of the London Bullion Market Association. It will continue to be kept under review in the light of market developments.

---

[1] The Code does not affect in any way the regulation of deposit-taking under the Financial Services and Markets Act 2000. The Code does not cover debt securities the issuance of which may involve the acceptance of *deposits* as these are defined as investments under the Financial Services and Markets Act. The Code does, however, cover wholesale deposits that are specified as investments in the Regulated Activities Order, as well as wholesale deposits that are not so specified.

[2] The Government made clear in January 1988 that ordinary foreign exchange and bullion transactions fall outside the Financial Services Act (1986). However, as explained by the Securities and Investments Board in consultation document 89, issued in August 1995, certain margined products do constitute investment business within the meaning of the Financial Services Act (1986); and the treatment of these products is the same under the Financial Services and Markets Act (2000).

[3] Other foreign exchange products, such as futures contracts, are classified as investment products.

Distribution

6. Firms should endeavour to make their counterparties aware that deals in the London market are undertaken in accordance with the Code and that it is available from the Bank of England's website (www.bankofengland.co.uk) or direct from the Bank of England, Threadneedle Street, London, EC2R 8AH.

Compliance and arbitration

7. Where a firm is concerned about a counterparty not adhering to the Code, it should approach the counterparty and, where appropriate, seek remedial action. Where disputes about matters of market practice relating to adherence to the Code cannot be resolved bilaterally, there are provisions in the foreign exchange market for arbitration to be carried out by an arbitration panel, which will be chosen on a case by case basis from a pool of the members of the Foreign Exchange Joint Standing Committee and other market participants. Details of this foreign exchange arbitration process are set out in Annex 3 of this Code. In the case of disputes in the bullion market, details of the arbitration arrangements can be obtained from the London Market Bullion Association[4] or the Bank of England. There are currently no arbitration procedures in the sterling wholesale deposit market.

The Role of the Financial Services Authority

8. **The NIPs Code covers business that is outside the scope of FSA regulation (except those deposits which are investments as specified in the Regulatory Activities Order)** and provides guidance on what is currently believed to constitute good market practice. The Inter-Professional Conduct Chapter of the FSA Handbook and the Conduct of Business Sourcebook also set out similar requirements for authorised firms in respect of investment business. If an authorised firm carries out both investment and non-investment business, it may find it more convenient to implement just one set of requirements where these cover the same types of functions but in relation to the different business lines. That one document would have to be the FSA's Handbook, given that the IPC has regulatory force, though the NIPS Code may provide useful, more detailed guidance in some circumstances. The NIPs Code has no statutory underpinning except where it refers to existing legal requirements but non-compliance (depending on the circumstances, seriousness and duration of the incidents) may raise issues such as the integrity or competence of the firm, which are relevant to the FSA's authorisation requirements. The FSA has participated in the development of this Code and expects management of authorised firms to take due account of it when conducting business in products covered by this code.

II GENERAL STANDARDS

Firms – and their employees – should act in accordance with the spirit as well as the letter of the Code when undertaking, arranging or advising on transactions in the wholesale markets. Managers of firms should ensure that the obligations imposed on

---

[4] The London Market Bullion Association, 6 Frederick's Place, London, EC2R 8BT; telephone 020 7796 3067; or mail@lbma.org.uk.

them and their staff by the general law are observed. Management and staff should also be mindful of any relevant rules and codes of practice of regulatory bodies, such as section 3.4 of the FSA's IPC.

Responsibilities

Of the firm

9. All firms are expected to act in a manner consistent with the Code so as to maintain the highest reputation for the wholesale markets in London.

10. Relevant staff should be familiar with the Code, conduct themselves at all times in a thoroughly professional manner and undertake transactions in a way that is consistent with the procedures set out in this Code.

11. All firms are responsible for the actions of their staff. This responsibility includes:
    - ensuring that any individual who commits the firm to a transaction has the necessary authority to do so;
    - ensuring that employees are adequately trained in the practices of the markets in which they deal/broke; and are aware of their own, and their firm's, responsibilities. Inexperienced dealers should not rely on a broker, for instance, to fill gaps in their training or experience; to do so is clearly **not** the broker's responsibility;
    - ensuring staff are made aware of and comply with any other relevant guidance that may from time to time be issued, which supplements or replaces this Code, and;
    - ensuring that employees comply with any regulatory requirements that may be applicable or relevant to a firm's activities in the wholesale markets.

12. When establishing a relationship with a **new** counterparty or client, firms should take steps to make them aware of the precise nature of the firm's liability for business to be conducted, including any limitations on that liability and the capacity in which they act. **In particular, broking firms should explain to a new client the limited role of brokers (see paragraphs 22 and 23 of this code).**

13. All firms should identify any potential or actual **conflicts of interest** that might arise when undertaking wholesale market transactions and take measures either to eliminate these conflicts or control them so as to ensure the fair treatment of counterparties.

14. All firms should **know their counterparty**. For principals this is essential where the nature of the business undertaken requires the assessment of creditworthiness. Before dealing with another principal for the first time in any product covered by this Code, firms should ensure that appropriate steps are taken (see paragraphs 24 to 25 and 78 to 83 of this Code).

15. As part of the 'know your counterparty' process principals should take great care to prevent their transactions in the wholesale markets being used to facilitate **money laundering**. To this end they should be familiar with the Guidance Notes published by the Joint Money Laundering Steering Group in March 2001 (as updated from time to time)[5]. These make clear the very limited responsibilities name passing brokers have in this area; in particular banks (and others that use brokers) should **not** seek to rely on brokers to undertake anything other than identity and location checks on their behalf.

---

[5] Available from the Joint Money Laundering Steering Group, Pinners Hall, 105–108 Old Broad Street, London, EC2N 1BX.

16. Each principal should assess the merits and risks of a transaction and decide if it needs to seek independent professional advice. All principals should accept responsibility for entering into wholesale market transactions and any subsequent losses they might incur.

17. Management of broking firms should advise their employees of the need to ensure that their behaviour could not be construed as having misled counterparties about the limited role of brokers (see paragraphs 22 and 23 of this code). Failure to be vigilant in this area may adversely affect the reputation of the broking firm itself.

Of the employee

18. When entering into or arranging individual deals, dealers and brokers should seek to ensure that they do not provide misleading information or misrepresent the nature of any transaction in any way. Dealers and brokers should disclose:

   - the identity of the firm for which they are acting, and its role, to their counter-parties/clients. This is particularly important, for instance, where an individual dealer acts for more than one company, or in more than one capacity.

   - the products in which they are proposing to deal.

   - facts believed to be material to completing a specific transaction before the deal is done, except where such disclosure would reveal confidential information about the activities of another firm. Unless specifically asked for more information, or clarification, a dealer at a principal will assume his counterparty has all the necessary information for this decision making process when entering into a wholesale market transaction.

19. When a deal is being arranged through a broker, the broker should act in a way that does not unfairly favour one client over another, irrespective of what brokerage arrangements exist between them and the broking firm.

Clarity of role

Role of principals

20. The role of firms acting as principal is to deal for their own account. It is the responsibility of the principal alone to assess the creditworthiness of its counterparties or potential counterparties whether dealing direct or through a broking firm. Principals should decide what credence, if any, is given to any information or comment provided by a broker to a dealer. It is for each principal to decide whether or not to seek independent professional advice.

21. Some firms may act as agent for connected or other companies as well as, or instead of, dealing for their own account. If so, such agents should:

   - always make absolutely clear to all concerned the capacity in which they are acting (e.g. if they also act as principal or broker).

   - declare at an early stage of negotiations the party for whom they are acting. It may be considered desirable to set out this relationship formally in writing for future reference.

   - ensure that all confirmations make clear when a deal is done on an agency basis.

   - when acting as agent for an unregulated principal, make clear at an early stage this qualification to potential counterparties; and include this on confirmations.

Role of brokers

22. Typically the role of the specialist wholesale market broking firms in London for non-investment products is to act as arrangers of deals[6]. They:

   - bring together counterparties on mutually acceptable terms and pass names to facilitate the conclusion of a transaction.

   - receive payment for this service in the form of brokerage (except where a prior explicit agreement between the management of all parties to a deal provides otherwise).

   - are not permitted, even fleetingly, to act as principal in a deal, or to act in any discretionary fund management capacity[7].

23. It is accepted that, in providing the service specified in the previous paragraph, individual brokers may be called upon to give advice or express opinions, usually in response to requests from individual dealers. While brokers should be mindful of the need not to reveal confidential information about the market activities of individual clients, there is no restriction on brokers passing, or commenting, on general information that is in the public domain. Equally, there is no responsibility upon a broker to volunteer general information of this type. Where information is sought or volunteered individual brokers should exercise particular care. For instance, brokers do not have sufficient information to be qualified to advise principals on the creditworthiness of specific counterparties and to do so is not their role.

III CONTROLS

Management should have in place, and review regularly, appropriate control procedures that their staff should follow. Further guidance on some of the aspects referred to below, together with some additional information that may be useful for market participants, can be found in Annex 1.

Know your counterparty

24. As noted in paragraph 14 within the section on General Standards, all firms should **know their counterparty**. It is necessary for a variety of reasons, including firms' own risk control and the need to meet their legal obligations (e.g. on money laundering) for firms to undertake 'know their counterparty' checks before dealing in any products covered by this Code.

25. For further information and guidance please refer to paragraphs 78 to 83 of Annex 1 of this Code. For FSA authorised firms, obligations in this area arise from the FSA Rulebook.

Dealing mandates

26. Dealing mandates can be useful in clarifying the nature of the counterparty relationship. A mandate might, for example, clarify whether the relationship is at

---

[6] In non-investment products, there is one exception to this rule, *namely* when broking firms are investing their own money. In such transactions, brokers should make clear to the relevant counterparties that they are acting as principal.

[7] The relationship between an institution offering a discretionary or advisory management service and its clients in any of the financial products described falls outside the scope of this Code and, if it constitutes investment business within the terms of the Financial Services and Markets Act 2000, should be in accordance with that Act.

arms length or advisory, and/or set out confirmation procedures, standard settlement instructions, and other control procedures. But a mandate may not be appropriate or necessary for all counterparty relationships. The decision to establish a mandate rests firmly with the management of each counterparty.

27. For further information and guidance please refer to paragraphs 89 and 90 of Annex 1 of this Code.

Confidentiality

28. Confidentiality is essential for the preservation of a reputable and efficient market place. Principals and brokers share equal responsibility for maintaining confidentiality. Principals or brokers should not, without explicit permission, disclose or discuss, or apply pressure on others to disclose or discuss, any information relating to specific deals which have been transacted, or are in the process of being arranged, except to or with the parties directly involved (and, if necessary, their advisers) or where this is required by law or to comply with the requirements of a supervisory body. All relevant personnel should be made aware of, and observe, this fundamental principle.

29. For further information and guidance please refer to paragraphs 84 to 88 of Annex 1 of this Code. For FSA authorised firms, paragraphs 2 and 3 of the third annex of the IPC sets out good market practice as regards confidentiality.

Taping

30. The use of tape-recording equipment in the offices of voice brokers and principals to record conversations by dealers, salespersons and brokers, together with back-office telephone lines used by those responsible for confirming deals or passing payment and other instructions is normal practice. Taping is also common where a firm's private banking division sells wholesale products.

31. Where electronic trading systems are used which allow the automatic capture of deal information taping may be superfluous.

32. Taping can assist in the:

- proper recording of the material terms of a transaction to which a firm is a party;
- speedy and effective resolution of differences and disputes;
- identification of instances of inappropriate behaviour, either on the part of its employees or those of its counterparties.

33. Firms which have installed or plan to install tape-recording equipment, should take steps to inform their clients that transactions will be recorded, and to comply with the other relevant provisions of any telecom privacy legislation in force.

34. A firm should make and implement a policy about the period of time for which it keeps tapes. The longer recordings are retained the greater the chances are that any subsequent disputes over transactions can be resolved satisfactorily. It is for firms to decide how long to keep such tapes; to date normal practice has been to keep them for at least two months. Recordings that cover any relevant aspects of a transaction about which there is a dispute should be retained until the problem has been resolved, following an agreement between the parties involved.

35. Management should seek to ensure that it is able to access all tapes promptly and that access to recording equipment and tapes, whether in use or in store, is strictly controlled so that they cannot be tampered with.

36. For FSA authorised firms, section 3.6 of the IPC sets out rules and guidance as regards taping.

Deals at non-current rates

37. Principals and brokers should take great care before entering into or arranging transactions at materially different non-current rates, including rolling-over an existing contract at the original rate. Experience suggests that these should only be undertaken after very careful consideration by both parties and approval, on a deal by deal basis, by their senior management. It is particularly important to ensure that there is no ambiguity in such transactions over the amounts that each counterparty is to pay and receive.

38. Failure to use current rates (where available in the relevant market) may result in:
   - the extension of unauthorised credit;
   - the firm unknowingly participating in the concealment of a profit or loss;
   - the perpetration of a fraud.

39. Senior management should ensure that, *before* the firm commits itself to such a transaction, proper procedures are in place to:
   - identify and bring to their attention non current rate transactions;
   - enable them to conclude that there are reasonable grounds for believing that the firm has not been put on notice that the reasons for the transaction are not justifiable and proper;
   - review appropriate documentation; and
   - confirm that all material terms of the non current rate transactions have been agreed in writing at a senior level by all relevant parties to the transaction.

40. These procedures are particularly important in the case of historic rate rollovers in FX markets. Where appropriate, spot rates should be determined immediately after completion of a forward foreign exchange transaction.

41. A clear audit trail should be provided to demonstrate that the application of non-market rates and/or prices in component(s) of a complex deal structure satisfy the legitimate requirements of counterparties to the transaction.

42. For FSA authorised firms, section 3.5 of the IPC sets out rules and guidance as regards transactions at non-market prices.

After-hours dealing

43. Extended trading after normal local hours has become accepted in some markets, most notably foreign exchange. Dealing after-hours into other centres forms an integral part of the operations of many firms both in London and elsewhere. Such dealing can involve additional hazards – whether undertaken direct or via a broker. For example, when dealing continues during the evening from premises other than the principal's dealing rooms, one of the principals involved might subsequently forget, or deny, having done a deal. Management should therefore issue clear guidelines to their staff, both on the kinds of deal which may be undertaken in those circumstances and on the permitted limits of any such dealing. All deals should be confirmed promptly – preferably by electronic message direct to the counterparty's offices. Management should consider installing answerphone facilities in the dealing area which dealers should use to record full details of all off-premises trades. These should be processed promptly on the next working day.

44. For FSA authorised firms, paragraphs 12 to 14 of the third annex of the IPC sets out good market practice as regards after-hours dealing.

Stop-loss orders

45. Principals may receive requests from branches, counterparties and correspondents to execute transactions – for instance to buy or sell a currency – if prices or rates should reach a specified level. These orders, which include stop-loss and limit orders from counterparties desiring around-the-clock protection for their own positions, may be intended to remain valid during the day, overnight, or until executed or cancelled. Management needs to establish clear policies and procedures for its traders who accept and execute stop-loss and limit orders. Management should ensure that the terms of such orders are agreed in accordance with these procedures. and that there is a clear understanding with the counterparty about the obligation it has assumed. Dealers handling such an instruction should have adequate lines of communication with the counterparty so that they can reach authorised personnel in case of an unusual situation or extreme price/rate movement.

Conflicts of interest

46. For FSA authorised firms, section 7.13 of the Conduct of Business Sourcebook sets out rules as regards conflicts of interest.

Dealing for personal account

47. Management should consider carefully whether any of their employees who deal in products covered by this code should be allowed to deal for own account in these products. Where allowed by management, it is their responsibility to ensure that adequate safeguards are established to prevent abuse. These safeguards should reflect the need to maintain confidentiality with respect to non-public price-sensitive information and to ensure that no action is taken by employees which might adversely affect the interests of the firm's clients or counterparties.

Deals using a connected broker

48. Brokers have a legal obligation to disclose the nature and extent of any material conflict between their own interests and their responsibilities to clients. To safeguard the independence of brokers they should give all their clients formal written notification of any principal(s) where a material connection exists (unless a client explicitly waives its rights to this information in writing); and notify any subsequent changes to this list of principals as they occur. For the purposes of this Code, a material connection would include situations where the relationship between the parties could have a bearing on the transaction or its terms, as a result for example of common management responsibilities or material shareholding links, whether direct or indirect. A shareholding of 10% or more in a broker is generally regarded as material; but, depending on the circumstances, a smaller holding may also represent a material connection.

49. Any deals arranged by a broker involving a connected principal should be at arm's length (i.e. at mutually agreed rates that are the same as those prevailing for transactions between unconnected counterparties).

Marketing and incentives

50. Firms should take care to ensure that advertisements for their services are directed so far as possible towards professionals.

51. Brokers should not make payments to banks for using their services although the provision of discount arrangements is a legitimate marketing technique, even if

these involve cross-product subsidisation between different parts of the same group.

52. For FSA authorised firms, sections 3.4.13 to 3.4.16 of the IPC set out rules and guidance as regards marketing and incentives.

Entertainment and gifts

53. A firm should establish a policy to ensure that neither it nor its employees should offer, give, solicit or accept any inducement from third parties. Where entertainment or gifts are offered in the ordinary course of business, management should:

   – establish a policy towards the giving/receiving of entertainments/gifts;
   – take reasonable steps to ensure that the policy is observed; and,
   – deal with gifts judged to be excessive but which cannot be declined without giving offence.

54. For further information and guidance please refer to paragraphs 101 to 103 of Annex 1 of this Code. For FSA authorised firms, sections 3.4.13 to 3.4.16 of the IPC set out rules and guidance as regards entertainment and gifts.

Gambling

55. Gambling with other market participants carries obvious dangers to the firm and individuals involved. Where it is allowed at all, it is strongly recommended that it is tightly restricted.

Drug and alcohol abuse

56. The judgement of those using drugs, alcohol and other substances that can give rise to abuse is likely to be impaired. Any dependancy will seriously diminish a member of staff's ability to function satisfactorily and may make them more vulnerable to outside inducement, for example to conduct business that is not necessarily in the best interests of the firm. Management should take all reasonable steps to educate themselves and their staff about both the signs and effects of the use of drugs and other substances that lead to abuse.

IV CONFIRMATION AND SETTLEMENT

Further information and guidance on the aspects referred to below can be found in Annex 1 of this Code.

Confirmation procedures

57. Prompt passing, recording and careful checking of confirmations minimises the possibility of errors and misunderstanding whether dealing direct or through brokers. Details should be passed as soon as practicable after deals have been done and checked upon receipt. The passing of details in batches is not recommended. For markets where standard terms are applicable eg under master documentation, it is recommended that confirmations conform to the formats specified for the market or instrument concerned. When electronic dealing systems are used there is no need to send confirmations.

58. For further information and guidance on confirmation procedures, please refer to paragraphs 108 to 117 of Annex 1 of this Code. For FSA authorised firms, para-

graphs 17 to 23 of the third annex of the IPC sets out good market practice as regards confirmations.

Payment/settlement instructions

59. Instructions should be passed as quickly as possible to facilitate prompt settlement. The use of standard settlement instructions is strongly recommended; their use can make a significant contribution to reducing both the incidence and size of differences arising from the mistaken settlement of funds.

60. For further information and guidance please refer to paragraphs 118 to 123 of Annex 1 of this Code. For FSA authorised firms, paragraphs 24 and 25 of the third annex of the IPC sets out good market practice as regards payment and settlement instructions.

Settlement of differences

61. If all the procedures outlined above are adhered to, the incidence and size of differences should be reduced; and those mistakes which do occur should be identified and corrected promptly. Failure to observe these principles could leave those responsible bearing the cost, without limit on size or duration, of any differences which arise. Except in the foreign exchange market, all differences must be settled in cash or, by mutual management agreement, by offset against brokerage due. In the absence of agreement otherwise, cash remains the default means of settlement.

62. For further information and guidance please refer to paragraphs 124 to 128 of Annex 1 of this Code. For FSA authorised firms, sections 3.7.4 to 3.7.8 of the IPC set out rules and guidance on settlement of differences.

ANNEX 1: DEALING PRINCIPLES AND PROCEDURES: STATEMENTS OF GOOD PRACTICE

Scope

Section I describes the coverage and status of the Code.

63. Whilst this Code is designed for the London markets, its provisions may extend beyond UK shores, for example where a UK broker arranges a deal involving an overseas counterparty. Where deals involving overseas counterparties are to be made on a different basis in any respect, for example because of distinct local rules or requirements, this should be clearly identified at the outset to avoid any possible confusion.

Procedures

Preliminary negotiation of terms

Firms should clearly state at the outset, prior to a transaction being executed, any qualifying conditions to which it will be subject.

64. Typical examples of qualifications include where a price is quoted subject to the necessary credit approval, finding a counterparty for matching deals or the ability to execute an associated transaction. For instance principals may quote a rate which is 'firm subject to the execution of a hedge transaction'. For the sake of

good order, it is important that firms complete deals as quickly as possible; the onus is on both sides to keep each other informed of progress or possible delays. If a principal's ability to conclude a transaction is constrained by other factors, for example opening hours in other centres, this should be made known to brokers and potential counterparties at an early stage and before names are exchanged.

Firmness of quotation

All firms, whether acting as principal, agent or broker, should make absolutely clear whether the prices they are quoting are firm or merely indicative. Prices quoted by brokers should be taken to be firm in marketable amounts unless otherwise qualified.

The following does not apply to authorised firms, for whom paragraphs 7 to 9 of the third annex of the IPC sets out good market practice as regards firmness of quotation.

65. A principal quoting a firm price (or rate) either through a broker or directly to a potential counterparty is committed to deal at that price (or rate) in a marketable amount provided the counterparty name is acceptable. In order to minimise the scope for confusion where there is no clear market convention, dealers quoting a firm price (or rate) should indicate the length of time for which the quote is firm.

66. It is generally accepted that when dealing in fast moving markets (like spot forex) a principal has to assume that a price given to a broker is good only for a short length of time. However, this practice would be open to misunderstandings about how quickly a price is deemed to lapse if it were adopted when dealing in generally less hectic markets, for example the forward foreign exchange or deposit markets, or when market conditions are relatively quiet. Since dealers have prime responsibility for prices put to a broker, the onus in such circumstances is on dealers to satisfy themselves that their prices have been taken off, unless a time limit is placed by the principal on its interest at the outset (e.g. 'firm for one minute only'). Otherwise, the principal should deal with an acceptable name at the quoted rate in a marketable amount.

67. For their part brokers should make every effort to assist dealers by checking from time to time with them whether their interest at particular prices (or rates) is still current. They should also do so when a specific name and amount have been quoted.

68. What constitutes a marketable amount varies from market to market but will generally be familiar to practitioners. If a broker is quoting on the basis of small amounts or particular names, the quotation should be qualified accordingly. Where principals are proposing to deal in unfamiliar markets through a broker, it is recommended that they first ask brokers what amounts are sufficient to validate normal market quotations. If their interest is in a smaller amount, the principal should specify this when initially requesting a price from or offering a price to the broker.

Concluding a deal

Principals are bound to a deal once the price and any other key commercial terms have been agreed. Oral agreements are considered binding. However, holding brokers unreasonably to a price is viewed as unprofessional and should be discouraged by management.

69. Where quoted prices are qualified as being indicative or subject to negotiation of commercial terms, principals should normally consider themselves bound to a

deal at the point where the terms have been agreed without qualification. Oral agreements are considered binding; the subsequent confirmation is evidence of the deal but should not override terms agreed orally. The practice of making a transaction subject to documentation is **not** good practice. In order to minimise the likelihood of disputes arising once documentation is prepared, firms should make every effort to agree all material points quickly during the oral negotiation of terms, and should include these on the confirmation. Any remaining details should be agreed as soon as possible thereafter.

70. Where brokers are involved, it is their responsibility to ensure that the principal providing the price (rate) is made aware immediately it has been dealt upon. As a general rule a deal should only be regarded as having been 'done' where the broker's contact is positively acknowledged by the dealer. A broker should never assume that a deal is done without some form of oral acknowledgement from the dealer. Where a broker puts a specific proposition to a dealer for a price (e.g. specifying an amount and a name for which a quote is required), the dealer can reasonably expect to be told almost immediately by the broker whether the price has been hit or not.

Passing of names by brokers

Brokers should not divulge the names of principals prematurely, and certainly not until satisfied that both sides display a serious intention to transact. Principals and brokers should at all times treat the details of transactions as absolutely confidential to the parties involved (see paragraphs 28 and 29 and 84 to 88 of this Code).

71. To save time and minimise frustration, principals should wherever practicable give brokers prior indication of counterparties with whom, for whatever reason, they would be unwilling to do business (referring as necessary to particular markets or instruments). At the same time brokers should take full account of the best interests and any precise instructions of the client.

72. To avoid subsequent awkwardness, principals (including agents) have a particular obligation to give guidance to brokers on any particular features (maturities etc.) or types of counterparty (such as non-financial institutions) which might cause difficulties. In some instruments, principals may also wish to give brokers guidance on the extent of the price differentiation across broad categories of counterparties. Where a broker is acting for an institution which is not supervised, he should disclose this fact as soon as possible; the degree of disclosure required in such a case will usually be greater. For instance, credit considerations may require that such names be disclosed to a principal first in order that the principal may quote a rate at which it is committed to deal. Equally, disclosure of difficult names may be necessary since this may influence the documentation.

73. In the sterling and currency deposit markets, it is accepted that principals dealing through a broker have the right to turn down a name wishing to take deposits; this could therefore require predisclosure of the name before closing the deal. Once a lender has asked the key question 'who pays?', it is considered committed to do business at the price quoted with that name, or an alternative acceptable name if offered immediately. The name of a lender shall be disclosed only after the lender has accepted the borrower's name. Conversely, where a borrower is taking secured money there may be occasions when it will wish to decline to take funds, through a broker, when the lender's name is passed.

74. For FSA authorised firms, section 3.7.3 of the IPC sets out rules and guidance on the passing of names.

Use of intermediaries

Brokers should not interpose an intermediary in any deal which could take place without its introduction.

75. An intermediary should only be introduced by a broker where it is strictly necessary for the completion of a deal, most obviously where a name switch is required because one counterparty is full of another's name but is prepared to deal with a third party. Any fees involved in transactions involving intermediaries should be explicitly identified by the broker and shown on the relevant confirmation(s).

76. Where a broker needs to switch a name this should be undertaken as promptly as possible, bearing in mind that this may take longer at certain times of the day; or if the name is a particularly difficult one; or if the deal is larger than normal. It is certainly not good practice to leave a deal overnight without acceptable names having been passed.

Fraud

77. There is a need for great vigilance by all staff against attempted fraud. This is particularly so where calls are received on an ordinary telephone line (usually in principal to principal transactions). As a precautionary measure, it is strongly recommended that the details of all telephone deals which do not include pre-agreed standard settlement instructions should be confirmed by a generally accepted electronic means without delay by the recipient, seeking an answer-back to ensure the deal is genuine.

Know your counterparty

78. *Before agreeing to establish a dealing relationship in any of these non-investment products, firms should be mindful of any reputational risks that might arise as a result.* In order to minimise the risks it is desirable for firms to have in place a clearly articulated approval process for their dealers and salespersons to follow before dealing with counterparties for the first time in any non-investment product. This process, which should be appropriately monitored by management, should apply both when granting an initial dealing line for a product, and subsequently if changing or extending it to other wholesale products. Such a process might include the following considerations, which will need to be tailored to the type of transaction being considered:

   - what information is available to firms on the legal capacity of the counterparty to undertake such transactions? Is this information sufficient to make an informed decision on the legal risks it might face if it undertakes such business with the counterparty?

   - who initiated the request for the product relationship? Might this decision have been influenced by any product advice given by the firm?

   - if advice is given, was this subject to a written agreement between the parties; if not, should it be? Are both parties clear what reliance the customer is placing upon that advice? What, if any, are the legal responsibilities the firm might owe to the customer to whom advice is given in subsequently undertaking transactions in that product? For instance, management might ask itself if it is being asked to advise on the customer's whole portfolio – which might put it in a different legal position than if it were advising on only part of the portfolio.

   - are there potential conflicts between the firm's interests and those of the potential customer? If there are how should they be managed; and does the customer need to be alerted?

- have appropriate legal agreements between the firm and the customer been enacted? Do they make clear the respective responsibilities of both parties for any losses? Do they make clear which party is responsible for decisions to close out trades undertaken?

79. Procedures should be in place to ensure that the information available to banks and other firms, upon which they will base their judgement on whether or not to open/extend a dealing relationship with a particular customer, is carefully assessed on a broad product by product basis.

80. Once a customer dealing relationship has been established in one, or more, non-investment product(s) it is strongly recommended that management at both parties periodically review it, against the above criteria. It is also in firms' own interests to review periodically the totality of their business relationship with each customer against the same criteria.

81. Firms may give advice that falls outside the authorisation requirement derived from the Financial Services and Markets Act (2000). Thus, giving advice on non-investment products does not normally constitute investment advice. Neutral information, such as historical data or economic developments, is not investment advice.

82. It is prudent for firms to maintain, as accurately as they can, records of conversations – both internal or with the investor – material to their relationship. Where these are in written form, records must be kept in line with statutory requirements. Where tapes are the only material record of specific transactions, or discussions leading up to specific such transactions, management should consider very carefully whether some or all of these should be retained for a similar length of time to written records, especially in the case of counterparties who may not have kept their own records, since disputes are more likely to escalate in the absence of a detailed and accurate audit trail of what was done and why.

83. More guidance on taping and recording of information may be found in paragraphs 30 to 36 of this Code. For FSA authorised firms, section 3.6 of the IPC sets out rules and guidance as regards taping.

Confidentiality

84. Where confidential or market sensitive information is routinely shared by a London based firm with other branches/subsidiaries within its group, it should be shared in accordance with established procedures. London management should be responsible for how such information is subsequently controlled – in particular they should make clear that such information should continue to be treated as being subject to the confidentiality provisions of the Code.

85. Care should be taken over the use of open loudspeakers in both brokers' offices and principals' dealing rooms as these may lead to confidentiality breaches.

86. Situations arise where sales/marketing staff from firms visit the offices of their counterparties; during such visits the customer may wish to arrange a transaction via the sales/marketing representative. Subject to proper controls this is perfectly acceptable. However, a principal's dealer should not deal from within the offices of a broker or another principal without proper authority. Brokers should not conduct business from outside their own offices. The only exception to these general rules might be when it is necessary for two unconnected institutions to share the same facilities as part of their agreed contingency arrangements. In such circumstances management should ensure appropriate arrangements are in place to protect counterparty confidentiality.

87. A principal should not place an order with a broker with the intention of ascertaining the name of a counterparty in order to make direct contact to conclude the deal; neither should direct contact be made to increase the amount of a completed trade arranged through a broker.

88. For FSA authorised firms, paragraphs 2 and 3 of the third annex of the IPC set out good market practice as regards confidentiality.

Dealing mandates

89. It is a matter for the two parties to agree what a mandate should and should not cover. It is recognised as best practice, however, that mandates should not be used to pass responsibility to another counterparty. They should not weaken the standard set out in paragraphs 9 to 23 of the Code, namely that all firms will be held responsible for the actions of their own staff and that it is the responsibility of each firm to ensure that any member of its own staff who commits it to a deal has the necessary authority to do so. A firm should not place any reliance on the ability of another to monitor that authority in the absence of a specific written agreement to accept such responsibility. Such an agreement raises important considerations and firms should ensure, before accepting such responsibility, that they have the ability to take on the tasks assigned to them.

90. If a mandate is to be adopted, it is important that proper thought is given to the manner in which the mandate is to be structured and administered. There should, for example, be periodic review of the terms of the mandate. As a general rule, the onus is on the counterparty to notify any change necessary to an existing mandate promptly.

Dealing with unidentified principals

91. There has been a growing trend towards discretionary management companies dealing in wholesale market products on behalf of their clients. For its own commercial reasons a fund manager may not wish to divulge the name of its client(s) when concluding such deals. This practice raises important conduct of business as well as prudential considerations, particularly in terms of principals' ability to know their counterparties and to assess their credit risk to those particular counterparties and to satisfy documentation requirements. Before any institution transacts business on this basis, its senior management should decide, as a matter of policy, whether they judge it appropriate to do so. In doing so, they should consider all the risks involved, and fully document the decision that they reach.

92. For FSA authorised firms, appendix 1 chapter LE of the Interim Prudential Sourcebook sets out rules as regards dealing with unidentified principals.

Terms and documentation, including Brokers' Terms and Conditions

93. It is now common for deals to be subject to some form of legal documentation binding the two parties to certain standard conditions and undertakings (which typically will take the form either of signed Master Agreements exchanged between the two parties or of standard Terms). Principals should have procedures in place to enable documentation to be completed and exchanged as soon as possible.

94. The following does not apply to authorised firms, for whom paragraphs 26 and 27 of the third annex of the IPC set out good market practice as regards Master Agreements.

95. It is in the interest of all principals to make every effort to progress the finalisation of documentation as quickly as possible. In some markets, documentation should be in place before any deals are undertaken. More generally, however, the aim should be for documentation to be in place within three months of the first deal being struck. Failure to agree documentation within this timescale should cause management to review the additional risks that this might imply for any future deals with the counterparty concerned. Factors which may influence management's views include whether they can take comfort on their legal position from the mutual confirmation of terms with a particular counterparty; or where the delay is in putting in place multiple master agreements for products that are, in the interim, subject to previously agreed documentation.

96. Some documentation in common usage provides for various options and/or modifications to be agreed by mutual consent. These should be clearly stated before dealing. Firms should make clear at an early stage if they are not intending to use standard terms documentation. Where changes are proposed these should also be made clear. Some outstanding transactions might still be subject to old documentation (e.g. the 1987 ISDA) that results in one-way payment provisions. The use of such provisions is not recommended. Banking supervisors worldwide have indicated that such transactions will not be eligible for netting for capital adequacy purposes.

Commission/brokerage

Brokers' charges are freely negotiable. Principals should pay brokerage bills promptly.

97. Where the services of a broker are used it is traditional practice for an appropriate brokerage package to be agreed by the directors or senior management on each side. Any variation on a particular transaction from those previously agreed brokerage arrangements should be expressly approved by both parties and clearly recorded on the subsequent documentation; this should be the exception rather than the rule. Brokers should never pay cash to a principal as an incentive to use its services (see also earlier section titled 'Marketing and incentives' (paragraphs 50 to 52)).

98. Although brokers normally quote dealing prices excluding commission/brokerage charges, there may be circumstances when the broker and principal may agree on an acceptable net rate; if so it is important that the broker subsequently informs the principal how that rate is divided between payments to counterparties and upfront commission. In such cases all parties need to be quite clear that this division will be determined no later than the time at which the deal is struck, and that a record is kept.

99. Some principals fail to pay due brokerage bills promptly. This is not good practice. Brokerage bills should be paid promptly. The Derivatives and Foreign Exchange Joint Standing Committees wrote to principals in London in May 1999 emphasising the importance of prompt payment.

100. For FSA authorised firms, paragraph 28 of the third annex of the IPC sets out good market practice as regards commission/brokerage.

Entertainment and gifts

101. Management may wish to consider the following points in formulating a policy on receiving and giving entertainment and gifts:

  ■ policies should contain specific reference to the appropriate treatment for gifts (given and received). This policy should specifically preclude the giving (or receiving) of cash or gifts that are readily convertible into cash;

- in determining whether the offer of a particular gift or form of entertainment might be construed as excessive, management should bear in mind whether it could be regarded as an improper inducement, either by the employer of the recipient or the supervisory authorities. Any grey areas should be cleared **in advance** with management at the recipient firms; and,

- firms should not normally offer entertainment if a representative of the host company will not be present at the event.

102. Management should have regard to the reputational risks to the firm and the London market generally of adverse comment/publicity generated by entertainment or gifts given or received.

103. The activities of dealers of some of the principals active in the markets may be governed by statute. For instance, offering hospitality or gifts to officers and members of UK local authorities and other public bodies is subject to the provisions of legislation that carries sanctions under criminal law. One of the most onerous requirements of this legislation is that any offer or receipt of hospitality is, prima facie, deemed to be a criminal offence, unless the contrary is proved.

Market conventions

Management should ensure that individual brokers and dealers are aware of their responsibility to act professionally at all times and, as part of this, to use clear, unambiguous terminology.

104. The use of clear language is in the interests of all concerned. Management should establish internal procedures (including retraining if necessary) to alert individual dealers and brokers who act in different markets (or move from one market to another) both to any differences in terminology between markets and to the possibility that any particular term could be misinterpreted. In those markets where standard terms and conditions have been published individual dealers and brokers should familiarise themselves with the definitions they contain.

105. Standard conventions for calculating the interest and proceeds on certain sterling and currency instruments, together with market conventions regarding brokerage, are set out in Annex 2. Similarly, market conventions in the bullion markets are set out in Annex 4.

Market disruption/bank holidays

106. There have been instances of general disruption to the wholesale markets which have, in turn, resulted in interruptions to the sterling settlement systems and consequent delays in sterling payments. It has been agreed that in such unexpected circumstances the Bank of England should determine and publish the interest rate(s) which parties to deals affected by such interruptions should use to calculate the appropriate interest adjustment (unless all the parties to the deal agree instead on some other arrangement – such as to continue to apply the existing rate of interest on the original transaction or as provided for in the relevant documentation). The Bank of England shall have absolute discretion in its determination of any interest rate(s), and shall not be required to explain its method of determining the same and shall not be liable to any person in respect of such determination.

107. Occasionally unforeseen events mean that market participants will have entered into contracts for a particular maturity date only to find, subsequently, that that day is declared a public holiday. It is normal market practice in London to extend

contracts maturing on a non-business day to the next working day. But to minimise possible disputes market participants may need to agree settlement arrangements for such deals with their counterparties in advance.

Confirmation procedures

Oral deal checks

Practitioners may find it helpful to undertake oral deal checks at least once a day, especially when using a broker.

108. Particularly when dealing in faster moving markets like foreign exchange, but also when dealing in other instruments which have very short settlement periods, many principals request regular oral deal checks – whether dealing through brokers or direct – prior to the exchange and checking of a written or electronically dispatched confirmation. Their use can be an important means of helping to reduce the number and size of differences particularly when dealing through brokers or for deals involving non-London counterparties. It is for each firm to agree with its broker(s) whether or not it wishes to be provided with this service and, if so, how many such checks a day it requires. If a single check is thought to be sufficient, this should be undertaken towards the end of the trading day as a useful complement, particularly where late deals are concerned, to the process of sending out and checking confirmations.

109. As a matter of common sense, the broker should always obtain acknowledgement from a dealer on completion of the check that all the deals have been agreed or, if not, that any identified discrepancies are resolved as a matter of urgency. Lack of response should not be construed as acknowledgement.

Written/electronic confirmations

In all markets, the confirmation provides a necessary final safeguard against dealing errors. Confirmations should be dispatched and checked carefully and promptly, even when oral deal checks have been undertaken. The issue and checking of confirmations is a back-office responsibility which should be carried out independently from those who initiate deals.

110. A confirmation of each deal should be sent out without delay and where possible electronically. This is particularly important if dealing for same day settlement. As a general rule, all participants in the wholesale markets should have, or be aiming to have, in place the capability to dispatch confirmations so that they are received and can be checked within a few hours of the deal being struck. Principals should enquire about any confirmations that have not been received within a reasonable period.

111. All confirmations should include the trade date, the name of the other counterparty and all other details of the deal, including where appropriate the commission charged by the broker. Some principals include their own terms and conditions of trading on their written confirmations. Where they are used, it is advisable to reference a particular master agreement on any written confirmation. To avoid misunderstandings, any subsequent changes should be brought specifically to the attention of their counterparties.

112. In many markets, it is accepted practice for principals to confirm directly all the details of transactions arranged through a broker; the broker should nevertheless also send a confirmation to each counterparty.

113. All counterparties are reminded that the prompt sending and checking of confirmations is also regarded as good practice in deals not arranged through a broker. Counterparties should check confirmations carefully and immediately upon receipt so that discrepancies can be quickly revealed and corrected. It is good practice to check within a few hours of receipt.

114. Firms should not send two confirmations (e.g. an initial one by the internet, telex, fax or other acceptable electronic means) followed by a written confirmation, which if posted could easily not arrive until after the settlement date and could cause confusion and uncertainty. For this reason, wherever practicable a single confirmation should be sent promptly by each party, if possible by one of the generally accepted electronic means now available, (for example SWIFT). Where this is not practicable, firms should indicate (e.g. on the preliminary confirmation) that a more detailed written version is to follow. It is not good practice to rely solely on an oral check.

115. Confirmations should not be issued by or sent to and checked by dealers. This is a back-office function. Where dealers do get involved in these procedures they should be closely controlled.

116. Certain automated dealing systems produce confirmations automatically. Provided these are received in the back office and entered into banks' internal systems, no additional confirmation need be sent.

117. Particular attention needs to be paid by all parties when confirming deals in which at least one of the counterparties is based outside London, and to any consequential differences in confirmation procedure.

Payment/settlement instructions

118. The use of standard settlement instructions (SSIs) continues to increase in London. International acceptance of the benefits of many SSIs is an important next step. In order to facilitate still greater usage of SSIs the BBA now maintains a directory of London based institutions that use them. Firms who do not already do so are encouraged to draw up plans to move towards using SSIs as soon as possible. A major advantage of using SSIs is that they remove the need to confirm payment details by phone.

119. The guidelines set out in Annex 3 of this Code set out a framework, which it is hoped principals will aim to adopt when using SSIs for wholesale market transactions. The guidance notes emphasise that SSIs should only be established or amended via confirmed letter, authenticated SWIFT message or SWIFT SSI/FX Directory Service and not by SWIFT broadcast. While many firms comply with this guidance, difficulties have been encountered where some insist on using SWIFT broadcasts. Broadcast messages remain unsuitable for the purpose of changing SSIs, are non-binding on recipients and should not be used by firms for this purpose. However, if a firm receives notice from a counterparty of the amendment of a SSI by a SWIFT broadcast, it should be free to act upon such notice if it wishes. It should seek authentication of the message by way of sending confirmation of the arrangement, making clear when and for what deals the new instructions will be implemented. Until that process is complete the original instructions will be deemed still to be operative.

120. Brokers should only be expected to pass payment instructions in very unusual circumstances or in certain deposit markets where the counterparty is, for example, a local authority. All such instructions should be passed with minimum delay.

121. Where SSIs are not being used, principals should ensure that any alterations to

original payment instructions, including the paying agent where this has been specifically requested, should be immediately notified direct to the counterparty. This notification should be supported by written, telex, or similar authenticated confirmation of the new instructions.

122. While it is important that payment instructions are passed quickly, it is equally important that principals have in place appropriate procedures for controlling the timing of their instructions to correspondent banks to release funds when settling wholesale market transactions. Failure to maintain effective controls over payment flows can significantly increase the risks that institutions face when dealing in the OTC wholesale markets.

123. For FSA authorised firms, paragraphs 24 and 25 of the third annex of the IPC set out good market practice as regards standard settlement instructions.

Settlement of differences

124. In all the wholesale markets (including foreign exchange) if a broker misses a price it should offer to close the deal at the next best price if held to the deal, and must then settle the difference arising by cheque. However, providing management on both sides agree, the difference may be offset against brokerage due or, subject to the conditions as set out in Annex 3 of this code, if it is a foreign exchange transaction, by points. **In the absence of mutual agreement to settle a difference by brokerage offset or points, principals should accept cash settlement. Principals should always be prepared to accept cash settlement, since to do otherwise would put the broker in breach of this Code. It is unprofessional for a dealer to refuse to accept a difference cheque and insist the deal is honoured**; individual brokers facing this situation should advise their senior management who, if necessary, should raise the matter with management of the client.

125. As noted above, the prompt dispatch and checking of confirmations is of great importance. Non-standard settlement instructions should be particularly carefully checked, and any discrepancies identified promptly upon receipt, and notified direct to the counterparty, or to the broker (in circumstances described earlier).

126. Where difference payments arise because of errors in the payment of funds, principals are reminded that they should not benefit from undue enrichment by retaining the funds. Technological developments have resulted in faster and more efficient mechanisms for the delivery and checking of confirmations. This means that when brokers pass payment instructions that cannot be cross-checked against direct confirmation details, their liability in the event of an error should be limited to 24 hours from when the deal was struck. This limit on the broker's liability is not intended to absolve brokers of responsibility for their own errors; rather it recognises that once payments do go astray the broker is limited in what action it can directly take to rectify the situation. In the foreign exchange and currency deposit markets arrangements have been drawn up to facilitate the payment of differences via the Secretary of the Foreign Exchange Joint Standing Committee[8].

---

[8] All requests for settlement via these arrangements should be marked for the attention of the Secretary, Foreign Exchange Joint Standing Committee, Bank of England Dealing Room (HO-1), Bank of England, Threadneedle Street, London EC2R 8AH. They should be accompanied by a written report of the circumstances resulting in the difference.

127. In the foreign exchange market only, and only with the explicit consent of banks, brokers may make use of 'points' to settle differences. Procedures for participants in points arrangements may be found in Annex 3 of this code.

128. For FSA authorised firms, sections 3.7.4 to 3.7.8 of the IPC set out rules and guidance on the settlement of differences.

ANNEX 2: STERLING WHOLESALE DEPOSIT MARKET

Market conventions

1 Calculation of interest and brokerage in the sterling deposit market

Interest

On deposits this is calculated on a daily basis on a 365-day year.

Interest on a deposit is paid at maturity, or annually and at maturity, unless special arrangements are made at the time the deal is concluded.

Brokerage

All brokerage is calculated on a daily basis on a 365-day year and brokerage statements are submitted monthly.

2 Calculation of interest in a leap year

The calculation of interest in a leap year depends upon whether interest falls to be calculated on a daily or an annual basis. The position may differ as between temporary and longer-term loans.

Temporary loans

Because temporary loans may be repaid in less than one year (but may, of course, be continued for more than a year) interest on temporary money is almost invariably calculated on a daily basis. Thus any period which includes 29 February automatically incorporates that day in the calculation; in calculating the appropriate amount of interest, the number of days in the period since the last payment of interest is expressed as a fraction of a normal 365-day year, not the 366 days of a leap year, which ensures that full value is given for the 'extra' day.

Examples:
Assume last previous interest payment 1 February (up to and including 31 January) and date of repayment 1 April (in a leap year). Duration of loan for final interest calculation = 29 days (February) + 31 days (March) = 60 days.
Calculation of interest would be

$$P \times \frac{r}{100} \times \frac{60}{365} =$$

Assume no intermediate interest payments. Loan placed 1 March and called for repayment 1 March the following year (leap year). Total period up to and including

29 February = 366 days. Calculation of interest would be

$$P \times \frac{r}{100} \times \frac{366}{365} =$$

This is in line with banking practice regarding interest on deposits, which is calculated on a 'daily' basis, and no conflict therefore arises.

Longer-term loans

The following procedure for the calculation of interest on loans which cannot be repaid in less than one year (except under a TSB or building society stress clause) was agreed between the BBA and the Chartered Institute of Public Finance and Accountancy on 12 December 1978.

(a) Fixed interest

The total amount of interest to be paid on a longer-term loan at fixed interest should be calculated on the basis of the number of complete calendar years running from the first day of the loan, with each day of any remaining period bearing interest as for 1/365 of a year.

Normal practice for the calculation of interest in leap years is to disregard 29 February if it falls within one of the complete calendar years. Only when it falls within the remaining period is it counted as an additional day with the divisor remaining at 365.

Example 3 1/2 year loan, maturing on 30 June of a leap year.

First 3 years' interest: $P \times \dfrac{r}{100} \times 3 =$

Final 6 months' interest: $P \times \dfrac{r}{100} \times \dfrac{182}{365}$

Certain banks, however, require additional payment of interest for 29 February in all cases, and it was therefore agreed that:

- both the original offer or bid, and the agent's confirmation, should state specifically if such payment is to be made; and
- the documentation should incorporate the appropriate phraseology.

Interest on longer-term loans should be paid half-yearly, on the half-yearly anniversary of the loan or on other prescribed dates and at maturity. **To calculate half-yearly interest payments** the accepted market formula is:

$$P \times \frac{r}{100} \times \frac{d}{365} =$$

Where d = actual number of days

Although, with the agreement of both parties, the following is sometimes used:

$$P \times \frac{r}{100} \times \frac{1}{2} =$$

(b) Floating rate

Interest on variable rate loans, or rollovers, which are taken for a fixed number of years with the rate of interest adjusted on specific dates, should be calculated in the same manner as for temporary loans.

ANNEX 3: FOREIGN CURRENCY WHOLESALE DEPOSITS AND SPOT AND FORWARD FOREIGN EXCHANGE

Arbitration arrangements in the foreign exchange market, including the role of the Foreign Exchange Joint Standing Committee

In the foreign exchange market, where a firm is concerned about a counterparty not adhering to the terms of this Code, it should generally approach the counterparty and, where appropriate, seek remedial action by the firm. Where disputes about matters relating to adherence with the Code cannot be resolved bilaterally, these can be brought to the attention of the FX JSC, who will implement an arbitration procedure.

Composition of the Panel, and nature of the ruling on a dispute

An arbitration panel would be selected on a case by case basis from a pool of members of the JSC, and other market participants. To ensure no conflicts of interest, panel members would be selected from the pool only once the disputing parties were known. The Panel would contain at least one member of the FX JSC, and the Bank of England would provide a Secretary for the panel. A ruling on a dispute by this panel would be binding.

Brokerage and other market conventions in the foreign exchange and currency deposit markets

Brokerage

(a) **General (foreign exchange and currency deposits)**
Brokerage arrangements are freely negotiable.
These arrangements should be agreed by directors and senior management in advance of any particular transaction.

(b) **Currency deposits**
Calculation of brokerage on all currency deposits should be worked out on a 360-day year.
Brokers' confirmations and statements relating to currency deposits should express brokerage in the currency of the deal.
In a simultaneous forward-forward deposit (for example one month against six months), the brokerage to be charged shall be on the actual intervening period (in the above example, five months).

Other Market Conventions – Currency deposits

Length of the year
For the purpose of calculating interest, one year is in general deemed to comprise 360 days; but practice is not uniform in all currencies or centres.

Spreads and quotations
Quotations will normally be made in fractions, except in short-dated foreign exchange dealings, where decimals are normally used.

Call and notice money
For US dollars (and sterling), notice in respect of call money must be given before noon in London. For other currencies, it should be given before such time as may be necessary to conform with local clearing practice in the country of the currency dealt in.

Guidelines for exchanging standard settlement instructions (SSIs)

While the parties to SSIs are free to agree changes to the detail on a bilateral basis, it is hoped that this framework will be useful and will be followed as closely as possible.

When **establishing** SSIs with a counterparty for the first time these should be appropriately authorised internally before being issued. SSIs should be established by post (and issued in duplicate, typically under two authorised signatories), or alternatively, by SWIFT SSI/FX Directory Service or authenticated SWIFT message.

Cancellation or amendment of SSIs should ideally be undertaken by SWIFT SSI/FX Directory Service, authenticated SWIFT or tested telex. SWIFT broadcast is **not** an acceptable means for establishing, cancelling or amending SSIs.

A mutually agreed **period of notice** for changing SSIs should be given regardless of the chosen channel for notification. Typically this will be between 10 working days and one month. Some parties may also wish to provide for changes to be made at shorter notice in certain circumstances.

Unless both initiator and recipient are subscribers to SWIFT SSI/FX Directory, **recipients** have a responsibility to acknowledge acceptance (or otherwise) of the proposed/amended SSI within the timescale agreed (see above). Failure to do so could result in a liability to compensate for any losses that result. In the case of written notification, this should be undertaken by the recipient signing and returning the duplicate letter. Recipients should also confirm the precise date on which SSIs will be activated (via SWIFT or tested telex).

Instructions should be issued for each currency and wholesale market product. Each party will typically nominate only one correspondent per currency for foreign exchange deals and one per currency for other wholesale market deals. The same correspondent may be used for foreign exchange and other wholesale market deals.

As a general rule, all outstanding deals, including maturing forwards, should be settled in accordance with the SSI in force at their value date (unless otherwise and explicitly agreed by the parties at the time at which any change to an existing SSI is agreed).

The SSI agreement for each business category should contain the following:

– the nature of the deals covered (for example whether they include same day settlement or only spot/forward forex deals).

– confirmation that a single SSI will apply for all such deals with the counterparty.

– the effective date.

– confirmation that it will remain in force 'until advised'.

– recognition that no additional telephone confirmation of settlement details will be required.

– recognition that any deviation from the SSI will be subject to an agreed period of notice.

When operating SSIs on this basis, the general obligations on both parties are to ensure that:

– they apply the SSI which is current on the settlement date for relevant transactions.

– confirmations are issued in accordance with this Code; the aim should be to send them out on the day a deal is struck.

– confirmations are checked promptly upon receipt in accordance with this Code. Any discrepancies should be advised by no later than 3.00 p.m. on the business day following trade date at the latest.

Requirements for participants in the forex market 'points' arrangements

The foreign exchange market is a professional market, in which firm prices are quoted. On some occasions, by the time a bank has agreed to deal at a price quoted by a broker, that price may have been withdrawn by the market maker who had indicated to the broker a willingness to deal at that rate. The broker might then seek to find a second bank prepared to conclude an offsetting transaction. 'Points' can be lent or borrowed to settle any difference that may arise.

The Wholesale Markets Brokers' Association and the Joint Standing Committee agree that the use of points can assist in the smooth functioning of the foreign exchange market.

Management in all banks (and other active market participants) should satisfy themselves that internal rules reduce the scope for differences. Dealers should also be discouraged from acting unprofessionally. In monitoring points usage, all parties should ensure that appropriate management controls are in place and that record keeping arrangements are sufficient to enable individual transactions involving points (both negative and positive) to be identified. The informal use of points between individual dealers and brokers is considered unacceptable. All differences should normally be settled within 30 days from the date the original deal was undertaken.

A broking firm should approach its clients at the appropriate management level to establish whether they wish to accept the broker's involvement in points arrangements. Banks that explicitly accept in writing the use of points will be assumed to have given their informed consent to the practice. Participating in points arrangements will not of itself commit any bank to lending points to brokers or to the use of positive points in lieu of cash payment for any differences. Any such decision should be taken quite separately by management.

For those banks that choose not to participate, a broking firm will need to consider whether, and on what terms, it is prepared to continue to provide a broking service. Where a service continues to be provided, the broking firm should take the following steps:

- advise the management of the banks that it may no longer provide a firm price service, i.e. that prices would be executed 'at best'; banks should take steps to inform their dealers that the broker cannot be held to a price.

- under normal circumstances settle any differences resulting from mistakes by cheque; where London banks are concerned, it is recommended that cheques be paid through the FX Joint Standing Committee's mechanism. As a matter of equity, banks should also accept that any differences resulting from mistakes on the part of their dealers should be payable to the broker through the same procedures (see footnote to paragraph 126).

- maintain an up-to-date list of names distinguishing those banks participating in points arrangements from those not participating, with copies provided to all appropriate members of staff.

On rare occasions individuals will inevitably make mistakes, when (positive) points may wrongly be taken by a broker from a deal involving a bank not participating in points arrangements. Systems should therefore be in place in each broking firm to identify any such errors promptly and to ensure that full rectification takes place immediately so that no positive points accrue to the benefit of the broker. Any such adjustment will leave the original deal undisturbed.

The Joint Standing Committee will keep the operation of the points framework under review. Disputes arising from points arrangements may be referred to the Committee's arbitration panel.

ANNEX 4: WHOLESALE BULLION SPOT, FORWARD AND DEPOSITS IN GOLD AND SILVER

Basic Market Definitions

The unit of trading for gold is one *fine* troy ounce and for silver is one troy ounce. In the case of gold, the unit represents pure gold irrespective of the fineness of a particular bar, whereas for silver it represents one ounce of material of which a minimum of 999 parts in every 1,000 will be silver. Fineness represents the scale that denotes the proportion of pure gold or silver in a bar or other item measured in parts per 1,000 while assay is the process by which the fineness is determined (as an example, a bar could assay at 996.4 fine).

The Troy Ounce is the traditional unit of weight used for precious metals. One troy ounce is equal to 1.0971428 ounces avoirdupois. The accepted conversion factors between troy and metric are that one kilo equals 32.1507465 troy ounces, and one troy ounce equals 0.0311035 kilos.

Fine Gold Content represents the actual quantity of gold in a bar. For example a good delivery bar may have a gross weight of 403.775 ounces. If it were of a fineness of say 996.4 fine, the fine gold content or net weight of gold would be $403.775 \times 0.9964 = 402.321$ fine ounces.

The basic unit for delivery of gold is the London Good Delivery Gold Bar. This must have a minimum fineness of 995 parts per 1000, and must have a gold content of greater than 350, and less than 430 fine ounces, with the bar weight being expressed in multiples of 0.025 of an ounce. Bars are generally close to 400 ounces or 12.5 kilograms.

The basic unit for delivery of silver is the London Good Delivery Silver Bar. This must be of a minimum fineness of 999 parts per thousand and, for bars produced after 1st January 2000, weigh between 750 and 1,100 ounces. Bars produced prior to 1st January 2000 must weigh between 500 and 1250 ounces. The weight of bars must be expressed in multiples of 0.1 of an ounce. Bars generally weigh around 1,000 ounces.

Both gold and silver Good Delivery Bars must conform to the specifications for Good Delivery set by the London Bullion Market Association (LBMA).

London Good Delivery Lists (LGD) are lists of refiners of gold and silver produced by the LBMA whose standards of production and assaying are such that their bars are acceptable in settlement against transactions conducted between LBMA members and with their clients. The lists are widely accepted as the international benchmark, providing the reliable standard for bars traded and delivered around the world. Assessment of applications for inclusion in the lists, together with their ongoing maintenance, is one of the core functions of the LBMA.

Details of the standards required for inclusion on the London Good Delivery Lists are published by the LBMA in the 'Good Delivery Rules for Gold and Silver Bars', with the lists themselves available on its web-site, www.lbma.org.uk.

Loco London. Bullion traders from all over the world have traditionally maintained precious metal accounts with members of the LBMA. This has meant that dealers around the world are able to settle bullion transactions between each other by transfers between London dealers such that most global 'over the counter' (OTC) gold and silver trading is cleared through the London Bullion Market Clearing.

This fact means that trading against a quotation for loco London delivery bullion, by and between dealers globally, makes the loco London price the common denominator in global bullion pricing, and the loco London bullion account the bullion equivalent of the currency nostro account.

Settlement and Delivery. The basis for settlement and delivery of the 'loco London' quotation is for delivery of a standard Good Delivery Bar at the London vault nominated by the dealer who made the sale.

While settlement or payment for a transaction will generally be in US dollars over an account in a New York bank, delivery of metal against transactions in gold and silver are in made in a number of ways. These include physical delivery at the vault of the dealer or elsewhere, by credit to an allocated or unallocated account with the dealer or through the London Bullion Clearing to the unallocated account of any third party.

In addition to delivery at its own vault, a dealer will arrange delivery of metal to any destination in the world and in any form of bar size or fineness.

Allocated Accounts are accounts maintained by dealers in client's names on which are maintained balances of identifiable bars of metal 'Allocated' to the customer's name and segregated from other metal held in the vault. The client has full title to this metal with the dealer holding it on the client's behalf as custodian.

Unallocated Accounts are accounts, the unit of which is one fine troy ounce of gold or one troy ounce of silver based upon a 995 fine LGD gold bar or 999 LGD silver bar respectively. The balance of an unallocated account represents the indebtedness between the parties and credit balances on client accounts are backed by the general stock of the bullion dealer with whom the account is held; the client in this scenario is an unsecured creditor. Should the client wish to receive actual metal, this is done by 'allocating' specific bars, the fine metal content of which is then debited to the unallocated account. Market convention is that bullion may be allocated on the day it is called for, with physical metal generally available for collection on the next business day.

Leases. Gold and silver may be placed on deposit, borrowed or lent, just like currency and with interest calculated on the basis of troy ounces of gold or silver. It is uncollateralised lending. In order to differentiate and to avoid confusion with forward swaps, this activity is termed 'leasing'. Firms therefore 'lend on the lease' or 'borrow on the lease'.

Forwards may be for a simple purchase or sale of metal for settlement beyond spot, an outright forward, or for forward swap transactions. Forward swaps are a simultaneous purchase and sale where one leg of the transaction is generally for spot value and the other forward, conducted at an agreed differential to the spot leg of the deal. They are in effect collateralised loans of metal. This leads to the terms 'borrowing on the swap', in the case where the spot is purchased and the forward sold, or 'lending on the swap' where the spot is sold and the forward purchased, in order to differentiate from leasing metal.

Market Conventions

Quoting Conventions. Prices are expressed in US dollars per fine troy ounce for gold and per troy ounce for silver. Prices against other currencies or in units of weight other than troy ounces are generally available on request.

Marketable Amounts. In the spot market the standard dealing amounts between market makers are 5,000 fine ounces in gold and 100,000 ounces in silver. The usual minimum size of transaction is 2,000 troy ounces for gold and 50,000 troy ounces for silver while dealers are willing to offer competitive prices for much larger volumes for clients.

In the forward market, subject to credit limits, London's market makers quote for at least 32,000 fine ounces for gold swaps versus US dollars, and for at least one million ounces of silver.

Spot and Forward Value Dates. Settlement and delivery for spot transactions is two good business days after the day of the deal where a good business day is one in which banks are open in London for delivery of the gold or silver and in New York for settlement of dollars.

The value dates for standard forward quotations are at calendar monthly intervals from spot. Should that day be a non-business day, the value will be for the nearest good business day except at month ends when the value date will be kept in the month which reflects the number of months being quoted for.

Gold and Silver Deposits

Market convention is for the interest payable on loans of gold or silver to be calculated in terms of ounces of metal which are converted to US dollars based on a US dollar price for the metal agreed at the inception of the lease transaction. The interest basis for gold and silver is a 360-day year.

Interest therefore equals: $B \times (R/100) \times (d/360) \times P$

Where B is ounces of bullion, R is the lease rate, d is the number of days and P is the Price of gold or silver agreed for calculation of interest.

Outright Forwards and Swaps

Market convention is for forward prices in gold and silver to be quoted in interest rate terms on the basis at which a dealer will borrow or lend metal on the swap.

A dealer therefore may quote three months forward at, say, 5.5 to 5.75.

This means that he will lend on the swap, i.e. sell spot and buy forward, and pay on the basis of 5.5% per annum over the spot price for the forward leg, or borrow on the swap, buy spot and sell forward, and charge on the basis of 5.75% per annum over the spot for the forward.

In this scenario, were the dealer to be asked to lend on the swap at 5.5 and the spot price were say $282.25 to 282.75, the dealer would, in accordance with market practice, base the deal at the middle of the spread. He would therefore sell the spot at $282.50, and buy the forward at a premium calculated as:

$282.50 \times 90/360 \times 5.5/100 = 3.88
The forward price therefore equals: $282.50 + $3.88 = $286.38

The outright forward purchase price is calculated as the spot bid price plus the forward swap bid and the forward sale price as the spot offered price plus the forward swap offer.

The London Gold and Silver Fixings

In addition to the two-way bid and offer quotations available in the OTC environment, London provides fixings for both gold and silver. The guiding principle behind the fixings is that all business, whether for large or small amounts, is conducted solely on the basis of the final fixed price. The fixings, while serving those who wish to do business at a globally published price, provide transparent benchmarks that are used around the world as a basis for a variety of transactions, including industrial contracts, averaging business and provide the basis for cashed settled swap and option transactions.

The Gold Fixing. Five members of the LBMA meet twice each London business day at 10.30 a.m. and 3.00 p.m. to fix the price of gold. Orders are placed by clients to the dealing rooms of members of the Fixing who net all orders before communicating that net interest to their representative at the Fixing. The gold price is then adjusted up and down until demand and supply is matched at which point the price is declared 'Fixed' and all business is conducted on the basis of that Fixing Price. Transparency at the Fixing is served by the fact that counterparties may be kept advised of price changes, together with the level of interest, while the Fixing is in progress and adjusts their interest accordingly.

The Silver Fixing. Three members of the LBMA conduct the Silver Fixing meeting by telephone at 12.00 noon each working day. The process then follows a similar pattern to gold, arriving at a Fixing Price when buying and selling orders are matched.

Other Products

Other products available from members of the LBMA including options and gold interest rate derivative transactions come under the definition of investment products and so are regulated by the Financial Services Authority. Details of these products are available in the Inter-Professionals Conduct (IPC) Chapter of the Financial Services Authority (FSA) Handbook.

Vaulting Facilities

Each Member of the LBMA which offers clearing services has either their own vault for the storage of physical bullion or the dedicated use of storage facilities with another party plus, in the case of gold, account facilities for allocated metal at the Bank of England

Clearing

The London Bullion Clearing is a daily clearing system of paper transfers whereby members offering clearing services utilise the unallocated gold and silver accounts they maintain between each other not only for the settlement of mutual trades, but for third party transfers. These are conducted on behalf of clients and other members of the London Bullion Market in settlement of their own loco London bullion activities. The system avoids the security risks and costs involved in the physical movement of bullion.

The Clearing operates on the basis of a code of market practice encapsulated in a 'Letter of Understanding' to which each member offering Clearing services is a signatory. The Letter sets out the framework under which the signatories operate the clearing system and covers two main areas;

- the right each signatory to the Letter has over any other signatory member to call on his unallocated account with the other member and

- the timing under which instruction for transfers and allocations may be given and effected.

Transfer instructions for members' own purposes and for client transfers may be made up to 4.00 p.m. London time on the day of settlement. Clearing members then have until 4.30 p.m. to effect transfers or call for allocation for credit purposes.

Availability of Official Market information

The Fixing prices for gold and silver are published immediately on the various new agencies. On Reuters, on 'XAUFIX = ' and 'XAGFIX = ' for gold and silver respectively.

GOFO. Prices for gold swaps are available from the Reuters page GOFO and, from these prices, rates for forwards and leases may be determined.

GOFO is the Gold Forward Offered Rate and is the rate at which dealers will lend gold on the swap against US dollars. As such it provides an international benchmark and is the basis for the pricing of gold swaps, forwards and leases. It is the gold equivalent of LIBOR.

From GOFO rates, indicative mid-market gold lease rates can be determined as:

Mid-market lease rate = (US dollar LIBOR less 0.0625%) minus (GOFO plus 0.125%)

This indicative mid-market lease rate is published on Reuters page LGLR.

GOFO mean is published each business day at 11.00 a.m. In order for the mean to be valid, rates from at least six Market Making Members of the LBMA must be available on the GOFO page at 11.00 a.m. The mean is then determined by rejecting the highest and lowest quotations and calculating the average of the remaining rates. The GOFO mean provides the benchmark for long term finance and loan agreements as well as for the settlement of gold Interest Rate Swaps and Forward Rate Agreements.

SIFO is the Silver Offered Rate and provides indicative forward rates for silver. However, as these are only indicative rates, the LBMA does not recommend that they be used as a benchmark to settle any transactions.

Standard Documentation

Given the variety of products provided by members of the market, and in order to avoid the problems inherent in a multiplicity of bilateral agreements to cover the transactions involved, the LBMA has developed and introduced a number of standard agreements. These cover the terms and conditions for operating allocated and unallocated accounts as well as forward, option and gold interest rate derivative transactions. Copies are available from the LBMA.

ANNEX 5: OTHER GENERAL GUIDANCE INCLUDING GOOD PRACTICES IN OBTAINING DATA FOR MARK TO MARKET PURPOSES

Good practices in obtaining data for mark to market purposes

This Schedule is intended to provide guidance for principals when obtaining external data for the purposes of marking to market OTC transactions and for those brokers whom may be supplying these data. A number of market participants have asked for clarification of where responsibilities lie, and of what is good, or sound, practice in the acquisition and supply of such data. It is clear that there is a wide range of practices among participants; this guidance is intended to outline the main principles which participants should consider, rather than to be overly prescriptive as regards methods.

The FSA's regulatory requirements will apply for firms authorised by the FSA.

The General Principles

■ Principals who engage in trading should undertake regular prudent and consistent valuation of their mark-to-market trading positions. For many such positions, quoted prices will be the best guide to a fair valuation.

■ Principals need to have in place appropriate procedures for the independent checking of mark-to-market trading positions by the middle and/or back office.

■ Brokers can play a useful role in the market as one of the sources of external data for valuation purposes. Where they do so, this service should be governed by the same considerations as apply to other relations between brokers and principals as described in paragraphs 20 to 23 of the Code. Firms may enter into specific bilateral agreements about the reliance to be placed on any service supplied but, absent these, all principals are responsible for their own actions.

Acquisition of Data

Where principals are seeking to acquire external data for valuation purposes, they should also consider the following:

- Where possible, prices (and volatilities) used in mark-to-market calculations should be checked by an area of the principal that is independent of the front office.

- Screen services, brokers and other third party providers can all be useful sources of data. In some areas such as where markets are particularly thin or illiquid, principals may consider exchanging historical data with other principals.

- Where independent prices are not available, a series of checks should be put in place to ensure that all prices are measured on a prudent basis.

- Screen prices showing the bid-offer spread are widely available for many products. Where available, these will often be the most appropriate source, though principals should also consider how these data have been constructed and what they represent. Are they, for example, the last actual trade and if so how long ago did it occur? From which market were they obtained and at what time? If the prices are not actual trades on what basis were they calculated (e.g. interpolation)? What size was the trade representative of? Is this price based on a liquid market?

- Where principals seek external data for specific transactions/instruments, they should specify in appropriate detail what data they require. Principals should state the appropriate characteristics on which they want the estimate to be based e.g. mid-market, indicative or firm prices, close-out prices, the size of deal for which the price is generally good.

Supply of Data by Brokers

In supplying data, brokers should consider:

- Whether appropriate back office controls are in place to ensure the data are appropriately calculated and recorded. The procedures for supplying data should be fully documented.

- Stating the precise conditions under which the estimates were constructed (mid-market, last trade, size etc.) They should also ensure that they provide data to principals on a consistent basis.

- Indicating an appropriate disclaimer of liability where appropriate in addition to the general presumption of the Code outlined above.

- Where possible, data should be provided by the broker's back office function independent of the brokers.

- Where data are provided by fax (or fax equivalent), particular care is taken to ensure that the appropriate procedures are followed.

- Where markets are particularly illiquid, whether the broker can give any guidance on, say, the number of principals trading the product to which the price refers.

- Subjecting the supply of data procedures to periodic compliance and internal and external audit review.

ANNEX 6: GOOD PRACTICE GUIDELINES FOR FOREIGN EXCHANGE TRADING[9]

Leading intermediaries in the foreign exchange market have agreed on a new set of good practice guidelines for foreign exchange trading. This is in response to a recommendation made in the report, published in April 2000, of the Financial Stability Forum Working Group on Highly-Leveraged Institutions, which was chaired by Sir Howard Davies.

Major commercial and investment banks have collaborated in drawing up the guidelines, which are to be incorporated in existing codes of market conduct. The collaboration was facilitated by a group of central banks, which have an interest in ensuring orderly conditions in financial markets. The guidelines have been discussed and endorsed by the bodies which are responsible for foreign exchange market standards in the main financial centres.

Trading Principles

We, the firms listed below, have reviewed the following principles and have incorporated them into our own guidelines and codes of conduct. We encourage both companies and industry organisations that are responsible for the writing of codes and best practices to consider this input during production of such documents. We encourage the market participants around the world to incorporate these principles in their own codes to the degree that their national and regional jurisdictions allow.

We recognise that all trading parties need to put heightened emphasis and sensitivity on market risk and credit management issues during times of market volatility. When an individual currency is experiencing high volatility, intermediaries should pay special attention to the financing of trades in that currency.

Foreign exchange managers have a particular responsibility in the execution of orders at volatile times. Intermediaries should take care to discuss with customers the risks of operating in these environments and the possible scrutiny of actions. Market makers may reserve the right to refuse customer transactions that they feel may further disrupt or have the intent to disrupt the market.

The handling of all orders, including stop losses, requires vigilance by foreign exchange managers to ensure that there is mutual agreement with customers on the basis on which orders are accepted. Frequent communication with customers about market developments, particularly with a view toward determining their individual trigger levels, is strongly encouraged.

The handling of customer orders requires standards that strive for best execution for the customer in accordance with such orders subject to market conditions. In particular, caution should be taken so that customers' interests are not exploited when financial intermediaries trade for their own accounts.

Institutions and other trading organisations should be attentive at all times to ensure the independence and integrity of any market-related research that they publish.

Financial intermediaries are encouraged to implement rigorous internal guidelines concerning the handling of rumours and possible false information. We strongly

---

[9] Statement issued on 22 February 2001 by sixteen leading intermediaries in the foreign exchange market: ANZ Bank; Banamex; Bank of Tokyo-Mitsubishi; Barclays; JPMorgan Chase; Citibank; DBS; Deutsche Bank; Goldman Sachs; HSBC; Morgan Stanley; Nomura Securities; Societe Generale; Standard Bank of South Africa; Standard Chartered; and UBS Warburg. Since the statement was issued, a number of other banks have also endorsed these guidelines.

endorse the model code[10] that dealers should not relay information they know is false or they suspect may be inaccurate.

Manipulative practices by banks with each other or with clients constitute unacceptable trading behaviour.

Foreign exchange trading management should prohibit the deliberate exploitation of electronic dealing systems to generate artificial price behaviour.

---

[10] Page 38 of the International Code of Conduct and Practice for the Financial Markets. Please refer to www.aciforex.com, Model Code.

Taylor Associates run programmes and tutorials for governments and government agencies, banks and corporations in the following general areas:

Hard Skills
- Foreign Exchange
- Capital Markets
- Derivatives
- Money Laundering
- Treasury
- Fixed Income
- Equities
- Technical Analysis
- Portfolio Management
- Credit Evaluation
- Risk
- General Finance and Accounting

Soft Skills
- Team Building
- Management Development
- Stress Management
- Project Management
- Consultancy Skills
- Selling Skills
- Presentation and Listening Skills
- Communication Skills
- Managing People
- Interviewing Techniques
- Leadership
- Diversity

To contact Taylor Associates:

Telephone/Fax: +44 (0) 1372 841096

E-mail: info@taylorassociates.co.uk

http://www.taylorassociates.co.uk

Index

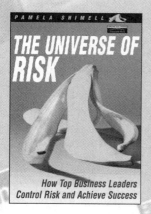
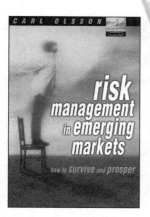
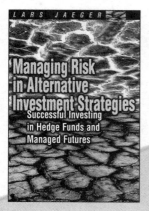